DATE DUE

Unless Recalled Earlier

Guide to Reference and Information Sources in the Zoological Sciences

Recent Titles in
Reference Sources in Science and Technology

GUIDE TO REFERENCE AND INFORMATION SOURCES IN THE ZOOLOGICAL SCIENCES

Diane Schmidt

Reference Sources in Science and Technology

LIBRARIES

UNLIMITED

A Member of the Greenwood Publishing Group

Westport, Connecticut • London

Library of Congress Cataloging-in-Publication Data

Schmidt, Diane, 1956–
   Guide to reference and information sources in the zoological sciences / Diane Schmidt.
      p. cm.—(Reference sources in science and technology)
   "A complete revision of A guide to the zoological literature: the animal kingdom, published in 1994 by George H. Bell and Diane B. Rhodes"—Preface.
      ISBN 1–56308–977–7 (pbk. : alk. paper)
      1. Zoology—Bibliography. I. Bell, George H. 1943– —Guide to the zoological literature. II. Title. III. Series.
Z7991.S36 2003
[QL45.2]
016.59—dc21   2003054568

British Library Cataloguing in Publication Data is available.

Library of Congress Catalog Card Number: 2003054568
ISBN: 1–56308–977–7

First published in 2003

Libraries Unlimited, 88 Post Road West, Westport, CT 06881
A Member of the Greenwood Publishing Group.
www.lu.com

Printed in the United States of America

3620944

523749954

CONTENTS

V

PREFACE

This is a complete revision of George H. Bell and Diane B. Rhodes's *A Guide to the Zoological Literature: The Animal Kingdom* (1994). This award-winning guide included nearly 2,000 books, journals, associations, and other resources dealing with taxonomic zoology worldwide. The present version retains most of the original taxonomic arrangement, but the coverage policy has changed. The most important materials on physiology and ecology are included, but only continentwide or regional taxonomic resources have been listed. The exception to this rule is that resources for North America include items for the countries of Canada, Mexico, and the United States. The numerous Web resources are integrated into the appropriate section such as handbooks or checklists, and they were selected using the same criteria as printed materials.

The author wishes to acknowledge the Research and Publication Committee of the University of Illinois at Urbana-Champaign Library, which provided support for the completion of this research. In addition, the author would like to thank Eleannor Maajid for her assistance in the final editing of the manuscript.

Introduction

What Is Zoology?

Zoology, according to *Henderson's Dictionary of Biological Terms,* 12th ed. (Lawrence, 2000), is "the science dealing with the structure, functions, behaviour, history, classification and distribution of animals" (688). Zoology can be treated as that portion of biology dealing with animals, as opposed to botany, which deals with plants, or microbiology, which deals with microorganisms. Using this definition, zoology could include anatomy, physiology, histology, cytology, and any of the other biological disciplines. In practice, however, the term is often restricted to what is now called "integrative biology," dealing with whole organisms rather than aspects of their beings. This would include systematics, ecology, evolution, and studies based on taxonomic group rather than function.

So, what is an animal? Animals, according to the same source just cited, are "multicellular eukaryotic organisms with wall-less, non-photosynthetic cells" (34). The dictionary definition of an animal is technical for a good reason. Although we all know an animal when we see one, this holds true only for the so-called higher animals. The invertebrates, those animals without a backbone, constitute a vast and highly variable backdrop to our knowledge of the animal kingdom. For instance, many of the 9,000 species of sponges look like slightly squishy rocks. Placozoans are another oddity, perhaps the simplest animals with only two layers of cells that look like amoebas with flagella. Compared to placozoans even immobile sponges seem complex. Other invertebrates are more familiar but their lifestyles may seem bizarre to vertebrates such as ourselves.

Older systems of classification divided living organisms into two kingdoms, the Plantae and the Animalia. Most biologists now follow either the Five Kingdom (Prokaryotae, Protoctista, Fungi, Plantae, and Animalia) or Three Domain (Archaebacteria, Eubacteria, and Eukaryota) systems. These higher-level discussions do not affect the definition of animals, except that in the Two Kingdom model, protozoa were included in the animal kingdom. The protozoa are excluded from consideration in this volume, although they were included in the first edition.

History of the Zoological Literature

For most of the historical period, the literature of zoology was the same as the literature of other forms of biology. People have been studying animals since the dawn of time although the intent and the degree of scientific validity of their conclusions have varied over the ages. It is instructive to compare some of the well-known encyclopedic works about animals. Aristotle's *Historia Animalium* (Thompson, 1910) is an easy choice for the first zoological encyclopedia. It was quite scientific for its time. Aristotle drew most of his conclusions based on data gathered by observation, although experimentation was not part of his research method. The compendium is arranged by general topic and the descriptions of animals are scattered throughout, with tidbits on octopus breeding, habits, description, diet, and use as bait grouped with the same topics for other animals. Considering the breadth of organisms and topics that Aristotle covered, it is amazing how much he got right.

In later years theology and scholasticism, the reliance on the study of the writings of authorities, became the dominant mode of thinking. Bestiaries, or compendia of writings on animals, were extremely popular throughout the medieval period. The first bestiary, the *Physiologus*, was written in the third century based on Egyptian, Hebrew, and Indian legends. It was copied, revised, and added to for centuries. These bestiaries had very little grounding in real life and were almost exclusively designed as religious allegory, not as a description of real animals. According to *Physiologus*, for instance, weasels give birth through their ears (males exiting through the right ear, females from the left), and the moral was that "Wicked things are engendered through the ears" (Curley, 1979, p. 50). The herbals, the botanical counterparts of bestiaries, retained some grounding in reality since the herbals were used to identify plants and their medicinal uses, but the writers of the bestiaries were free to let their imaginations run free.

Bestiaries were popular literature for centuries, but at the same time there was a more serious attempt to study animals. Albertus Magnus (1193–1280), the Dominican saint, was one of the most famous scholars of the thirteenth century. His *De Animalibus* summarized his contemporary's state of knowledge of the animal world, with many glosses provided by Albertus Magnus himself. Books 22–26, *On the Nature of Animals,* divided the animals into humans, quadrupeds, serpents, birds, aquatic animals, and vermin. Within each class he arranged the animals in alphabetical order. To our modern eyes this often leads to odd juxtapositions. For instance, hippos, fish, and sea urchins are all considered aquatic animals; the vermin (bloodless animals) include frogs and toads as well as insects. Albertus was far more skeptical, in a medieval way, than the bestiary authors. He finds the story that the gaze of a basilisk kills only if the person meets the basilisk's eye first, rather than the other way around, to be quite senseless, and besides Avicenna doesn't believe it either (Kitchell and Resnick, 1999, p. 1720).

Even as late as 1607, when Edward Topsell's *History of Four-footed Beasts* was published, the state of knowledge of the animal kingdom had not advanced significantly. Topsell's book was a translation of Konrad Gesner's *Historia Animalium* (originally published 1551–87). Gesner and Topsell had eliminated the religious allegory but retained the scholastic method. They repeated many of the inaccurate folktales and spurious medical uses reported by previous authorities rather than relying on direct observation of the animals, although in some cases they reported quite accurate information. Topsell, for instance, correctly identified several types of foxes (though not as species; that was to come later) but solemnly repeated the story first found in the *Physiologus* that foxes would play dead to catch crows. Like Albertus Magnus, Topsell occasionally expressed doubts about the stories he related (South, 1981).

Change was in the air, however, and science was gaining momentum. Over the next two hundred years the study of biology made great advances, including William Harvey's investigation of the circulatory system, Anton van Leeuwenhoek's examination of microscopic animals, and Robert Hooke's discovery of the nature of cells (Moore, 1993). Another important event in the creation of the modern period in terms of zoology occurred with the development of new systems of classification. In the late seventeenth century John Ray realized that the basic population unit for living organisms was the species (Magner, 2002). This was followed by Carolus Linneaus's publication of *Systema Naturae* (the tenth and definitive edition was published in 1758).

Linnaeus's *Systema Naturae* organized about 4,000 plant and animal species in a hierarchical classification system from kingdom to species, organized by morphological characteristics. Previously authors had a great deal of difficulty deciding how to arrange animal species, as seen in the examples above. The most common system seemed to be alphabetical, except that it changed from language to language. Linneaus introduced another idea, binomial nomenclature, that helped solve the language problem, as well. This innovation created a theoretically stable scientific name used by all biologists whatever their native tongue. A dog was *Canis familiaris* whether you were in France, Sweden, or China, and its place among the other dogs did not change either. According to the logic of Linneaus's morphological classification, the dog *Canis familiaris* closely resembles the wolf *Canis lupus* and is less similar to the red fox *Vulpes vulpes* but all three species are similar enough to belong to the family Canidae.

It would be another hundred years before Darwin and Wallace published their joint paper on evolution in 1858, but after Linneaus's time taxonomy as a science was well established, the Age of Exploration had begun, and things were never to be the same again. *On the Origin of Species* established the facts of natural selection and evolution although the details continue to be debated. This understanding of evolutionary relationships has led to changes in Linnaeus's classification system. For instance, Linnaeus classed amphibians and reptiles together in the Amphibia but he divided them according to their form into serpents (without feet) and reptiles (with feet). Amphibians and reptiles are now organized according to their phylogeny rather than their shape. Also, to take the dog, wolf, fox example listed above, under our modern evolutionary view we would say that dogs are closely related to wolves and less closely related to foxes.

Taxonomy

Many of the resources covered in this volume deal with animal taxonomy, so some definitions are in order. *Systematics* is a broad field that attempts to identify patterns in organisms and covers both taxonomy and evolutionary biology. The term is sometimes used as a synonym for taxonomy. *Taxonomy* is the theory and practice of classifying and naming organisms. *Classification* is the process of ranking groups of organisms in a hierarchical arrangement. *Taxon* (plural *taxa*) is a taxonomic group of any level, such as genus, order, family, or kingdom. *Nomenclature* is the system that describes how species and other higher groups are to be named, including which names are valid and how to Latinize terms from other languages. Animal taxonomists follow the rules laid out in the *International Code of Zoological Nomenclature* (see chapter 1). All currently accepted scientific names and descriptions began with Linnaeus's publication of the tenth edition of *Systema Naturae.*

Taxonomy is often divided into two areas, descriptive taxonomy and phylogenetic taxonomy. *Descriptive taxonomy,* as its name suggests, identifies and describes species and other groups. The literature of descriptive taxonomy is widely distributed. Taxonomists must refer back to the original description of a species, which may have been published at any time since Linnaeus's original work and in a wide range of books, journals, bulletins, monographs, and other often obscure sources. Various experts in families or orders of animals have then compiled catalogs, handbooks, or checklists that attempt to sort out the classification and nomenclature of that group, but such works are invariably outdated soon after publication as new species are discovered and other revisions made, which are then published in the same types of articles and books, and the cycle begins again. *Phylogenetic taxonomy* (or phylogenetics) attempts to trace the evolutionary relationships of organisms. Most modern phylogenetics is based on *cladistics*, in which taxonomists attempt to identify *clades,* groups of organisms that contain the set of all descendants of a particular ancestor and no other organisms. The dinosaur clade, for instance, would include dinosaurs and birds but not turtles, even though dinosaurs and turtles are both reptiles. After all, birds are descended from dinosaurs, but turtles and dinosaurs had different reptilian ancestors. Phylogenies, then, are branching family trees showing the relationships of organisms.

For a long time, taxonomy has been viewed by nontaxonomists as a boring activity, lacking in prestige and interest. Taxonomists turned away from purely descriptive taxonomy to phylogenetic taxonomy, and the money went even farther afield, to cutting-edge subjects such as molecular biology or genomics. This lack of prestige certainly isn't because the taxonomists' work is done; we don't know how many living species are out there, but estimates range from 4 million to 100 million species. Most authorities estimate there are 10 to 13 million species of which only about 1.4 million have been described to date, with thousands of new species added to the collection each year. Newsworthy discoveries are made annually, from the discovery of an entirely new order of insects (the Mantophasmatodea) while this volume was being written, to bizarre marine animals such as a second species of coelacanth. In addition, taxonomy is not just an academic pursuit followed by old duffers in dusty museums. The classification of species has an impact on people from birders who like it when species are split in two (more species for their life lists!) to developers who are not happy when rare subspecies are reclassified as species (and are thus eligible for protection under the Endangered Species Act).

As one might expect, with over 1.4 million described species plus unknown millions yet to be described, the job of keeping track of the literature of taxonomy is a difficult one. Individual taxonomists and zoologists can keep up with the literature of their own narrow field, but for the student or nontaxonomist, the task can be daunting. The primary index for zoology, *Zoological Record,* has been published since 1864. It indexes 4,500 journals plus conference proceedings, books, newsletters, and technical reports (see chapter 1 for more detail). The electronic archive, going back to 1978, contains over 1.5 million records. Even this resource doesn't cover the entire literature of zoology. As a result, many taxonomists have created specialized taxonomic bibliographies and lists of the original descriptions of plant and animal species. Many of these are listed in the appropriate chapters in this volume.

Despite the obvious advantages of the Web for organizing and making vast quantities of data available, its use by taxonomists is only beginning to take off. Many authors have created authoritative Web sites describing the classification of the group of organisms that they study, but most of these relate to small taxa. There is no *Zoological Record* equivalent for Web sites, so the sites are difficult to locate. Many, but not all, of them are annotated in this volume. Because one of the chief characteristics of the Web is its changeability, an associated Web site at http://www.library.uiuc. edu/bix/zoology/ will monitor the URLs and fates of the sites annotated in this volume.

A number of authors have begun to call for the creation of a large-scale Web taxonomy system (e.g., Godfray, 2002), and several projects are currently underway. These projects are discussed in chapter 1 and include initiatives such as the Global Biodiversity Information Facility, Species 2000, the All Species Foundation, the Global Taxonomy Initiative, and others. Their success should help revitalize the field of taxonomy and will certainly make the task of finding taxonomic information much easier. At the time of writing, however, each project was in its infancy. For the near future, the literature of zoology will continue to be primarily print based.

About This Book

Although the preceding discussion has centered on the technical aspects of taxonomy or nomenclature, these works are not the only ones discussed in this volume. Also included are encyclopedias and dictionaries, handbooks that survey the diversity of a particular taxon of animals or of the animals of a particular geographical area, identification guides, journals, associations, and other useful tools. A very select group of works discussing the biology of various taxa, especially the so-called lower animals, is also included, as well as a very few books covering other topics such as animal ecology or behavior. Most of these are annotated in chapter 1. Paleontological materials are generally not covered, nor are materials on applied fields such as veterinary medicine, agriculture, or pest control, although they often include useful information on individual species. Note that most of the major taxonomic revisions are published as journal articles and are thus excluded from the purview of this volume, but you should be able to identify them by using the other resources listed.

Resources Included

The arrangement of the book covers the periodical literature first, followed by monographic works. A final section covers relevant associations. An associated Web page at http://www.library.uiuc.edu/bix/zoology/ will monitor all sites and keep URLs up to date.

Indexes, Abstracts, and Bibliographies

This section includes article indexes, abstracts, databases, and book-length bibliographies.

Journals

Core journals and review publications are listed in this section. The lists are extensive but not intended to be comprehensive.

Guides to the Literature

Guides to the literature are books such as this one, which help readers identify major resources. Several are listed in chapter 1 and other chapters where available. This section also includes major Web directories with links to other pages of interest; also see the associated Web site at http://www.library.uiuc.edu/bix/zoology/.

Biographies and Histories

Only relatively comprehensive biographies covering multiple individuals and broad histories are annotated in this volume.

Checklists and Classification Schemes

There are two kinds of checklists: those that lists the valid and/or invalid scientific names for a particular taxon, and those that list all the species of a particular geographical region. Both are included in this section, along with books that outline the classification of a taxon.

Dictionaries and Encyclopedias

It is often difficult to distinguish between dictionaries and encyclopedias, so they are combined. Dictionaries provide definitions of words and may discuss their derivation. Encyclopedias generally have lengthier essays on topics and cover a broad range of topics.

Handbooks

Handbooks are the largest category of items covered in this book. The term means a number of things, but as treated here includes faunas (surveys of the animals of a particular region), overviews of a particular order, and general works that do not fit in any of the other categories used. The term "handbook" often refers to an identification guide, but these are treated in the Identification Tools section (see later). For the most part, only handbooks covering an entire order are included, although family level handbooks are included for major families or if there is no comparable work for the entire order. The geographical handbooks are almost all continentwide or at least cover multiple countries. The following biogeographical headings were used, rather than geopolitical terms:

North America (including Canada, Mexico, and the United States)

Africa (including Madagascar, the Seychelles, and other islands in the Indian Ocean)

Antarctica

Asia (with India, Indonesia, Malaysia, the Philippines, and Borneo)

Australasia (Australia, New Zealand, the Celebes, and Papua/New Guinea)

Central and South America (including the Caribbean islands)

Europe (including the Middle East, northern Africa, and Iceland)

Pacific Islands (including Hawaii)

Identification Tools

Identification tools include field guides, manuals, and taxonomic keys. All these resources are devised to help identify species or other taxa and range from the small portable field guides designed for the use of nonspecialists to detailed technical manuals and keys for the use of professionals.

Textbooks

Textbooks are useful not only as texts for a course, but also for general reference. Core texts are listed in this section.

Associations

Associations, societies, and other organizations that work with a particular group of organisms are included in this section. Only professional organizations are listed.

References

Curley, Michael J. 1979. *Physiologus*. Austin: University of Texas Press.

Godfray, H. Charles J. 2002. Challenges for taxonomy. *Nature* 417 (6884): 17–19.

Kitchell, Kenneth F. Jr. and Irven Michael Resnick, trans. 1999. *On Animals: A Medieval Summa Zoologica*. Baltimore: Johns Hopkins University Press.

Lawrence, Eleanor. 2000. *Henderson's Dictionary of Biological Terms*. 12th ed. New York: Prentice Hall.

Magner, Lois N. 2002. *A History of the Life Sciences*. 3rd ed. New York: Marcel Dekker.

Moore, John A. 1993. *Science as a Way of Knowing: The Foundations of Modern Biology*. Cambridge, MA: Harvard University Press.

South, Malcolm, ed. 1981. *Topsell's Histories of Beasts*. Chicago: Nelson-Hall.

Thompson, D'Arcy Wentworth. 1910. *Historia Animalium*. Oxford: The Clarendon Press.

1

General Reference Sources

This chapter covers general resources that may be useful for zoologists, including very general biology or science resources such as *Science Citation Index* and also resources that cover zoology in general. Consult this chapter in association with other chapters, because the very broad materials such as *Zoological Record* or *Grzimek's Animal Life Encyclopedia* are annotated here but not cross-referenced in the subject chapters.

Indexes, Abstracts, and Bibliographies

AGRICOLA (AGRICultural OnLine Access). Washington, DC: National Agricultural Library, 1970– . Updated daily. URL: http://www. nalusda.gov/ag98/. (Accessed August 25, 2003).

The online equivalent of *Bibliography of Agriculture,* produced by the National Agriculture Library (NAL). This database covers journal articles, book chapters, government documents, technical reports, and proceedings. The material primarily comes from the holdings of NAL, although some other material is also included. AGRICOLA is a useful source of information on animals of economic importance, particularly insects. You will also find information on interactions of wildlife with livestock and similar subjects. Because AGRICOLA is produced by a government agency, it is inexpensive and available from a number of vendors in several formats such as online, on CD-ROM, and through the Web. The database can be searched for free at the URL listed above. However, this

11

search engine is very clumsy so most users are better off checking to see what other access methods are available to them. NAL also publishes an annual *List of Journals Indexed in AGRICOLA*. It can also be accessed at no charge on the Web, at http://www.nalusda.gov/indexing/ljiarch.htm.

Animal Behavior Abstracts. Vol. 1– . Bethesda, MD: Cambridge Scientific Abstracts, 1972– . Quarterly. Price varies. ISSN 0301-8695.

This specialized index covers all aspects of animal behavior, both psychological and biological studies in areas such as behavioral ecology, neurobiology, genetics, and applied ethology. It is also available as part of the *Biological Sciences Collection* (see below) online, on CD-ROM, and on the Web.

Aquatic Sciences and Fisheries Abstracts. Part 1: Biological Sciences and Living Resources. Vol. 8– . Bethesda, MD: CSA, 1978– . Monthly. Price varies. ISSN 0140-5373.

Another specialized index from CSA. This index covers all aspects of marine, freshwater, and brackish water organisms, including their biology and exploitation. Legal and socioeconomic issues relating to marine organisms are also included. The index contains author, subject, taxonomic, and geographical indexes. Part 2, *Ocean Technology, Policy, and Non-Living Resources,* and Part 3, *Aquatic Pollution and Environmental Quality,* are also available. The three sections are available online, on CD-ROM, and on the Web as a stand-alone database and as part of the *Aquatic Sciences and Fisheries Abstracts Database* and the *Biological Sciences Database* (see below).

Biological Abstracts. Vol. 1– . Philadelphia: BIOSIS, 1926– . Biweekly. $8,980 (main series); $3,470 (cumulative indexes). ISSN 0006-3169.

Biological Abstracts is half of the *BIOSIS Previews* database, which also includes *Biological Abstracts/RRM* (below). *Biological Abstracts* is the most comprehensive biological database available and covers the literature of biology and biomedicine from around the world. Only journal articles reporting on original research are covered in the main title; reviews, proceedings, and the like, are covered in the companion title. It is a good choice for searching most areas of zoology. The print version is in two main parts: the abstracts section and several indexes. The abstracts are arranged by broad subject categories. The indexes include author, biosystematic, generic, and subject keywords and are used to find the abstract number.

The emphasis in recent years has been away from the print index and toward the database, which is available as the combined *BIOSIS Previews* database and also as separate *BA on CD* and *BA/RRM on CD* CD-ROMs. In the past, the BIOSIS database used keywords and numerical Concept Codes for broad subject categories such as pollution. Since 1998, the indexing has changed to a new Relational Indexing system. The new indexing system has many specialized fields for categories such as organisms, diseases, molecular sequence data, methods, geopolitical locations, and many others. Further enhancements to the indexing were made in 2003. The BIOSIS Web site at http://www.biosis.org/ has extensive information and free training publications in Adobe Acrobat format. The database is available from several vendors online as part of *BIOSIS Previews* and on CD-ROM as *BA on CD*. In addition, OCLC's FirstSearch system offers a student version titled *BasicBIOSIS,* which has a four- to five-year rolling file indexing about 360 major journals. BIOSIS also publishes two useful resources to help users make the most out of the database: the *BIOSIS Search Guide* and the *BIOSIS Serial Sources.*

Biological Abstracts/RRM (Reports, Reviews, Meetings). Vol. 18– . Philadelphia: BIOSIS, 1980– . Monthly. $4,400. ISSN 0192-6985.

BA/RRM is a companion to *Biological Abstracts.* It provides coverage of material not covered in *Biological Abstracts* such as editorials, reports, bibliographies, proceedings, symposia, books, chapters, review journals, translated journals, nomenclature rules, and so on. Proceedings are less important in zoology than they are in many other scientific fields, but they can also be difficult to track down. *BA/RRM* is also valuable because of the review articles and other types of literature not covered in the main title. *BA/RRM* is arranged like *Biological Abstracts* in broad subject categories with five indexes. Formerly titled *Bioresearch Index.* Available online as part of *BIOSIS Previews* (see above) and on CD-ROM as *BA/RRM on CD.*

Biological and Agricultural Index. Vol. 1– . New York: Wilson, 1916/18– . Monthly. Price varies. ISSN 0006-3177.

This index and *Biology Digest,* below, are suitable choices for undergraduate and high school students and the general public. It covers 225 core journals that are available at most four-year colleges and universities and is complementary to *General Science Index* (see below). *Biological and Agricultural Index* indexes journals more comprehensively than *Biological Abstracts,* covering items such as book reviews and letters to the editor that are not included in *Biological Abstracts.* The print index has alphabetical subject and author indexes. Available online, on CD-ROM, and on the Web.

Biology Digest. Vol. 1– . Medford, NJ: Plexus, 1974– . Monthly, September to May. $149. ISSN 0095-2958.

   Biology Digest covers around 300 biological journals and, like *Biological and Agricultural Index,* is appropriate for undergraduates and the general public. Unlike its competitor, however, it includes original abstracts aimed at summarizing articles for students. The abstracts are arranged by broad subject, like *Biological Abstracts.* Zoology is covered in the "Diversity of Life" section. There are author and keyword indexes in each issue, which cumulate every six months. Available from several vendors online, on CD-ROM, and on the Web.

CAB Abstracts. Wallingford, UK: CAB International, 1973– . Monthly. Price varies.

   This database contains records from nearly 50 CABI (Commonwealth Agricultural Bureaux International) abstract journals. It covers over 10,000 journals, books, technical reports, theses, proceedings, patents, and other document types. The truly international and multilingual coverage is an important source for applied research in zoology, entomology, nematology, parasitology, and veterinary medicine. It is available online as *CABA,* and on CD-ROM as *CABCD* for the full database; also available on CD-ROM in sections dealing with particular narrower subjects.

Chemical Abstracts. Vol. 1– . Columbus, OH: Chemical Abstracts Service, 1907– . Weekly. $21,600 (for academic institutions). ISSN 0009-2258.

   Chemical Abstracts is the most important index for chemistry. It scans over 8,000 scientific and engineering journals, plus patents, conference proceedings, reports, and monographs. Many facets of biochemical zoology or molecular biology are covered in this index, so it is a useful tool for biologists. Available online and on CD-ROM in several versions with varying starting dates, and there are several Web access methods. For academic institutions, the most common access is probably *SciFinder Scholar,* which allows simultaneous searching of *Chemical Abstracts* and several other databases including PubMed (see *Index Medicus,* below). OCLC FirstSearch also provides a limited edition of the database aimed at students, called the *CA Student Edition.* CAS also publishes the *Chemical*

Abstracts Service Source Index (CASSI), which is particularly useful in its multivolume cumulated version covering 1907 to date.

CSA Biological Sciences Collection. Bethesda, MD: Cambridge Scientific Abstracts, 1980– . Price varies.

This database is the combination of 28 abstracting journals from Cambridge Scientific Abstracts. Sections of particular interest to zoologists include *Animal Behavior Abstracts, Chemoreception Abstracts, Entomology Abstracts* (see chapter 3 of this volume), *Genetics Abstracts, Microbiology Abstracts* (three sections), and *Neurosciences Abstracts.* The Biological Sciences Collection, aimed at the collegiate or research level, is a less expensive and less comprehensive alternative to *Biological Abstracts.* It is available online, on CD-ROM, and on the Web.

Current Awareness in Biological Sciences. Vol. 1– . Amsterdam: Elsevier, 1954– . 144/yr. $9,296. ISSN 0733-4443.

This index is a compilation of 12 print sections of the *Current Advances* series, which are also available individually. It includes sections on ecology, genetics, neuroscience, physiology, and others of interest to zoologists and is aimed at researchers. CABS covers about 1,700 international journals and was formerly called *International Abstracts of Biological Sciences.* It is available online as *Elsevier BIOBASE,* which also includes material not found in the print version.

Current Contents/Agriculture, Biology, and Environmental Sciences. CC/ABES.). Vol. 1– . Philadelphia: Institute for Scientific Information, 1970– . Weekly. $795. ISSN 0011-3379.

The original print *Current Contents* is simply a weekly compilation of tables of contents (TOCs) of major journals and book series. The TOCs are arranged by subject with subject and author indexes, as well as publisher addresses. Subjects covered in *CC/ABES* include agriculture, botany, entomology, ecology, mycology, ornithology, veterinary medicine, and wildlife management. It is now available online, on CD-ROM as *Current Contents Search* (available in several combinations of sections), on the Web, and on weekly diskettes from ISI. The database version is more like a standard article database, with abstracts and added keywords, although the TOCs are included. Most implementations of the database also allow users to set up profiles and get weekly updates for subject terms or journals of interest.

Current Contents/Life Sciences. Vol. 1– . Philadelphia: Institute for Scientific Information, 1958– . Weekly. $850. ISSN 0011-3409.

Companion to *CC/ABES,* above, covering topics such as biochemistry, biomedical research, biophysics, endocrinology, genetics, immunology, microbiology, neurosciences, and pharmacology. There are two versions, containing 1,200 and 600 titles. Like its companion series, *CC/LS* is available online, on CD-ROM, on the Web, and on diskette (see above).

Ecological Abstracts. Vol. 1– . Norwich, UK: Elsevier, 1974– . Monthly. $2,056. ISSN 0305-196X.

This specialized index covers all aspects of ecology, including aquatic, terrestrial, and applied. Aimed at researchers, it scans about 3,000 journals, plus books, proceedings, and other sources. There are annual subject, organism, regional, and author indexes. It is available online and on CD-ROM as part of *Geobase. Ecology Abstracts,* below, is similar in coverage. Includes 14,000 items.

Ecology Abstracts. Vol. 1– . Bethesda, MD: Cambridge Scientific Abstracts, 1975– . Monthly. Price varies. ISSN 0143-3296.

Another of the Cambridge Scientific Abstracts specialized indexes, *Ecology Abstracts* covers journal articles in all aspects of ecology, conservation, and biodiversity. Available online and on CD-ROM as part of the *Biological Sciences Collection.* Formerly titled *Applied Ecology Abstracts.* 1,300 items added per month; 215,500 items in database in mid-2000.

Index Medicus. New series, Vol. 1– . Washington, DC: National Library of Medicine, 1975– . Monthly. $522. ISSN 0019-3879.

Index Medicus and its various electronic formats (AKA MEDLINE, PubMed, and formerly Grateful Med) is the best-known index for the biomedical sciences, including veterinary medicine. For zoologists, it is useful for its coverage of pests of medical importance, for wildlife diseases, and medical entomology.

Like AGRICOLA (above), it is available for free searching on the Web as PubMed (1966 to date) at http://www.ncbi.nlm.nih.gov/entrez/query.fcgi. The PubMed database is designed for researchers and covers more journals than the regular MEDLINE database. PubMed also offers links to protein and gene sequence databases such as GenBank, plus live links to electronic journals. You will be able to connect to most of these electronic journals only if your library or institution has subscribed to them, however. There are also a number of other features, such as the ability to set up Current Awareness searches through the "Cubby" feature. In addition, there are useful services such as browseable databases for journal titles and medical subject headings, and citation matching services. The *OldMEDLINE* database offers free searching of articles (1958–65) at http://gateway.nlm.nih.gov/. MEDLINE is also available from numerous other online and CD-ROM vendors.

Index to Scientific and Technical Proceedings. Vol. 1– . Philadelphia: Institute for Scientific Information, 1975– . Monthly. $2,885. ISSN 0149-8088.

Most scientific meetings publish their results as abstracts, proceedings, or papers. Finding these items can be very difficult, so indexes such as this can be useful, although *Biological Abstracts/RRM* (above) covers the biological sciences more completely. The papers are listed by broad subject categories and there are indexes for subject, sponsor, author, meeting location, and corporations.

Index to Scientific Reviews. Vol. 1– . Philadelphia: Institute for Scientific Information, 1974– . Semiannual. $1,855. ISSN 0360-0661.

A multidisciplinary index to review articles found in books and journals. It is actually a subset of the *Science Citation Index* (below). Review articles are also indexed in *BA/RRM* (above) and in most other indexes or databases. The *Index to Scientific Reviews* is also available separately on CD-ROM and as part of the *Science Citation Index* in its various incarnations.

Monthly Catalog of United States Government Publications. Vol. 1– . Washington, DC: U.S. Government Printing Office, 1895– . Monthly. $229. ISSN 0362-6830.

Government documents are published by most departments of the federal government, and they are excellent sources of information in several areas such as biodiversity and endangered species. The *Monthly Catalog,* arranged by governmental department, is the most important means of discovering government documents. There are author, title, subject, and series/report indexes in each issue. The catalog is available online, on CD-ROM, and on the Web. Many online government publications are available from the FirstGov site at http://firstgov.gov/. This site is designed to provide the public with easy access to all online U.S. federal government resources.

National Technical Information Service (NTIS). Washington, DC: National Technical Information Service, 1990s– . URL: http://www.ntis. gov/search.htm. (Accessed August 25, 2003).

This site lists over 750,000 technical reports available from the National Technical Information Service (NTIS), including research supported by federal grants and some state and local governments. Some international agencies are also represented. It is available online, on CD-ROM, and on the Web. Material published after 1990 is freely searchable at NTIS's Web site. The print version, *Government Reports Announcements and Index (GRAI),* is no longer being published.

PASCAL. Paris: Institut de l'Information Scientifique & Technique, 1973– .

This French database corresponds to the print *Bibliographie Internationale* (previously titled *Bulletin Signaletique*). It is in French and English and has international coverage of all science and technical areas, including zoology. Available online and on CD-ROM.

Referativnyi Zhurnal: Biologiya. Vol. 1– . Moscow: Vsesoyuznyi Institut Nauchno Tekhnicheskoi Informatsii (VINITI), 1958– . Monthly. Price varies. ISSN 0034-2300.

The most important Russian scientific index. Abstracts are arranged in broad subject categories, with annual author and scientific name indexes.

Science Citation Index. Vol. 1– . Philadelphia: Institute for Scientific Information, 1961– . Bimonthly. $11,730. ISSN 0036-827X.

A unique multidisciplinary index to the literature of science. The citation index groups all articles that have referenced the same earlier work and so provides a different sort of access to the literature. It is used to trace the scientific "lineage" of ideas, to determine whether a particular article is used, and in a number of other ways. It can also be used as a normal interdisciplinary index for current articles. There are citation, source, corporate, and subject (keyword) indexes. Covers about 4,500 journals. Available online, on CD-ROM, and on the Web (as *Web of Knowledge,* formerly *Web of Science*) from ISI.

SciTechResources.gov. Springfield, VA: National Technical Information Service. URL: http://www.scitechresources.gov/. (Accessed August 25, 2003).

This site is designed to permit scientists and interested laypeople to access the vast amount of scientific information developed by U.S. government agencies. It is similar to the FirstGov site listed above. Users can search by agency, subject, or document type and can also limit their search to only general interest material (the "Citizen Search"). Search results include a brief summary of each site's content and type (e.g., Web portal or maps and charts) and a link to the actual site. Created by National Technical Information Service (NTIS).

Wildlife Worldwide. Baltimore: National Information Services Corp, 1992– . Quarterly. ISSN 1070-5007. CD-ROM.

Wildlife Worldwide is a combination full-text database and index covering the literature of wildlife around the world. It consists of several collections, including the database equivalent of the U.S. Fish and Wildlife print publication *Wildlife Review* (1971–present), Wildlife Database (1960–present), the entire WIS (HERMAN) index from the Wildlife Information Service (1935–present), Waterfowl and Wetlands Database (1968–94), the BIODOC file from the National University of Costa Rica (1980–present), Swiss Wildlife Information Service (1974–present), three databases from the IUCN (the World Conservation Union), and other material. Formerly titled *Wildlife & Fish Worldwide.*

Zoological Record. Vol. 1– . Philadelphia: BIOSIS, 1864– . Annual. $4,500 (all 20 sections). ISSN 0144-3607.

Zoological Record is the most comprehensive zoological index in the world, published by the same company as *Biological Abstracts.* It includes books and proceedings, and articles from over 6,500 periodicals. There is exhaustive coverage for systematic zoology, in addition to coverage of all other areas of zoology such as behavior, ecology, and physiology. The index is published in 20 sections, each corresponding to a class or phylum such as Insecta, Annelida, or Trilobyta. The sections are available separately or as part of the entire series. Because the print *Zoological Record* is published only once a year, it is basically a retrospective tool, although the electronic database is updated more often and can be used for current awareness. Citations (without abstracts) are listed by author, and there are subject, geographical, paleontological, and systematic indexes. *ZR* is also available online and on CD-ROM. The *Zoological Record Search Guide* and the *Zoological Record Serial Sources* are helpful aids, similar to the *Biological Abstracts* guides mentioned above.

Historical Periodical Indexes

The bibliographies and indexes listed here concentrate on the period before indexes such as *Biological Abstracts* or *Zoological Record* began in the late nineteenth and early twentieth centuries. Taxonomists, in particular, often need access to the early literature and will find these resources invaluable.

Bibliographia Zoologica. Vol. 1–43. Zurich: Sumptibus Concilii Bibliographici, 1896–1934.

Covers the literature of zoology from 1895 to 1934. From 1896 to 1912, this bibliography was published as a supplement to *Zoologischer Anzeiger* and continued the "Litteratur" section found in its earlier volumes.

British Museum (Natural History). **List of Serial Publications in the Libraries of the Department of Zoology and Entomology.** London: British Museum (Natural History), 1967. 281 p. (Publication 664).

This list is useful when confronted with the abbreviation of an old, obscure journal. The collections of the British Museum were very complete, making this list very comprehensive.

Carus, J. Victor, and Wilhelm Engelmann, eds. **Bibliotheca Zoologica I.** Leipzig: Englemann, 1861. 2 vol.

A continuation of *Bibliotheca Historico-Naturalis,* below; continued by Taschenberg's *Bibliotheca Zoologica II.* This work covers the years 1846 to 1860.

Englemann, W. **Bibliotheca Historico-Naturalis: Verzeichniss der bücher über naturgeschichte, welche in Deutschland, Scandinavien, Holland, England, Frankreich, Italien und Spanien in den jahren 1700–1846 erschienen sind.** Leipzig: Englemann, 1846. 786 p.

This bibliography covers works from 1700 to 1846 in natural history. It is arranged by broad subject headings, and alphabetically by author within each category. The categories are also divided into two sections, those published in Germany and those published elsewhere.

Harvard University, Museum of Comparative Zoology. *Catalogue of the Library of the Museum of Comparative Zoology, Harvard University.* Vol. 1–8. Boston: Hall, 1968. $835. ISBN 081610767X (set). **Supplement.** Vol. 1– , 1976– . $140. ISBN 0816108110 (sup. 1).

Like the British Museum's catalog listed above, this work is useful for verifying citations and journal titles. It contains an alphabetical listing of manuscripts, photographs, and maps as well as books and journals in Harvard's Library of the Museum of Comparative Anatomy.

International Catalogue of Scientific Literature: N, Zoology. 1st–14th annual issues. London: Harrison, 1902–16.

An outgrowth of the *Catalogue of Scientific Papers* published by the Royal Society of London, this catalog was designed as a complete record of scientific literature. It was published in 20 sections, of which section N covered zoology. Entries are arranged by author's name, and there is a subject index.

Reuss, Jeremias David. **Repertorium Commentationum a Societatibus Litterariis Editarum...T. 1, Historia Naturalis, Generalis et Zoologia.** Gottingae: Dieterich, 1801. (Reprint: New York: Burt Franklin, 1961).

An index to society publications in zoology up to 1800. Most of the citations are to eighteenth-century works, and most are arranged by taxonomic groups.

Taschenberg, O., comp. **Bibliotheca Zoologica II.** Leipzig: Englemann, 1887–1923. 19 vol. in 9.

A continuation of *Bibliotheca Zoologica I* and *Bibliotheca Historico-Naturalis* (above) that covers the years 1861 to 1880.

Zoologischer Bericht. Bd. 1–55. Jena: Fischer, 1922–43/44. 55 vol.

This index was published in German but covers the literature of zoology worldwide. It is arranged in broad subject categories, and citations are in alphabetical order by author. There are also extensive abstracts (in German), and each volume has author and subject indexes.

Journals

Animal Behaviour. Vol. 1– . London: Academic Press, 1952– . Monthly. $801. ISSN 0003-3472.

Publishes long reviews, research articles, and book reviews in all aspects of animal behavior. There is also a Forum section listed in each issue, which lists opinion articles that are only available from the journal's home page at http://www.academicpress.com/anbehav/forum. The

Forum articles are freely accessible to all, not just subscribers to the journal. It is published for the Association for the Study of Animal Behaviour in the United Kingdom and the Animal Behavior Society of North America.

Behavioral Ecology. Vol. 1– . New York: Oxford University Press, 1990– . Bimonthly. $450. ISSN 1045-2249. Available electronically.

Publishes articles, reviews, and brief correspondence in both theoretical and empirical studies in the field, which is defined broadly as the use of ecological and evolutionary processes to explain behaviors, the use of behavioral processes to predict ecological patterns, and studies relating behavior to the environment. In addition to the abstract published in the journal, each article has an author-prepared Lay Summary that is only available on the journal's Web site at http://beheco.oupjournals.org/supplemental/. The summaries are designed to show nonscientists what the article is about and why it is important. The official journal of the International Society for Behavioral Ecology.

Behavioral Ecology and Sociobiology. Vol. 1– . Heidelberg, Germany: Springer-Verlag, 1976– . Monthly. $2,252. ISSN 0340-5443. Available electronically.

Publishes reviews and original research articles dealing with theoretical and empirical studies of animal behavior, with emphasis on the function and evolution of behavior. Some articles have freely available electronic supplementary material posted on the journal's Web site at http://link.springer.de/journals/bes.

Behaviour: An International Journal of Behavioural Biology. Vol. 1– . Leiden, Netherlands: E. J. Brill, 1947– . Monthly. $596. ISSN 0005-7959. Available electronically.

Publishes both theoretical and empirical studies in all areas of behavior, including causes, development, and evolution of animal and human behavior. Most articles are about animal behavior, however.

Bulletin of the Natural History Museum: Zoology Series. Vol. 1– . London: Intercept, 1949– . Semiannual. $155. ISSN 0968-0470.

Most papers in the *Bulletin* are the results of research carried out on the collections of the famous Natural History Museum. Many of the articles cover systematics. Formerly titled *Bulletin of the British Museum of Natural History: Zoological Series*.

Canadian Journal of Zoology/Revue Canadienne de Zoologie. Vol. 1– . Ottawa: National Research Council of Canada, 1929– . Monthly. $954. ISSN 0008-4301. Available electronically.

Publishes articles, notes, reviews, and comments in English and French, in areas of zoology such as behavior, biochemistry, physiology, developmental biology, ecology, genetics, pathology, and systematics. Each issue is arranged in sections by subject area. Most articles are in English, with French and English abstracts.

Integrative and Comparative Biology. Vol. 42– . McLean, VA: Society for Integrative and Comparative Biology, 2002– . Bimonthly. $505. ISSN 1540-7063. Available electronically.

Publishes invited papers from symposia sponsored by the Society for Integrative and Comparative Biology (formerly the American Society of Zoologists) on topics such as behavioral ecology, physiology, and others. There are also a few book reviews. Formerly *American Zoologist.*

Journal of Animal Ecology. Vol. 1– . Oxford, UK: Blackwell Science, 1932– . Bimonthly. $610. ISSN 0021-8790. Available electronically.

Publishes original research papers, comments, and occasional reviews on all aspects of animal ecology. Published for the British Ecological Society.

Journal of Experimental Zoology. Vol. 1– . New York: Wiley-Liss, 1904– . 18/yr. $5,534. ISSN 0022-104X. Available electronically.

Publishes the results of original research in zoology. Issues are arranged by subjects such as neurobiology, cell biology, genetics, and physiology. A subscription comes with four issues of *Molecular and Developmental Evolution (MDE),* which covers experimental approaches to evolution and development.

Journal of Wildlife Management. Vol. 1– . Bethesda, MD: The Wildlife Society, 19– . Quarterly. $200. ISSN 0022-541X.

Covers research papers and reviews on many issues in wildlife management such as nutrition. Subscription price includes *Wildlife Monographs,* which publishes papers too long for the journal. An official publication of the Wildlife Society.

Journal of Zoological Systematics and Evolutionary Research. Vol. 32– . Berlin: Blackwell Wissenschaft, 1994– . Quarterly. Price not available. ISSN 0947-5745. Available electronically.

Publishes papers in English, French, and German on zoological systematics and evolution. Formerly titled *Zeitschrift für zoologische Systematik und Evolutionsforschung.*

Journal of Zoology. Vol. 211– . Cambridge, UK: Cambridge University Press, 1987– . Monthly. $900. ISSN 0952-8369. Available electronically.

This venerable publication has been around for nearly 200 years in various incarnations. It publishes articles and reviews in all areas of zoology from behavior to physiology. It is published for the Zoological Society of London and incorporates the *Proceedings of the Zoological Society of London* (founded in 1830) and the *Transactions of the Zoological Society of London* (founded in 1833).

Physiological and Biochemical Zoology: PBZ. Vol. 72– . Chicago: University of Chicago Press, 1999– . Bimonthly. $445. ISSN 0031-935X. Available electronically.

Publishes research papers and technical comments in a variety of areas, such as thermoregulation, respiration, evolutionary physiology, and biochemistry. Sponsored by the Division of Comparative Physiology and Biochemistry of the Society for Integrative and Comparative Biology.

Systematic Biology. Vol. 1– . New York: Taylor and Francis, 1952– . Quarterly. $143. ISSN 1063-5157. Available electronically.

Publishes articles, announcements, historical essays, book reviews, and Points of View (short discussions of controversial topics) on a wide range of topics in systematic biology. Formerly titled *Systematic Zoology,* and although the title reflects a broader mission, almost all articles are still about animal systematics. The journal of the Society of Systematic Biologists.

Wildlife Society Bulletin. Vol. 1– . Bethesda, MD: The Wildlife Society, 1973– . Quarterly. $105. ISSN 0091-7648.

Articles covering all areas of interest to wildlife management are covered. Each issue features a "Special Coverage" section focusing on a single topic such as the effect of predation on avian recruitment in addition to regular articles arranged by broad subject. Regular departments include opinions, policy news, perspectives, obituaries, a bibliography of recent publications, and "The Lighter Side." The journal is unusual in that many of the articles include a photograph of the author(s), often taken in the field.

Zoological Journal of the Linnean Society. Vol. 48– . Cambridge, UK: Blackwell Science, 1969– . Monthly. $1,357. ISSN 0024-4082. Available electronically.

Publishes original papers on zoology with an emphasis on the diversity, systematics, and evolution of extinct and living animals. Published for the Linnean Society of London. Formerly *Journal of the Linnean Society: Zoology.* Formerly published by Academic Press.

Zoologica Scripta. Vol. 1– . Cambridge, UK: Blackwell Science, 1971– . Quarterly. $785. ISSN 0300-3256. Available electronically.

Publishes papers, review articles, and debate comments and replies dealing with zoological diversity and systematics. Published for the Norwegian Academy of Science and Letters and the Royal Swedish Academy of Sciences.

Zoologischer Anzeiger. Vol. 1– . Jena, Germany: Gustav Fischer Verlag, 1978– . Quarterly. $435. ISSN 0044-5231. Available electronically.

This journal publishes original research articles and book reviews on comparative zoology with special emphasis on morphology, systematics, biogeography, and evolutionary ecology.

Zoomorphology: An International Journal of Comparative and Functional Morphology. Vol. 96– . Heidelberg, Germany: Springer International, 1980– . Quarterly. $1,244. ISSN 0720-213X. Available electronically.

The journal publishes original papers based on morphological investigation of invertebrates and vertebrates.

Guides to the Literature

Balay, Robert, and Vee Friesner Carrington, eds. **Guide to Reference Books.** 11th ed. Chicago: American Library Association, 1996. 2,020 p. $275. ISBN 0838906699.

Earlier editions of this classic were edited by Eugene Sheehy, but all editions are highly regarded. The guide covers all subject areas and has about 15,500 items, of which about 100 are zoological. It is particularly strong in U.S. sources, but because it is updated at long intervals (the 10th edition was published in 1986), it may be out of date.

Biological Abstracts, Inc. **BiologyBrowser.** Philadelphia: BIOSIS, 1992– .
URL: http://www.biologybrowser.org/ (Accessed August 25, 2003).

A collection of free resources for biologists, some of them produced by
BIOSIS. The site also includes a collection of Web sites, several discussion
forums, a list of conferences, and other material. The Web site directory can
be searched or browsed by geographical location, organism, or subject.

Malinowsky, H. Robert. **Reference Sources in Science, Engineering,
Medicine, and Agriculture.** Phoenix: Oryx, 1994. 355 p. $42.95 (paper).
ISBN 0897747429; 0897747453 (paper).

Although slightly dated by now, this guide provides information on
about 2,400 reference sources in the scientific fields. The author includes
general information on the serial price increase problem, scientific communication, and types of reference sources. The remaining chapters cover
resources for the various subject areas, including about 100 major sources
for zoology. The annotations are brief and designed for the use of both
librarians and students.

Mullay, Marilyn, and Priscilla Schlicke. **Walford's Guide to Reference
Material, Vol. 1: Science and Technology.** 8th ed. London: Library Association, 1999. ISBN 185604341X (Vol. 1).

The classic British guide to reference sources. It is intended to be a one-
stop shop for identifying the major reference materials, including articles,
microfilm, CD-ROMs, and Web sites. Use as a complement to the U.S.
Guide to Reference Books, because it is particularly strong in the British
and English-language European sources. Lists about 270 sources in zoology and another 100 natural history sources.

Schmidt, Diane. **A Guide to Field Guides: Identifying the Natural History of North America.** Englewood, CO: Libraries Unlimited, 1999. 304
p. $65. ISBN 1563087073.

This comprehensive guide describes over 1,300 field guides to North
American plants and animals. Most are in print, although a few out-of-
print classics are also included. The descriptions of the guides are brief,
listing the number of species identified in the guide, the type of illustrations, and the presence of taxonomic keys, range maps, and checklists.

Schmidt, Diane. **International Field Guides.** Urbana: University of Illinois, 1998– . URL: http://door.library.uiuc.edu/bix/fieldguides/main.htm
(Accessed August 25, 2003).

This frequently updated site is a companion to the print guide to North American field guides listed above. Over 1,500 field guides from all parts of the world outside of North America are described. Most are in English, and most are readily available in North America. The descriptions follow the same format listed above.

Schmidt, Diane, Elisabeth B. Davis, and Pamela F. Jacobs. **Using the Biological Literature: A Practical Guide.** 3rd ed. New York: Marcel Dekker, 2002. 474 p. $85. ISBN 0824706676.

An annotated guide to resources for all the biological sciences, with separate chapters on entomology and zoology. Each chapter identifies resources such as indexes, dictionaries and encyclopedias, handbooks, journals, and associations. Major Web sites are also listed, and an associated Web site at http://www.library.uiuc.edu/biologicalliterature/ keeps the URLs updated.

Wyatt, H. V., ed. **Information Sources in the Life Sciences.** 4th ed., rev. New Providence, NJ: Bowker/Saur, 1997. (Guides to Information Sources). 264 p. $95. ISBN 1857390709.

A British student's guide to the life sciences literature. The authors discuss a number of general topics such as scientific fraud, invisible colleges, and the types of scientific literature (newsletters, encyclopedias, statistics, etc.) that are not covered in the other guides to the literature mentioned in this section. They also discuss the literature of various disciplines, including zoology. The major resources are listed and briefly described.

Biographies and Histories

American Men and Women of Science: A Biographical Directory of Today's Leaders in Physical, Biological and Related Science. 21st ed. New York: Bowker, 2001. 8 vol. $1,151.25 (set). ISBN 0835243443 (set).

This directory provides brief biographies of 120,000 living scientists and engineers from the United States and Canada, including birthplace and date, spouse and children's names, scientific field, education, honors and awards, research focus, professional memberships, and addresses.

Bynum, W. F., et al., eds. **Dictionary of the History of Science.** Princeton, NJ: Princeton University Press, 1985 reprint. 494 p. $28.95 (paper). ISBN 0691023840 (paper).

Seven hundred signed articles discuss the key ideas and core features of recent Western science in all fields. The dictionary includes a brief annotated bibliography and biographical index.

Concise Dictionary of Scientific Biography. 2nd ed. New York: Scribners, 2000. 1,097 p. $168.75. ISBN 0684806312.

This is an abridgement of the authoritative and comprehensive *Dictionary of Scientific Biography* (below), complete through supplement 11, and includes an index.

Dewsbury, Donald A., ed. **Leaders in the Study of Animal Behavior: Autobiographical Perspectives.** Lewisburg, PA: Bucknell University Press, 1985. 512 p. $65. ISBN 0838750524.

This is a collection of autobiographical essays written by the major figures in the study of animal behavior, including luminaries such as Konrad Lorenz, John Maynard Smith, Edward O. Wilson, Niko Tinbergen, and Irenaus Eibl-Eibesfeldt.

Evans, Howard Ensign. **Pioneer Naturalists: The Discovery and Naming of North American Plants and Animals.** New York: Holt, 1993. 294 p. $22.50. ISBN 0805023372.

Evans, an entomologist and popular science writer, tells the story of a number of North American species and the naturalists who named them. There are fascinating biographies of people as well known as John James Audubon or as little known as Philip Reese Uhler. Although the book covers only about 50 species and/or people, the chronology and bibliography provide a good starting point for further research.

Gillispie, Charles Coulston, ed. **Dictionary of Scientific Biography.** New York: Scribners, 1981. 9 vol. $1,800 (set). ISBN 068480588X (set).

This major biographical dictionary covers all areas of science with over 5,000 lengthy, detailed entries and citations to portraits of the most famous scientists. Includes bibliographies and index. For the abridged edition, see the *Concise Dictionary of Scientific Biography*, above.

Houck, Lynne D., and Lee C. Drickamer, eds. **Foundations of Animal Behavior: Classic Papers with Commentaries.** Chicago: University of Chicago Press, 1996. 843 p. $105; $37.50 (paper). ISBN 0226354563; 0226354571 (paper).

Includes 44 classic papers in animal behavior by well-known authors from Charles Darwin to John Maynard Smith. The papers are arranged in four broad categories, and each section has a commentary by modern researchers.

Journal of the History of Biology. Vol. 1– . Norwell, MA: Kluwer, 1968– . Triennial. $270. ISSN 0022-5010. Available electronically.

The emphasis in this journal is on the developments during the nineteenth and twentieth centuries in biology. It is aimed at both practicing biologists and historians of science. The journal publishes articles, essay reviews covering topics such as the 25th anniversary of E. O. Wilson's *Sociobiology,* and book reviews.

Kisling, Vernon N., Jr., ed. **Zoo and Aquarium History: Ancient Animal Collections to Zoological Gardens.** Boca Raton, FL: CRC Press, 2001. 415 p. $79.95. ISBN 084932100X.

An in-depth examination of the history of zoos and aquaria around the world. The authors begin with a chronological discussion of animal collections and menageries in the ancient world from earliest times to the Renaissance. More recent zoo history is divided by geographical locations. Europe and North American zoos receive the most attention, but all parts of the world are covered. A number of interesting side issues are discussed, such as our fascination with pandas and other "charismatic megafauna."

Melville, R. V. **Towards Stability in the Names of Animals: A History of the International Commission on Zoological Nomenclature, 1895–1995.** London: ICZN, 1995. 92 p. ISBN 0853010056.

Although this is a rather esoteric history, it covers an important facet of zoology. The author, who was the secretary of the International Commission on Zoological Nomenclature for many years and also one of the editors of *Official Lists and Indexes of Names and Works in Zoology* (below), discusses efforts to stabilize nomenclature from pre-Linnean times to the present. Many of the major taxonomists of early times are mentioned, and numerous portraits are included.

Porter, Roy, and Marilyn Bailey Ogilvie, eds. **The Biographical Dictionary of Scientists.** 3rd ed. New York: Oxford University Press, 2000. 6 vol. $125. ISBN 0195216636.

This set contains biographical information for over 1,200 scientists from a wide range of scientific fields, including zoology. There are several appendixes such as seven chronological reviews of developments in various scientific areas, an extensive glossary, a list of Nobel laureates, and a comprehensive index.

Dictionaries and Encyclopedias

Allaby, Michael, ed. **Dictionary of Zoology.** 2nd ed. New York: Oxford University Press, 1999. 508 p. (Oxford Paperback Reference). $15.95 (paper). ISBN 0192800760 (paper).

This dictionary is a revised edition of *Concise Oxford Dictionary of Zoology,* which was based on the 1985 *Oxford Dictionary of Natural History* (below). It features short definitions of terms used by zoologists, drawn from subjects such as anatomy, physiology, and ecology. About half the entries are either common or scientific names of animals, including higher-level taxa such as families and orders. There are also brief biographies of prominent zoologists. The inclusion of the taxonomic groups is rare in a dictionary, making this a useful general dictionary for budding zoologists.

Barrows, Edward M. **Animal Behavior Desk Reference: A Dictionary of Animal Behavior, Ecology, and Evolution.** 2nd ed. Boca Raton, FL: CRC, 2001. 922 p. $149.95. ISBN 0849320054.

Containing terms used in animal behavior and related subjects, this dictionary is unusual in that it cites the original author or source of the terms defined. The author emphasizes conceptual terms, not taxonomic or anatomical terms. Many of the terms are gathered together under a main heading (the types of biotopes are clustered under the main entry for biotope, for instance). There are appendixes listing organism names in hierarchical format using the three-domain system and associations interested in the areas covered by the desk reference.

Burnie, David. **The Kingfisher Illustrated Animal Encyclopedia.** New York: Kingfisher, 2000. 319 p. $27.95. ISBN 0753452839.

Although aimed at older children, this one-volume encyclopedia offers a good survey of the animal kingdom. Arranged in taxonomic order, it contains colorful photographs of representative or interesting species. As might be expected, the more charismatic groups of animals such as birds and mammals are covered in more depth than squishy liver flukes and their kin, but this encyclopedia provides more coverage of invertebrates than many competing children's encyclopedias.

Encyclopedia of Life Sciences. New York: Nature Publishing Group, 2001. 20 vol. $4,200. ISBN 1561592749.

A massive new reference tool for biologists, this encyclopedia contains 4,000 articles written by over 5,000 well-known experts. The encyclopedia is strongest in molecular biology and similar fields; there are few taxonomic groups represented in articles. Also available online (by subscription only), the continuously updated *ELS Online* will provide direct links from references to primary literature and other resources.

Grzimek, Bernhard, et al., eds. **Grzimek's Animal Life Encyclopedia.** 2nd ed. Detroit: Gale, 2003. 17 vol. $1,595 (set). ISBN 0787653624 (set).

There is no encyclopedia to compare with this classic, which was originally published in Germany in the 1960s. All groups of animals are covered in the 17 volumes, with many color illustrations and photographs. Articles include both general topics such as bird migration as well as taxonomic articles on each major taxon.

Henderson, Isabella Ferguson. **Henderson's Dictionary of Biological Terms.** 12th ed. Eleanor Lawrence, ed. London: Prentice Hall, 2000. 719 p. ISBN 0582414989 (paper).

A classic biology dictionary, the latest edition provides definitions of over 23,000 terms in all areas of biology, including zoology. Appendixes cover outlines of the plant, fungi, protoctista, and animal kingdoms and the bacteria and archaea domains, plus virus families and the Greek or Latin origin of common word elements used in biological terms. This dictionary is aimed at a more advanced audience than the similar *Oxford Dictionary of Biology,* below.

Hine, Robert, ed. **The Facts on File Dictionary of Biology.** 3rd ed. New York: Facts on File, 1999. 361 p. $44; $17.95 (paper). ISBN 0816039070; 0816039089 (paper).

Contains 3,300 entries covering all aspects of biology, defining the most commonly used biological terms; includes an appendix with charts of the animal and plant kingdoms and amino acid structures. Aimed at a high school audience.

Immelmann, Klaus, and Colin Beer. **A Dictionary of Ethology.** Cambridge, MA: Harvard University Press, 1989. 336 p. $60. ISBN 0674205065.

Although now out of print, this is still one of the best dictionaries for animal behavior. The definitions are lengthy and nontechnical, and although most are from classical ethology, terms used in behavioral ecology and sociobiology are also found. The dictionary is a translation of the German *Wörterbuch der Verhaltensforschung.*

Jaeger, Edmund C. **A Source-Book of Biological Names and Terms.** 3rd ed. Springfield, IL: Charles C. Thomas, 1978. 360 p. $61.95. ISBN 0398009163.

The classic source for definitions of word elements that are used in biology, both nomenclature and technical terms. Rather than define each word, Jaeger defines elements (e.g., pter = wing; arg = white or swift-footed) and gives their derivation and examples of their use. A very useful tool for the beginning taxonomist.

Jeffrey, Charles. **Biological Nomenclature.** 3rd ed. London: Edward Arnold, 1989. 86 p. ISBN 0713129832 (paper).

This little guide covers nomenclature for microorganisms, plants, and animals, including cultivated plants and domestic animals. It discusses general principles as well as specific practices in the use of nomenclature, and although now out of print is one of the standard sources for guidance in the proper use of nomenclature.

Leven, Simon Asher, ed. **Encyclopedia of Biodiversity.** San Diego: Academic, 2001. 5 vol. $1,295. ISBN 0122268652 (set).

This encyclopedia covers a wide range of topics, from individual taxonomic groups and ecosystems to evolution, ecology, genetics, and systematics to conservation, public policies, and human effects. Not all taxa are covered, but the articles offer a nice overview of what is known about the number and variety of species in most major taxa as well as the ecology and abundance of the organisms.

Lincoln, R.J., and G.A. Boxshall, eds. **Cambridge Illustrated Dictionary of Natural History.** Cambridge, MA: Cambridge University Press, 1987. 413 p. $49.95. ISBN 0521305519 (paper).

Contains short definitions of scientific names of organisms and terms from ecology, plus cross-references for common names. The major taxonomic groups of microorganisms, flowering plants, and animals are covered down to the order; flowering plants, vertebrates, and economically important insects are covered to the family. There are also over 700 line illustrations of organisms. The dictionary is partly updated by Allaby's *Dictionary of Zoology,* above.

Lincoln, Roger J., Geoff Boxshall, and Paul Clark. **A Dictionary of Ecology, Evolution, and Systematics.** 2nd ed. New York: Cambridge University Press, 1998. 361 p. $30 (paper). ISBN 0521591392; 052143842X (paper).

The dictionary could just as well be titled a dictionary of natural history, because the terms defined in it are primarily from that broadly defined field. Definitions are brief and include cross-references. Although technical systematics terms are defined, animal taxa are not, unlike Allaby's *Dictionary of Zoology,* above. There are 21 appendixes providing a number of useful tables and lists such as the geological time scale, taxonomic hierarchy, the Beaufort wind scale, proof correction marks, and acronyms and abbreviations.

Lipton, James. **An Exaltation of Larks: The Ultimate Edition.** New York: Viking, 1991. 324 p. ISBN 0670300446.

This unusual resource lists the "proper" terms referring to groups of animals, humans, or objects. Here you can find plurals such as "a drift of hogs" or "a knot of toads," all with citations to original, often medieval, sources. The author also offers a number of tongue-in-cheek modern versions such as "an advance of authors" or "a buttonhole of lobbyists." A similar British publication, Rex Collings, *A Crash of Rhinoceroses,* includes a number of British dialect terms.

Nature Encyclopedia. New York: Oxford University Press, 2001. 472 p. $65. ISBN 0195218345.

This colorful encyclopedia covers plants, animals, and geology. Numerous animals are described and illustrated, listed by their common names. American readers should be aware that the encyclopedia was first published in the UK, so some common species are listed under their British or European common name, rather than the one that Americans are accustomed to. The encyclopedia is a good single source for basic information on a variety of animals.

Nomenclatural Glossary for Zoology. BIOSIS, 1996. URL: http://www.biosis.org.uk/free_resources/nomglos.html (Accessed August 25, 2003).

This glossary is designed to aid indexers in the production of nomen-clatural entries for the Zoological Record but is valuable for anyone need-ing definitions of the often technical terminology used in taxonomy. It covers about 400 terms such as holotype, nomen imperfectum, or tau-tonymy. The glossary is consistent with the *International Code of Zoolog-ical Nomenclature,* 4th ed. (see below).

Oxford Dictionary of Biology. 4th ed. Oxford: Oxford University Press, 2000. 640 p. $14.95 ISBN 0192801023 (paper).

A comprehensive illustrated dictionary covering over 4,700 entries in all areas of biology. Most of the definitions are brief, but there are also a number of charts, timetables, and longer essays on topics such as geneti-cally modified organisms. In addition, appendixes provide a simplified outline of the classification of plants and animals and a geological time chart. Students will find this dictionary useful, and at the paperback price they can even afford a copy for themselves. One minor caveat is that this edition uses the British spellings of terms such as "behaviour" and "colour."

Tsur, Samuel A. **Elsevier's Dictionary of the Genera of Life.** New York: Elsevier, 1999. 556 p. $152.50. ISBN 0444829059.

About 5,300 genera of bacteria, fungi, plants, and animals are listed in this dictionary. Each entry lists the genus, the family, or order (including common names of the taxa), and a brief description with distribution and one or more sample species. There is a distinct medical tinge to the dic-tionary, because most of the sample species are of medicinal or disease-carrying importance. In fact, because genera are often quite variable and widespread, the medical orientation occasionally causes misleading entries. The dictionary is still useful as a source of information about thou-sands of genera, but users might also check Allaby's *Dictionary of Zool-ogy, above.*

Textbooks

Alcock, John. **Animal Behavior: An Evolutionary Approach.** 7th ed. Sunderland, MA: Sinauer, 2001. 543 p. $79.95. ISBN 0878930116.

Covers both the proximate causes, such as environmental aspects and neurobiology, and the evolution of animal behavior. Examples are taken both from invertebrates and vertebrates, and there are color photographs.

The text is aimed at undergraduate students and includes discussions on controversies in animal behavior and the tentative nature of scientific conclusions. The author has also written a number of books on animal behavior for a general audience.

Alexander, R. McNeill. **Animals.** New York: Cambridge University Press, 1990. 509 p. $105. ISBN 0521343917; 052134865X (paper).

Surveys the animal kingdom, from single-celled animals to mammals, suitable for undergraduate students. The taxonomy, structure, physiology, and natural history of each group is discussed. This work is a revised version of Alexander's earlier texts, *The Invertebrates* and *The Chordates.*

Harris, C. Leon. **Concepts in Zoology.** 2nd ed. New York: HarperCollins College, 1996. 891 p. ISBN 0673992438.

This general text emphasizes the concepts involved in zoology, rather than the details. Each chapter starts out with a conceptual outline and ends with a summary, list of key terms, chapter test, and further readings. Subjects covered include basic cellular and molecular biology, physiology, ecology and evolution, and diversity. About half of the book consists of a survey of the animal kingdom.

Hickman, Cleveland P., Larry S. Roberts, and Allan Larson. **Animal Diversity.** 2nd ed. Boston: McGraw-Hill, 2000. 429 p. $75.30. ISBN 0070122008.

An undergraduate-level survey of the animal kingdom, this text is suitable for one-semester courses. It covers diversity, evolutionary relationships, adaptations, and environmental interactions. After beginning chapters introducing the science of zoology, and the evolution, anatomy, and classification of animals, the bulk of the book consists of chapters covering each of the major taxa from protists to mammals. The text has a profusion of colorful illustrations and numerous sidebars. Each chapter concludes with a summary, review questions, selected references, and links to the Web. The links are also freely available at the book's Web site, http://www.mhhe.com/biosci/pae/zoology/animaldiversity/.

Hickman, Cleveland P., Larry S. Roberts, and Allan Larson. **Integrated Principles of Zoology.** 11th ed. Boston: McGraw-Hill, 2001. 899 p. $95.94. ISBN 0072909617.

Like most other zoology textbooks, this one covers basic biology, genetics, physiology, and ecology as well as the diversity of animal life.

Each chapter concludes with a summary, review questions, and selected references. The text is supported by several multimedia products, including a tutorial CD-ROM, an Online Learning Center Web site at http://www.mhhe.com/biosci/pae/zoology/hickman11/, and a Visual Resource Library CD-ROM. For undergraduates, but more advanced than Miller and Harley, below.

Krebs, J. R., and N. B. Davies, eds. **Behavioural Ecology: An Evolutionary Approach.** 4th ed. Cambridge, MA: Blackwell Science, 1997. 456 p. $75.95. ISBN 0865427313.

A graduate and upper-level undergraduate text with contributions by experts in behavioral ecology. The text is in three parts, titled "Mechanisms and Individual Behaviour," "From Individual Behaviour to Social Systems," and "Life Histories, Phylogenies and Populations." The same editors have also created an introductory text, *Introduction to Behavioural Ecology.*

Mayr, Ernst, and Peter D. Ashlock. **Principles of Systematic Zoology.** 2nd ed. New York: McGraw-Hill, 1991. 475 p. ISBN 0070411441.

Mayr is one of the best-known taxonomists, and this is a classic text for taxonomy. The second edition is divided into two sections, microtaxonomy (at the species level and below) and macrotaxonomy (above the species level). A third section, methodological issues, covers more general topics such as systematics collections, publications, and the rules of nomenclature. The authors provide both practical advice and general philosophy and concepts.

Miller, Stephen A., and John P. Harley. **Zoology.** 5th ed. New York: McGraw-Hill, 2001. ISBN 0071124071.

An undergraduate text covering general biology, systematics, and comparative form and function of animals. Some of the chapters are only available from the publisher's Web site to purchasers of the text.

Nielsen, Claus. **Animal Evolution: Interrelationships of the Living Phyla.** 2nd ed. New York: Oxford University Press, 2001. 563 p. $115.50; $55.00 (paper). ISBN 0198506813; 0198506821 (paper).

A survey of the animal kingdom, with emphasis on the phylogenetic relationships among the extant animal phyla. The author uses both morphogenic traits and molecular biology to piece together the evolutionary relationships between the groups. Each group is described in detail, with emphasis on anatomy, development, and embryology. There are numerous illustrations, lengthy bibliographies, and a list of future research subjects for each phyla. Final chapters deal with problematic taxa, cladistical analyses using numerical data, and molecular phylogeny. The book is intended as a supplement to systematic zoology courses.

Ridley, Mark. **Animal Behavior: An Introduction to Behavioral Mechanisms, Development, and Ecology.** 2nd ed. Boston: Blackwell Scientific, 1995. 288 p. $74.95. ISBN 0865423903 (paper).

An introductory textbook to classical animal behavior. Each chapter includes a summary and further reading. The text is organized around the underlying questions of animal behavior such as mechanisms, evolutionary history, and development of behavior. There are many illustrations, including numerous black-and-white photographs by Niko Tinbergen.

Schuh, Randall T. **Biological Systematics: Principles and Applications.** Ithaca, NY: Cornell University Press, 2000. 236 p. $49.95. ISBN 0801436753.

Presents systematic theory based on cladistics and the principle of parsimony. It is in three sections, covering background information, cladistic methods, and the application of cladistic results. There is also a glossary and an appendix listing software for phylogenetic analysis, and each chapter has a bibliography. The background chapters provide a nice overview of the history and practice of nomenclature and systematics, but the bulk of the book is aimed at advanced graduate students.

Simpson, George Gaylord. **Principles of Animal Taxonomy.** New York: Columbia University Press, 1990. 247 p. ISBN 023109650X (paper).

A reprint of a classic text by one of the grand old men of evolution and taxonomy. Rather than being a by-the-numbers manual, this is a philosophical discussion of taxonomy, its history and practice. Even though the picky details of taxonomies have changed since the book was first published in 1961 and Simpson does not discuss cladistics in any detail, this is still a valuable text for new taxonomists.

Wilson, Edward O. **Sociobiology: The New Synthesis.** 25th anniv. ed. Cambridge, MA: Belknap Press of Harvard University Press, 2000. 697 p. $85; $29.95 (paper). ISBN 0674000897; 0674002350 (paper).

Although many of the conclusions of human sociobiology remain controversial, animal sociobiology is widely accepted. This massive compilation helped launch the field and is one of the best-known works in the field. There were few changes for the anniversary edition.

Winston, Judith E. **Describing Species: Practical Taxonomic Procedure for Biologists.** New York: Columbia University Press, 1999. 518 p. $71; $36.50 (paper). ISBN 0231068247; 0231068255 (paper).

The publisher refers to this guide as "a *Strunk & White* of species description," which about sums it up. Like the classic style manual, *Describing Species* provides a detailed guide to the minutiae of writing, in this case of creating good taxonomic descriptions for plants and animals. Introductory chapters cover the whys and hows of taxonomy and nomenclature, followed by sections on recognizing species (including how to do a literature search). The bulk of the book consists of detailed information on writing species descriptions: headings and synonyms, etymology of species names, type and voucher material, diagnosis, the parts of the full description, and how and where to publish. There are also chapters on subspecies, genera, creating dichotomous keys, descriptions of higher taxa, common problems, and further studies. An excellent reference for taxonomists of all levels of expertise.

Checklists and Classification Schemes

Animal Identification: A Reference Guide. London: British Museum (Natural History); New York: Wiley, 1980. 3 vol. ISBN 0471277657 (vol. 1); 0471277665 (vol. 2); 0471277673 (vol. 3).

This set identifies primary sources dealing with the taxonomy or identification of animal groups. Most of the sources are quite technical, although many field guides and other general works are included. Each volume is arranged by taxonomic group, with sections for general works, more narrow taxonomic treatments and geographical areas. Volume 1 covers marine and brackish water animals; Volume 2, land and freshwater animals excluding insects; and Volume 3 covers insects. Although the set is out of date, it is still a good starting point for identifying sources.

Bulletin of Zoological Nomenclature. Vol. 1– . London: International Commission on Zoological Nomenclature, 1943– . Quarterly. $200. ISSN 0007-5167.

The *Bulletin* contains requests to set aside the provisions of the International Code of Zoological Nomenclature in cases where their strict observance would cause confusion, plus comments on these requests. The commission then makes a ruling (called an Opinion), which is also published. The *Bulletin* also contains articles and notes relevant to zoological nomenclature.

International Code of Zoological Nomenclature = Code International de Nomenclature Zoologique. 4th ed. London: International Trust for Zoological Nomenclature, 1999. 306 p. ISBN 0853010064.

The International Code provides the rules for establishing nomenclature for animals. It is periodically updated and can be overruled only by the International Commission on Zoological Nomenclature through applications published in the *Bulletin of Zoological Nomenclature,* above. The code is available in German, Japanese, Russian, and Spanish versions, and Chinese and Ukrainian translations are planned. See also the *Official Lists and Indexes of Names and Works in Zoology,* below.

Index to Organism Names. Philadelphia: BIOSIS. URL: http://www. biosis.org/free_resources/ion.html. (Accessed August 25, 2003).

This searchable index contains nomenclature taken from the BIOSIS organization (publishers of *Biological Abstracts* and *Zoological Record*) and several other groups. The index provides basic information on nomenclature and hierarchy for plant and animal names, plus counts of the number of times the animal name occurred in volumes of the *Zoological Record,* which reflects the frequency the name is used in the literature. Currently, the database includes bacteria, algae, mosses, fungi, and animals. The Index consists of the publicly available portions of the *TRITON* database (Taxonomy Resource and Index to Organism Names), which is currently in development by BIOSIS.

Maddison, D. R., and W. P. Maddison. **The Tree of Life: A Multi-Authored, Distributed Internet Project Containing Information about Phylogeny and Biodiversity.** 1998. http://tolweb.org/tree/. (Accessed August 25, 2003).

The Tree of Life covers all groups of organisms, living and extinct. Most of the groups are treated only to the generic level. All of the treatments include extensive bibliographies dealing with the systematics of that group, and most also include photos or drawings of representative species, plus links to other Web sites dealing with the taxon. *The Tree of Life,* unlike some of the other comprehensive Web sites listed here, is aimed at researchers and advanced students.

Margulis, Lynn, and Karlene V. Schwartz. **The Five Kingdoms: An Illustrated Guide to the Phyla of Life on Earth.** 3rd ed. New York: W. H. Freeman, 1998. 520 p. $29.95 (paper). ISBN 071673026X; 0716730278 (paper).

Provides an introduction to the five kingdoms of Monera, Protoctista, Fungi, Animalia, and Plantae. This reference discusses classification schemes, the general features of each kingdom, an illustrative phylogeny, and a bibliography of suggested reading for each phylum. An appendix lists genera, including genus, phylum, and common name, for each. Also available on CD-ROM. This guide provides a nice overview of the five-kingdom classification scheme, which is widely (although not universally) accepted. It is useful both as a reference to the phyla of living organisms and also as a text for high school and undergraduate students.

NCBI Taxonomy Homepage. Bethesda, MD: NCBI, 2000– . URL: http://www.ncbi.nlm.nih.gov/Taxonomy/taxonomyhome.html/. (Accessed August 25, 2003).

This page was created to publicize the names of the 103,048 species (as of September 25, 2003) of organisms with gene sequences listed in GenBank. Although less than 25% of the species represented in GenBank are metazoans, this still represents a large number of animals. The taxonomy home page is not a taxonomic authority, but it serves as a useful guide to the current state of the field and contains many links to other taxonomic resources, both on the Web and in print.

Nomenclator Zoologicus. Vol. 1–4. London: Zoological Society of London, 1939–40. sup. 5– .

This list provides bibliographic citations to all names of genera and subgenera published since the 10th edition of Linneaus's *Systema Naturae* in 1758. The four volumes of the main work cover the period 1758 to 1935, with supplements occurring approximately every decade thereafter. The most recent supplement is number 9 (1978–94) published in 1996. The combined volumes include over 300,000 names listed alphabetically with the original citation and an indication of which animal group the name belongs to. Only the supplements are in print.

Melville, R. V., and J. D. D. Smith, eds. **Official Lists and Indexes of Names and Works in Zoology.** London: International Trust for Zoological Nomenclature, 1987. 366 p. ISBN 0853010048.

This list contains over 9,000 scientific names and titles of works that have been voted on by the International Commission on Zoological

Nomenclature and published in the *Bulletin of Zoological Nomenclature* up to the end of 1985. A supplement was published in 2001 providing another 2,385 entries from 1985 to 2000. There are four main sections: family-group names, generic names, specific names, and titles of works in addition to a systematic index and bibliographic references. The main title contains material from earlier editions of *Official Index of Rejected and Invalid Family Group Names in Zoology, Official Index of Rejected and Invalid Works in Zoological Nomenclature, Official List of Family Group Names in Zoology,* and *Official List of Works Approved as Available for Zoological Nomenclature.*

Sherborn, Charles Davies. **Index Animalium: Sive, Index Nominum quae ab A.D. MDCCLVIII Generibus et Speciebus Animalium Imposita Sunt, Societabus Eruditorum Adiuvantibus.** Bath, UK: Chivers, 1969. 1195 p.

First published from 1902 to 1933, this index provides a list of animals named from 1758 to 1800, with citations to the first description. There is also an extensive bibliography of works used to compile the index and an index to generic names listing the species names associated with them.

Handbooks

2000 IUCN Red List of Threatened Species. Cambridge, UK: International Union for Conservation of Nature and Natural Resources, 2000. URL: http://www.redlist.org/. (Accessed August 25, 2003).

For over 40 years, the IUCN Red Lists have provided taxonomic, conservation status, and distribution information for endangered plant and animal species worldwide. Separate Red Lists were available for various groups such as birds or fishes. However, beginning with the 2000 edition, the lists have been combined and will only be available electronically. They are available for free, on the Web at the URL listed above, and on CD-ROM for a fee. The Web site provides a great deal of information on the IUCN's programs, the criteria used for listing a species, references, and extensive links to other sites that provide information on the listed species.

Altman, Philip L., and Dorothy S. Dittmer, eds. **Biology Data Book.** 2nd ed. Bethesda, MD: Federation of American Societies for Experimental Biology, 1972–74. (Biological Handbooks series). ISBN 0913822078 (vol. 2); 0913822086 (vol. 3).

This set is out of print but still useful. Volume 1 covers genetics, cytology, reproduction, development, and growth; Volume 2 covers biological regulators, the environment and survival, parasitism, and neurobiology; Volume 3 has data on nutrition, metabolism, respiration, and body fluids. There are related volumes on respiration and nutrition. Each volume contains a detailed table of contents and index, and Volume 3 has an appendix listing scientific and common names of about 2,000 flowering plants and animals.

Animal Anatomy on File. Rev. ed. New York: Facts on File, 1999. 1 vol. $185 (binder); $249 (CD-ROM). ISBN 0816038759 (binder); 0816042187 (CD-ROM).

Contains over 250 images of animal anatomy for over 50 species of animals, from sponges to vertebrates. Both external and internal anatomy is covered, and the illustrations are labeled. The illustrations are designed to be readily photocopied for use in classroom discussions or tests, so they are fairly basic outline drawings. See also *Life Sciences on File,* below.

Ax, Peter. **Multicellular Animals: A New Approach to the Phylogenetic Order in Nature.** 2 vol. New York: Springer, 1996– . $99 (vol. 1); $199 (vol. 2). ISBN 3540608036 (vol. 1); 3540674063 (vol. 2).

This set presents a phylogeny of all metazoan animals, the first attempt at a comprehensive arrangement. Volume 1 introduces the concepts and history of phylogenetic systematics and details the phylogenies of the Porifera through the Plathelminthes; Volume 2 covers the Trochozoa through Arthropoda. A proposed third volume will cover the remaining taxa. For each taxa, the author provides phylogenies, illustrations of representatives, and a discussion of anatomy, development, and other topics that demonstrate the phylogenies. The work is a translation of the author's *System der Metazoa.*

Barnes, R. S. K., ed. **The Diversity of Living Organisms.** Malden, MA: Blackwell Science, 1998. 345 p. $60.95 (paper). ISBN 0632049170 (paper).

A synoptic guide to all classes of existing organisms, from prokaryotes to mammals. There are numerous black-and-white illustrations, demonstrating basic body plans for each class, and brief synoptic descriptions. The book is particularly useful for the lesser-known taxa, because it discusses all classes of organisms in the same depth. In fact, the Malacostraca (higher crustaceans) merit more verbiage than the Reptilia.

Blackwelder, Richard E., and George S. Garoian. **CRC Handbook of Animal Diversity.** Boca Raton, FL: CRC Press, 1986. 555 p. $311. ISBN 0849329922.

This handbook is intended as a reference to all aspects of animals that can be studied comparatively, especially such topics as anatomy, physiology, and classification. The handbook is arranged by topic such as life cycles, morphology, and behavior. Each chapter contains comparative data or summary statements about anything from reproduction across the animal kingdom to digestive organs.

Clewis, Beth. **Index to Illustrations of Animals and Plants.** New York: Neal-Schuman, 1991. 217 p. ISBN 1555700721.

Finding illustrations of plants and animals can be tricky. This index lists 62,000 plants and animals from around the world found in 142 books. The species are listed by common name, with indexes for scientific name and book title. The index updates both Munz and Thompson (below), covering books published in the 1980s.

Geigy Scientific Tables. 8th ed., rev. 6 vol. West Caldwell, NJ: Ciba-Geigy, 1981–92. ISBN 0914168509.

Although now out of print, this set of tables is still extremely useful. The set includes tables for units of measurement, body fluids, nutrition, statistics, mathematical formulas, physical chemistry, blood, somatometric data, biochemistry, inborn errors of metabolism, pharmacogenetics and ecogenetics, heart and circulation, and bacteria and protozoa. This set and the *Biology Data Book* (above) are the standard sources for tabular data.

Grassé, P. P., ed. **Traité de Zoologie: Anatomie, Systématique, Biologie.** Paris: Masson, 1948– . 17 vol. Price varies.

A classic treatise on the biology of animals, both fossil and living, arranged systematically by taxonomic divisions. All aspects of animal biology are covered, such as reproduction, physiology, behavior, and taxonomy. The handbook is written in French, and volumes are published out of sequence. There are extensive bibliographies. It is comparable to *Handbuch der Zoologie,* below.

Halstead, Bruce W. **Poisonous and Venomous Marine Animals of the World.** 2nd ed., rev. Princeton, NJ: Darwin, 1988. 1,168 p. $250. ISBN 0878500502.

Originally published in three volumes, this massive handbook covers the toxic marine invertebrates and vertebrates of the world. For each group of organisms, data is presented on species reported as venomous with their common names, distributions, and sources. The author also provides information on the biology of the organisms, the morphology of the venom apparatus, the mechanism of intoxication, medical aspects, public health aspects, toxicology, pharmacology, and chemistry.

Handbuch der Zoologie: Eine Naturgeschichte der Stamme des Tier-reiches. 2nd ed. Willy Kükenthal, ed. Berlin: W. de Gruyter, 1968– . Price varies.

A multivolume treatise covering the animal kingdom. It is arranged in systematic order, from the protozoa to the mammals. It is similar to *Traité de Zoologie,* above. The handbook contains detailed information on each group, including numerous illustrations and lengthy bibliographies. Most of the volumes are in German, but some of the more recent ones are in English. The first edition was started in 1923 and completed in 1967, and to date the second edition contains volumes for the Pogonophora, the insects, and selected volumes for the mammals.

InfoNatura: Birds and Mammals of Latin America. Version 1.0. Arlington, VA: NatureServe, 2001. URL: http://www.natureserve.org/infonatura/ (Accessed August 25, 2003).

This site provides conservation-oriented information on more than 5,500 species of birds and mammals of Latin America and the Caribbean. The database is searchable by English common name and scientific name or by higher taxa. The species accounts include taxonomic information such as English, Spanish, and Portuguese common names, global conservation (IUCN and CITES) status, distribution, and references. InfoNatura is a product of NatureServe (see below) in collaboration with Conserva-tion Data Centers in 12 Latin American and Caribbean countries.

Integrated Taxonomic Information System (ITIS). Washington, DC: U.S. Department of Agriculture, 1998– . URL: http://www.itis.usda.gov/ (Accessed August 25, 2003).

ITIS is a database of authoritative names for organisms, primarily plants and animals from North America but also from around the world. It is the result of a partnership of several federal agencies, including NOAA, USDA, USGS, and the Smithsonian Institute. The scientific names are taken from authoritative sources selected by taxonomic experts. The database can be queried by common or scientific name and includes both valid and invalid names. Results include the status of the name, taxonomic hierarchy, references, and distribution. Portions of the database can also be downloaded.

Lehner, Philip N. **Handbook of Ethological Methods.** 2nd ed. New York: Cambridge University Press, 1996. 672 p. ISBN 0521554055.

A compilation of the techniques for studying animal behavior, this handbook is the most comprehensive guide to experimental and statistical methods for the field. The author includes a general overview of the study of animal behavior, followed by sections on data collection, analysis, and interpretation. There are numerous examples and illustrations, and appendices with statistical tables, an overview of the use of computers in ethology, ethological ethics, and guidelines for the use of animals in research.

Life Sciences on File. Rev. ed. New York: Facts on File, 1999. 1 vol. $185 (binder); $185 (CD-ROM). ISBN 0816038724 (binder); 0816042160 (CD-ROM).

A loose-leaf binder containing over 1,000 reproducible diagrams and drawings covering life sciences topics. The set is in six sections titled Unity of Life, Continuity, Diversity, Maintenance, Human Biology, and Ecology. The Diversity section covers classification and has illustrations of the major groups of plants and animals. There is also a chronology and glossary. *Animal Anatomy on File,* above, is part of the same series.

Munz, Lucile Thompson, and Nedra G. Slauson. **Index to Illustrations of Living Things Outside North America: Where to Find Pictures of Flora and Fauna.** Hamden, CT: Archon Books, 1981. 441 p. ISBN 0208018573.

A companion volume to Thompson's *Index to Illustrations* (below) and updated by Clewis, above. The index is arranged by common name and lists illustrations of 9,000 species of animals and plants from 206 books. There is a scientific name index and a bibliography of sources.

NatureServe Explorer: An Online Encyclopedia of Life. Version 1.6. Arlington, VA: NatureServe, 2001. URL: http://www.natureserve.org/explorer. (Accessed August 25, 2003).

A database of conservation information on over 50,000 plants, animals, and ecological communities of North America. The data included in each species account includes taxonomic information, global and national conservation status, distribution, management, natural history, and references. NatureServe is a nonprofit organization developed by the Nature Conservancy and the Natural Heritage Network to advance the application of biodiversity information to conservation. It is also involved in the InfoNatura project, above.

Poole, Trevor, ed. **The UFAW Handbook on the Care and Management of Laboratory Animals.** 7th ed. Malden, MA: Blackwell Science, 1999. 2 vol. $300 (set). ISBN 0632051329 (vol. 1); 0632051310 (vol. 2); 0632051337 (set).

This is the standard handbook dealing with laboratory animal welfare. UFAW (the Universities Federation for Animal Welfare) is an international organization, and its recommendations are widely followed. This handbook provides detailed information on caring for the entire range of laboratory animals, with Volume 1 covering terrestrial vertebrates and Volume 2, aquatic and amphibian vertebrates and invertebrates. Entries provide standard biological data such as temperature requirements and normal concentrations of hormones in the blood for each type of animal as well as housing requirements, proper feeding, and instructions on how to handle animals.

Species 2000. International Union of Biological Sciences. URL: http://www.sp2000.org/. (Accessed August 25, 2003).

"Species 2000 has the objective of enumerating all known species of plants, animals, fungi and microbes on Earth as the baseline dataset for studies of global biodiversity." Eighteen organizations have formed a federation to combine existing taxonomic databases created by their members. The Web site contains information about the Species 2000 initiative, as well as two versions of the database. One, the "Catalogue of Life," is a reference version stabilized every year. It is also available on CD-ROM. The "Dynamic Checklist" contains the same information, but is continually updated. Another section, the "Names Service," provides information on accepted and invalid nomenclature, including groups of organisms not included in the catalog or checklist. As of August 2003, the Catalogue of Life included 304,000 species, but not all taxa are represented.

Style Manual Committee, Council of Biology Editors. **Scientific Style and Format: The CBE Manual for Authors, Editors, and Publishers.** 6th ed. New York: Cambridge University Press, 1994. 825 p. $60. ISBN 0521471540.

This manual provides guidance on scientific writing, from basic punctuation and spelling to special scientific conventions (chemical names, subatomic particles, drugs, viruses, and so on). There are also instructions on writing for books and journals, and appendixes listing the abbreviated forms of journal titles and publisher names, plus an annotated bibliography of other useful works. The manual was formerly titled the *CBE Style Manual.*

Synopsis and Classification of Living Organisms. Sybil P. Parker, Editor in Chief. New York: McGraw-Hill, 1982. 2 vol. ISBN 0070790310 (set).

Although now out of print, this set is a standard reference for higher-level taxonomy. The systematic positions and affinities of all living organisms are presented in brief articles for all taxa from the kingdom to the family level. An appendix discusses the history and role of nomenclature in the taxonomy and classification of organisms, and provides classification tables.

Das Tierreich. Vol. 1– . Berlin: Walter de Gruyter, 1897– . Irregular. Price varies. ISSN 0040-7305.

Published for the Deutchen Zoologischen Gesellschaft, this serial was designed to create a systematic treatment of all groups of the animal kingdom. After World War II it became clear this was not feasible, so the serial was redesigned as a sequence of systematic monographs published with no attempt to survey the entire animal kingdom. Recent monographs cover the dragonflies, chameleons, and the Serrolecaniini (a tribe of insects).

Thompson, John W. **Index to Illustrations of the Natural World: Where to Find Pictures of the Living Things of North America.** Hamden, CT: Shoe String Press, 1983. Reprint of the 1977 ed. 265 p. ISBN 0208020381.

This book indexes illustrations to more than 6,200 North American plants and animals from 178 books. The arrangement is by common name with a scientific name index. Companion to Munz, and updated by Clewis, both above.

Tudge, Colin. **The Variety of Life: A Survey and a Celebration of All the Creatures That Have Ever Lived.** New York: Oxford University Press, 2000. 684 p. $60. ISBN 0198503113.

Another nice survey of living organisms. Unlike *The Diversity of Living Organisms,* above, Tudge discusses general topics in taxonomy as well as describing organisms. Macrofauna such as reptiles and mammals are covered in more detail than microorganisms and plants. Also, Tudge includes extensive information on extinct groups such as dinosaurs. The book is written in an informal manner and the author clearly enjoyed his work.

University of California, Berkeley. Museum of Paleontology. **Phylogeny of Life.** URL: http://www.ucmp.berkeley.edu/exhibit/phylogeny.html. (Accessed August 25, 2003).

This Web site provides an introduction to the exhibits in the phylogeny wing at the Museum of Paleontology. The Web List of Taxa is an index to the organisms covered in the exhibits. Almost all taxa of organisms, from viruses to animals, are included with a brief introduction to the taxonomy, ecology, and life history of organisms in the group. There are also illustrations, short lists of Web sites for further research, information on the paleontology of the taxa, and links to an online glossary. This is an excellent site for information on obscure taxa of animals. Although most groups are discussed only at the level of the phylum, taxa such as the insects or mammals are taken to the family level.

Wood, Phyllis. **Scientific Illustration: A Guide to Biological, Zoological, and Medical Rendering Techniques, Design, Printing, and Display.** 2nd ed. New York: Van Nostrand Reinhold, 1994. 158 p. $29.95. ISBN 0442013167 (paper).

A lavishly illustrated guide to preparing illustrations for scientific purposes. The author provides detailed guidance on basic drawing techniques such as perspective, light and shadow, and other matters in addition to demonstrating how to lay out materials, prepare illustrations for publication, and preparing exhibits. There is also a chapter on computer graphics by Patrick McDonnell and a career guide. Zweifel, below, covers many of the same topics, but this guide has more illustrations and includes the material on computer graphics.

Zweifel, Frances W. **A Handbook of Biological Illustration.** 2nd ed. Chicago: University of Chicago Press, 1988. 160 p. (Chicago Guides to Writing, Editing, & Publishing). $14. ISBN 0226997014 (paper).

Although written before the advent of computer graphics, this little handbook is the classic guide to preparing biological illustrations. The author demonstrates the standard techniques for preparing black-and-white drawings, lettering, photographs, graphs, and maps. He also provides information on preparing items for poster sessions and mounting and packing illustrations. The handbook is designed for the use of illustrators rather than authors, but it is a good introduction to the art of illustrating.

Geographical Section

Asia

The Fauna of India and the Adjacent Countries. Delhi: Zoological Survey of India, 1947– . Vol. price varies.

Originally published as *The Fauna of British India, Including Ceylon and Burma* from 1888–1946, this series is currently being reprinted. After India gained its independence, the title of the series was changed and work on the catalog continued by the Zoological Survey of India. The series is divided into subseries covering various taxa such as Aranea, reptiles, or Plathelminthes.

Zhongguo dong wu zhi (Fauna Sinica). Beijing: Ke xue chu ban she, 1970– . Vol. price varies.

An important Chinese series. All volumes are in Chinese, but have a short English abstract as well as including scientific and English common names. Most taxa have been published.

Australasia

Zoological Catalogue of Australia. Canberra: Australian Govt. Pub. Service, 1983– . Vol. price varies.

Published out of systematic sequence, this series covers all the animals of Australia, from the Hemichordata to the vertebrates. It is currently up to Volume 37.2 covering the birds. Each entry includes synonymy, type specimen and locality, a summary of distribution and ecology, and bibliography for each species. Later volumes were published by CSIRO. It is expected to contain about 90 volumes when finished. To date, volumes covering most of the vertebrates and some invertebrate groups, especially the arthropods, have been published.

Europe

Fauna of the USSR. Jerusalem: Israel Program for Scientific Translations, 1960– . Vol. price varies.

This ongoing series is a translation of *Fauna USSR,* which began publication in 1911. The catalog covers specific taxa of the animals of the former Soviet Union. Most of the translations have been published by the Israel Program for Scientific Translations and are available as individual subseries. Organisms covered in the English version of the catalogue include most insects, polychaetes, crustacea, fishes, and mammals.

Hayward, P. J., and J. S. Ryland. **Handbook of the Marine Fauna of North-West Europe.** New York: Oxford University Press, 1995. 800 p. $60. ISBN 0198540558 (paper); 019854054X.
An identification guide to 1,500 species of the marine fauna of the British Isles, from sponges to fish. Covers 20 major invertebrate phyla in addition to the fishes. Includes keys, line drawings, and brief species accounts.

Identification Tools

Numerous field guides and manuals are available that identify the common animals of a region (or even more general guides to the geology, plants, and animals of a region). These guides can be found in the Schmidt's guides to field guides listed above, under either "Animals" or "Flora and Fauna." Especially, see the following field guide series:

Audubon Society Field Guides. New York: Knopf. Feature color photographs rather than illustrations.

Ecotravellers' Wildlife Guides. San Diego: Academic Press. Guides to popular ecotourist destinations, such as the Amazon, New Zealand, or Hawaii, identifying animals from insects to

Golden Field Guides. New York: Golden Books. Guides cover the entire United States.

HarperCollins. London: HarperCollins. The largest publisher of field guides for Britain and the world.

Peterson Field Guide Series. Boston: Houghton Mifflin. The original field guide series; still excellent.

Pictured Key Series. Dubuque, IA: W. C. Brown. Illustrated keys to many types of organisms.

Other publishers that publish reliable, highly regarded guides for other locations include Angus & Robertson (Australia); New Holland (many locations, co-published in the United States by Ralph Curtis Books); Pica Press/Christopher Helm (bird taxonomic guides; see chapter 7); Reed (Australia); Struik (Southern Africa); among others.

Wernert, Susan J. **Reader's Digest North American Wildlife.** Updated ed. Pleasantville, NY: Reader's Digest Association, 1998. 559 p. $29.95. ISBN 0762100206.

This hefty guide covers over 2,000 species of plants and animals. There are brief illustrated keys, color illustrations, and range maps for most groups.

Winchester, A.M., and H.E. Jaques. **How to Know the Living Things.** 2nd ed. Dubuque, IA: W.C. Brown, 1981. 173 p. (Pictured Key Nature Series). $30. ISBN 0697047806 (paper); 0697047784.

An illustrated key to all groups of living organisms, from viruses to plants. Most groups are keyed to the level of the order, and representative species are illustrated.

Associations

American Association for Zoological Nomenclature (AAZN). c/o National Museum of Natural History, MRC 168, Smithsonian Institution, Washington, DC 20560. Phone: (202) 382-1802. URL: http://www.iczn.org/aazn.htm (Accessed August 25, 2003).

American Institute of Biological Sciences (AIBS). 1444 I St. NW, Ste. 200, Washington, DC 20005-2210. Phone: (202) 628-1500; Fax: (202) 628-1509. E-mail: jkolber@aibs.org. URL: http://www.aibs.org (Accessed August 25, 2003).

American Zoo and Aquariums Association. 8403 Colesville Rd., Ste. 710, Silver Spring, MD 20910-3314. Phone: (301) 562-0777; Fax: (301) 562-0888. E-mail: sbutler@aza.org. URL: http://www.aza.org (Accessed August 25, 2003).

Animal Behavior Society. Indiana University, 2611 East 10th Street #170, Bloomington, IN 47408-2603. Phone: (812) 856-5541; Fax: (812) 856-5542. E-mail: aboffice@indiana.edu. URL: http://www.animalbehavior.org (Accessed August 25, 2003).

Council of Biology Editors (CBE). c/o Drohan Management Group, 11250 Roger Bacon Dr., Ste. 8, Reston, VA 20190-5202. Phone: (703) 437-4377; Fax: (703) 435-4390. E-mail: cbehdqts@aol.com.

Federation of American Societies for Experimental Biology (FASEB). 9650 Rockville Pike, Bethesda, MD 20814-3998. Phone: (301) 530-7090; Fax: (301) 530-7049. E-mail: admin@faseb.org. URL: http://www.faseb.org (Accessed August 25, 2003).

International Commission on Zoological Nomenclature (ICZN). Natural History Museum, Cromwell Rd., London SW7 5BD, UK. Phone: 44 20 79425653. E-mail: iczn@nhm.ac.uk. URL: http://www.iczn.org (Accessed August 25, 2003).

International Union of Biological Sciences (IUBS). 51, blvd. de Montmorency, F-75016 Paris, France. Phone: 33 1 45250009; Fax: 33 1 45252029. E-mail: lub@paris7.jussieu.fr. URL: http://www.iubs.org. (Accessed August 25, 2003).

National Science Collections Alliance (NSC). 1725K St. NW, Ste. 601, Washington, DC 20006-1401. Phone: (202) 835-9050; Fax: (202) 835-7334. E-mail: asc@ascoll.org. URL: http://www.nscalliance.org. (Formerly Association of Systematics Collections). (Accessed August 25, 2003).

Society for Conservation Biology (SCB). University of Washington, Box 351800, Seattle, WA 98195-1800. Phone: (206) 616-4054; Fax: (206) 543-3041. E-mail: conbio@u.washington.edu. URL: http://conbio.net (Accessed August 25, 2003).

Society for Experimental Biology (SEB). Burlington House, Piccadilly, London W1V OLQ, UK. Phone: 44 171 4398732; Fax: 44 171 2874786. E-mail: seb@sebiol.demon.co.uk. URL: http://www.sebiology.org (Accessed August 25, 2003).

Society for Integrative and Comparative Biology (SICB). 1313 Dolley Madison Blvd., Ste. 402, McLean, VA 22101-3926. Phone: (703) 790-1745, Fax: (703) 790-2672. E-mail: sicb@burkInc.com. URL: http://www.sicb.org. (Formerly American Society of Zoologists.) (Accessed August 25, 2003).

Society of Systematic Biologists (SSB). EEB U-3043, University of Connecticut, Storrs, CT 06269-3043. Phone: (860) 486-4640; Fax: (860) 486-6364.URL: http://systbiol.org. (Formerly Society of Systematic Zoology.) (Accessed January 30, 2003).

2

Invertebrates (Excluding Arthropods)

The invertebrates are a large and diverse group of organisms whose taxonomy is still being debated. Depending on which system is used, there are between 35 and 40 phyla of invertebrates containing about 140,000 species compared to the 42,000 species in the single chordate phylum. The invertebrates display an amazing range of body types and lifestyles, ranging from the very simple Placozoa with only a few hundred cells to the complex giant squid *Architeuthis,* which grows to 18 meters in length and is possibly the largest invertebrate ever. Some invertebrate phyla, such as the mollusks and the echinoderms, are well known and have thousands of identified species; others such as the Echiura are so obscure that the average well-read biologist may never have heard of them. Some phyla have not been studied in detail, so particular resources listed in this chapter may be rather old. Information on many of the minor phyla are only found in the more general resources, so check them as well. Also, the names and hierarchical position of some taxa have changed, so the list here provides a partial list of other names.

The Protozoa were traditionally included in the animal kingdom, although all of the more modern systems such as the Five Kingdom or Three Domain systems class them separately. They are not covered in this guide. In addition, it has been estimated that 86% of all described species are insects, so the Arthropoda have been given their own separate chapter. The Hemichordata, which have a stomochord similar to the chordate notochord but are generally believed to be more closely related to the echino-

53

derms, are covered in this chapter. However, the Urochordata and Cephalochordata are included in chapter 4 on the vertebrates.

Classification of Invertebrates (from Brusca and Brusca, 1990)

Porifera (sponges; 9,000 species)

Cnidaria (sea anemones, corals, and jellyfish; 9,000 species)

Ctenophora (comb jellies; 100 species)

Onchyphora (velvet worms; 80 species)

Tardigrada (water bears; 400 species)

Annelida (segmented worms; 15,000 species)

Pogonophora (tube worms or bearded worms, often combined with Vestimentifera; 135 species)

Vestimentifera (giant tube worms; 8 species)

Echiura (spoon worms; 135 species)

Mollusca (snails, clams, octopi, etc.; 50,000 species)

Sipuncula (peanut worms; 250 species)

Nemertea (ribbon worms; 900 species)

Platyhelminthes (flatworms, tapeworms, and flukes; 20,000 species)

Lophophorates (brachiopods and bryozoans; 4,300 species)

Chaetognatha (100 species)

Echinodermata (sea urchins and starfish; 7,000 species)

Pseudocoelomates (rotifers, nematodes, Acanthocephala, etc.; 21,900 species)

Placozoa (1 species)

Monoblastozoa (1 species)

Mesozoa (Rhombozoa and Orthonectida, 100 species)

Hemichordata (acorn worms and pterobranchs, 100 species)

Indexes, Abstracts, and Bibliographies

Aquatic Sciences and Fisheries Abstracts: Biological Sciences and Living Resources.

See chapter 1 for full annotation. Because many invertebrates live in marine environments, this is a valuable index for invertebrate zoologists.

Helminthological Abstracts. Vol. 1– . Wallingford, Oxon, UK: CAB International, 1932– . Monthly. $990 (print only); $855 (Internet only). ISSN 0957-6789.

The abstracting journal covers articles, reports, conferences and books dealing with all aspects of parasitic helminths worldwide. There are monthly and annual author and subject indexes. *Helminthological Abstracts* is also available on the Internet, updated weekly, with a 10-year back file. It is also available as part of the complete *CAB Abstracts* database (see chapter 1).

Journals

Advances in Parasitology. Vol. 1– . San Diego: Academic Press, 1963– . Irregular. $166 (vol. 52). ISSN 0065-308X.

A review journal containing lengthy articles in all areas of parasitology. Subjects include medical studies, biological and taxonomic studies, and life histories. Special thematic volumes cover a specific topic such as the applications of geographical information systems in epidemiology.

Invertebrate Biology. Vol. 114– . Lawrence, KS: American Microscopical Society, 1995– . Quarterly. $85. ISSN 1077-8306.

Publishes articles and occasional long reviews on all aspects of invertebrate biology, including metazoans and protozoans. Formerly *Transactions of the American Microscopical Society.*

Invertebrate Neuroscience: IN. Vol. 1– . Heidelberg: Springer Verlag, 1995– . Quarterly. $469. ISSN 1354-2516. Available electronically.

Publishes peer-reviewed research papers, short communications, methods papers, and reviews describing recent advances in the field of invertebrate neuroscience, with emphasis on studies using molecular and cell biology methods. Electronic supplementary material, such as sequence data, alignments and sequence comparisons, animations, and short videos, appears only in the electronic version.

Invertebrate Reproduction and Development. Vol. 15– . Rehovot, Israel: Balaban, 1989– . Bimonthly. $425. ISSN 0792-4259.

Publishes original papers and reviews on the sexual, reproductive, and developmental biology of invertebrates. Formerly *International Journal of Invertebrate Reproduction and Development.*

Invertebrate Systematics. Vol. 16– . Melbourne: Commonwealth Scientific and Industrial Research Organization with the cooperation of the Australian Academy of Science, 2001– . 8/yr. $675. ISSN 0818-0164. Available electronically.

Publishes articles on the systematics of invertebrates from around the world. Most of the papers concern major revisions of taxonomic groups, although articles on species of economic or conservation interest are also welcomed. The journal also publishes methodological papers and reviews. Sample articles from select issues are available at http://www.publish. csiro.au/journals/samples.cfm. Formerly *Invertebrate Taxonomy.*

Journal of Invertebrate Pathology. Vol. 7– . New York: Academic Press, 1965– . Bimonthly. $950. ISSN 0022-2011. Available electronically.

Publishes original research articles and notes on the diseases of invertebrates, including the suppression of diseases in beneficial species and the use of diseases in controlling undesirable species as well as articles dealing with the etiology of invertebrate diseases. Formerly *Journal of Insect Pathology.*

Systematic Section

Platyhelminthes

Comparative Parasitology. Vol. 67– . Lawrence, KS: Helminthological Society of Washington, 2000– . Semiannual. $55. ISSN 1525-2647.

Publishes brief research notes and full articles on all aspects of parasitology. Formerly *Journal of the Helminthological Society of Washington.*

Helminthologia. Vol. 1– . Bratislava. ČSAV vo Vydavatelstve Slovenskej akadémie vied, 1959– . ISSN 0440-6605.

Publishes original articles in all aspects of helminthology, including agronomy, veterinary medicine, and human medicine.

Mollusca

American Malacological Bulletin. Vol. 1– . Hattiesburg, MS: American Malacological Union, 1983– . Two no. a year. ISSN 0740-2783.

Publishes articles and symposia reports in all areas of malacology. Cumulative author and taxonomic indexes and tables of contents from 1983 to 1998 are available on the American Malacological Society's Web site at http://erato.acnatsci.org/ams/publications/amb.html.

Journal of Conchology. Vol. 1– . Bromborough, UK: Conchological Society of Great Britain and Ireland, 1879– . 2 no. a year (irregular). $62. ISBN 0022-0019.

The oldest continuously published journal of molluscan studies. It contains scientific papers and short communications on mollusks with emphasis on promoting conservation, biogeography, and taxonomy. Both living and fossil mollusks are included. Also includes the official proceedings of the society, obituaries, and book reviews. Formerly *Quarterly Journal of Conchology*.

Journal of Molluscan Studies. Vol. 1– . Oxford, UK: Oxford University Press, 1893– . Quarterly. $340. ISSN 0260-1230. Available electronically.

Published for the Malacological Society of London, this journal publishes articles in the area of molluscan biology. It features both new topics such as molecular genetics and cladistic phylogenetics but also continues to publish articles on basic ecology and systematics.

Malacologia. Vol. 1– . Ann Arbor: Institute of Malacology, 1962– . Biannual. ISSN 0076-2997.

Publishes original research on most aspects of molluscan biology, except physiology and biochemistry. The journal also publishes symposia occasionally. Articles are written in English, French, German, or Spanish with an English abstract.

Malacological Review. Vol. 1– . Ann Arbor: Museum of Zoology, University of Michigan, 1968– . $33. ISSN 0076-3004.

Publishes original research articles on both descriptive and experimental subjects and review articles. Articles are published in English, French, and German.

Molluscan Research. Vol. 15– . Sydney South, Australia: Malacological Society of Australasia, 1994– . Irregular. $50. ISSN 0085-2998.

Publishes general and theoretical papers relating to mollusks. Papers concerning specific geographical areas or new taxa usually focus on the region around Australia. Formerly *Journal of the Malacological Society of Australia*.

The Nautilus. Vol. 3– . Sanibel, FL: Bailey-Matthews Shell Museum, 1889– . Quarterly. $56. ISSN 0028-1344.

Publishes research articles and reviews in various areas of the biology, ecology, and systematics of mollusks as well as brief notes, notices of meetings, and other news items. Formerly *Conchologists' Exchange.*

The Veliger. Vol. 1– . Berkeley, CA: California Malacozoological Society, 1958– . Quarterly. $82. ISSN 0042-3211.

Publishes articles, short articles, notes, and book reviews in all areas of molluscan research. Tables of contents and supplementary data are available at the journal's site at http://www.veliger.org/contents.html.

Echinodermata

Echinoderm Studies. Vol. 1– . Rotterdam: A. A. Balkema, 1983– . Irregular. $115 (vol. 6). ISBN 9058093018 (vol. 6).

Publishes review articles in all areas of echinoderm biology and taxonomy. Volume 6 was published in 2001, and earlier volumes came out every three to four years.

Pseudocoelomates

Journal of Nematology. Vol. 1– . Lawrence, KS: Allen Press, 1969– . Quarterly. $110. ISSN 0022-300X.

The official journal of the Society of Nematologists. The journal publishes original papers dealing with basic, applied, descriptive, or experimental nematology. Comes with supplement, *Annals of Applied Nematology.*

Nematology: International Journal of Fundamental and Applied Nematological Research. Vol. 1– . Leiden: Brill, 1999– . 8/yr. $595. ISSN 1388-5545. Available electronically.

The primary European journal for nematology, this journal publishes research articles, opinion pieces, short communications, abstracts of proceedings, symposia reports, and occasional book reviews in all areas of nematological research. It was formed by the merger of *Fundamental and Applied Nematology* and *Nematologica.*

Biographies and Histories

Abbott, R. Tucker. **American Malacologists: A National Register of Professional and Amateur Malacologists and Private Shell Collectors**

and Biographies of Early American Mollusk Workers Born between 1618 and 1900. Falls Church, VA: American Malacologists, 1973. 1st ed., 1973–74. 494 p. ISBN 0913792020.

This directory provides biographical information on 400 deceased and 1,000 living amateur and professional malacologists. The deceased individuals included research workers, shell collectors, and people who had mollusk species named after them. The biographies are brief, but citations are included for the deceased individuals; living individuals provided their own data. A 100-page supplement was published in 1975, and the second edition, covering only living individuals not included in the first edition, was published in 1987 as *Register of American Malacologists.*

Dictionaries and Encyclopedias

Boury-Esnault, Nicole, and Klaus Rützler, eds. **Thesaurus of Sponge Morphology.** Washington, DC: Smithsonian Institution Press, 1997. 55 p. (Smithsonian Contributions to Zoology, no. 596).

An illustrated glossary to terms relating to sponge morphology. Sponge taxonomy is in its infancy, so this glossary was developed to help avoid misunderstandings due to imprecise use of terms. The definitions are arranged by broader topic such as cytology or spicule type and paired with illustrations. The volume also includes brief guidelines on preparing sponges for study and a bibliography.

Okáli, Ilja, Miroslava Dulová, and Pavel Mokrán. **Elsevier's Dictionary of Invertebrates (Excluding Insects): In Latin, English, French, German and Spanish.** New York: Elsevier, 2000. 449 p. $147.50. ISBN 0444505350.

A multilanguage dictionary providing the standard common names for over 4,600 taxa of noninsect invertebrates. The dictionary also lists selected obsolete or regional names and includes both British and North American names where different. Each entry also includes a taxonomic code allowing users to identify the broader taxonomic categories for each invertebrate. There are common name indexes for each language as well. The emphasis is on European organisms, so many of the less well-known invertebrates from other parts of the world are not included. The entries are by necessity brief and fairly cryptic, so users have to refer to the tables of abbreviations and taxonomic codes frequently.

Preston-Mafham, Rod, and Ken Preston-Mafham. **The Encyclopedia of Land Invertebrate Behaviour.** Cambridge, MA: MIT Press, 1993. 320 p. $62. ISBN 0262161370.

This colorful encyclopedia discusses the behavior of land invertebrates, including insects. Chapters cover the major types of behavior, including sexual, egg laying, parental care, feeding, and defense. Within each chapter, the discussion is arranged by type of behavior and type of invertebrate. Because the behavior of some groups of invertebrates is not well known, not all taxa are covered equally. However, readers can find information on gastropods, millipedes and centipedes, arachnids, insects, crustaceans, platyhelminths, Onchyphora, and others.

Stachowitsch, Michael. **The Invertebrates: An Illustrated Glossary.** New York: Wiley-Liss, 1992. 676 p. $340; $180 (paper). ISBN 0471832944; 0471561924 (paper).

An anatomical glossary containing over 10,000 entries and 1,100 figures in two sections. The first section is arranged by phyla or class and defines anatomical features of most of the invertebrate groups except protozoans and terrestrial arthropods. The second section defines adjectives describing anatomical characteristics (i.e., endoparasitic or nacreous). The German equivalent of each term is also given in both sections because many of the terms were originally coined in German and many of the original invertebrate descriptions were written in the same language.

Textbooks

Anderson, D. T., ed. **Invertebrate Zoology.** 2nd ed. New York: Oxford University Press, 2002. 476 p. $45. ISBN 0195513681 (paper).

A multiauthored text designed for one-semester courses. Each chapter is written by a different author and covers a major phylum, from Porifera to the protochordates, including arthropods. Topics such as basic body plan, structure and function, fossil members, and classification are covered.

Barnes, R. S. K., et al. **The Invertebrates: A Synthesis.** 3rd ed. Malden, MA: Blackwell Science, 2001. $79.95 (paper). ISBN 0632047615 (paper).

An undergraduate textbook that provides a systematic treatment of the invertebrate phyla. The authors begin with introductory material talking about evolution in general and the evolution of the invertebrates in particular. Further chapters discuss the individual phyla from protozoa to Crustacea (but excluding the insects). The discussion of each phyla is fairly brief and includes the derivation of the name, diagnostic and special features, and classification. Over half of the text is taken up by a description of invertebrate functional biology, including topics such as feeding, locomotion, and development. Each chapter ends with a list of items for further reading.

Brusca, Richard C., and Gary J. Brusca. **Invertebrates.** Sunderland, MA: Sinauer Associates, 1990. 922 p. $96.95. ISBN 0878930981.

Although it is described as an introductory textbook, this text is also a very valuable reference on the invertebrates from the metazoa to the Chordata. It is organized into three sections: body architecture, developmental patterns and life history strategies, and phylogenetic relationships. For many years it was the standard reference for invertebrate systematics, and although the consensus about phylogenetic relationships has changed, *Invertebrates* is still an excellent source of information.

Buchsbaum, Ralph, Mildred Buchsbaum, John Pearse, and Vicki Pearse. **Animals without Backbones.** 3rd ed. Chicago: University of Chicago Press, 1987. 572 p. $29 (paper). ISBN 0226078736; 0226078744 (paper).

Designed for undergraduates, nonmajors, and students in related fields such as paleontology, this text has been a classic since its original publication in 1938. There are many black-and-white photographs and illustrations, so it is a particularly good source for illustrations. Pearse's *Living Invertebrates,* below, is a more advanced text by the same authors.

Clarkson, E. N. K. **Invertebrate Palaeontology and Evolution.** 4th ed. Malden, MA: Blackwell Science, 1998. 452 p. $66.95. ISBN 0632052384.

This paleontology text provides a good overview of the invertebrates and their evolution. Part 1 covers the principles of paleontology; Part 2 discusses each major invertebrate phyla. A final chapter discusses trace fossils and exceptional faunas such as the well-known Burgess Shale fossils. A three-volume CD-ROM set, *Macrofossils on CD-ROM,* is also available for use as a supplement or stand-alone product. The CD-ROM contains records for over 1,000 key fossil genera, including images and basic information on range, stratigraphy, paleoecology, and more.

Meglitsch, Paul A., and Frederick R. Schram. **Invertebrate Zoology.** 3rd ed. New York: Oxford University Press, 1991. 623 p. $72.95. ISBN 0195049004; 0195539419 (paper).

This revision of a classic text takes a strongly phylogenetic approach, with little introductory information. Each chapter covers a different phyla, from protozoa to chordates, including arthropods. The text covers body plan, classification, biology, and phylogeny. The text was designed to be used in conjunction with *Illustrated Invertebrate Anatomy* (see Handbooks, above).

Moore, J., and Raith Overhill. **An Introduction to the Invertebrates.** New York: Cambridge University Press, 2001. 355 p. (Studies in Biology). $70; $24 (paper). ISBN 0521770769; 0521779146 (paper).

A concise guide to the invertebrates, designed as a supplement for biology courses. The body plan of each phyla, including arthropods, is examined in detail. Each chapter also discusses the taxonomy of the phylum. There are many sidebars covering general topics such as how muscles work or the types of nerves and brains found in animals.

New, T. R. **Introduction to Invertebrate Conservation Biology.** New York: Oxford University Press, 1995. 194 p. (Oxford Science Publications). $35 (paper). ISBN 0198540523; 0198540515 (paper).

Invertebrate conservation is rarely discussed in either conservation or invertebrate textbooks; after all, most invertebrates are not "charismatic megafauna" that catch the public's attention. This text discusses the need for invertebrate conservation, including appropriate approaches and priorities, captive breeding, regulations, and case histories.

Pearse, Vicki, John Pearse, Mildred Buchsbaum, and Ralph Buchsbaum. **Living Invertebrates.** Palo Alto, CA: Blackwell Scientific, 1987. 848 p. $54.95. ISBN 0865423121.

A companion to Buchsbaum's *Animals without Backbones,* designed for advanced students. This text is also lavishly illustrated and covers many of the same topics, with the addition of a classification guide for each phylum down to the class or order.

Pechenik, Jan A. **Biology of the Invertebrates.** 4th ed. Boston: McGraw-Hill, 2000. 578 p. $105.80. ISBN 0070122040.

Unlike many invertebrate textbooks, this one covers all 35 or 40 phyla, although some are discussed only very briefly. The author emphasizes functional morphology in his discussion. Each chapter includes topics for further discussion, classification to the family, general references, and a listing of Web resources.

Roberts, Larry S., and John Janovy. **Gerald D. Schmidt and Larry S. Roberts' Foundations of Parasitology.** 6th ed. Boston: McGraw-Hill, 2000. 688 p. $84.38. ISBN 0697424308.

A text designed for undergraduate courses, this classic text provides an overview of the orders of parasitic invertebrates. Introductory chapters discuss the ecology, evolution, immunology, and classification of parasites. The remainder of the book covers each taxon, from protozoa to ticks, with emphasis on the biology of the organisms rather than on their diagnosis. Each chapter includes an outline of the classification of the taxon, references, and Web URLs. A supplemental *Electronic Atlas of Parasitology* is available on CD-ROM. It contains photomicrographs of parasites.

Ruppert, Edward E., and Robert D. Barnes. **Invertebrate Zoology.** 6th ed. Philadelphia: Saunders College, 1994. 1,056 p. $93.50. ISBN 0030266688.

Like most invertebrate zoology texts, this takes a taxonomic approach to the subject and covers protozoa to protochordates. Each chapter starts with a discussion of principles and emerging patterns, and then covers topics such as anatomy, biology, and classification. Many of the chapters are further subdivided to the class.

Willmer, Pat. **Invertebrate Relationships: Patterns in Animal Evolution.** New York: Cambridge University Press, 1990. 400 p. $38 (paper). ISBN 0521330645; 0521337127 (paper).

This text presents the relationships between invertebrate phyla and of the phylogenetic pattern of the animal kingdom. After discussing the current state of knowledge and the available evidence for invertebrate phylogeny, the author covers each invertebrate phylum in detail.

Checklists and Classification Schemes

Systematic Section

Porifera

Hooper, John N. A., and R. W. M. van Soest. **Systema Porifera: A Guide to the Classification of Sponges.** New York: Kluwer Academic/Plenum, 2002. 2 vol. $595 (set). ISBN 0306472600 (set).

This book presents a major revision of the classification of the more than 2,000 genera of Porifera as well as a review of the taxonomic literature of the phylum. There are descriptions of each class, order, and family and keys to many families and genera.

Penney, James Theophilus, and A. A. Racek. **Comprehensive Revision of a Worldwide Collection of Freshwater Sponges (Porifera: Spongillidae).** Washington, DC: Smithsonian Institution Press, 1968. 184 p. (United States National Museum Bulletin, no. 272).

A classic revision of sponge classification based on the collections of James Penney, who died before the work could be finished. There are keys to genera and a very extensive bibliography.

Cnidaria and Ctenophora

Cairns, S. D., et al. **Common and Scientific Names of Aquatic Invertebrates from the United States and Canada. Cnidaria and Ctenophora.** Bethesda, MD: American Fisheries Society, 1991. 75 p. (American Fisheries Society Special Publication, no. 22). $33. ISBN 0913235741 (paper).

A list of approved common and scientific names for Cnidaria and Ctenophora from North America, this guide also includes a useful bibliography for background information and identification of the two phyla. The layout of the list is similar to that of the sibling publication on mollusks, described below, and also ends with several color photos demonstrating the variety of Cnidaria and Ctenophora species in North America.

Fautin, Daphne G. 2002. **Hexacorallians of the World: Sea Anemones, Corals, and Their Allies.** URL: http://hercules.kgs.ku.edu/hexacoral/anemone2/index.cfm. (Accessed August 25, 2003).

This site provides an authoritative list of several orders of cnidarians, specifically the Actiniaria, Antipatharia, Ceriantharia, Corallimorpharia, Ptychodactiaria, Scleractinia, and Zoanthidea. A vast amount of data can also be found here, including the usual catalog information (first description, synonymy, type specimen and location, distribution, and so on) as well as images and several classification schemes.

Mills, C. E. 2001. **Ctenophores.** URL: http://faculty.washington.edu/cemills/Ctenophores.html. (Accessed August 25, 2003).

The author, a scientist at the University of Washington, has created a Web page with extensive information on the Ctenophora. The site includes a list of all valid names of the Ctenophora as well as general information about the comb jellies.

Annelida

Reynolds, John W., and David G. Cook. **Nomenclatura Oligochaetologica: A Catalogue of Names, Descriptions, and Type Specimens of the Oligochaeta.** Fredericton: University of New Brunswick, 1976. 217 p. ISBN 0920114016.

Earthworms are the most familiar Oligochaetes, but like many other groups of invertebrates their systematics and nomenclature are in a state of confusion. This catalog lists genera and species names separately in alphabetical lists. Each name is given with the original author and publication, and the location of type specimens is also provided for species names. The introduction is in English, French, German, Portuguese, Russian, and Chinese. Appendixes list the full names of authors, journals, and museums that are abbreviated in the text. Supplements were published in 1981, 1989, and 1993.

Mollusca

Committee on Scientific and Vernacular Names of Mollusks of the Council of Systematic Malacologists. **Common and Scientific Names of Aquatic Invertebrates from the United States and Canada. Mollusks.** 2nd ed. Bethesda, MD: American Fisheries Society, 1998. 526 p. (American Fisheries Society Special Publication, no. 26). $59.00; $52.00(CD-ROM). ISBN 1888569018; 1888569093 (CD-ROM).

Provides the standard names for mollusks of North America. This second edition contains an alphabetical list of families followed by a systematic list of taxa that follows the most recent phylogenetic analyses. Nine appendixes providing annotations, lists of endangered, threatened, extinct, and invasive species, information on the biology and ecology of mollusks, guidelines for collecting mollusks, suggested keys and guidebooks, and major mollusk collections in North America. The book finishes off with a section of color photographs demonstrating the biodiversity of North American mollusks. The CD-ROM provides the full text of the print volume in PDF format. There is enough non-nomenclatural information in the checklist to make it very useful as a general guide to molluscan biology and bibliography.

Current Classification of Recent Cephalopoda. Smithsonian Institution National Museum of Natural History. URL: http://www.mnh.si.edu/cephs/newclass.pdf (Accessed August 25, 2003).

This 59-page PDF file provides a classification of cephalopods based on the latest literature. It was apparently prepared by staff at the Smithsonian, but no authors are credited. The author, date, type location, and type repository for each species or subspecies is given, although no synonyms are listed.

Goto, Yoshihiro, and Guido T. Poppe. **A Listing of Living Mollusca.** Ancona: L'informatore piceno, 1996. 2 vol. in 4 (Tools in Malacology). ISBN 8886070233.

An expansion of Vaught's *Classification of the Living Mollusca,* below. The authors reviewed the malacological literature, accepting the majority opinion in case of doubt and adding about 300 genera not listed in Vaught. Part 1, in two volumes, contains an alphabetical listing of species, with author, date, higher taxa, species number, and selected references. Part 2, also in two volumes, provides a systematic list based on Vaught's work. The listings in Part 2 contain detailed species number (taken from Part 1), the citation for the original description, general range information, and general references.

Vaught, Kay Cunningham. **A Classification of the Living Mollusca.** Melbourne, FL: American Malacologists, 1989. 195 p. ISBN 0915826216 (paper); 0915826224.

This compilation of family and generic names of living mollusks was prepared by an amateur malacologist with the assistance of two of the best-known authorities in the field, R. Tucker Abbott and Kenneth J. Boss. The names are in systematic order with an alphabetical index. The list of references is lengthy.

Voss, Nancy A., et al., eds. **Systematics and Biogeography of Cephalopods.** Washington, DC: Smithsonian Institution Press, 1998. 2 vol. (Smithsonian Contributions to Zoology, no. 586). No ISBN.

Resulting from the international workshop on Systematics and Biogeography of Cephalopods, this two-volume catalog provides information on the distribution and taxonomy of the cephalopods. Volume 1 includes several chapters discussing the use of various morphological characters in cephalopod systematics as well as species accounts for the Sepiidae, Loliginidae, Enoploteuthidae, Pyroteuthidae, and Ancistrocheiridae. Volume 2 covers the families Onychoteuthidae, Histioteuthidae, Ommastrephidae, and Octopodidae as well as providing an annotated list of currently accepted classification of cephalopods.

Wood, James B. **CephBase.** Galveston, TX, 1998– . URL: http://www.
cephbase.utmb.edu/ (Accessed August 25, 2003).

This Web site provides access to several databases containing information about the cephalopods, both life histories and classification. The
"Species Search" interface allows users to search by common or scientific
name, and the records include the classification, common name, distribution, images, predators and prey, references, type specimens, and links to
other Web sites for each species. There are now 785 species covered in the
databases.

Sipuncula

Hallan, Joel, and Edward B. Cutler. **Sipuncula Taxa with Synonyms.**
URL: http://www.mcz.harvard.edu/Departments/InvertZoo/as.fldr/cutler/
siptaxa.htm (Accessed August 25, 2003).

The classification system on this page was taken from Cutler's *The
Sipuncula: Their Systematics, Biology, and Evolution* (see below).

Echinodermata

Classification of the Extant Echinodermata. California Academy of
Sciences. URL: http://www.calacademy.org/research/izg/echinoderm/
classify.htm (Accessed August 25, 2003).

This page provides a list of the families of echinoderms. There are links
to images of some of the echinoderms, principally the starfish. The main
CAS Echinoderm Webpage (http://www.calacademy.org/research/izg/
echinoderm/) has basic information on echinoderms, meeting information, and an extensive list of Web pages.

Handbooks

Abramson, Charles I. **Invertebrate Learning: A Laboratory Manual
and Source Book.** Washington, DC: American Psychological Association, 1990. 100 p. $19.95. ISBN 1557981000 (spiral bound).

Invertebrates aren't known for their intellectual prowess, but this manual provides experiments that can be used to demonstrate they can learn.
The manual is designed for use in animal behavior courses. It is arranged
by type of experiment (habituation, classical condition, and operant con-
ditioning), and experiments are detailed for common organisms such as

protozoa, earthworms, planaria, bees, and ants. Appendixes provide further information on getting started with invertebrate learning experiments, covering supply houses, references, apparatus construction, and similar topics.

Adiyodi, K. G., and R. G. Adiyodi, series eds. **Reproductive Biology of Invertebrates.** New York: Wiley-Liss, 1983– . Vol. price varies.

A multivolume treatise covering all aspects of invertebrate reproduction. The editors have chosen a thematic, rather than a phylogenetic treatment of the subject, so each volume covers a particular topic rather than group of invertebrates. To date, the volumes include Volume 1, *Oogenesis, Oviposition, and Oosporption;* Volume 2, *Spermatogesis and Sperm Function;* Volume 3. *Accessory Sex Glands;* Volume 4, pt. A–B, *Fertilization, Development, and Parental Care;* Volume 5, *Sexual Differentiation and Behaviour;* Volume 6, pt. A–B, *Asexual Propagation and Reproductive Strategies;* Volume 7, *Progress in Developmental Biology;* Volume 8, *Progress in Reproductive Endocrinology;* Volume 9, pt. A–C, *Progress in Male Gamete Ultrastructure and Phylogeny;* Volume 10, pt. A–B, *Progress in Developmental Endocrinology;* and Volume 11, *Recent Progress in Vitellogenesis* (published in 2001).

Anderson, D. T. **Atlas of Invertebrate Anatomy.** Sydney, Australia: UNSW Press, 1996. 34 p.; 82 p. of plates. $34.50. ISBN 0868402079.

Provides line drawings of invertebrate anatomy for use in courses. The specific animals illustrated are found in Australia, but are similar to species used in dissections in other parts of the world. The author provides general information about the illustrated species and plates illustrating several views of the organism's anatomy. The phyla include Porifera, Cnidaria, Ctenophora, Platyhelminthes, Nemertea, Endoprocta, Nematoda, Acanthocephala, Sipuncula, Annelida, Uniramia, Crustacea, Chelicerata, Mollusca, Ectoprocta, Phoronida, Brachiopoda, Chaetognatha, Echinodermata, Hemichordata, and Chordata.

Conn, David Bruce. **Atlas of Invertebrate Reproduction and Development.** 2nd ed. New York: Wiley, 2000. 300 p. $195. ISBN 0471237965.

Covers 10 of the phyla of invertebrates that are most often used as experimental models in developmental biology. The author discusses the reproductive strategies and developmental patterns for each phyla, then provides detailed black-and-white photographs of representative species' reproductive anatomy and development. There is an extensive glossary, and the author also includes appendixes listing methods for studying invertebrate reproduction and sources for prepared slides and specimens.

Freeman, W. H., and Brian Bracegirdle. **An Atlas of Invertebrate Structure.** London: Heinemann Educational, 1971. 129 p. ISBN 0435603159.

The major groups of invertebrates, including insects, are covered in this laboratory atlas. It contains both black-and-white photographs and interpretive line drawings of the structures. For some species, the authors included illustrations of external views, dissections, and photomicrographs.

Frye, Fredric L. **Captive Invertebrates: A Guide to Their Biology and Husbandry.** Malabar, FL: Krieger, 1992. 135 p. $29.50. ISBN 0894645552.

A guide for both amateurs and professionals, this handbook covers the care of invertebrates such as arachnids, millipedes, insects, crustaceans, mollusks, and flatworms that are kept as pets or used as scientific model organisms. Chapters include building accommodations for captive invertebrates and culturing their food, and chapters covering the requirements of individual groups. Each chapter or section is headed by a quote from luminaries ranging from Archie the cockroach to Matsuo Basho.

Giese, Arthur C., and John S. Pearse, eds. **Reproduction of Marine Invertebrates.** New York: Academic Press, 1974– vol. 1–6, 9.

This treatise takes a systematic approach to describing the reproduction and development of marine invertebrates, with each volume covering a particular phylum or group of phyla. Each chapter is written by a different author and discusses topics such as asexual and sexual reproduction, development, metamorphosis, and more. The existing volumes include Volume 1, *Acoelomate and Pseudocoelomate Metazoans;* Volume 2, *Entoprocts and Lesser Coelomates;* Volume 3, *Annelids and Echiurans;* Volume 4, *Molluscs: Gastropods and Cephalopods;* Volume 5, *Molluscs: Pelecypods and Lesser Classes;* Volume 6, *Echinoderms and Lophophorates;* and Volume 9, *General Aspects: Seeking Unity in Diversity.* Volumes 7 and 8, covering nonmalacostracan arthropods and malacostracan arthropods, respectively, were never published.

Harrison, Frederick W., series ed. **Microscopic Anatomy of Invertebrates.** New York: Wiley-Liss. 15 vol. 1991–97. Price varies.

The 15 volumes in this treatise present the microscopic anatomy of all invertebrate groups, from protozoa to the invertebrate members of the chordates. The emphasis is on functional morphology. Each volume covers a particular invertebrate group, and chapters follow a standard format. The chapters cover external anatomy, epithelia, glands, connective tissues, vascular elements, digestive systems, respiratory structures, excretory structures, reproduction, immune system, and the nervous system. The volumes include Volume 1, *Protozoa;* Volume 2, *Placozoa, Porifera, Cnidaria, and Ctenophora;* Volume 3, *Platyhelminthes and Nemertina;* Volume 4, *Aschelminthes;* Volume 5, *Mollusca I;* Volume 6, *Mollusca II;* Volume 7, *Annelida;* Volume 8, *Chelicerate Arthropoda;* Volume 9, *Crustacea;* Volume 10, *Decapod Crustacea;* Volume 11, *Insecta;* Volume 12, *Onchyphora, Chilopoda, and Lesser Protostomata;* Volume 13, *Lophophorates and Entoprocta;* Volume 14, *Echinodermata;* and Volume 15, *Hemichordata, Chaetognatha, and the Invertebrate Chordates.*

Higgins, Robert P., and Hjalmar Thiel, eds. **Introduction to the Study of Meiofauna.** Washington, DC: Smithsonian Institution Press, 1988. 488 p. $59.25. ISBN 0874744881.

The meiofauna are the smallest of the benthic organisms found in the ocean, those smaller than 1 mm. About 22 of the 40 animal phyla are found in the meiofauna. In some cases, only the larval forms are small enough to qualify as meiofauna, but in others, adult forms also fit the definition. This volume provides a history of meiofaunal research, methods for studying the organisms, and chapters covering each invertebrate taxa. The taxonomic chapters are designed to summarize knowledge about the meiofauna groups rather than as an identification aid, but there are illustrations of representative species for most of the phyla.

Hyman, Libbie Henrietta. **The Invertebrates.** New York: McGraw-Hill, 1940–67. 6 vols. (McGraw-Hill Publications in the Zoological Sciences).

A major classic in the field of invertebrate zoology, this series was intended to cover all of the invertebrates from protozoa to arthropods. The author died before that was possible, although she completed volumes up to the first half of the mollusks. Each phyla is described in detail, with many black-and-white illustrations. The text covers morphology, taxonomy, physiology, embryology, and life cycles for the taxa. The volumes include Volume 1, *Protozoa through Ctenophora;* Volume 2, *Platyhelminthes and Rhynchocoela, the Acoelomate Bilateria;* Volume 3, *Acanthocephala, Aschelminthes, and Entoprocta, the Pseudocoelomate Bilateria;* Volume 4, *Echinodermata, the Coelomate Bilateria;* Volume 5, *Smaller Coelomate Groups;* and Volume 6, *Mollusca I.*

Kaestner, Alfred. **Invertebrate Zoology.** New York: Interscience, 1967–70. 3 vol. ISBN 0471454176 (vol. 3).

This treatise was designed as a less technical review of the invertebrates than Hyman's *The Invertebrates* (see above). Three volumes were published: Volume 1, *Porifera, Cnidaria, Platyhelminthes, Aschelminthes, Mollusca, Annelida and Related Phyla;* Volume 2, *Arthropod Relatives, Chelicerata, Myriapoda;* and Volume 3, *Crustacea.* A final volume, *Lophophorates and Deuterostomes,* was planned but has not yet been published. Translation of the second edition of the author's *Lehrbuch der speziellen Zoologie.*

Lincoln, Roger J., and J. Gordon Sheals, comps. **Invertebrate Animals, Collection and Preservation.** New York: Cambridge University Press, 1979. 150 p. ISBN 0521228514; 0521296773 (paper).

This little book provides techniques for collecting and preserving invertebrates. It is designed for the use of British Museum of Natural History staff but is useful for other researchers and students as well. The book is in three parts, covering the invertebrates by taxa, collecting methods and apparatus in general, methods for killing and preserving invertebrates, and general information on maintaining a collection.

Pierce, Sidney K., Timothy K. Maugel, and Lois Reid. **Illustrated Invertebrate Anatomy: A Laboratory Guide.** New York: Oxford University Press, 1987. 307 p. $49.95. ISBN 0195040716.

A photographic manual of invertebrate anatomy, with black-and-white photographs and line drawings. The authors include Protozoa, Porifera, Cnidaria, Ctenophora, Platyhelminthes, Nemertinea, Nematoda, Rotifera, Brachiopoda, Sipuncula, Echiura, Annelida, Mollusca, Arthropoda (Chelicerata and Crustacea only), Echinodermata, and Chordata.

Smith, Douglas G. **Pennak's Freshwater Invertebrates of the United States: Porifera to Crustacea.** 4th ed. New York: Wiley, 2001. 638 p. $120. ISBN 0471358371.

A handbook-cum-identification guide providing information on each of the major phyla of freshwater invertebrates. The first three editions of this highly regarded guide were written by Robert Pennak, and the fourth edition follows the format of the original versions with extensive revision of keys. This edition also excludes the Protozoa and aquatic insects, but does cover arachnids such as water mites. The chapters are lavishly illustrated with line drawings and black-and-white photographs, and they provide information on the classification, physiology, and natural history of the phyla. Each chapter concludes with an illustrated key to either common genera or species and extensive references. This is one of the standard handbooks covering the invertebrates, and it gathers together a vast amount of information on the invertebrates.

Teichert, Curt, ed. **Treatise on Invertebrate Paleontology.** 2nd ed., rev. and enl. Boulder, CO: Geological Society of America, 1970– .

The first edition of this massive set was published from 1953 to 1981 by Raymond Moore. The standard compendium of information on invertebrate paleontology, it is useful for students of living invertebrates as well because it summarizes the biology and classification of all the invertebrate phyla. It is in several sections designated by letters (part H for Brachiopoda, for instance). Most sections consist of several volumes as well. The standard treatment for each group is to discuss morphological features, ontogeny, classification, geographical distribution, evolutionary trends and phylogeny, and systematics for genera and higher taxa.

Thorp, James H., and Alan P. Covich, eds. **Ecology and Classification of North American Freshwater Invertebrates.** 2nd ed. San Diego: Academic, 2001. 1,056 p. $79.95. ISBN 0126906475.

As the title suggests, this book focuses on the ecology and classification of freshwater invertebrates, including insects but excluding parasitic invertebrates. The chapters covering the various taxa were written by different authors and follow a similar pattern. Most include an introduction, followed by sections on anatomy and physiology, development, ecology, collection, classification, and identification of the phyla plus references. Some chapters include taxonomic keys as well.

Systematic Section

Porifera

Bergquist, Patricia R. **Sponges.** London: Hutchinson, 1978. 268 p. ISBN 0520036581.

This handbook covers all aspects of sponge biology and classification, including anatomy, reproduction, ecology, biochemistry, and paleontology. There are numerous black-and-white photographs and line drawings of sponges and their organs. The author also provides a glossary, an extensive bibliography, and a list of general references.

van Soest, Rob W. M., Theo M. G. van Kempen, and Jean-Claude Braekman. **Sponges in Time and Space: Biology, Chemistry, Paleontology: Proceedings of the 4th International Porifera Congress, Amsterdam, Netherlands.** Rotterdam: A. A. Balkema, 1994. 515 p. $123. ISBN 9054100974.

The proceedings are arranged in five categories: Paleospongology, Systematics and Classification, Biogeography and Faunistics, Ecology and Life History Studies, and Natural Products Chemistry. There is also a list of participants and an index to the scientific names covered in the book. The International Porifera Congress meets once every seven or eight years.

Cnidaria

Arai, Mary N. **A Functional Biology of Scyphozoa.** New York: Chapman & Hall, 1997. 316 p. $157. ISBN 0412451107.

The Scyphozoa are the true jellyfish. This text covers topics such as locomotion, feeding, nutrition, metabolism, reproduction, growth, physical ecology, and biological interactions. An appendix lists the classification of the scyphozoans mentioned in the book.

Shick, Malcolm J. **A Functional Biology of Sea Anemones.** New York: Chapman & Hall, 1990. 395 p. ISBN 0412331500.

Covers the biology of sea anemones, including nutrition, metabolism, excretion, growth, reproduction, and ecology. The author also provides an appendix showing the classification of living anthozoans, the class of cnidarians that includes the sea anemones.

Pogonophora

Ivanov, A. V. **Pogonophora.** New York: Consultants Bureau, 1963. 479 p.

A translation from the Russian, this text covers all aspects of the biology and classification of this group of invertebrates. The author includes all 80 species of Pogonophora known at the time, many of them named by Ivanov himself. The systematic account includes keys, descriptions, and bibliography as well as many line drawings. The translated version includes some updated information based on studies prepared after the Russian publication in 1960.

Nemertea

Gibson, Raymond. **Nemerteans.** London: Hutchinson, 1972. 224 p. ISBN 0091119901; 009111991X (paper).

The nemertean worms are largely free-living marine organisms. The author discusses their classification, anatomy and physiology, asexual reproduction and regeneration, sexual reproduction, ecology and distribution, and phylogenetic relationships. There is also an appendix outlining the classification of the Nemertea to the family level.

Platyhelminthes

Yamaguti, Satyu. **Synopsis of Digenetic Trematodes of Vertebrates.** Tokyo: Keigaku, 1971. 2 vol.

An update of Volume 1 of *Systema Helminthum* (below), this two-volume set contains the same kinds of information about the trematodes. Volume 1 contains the text, and Volume 2 has 350 plates, all redrawn from the original. The author's *Synoptical Review of Life Histories of Digenetic Trematodes of Vertebrates,* below, includes more information about the trematodes.

Yamaguti, Satyu. **A Synoptical Review of Life Histories of Digenetic Trematodes of Vertebrates: with Special Reference to the Morphology of Their Larval Forms.** Tokyo: Keigaku, 1975. 590 p.

A companion to the author's *Synopsis of Digenetic Trematodes of Vertebrates,* above. The author has gathered together the information on the morphology and life histories of larval trematodes. Like the companion volume, the genera are arranged by host rather than the more usual systematic arrangement.

Yamaguti, Satyu. **Systema Helminthum.** New York: Interscience, 1958–63. 5 vol. in 7.

The author gathered together the descriptions of all genera of helminths known at the time. The set is organized by host and then by developmental and morphological characteristics rather than taxonomy and does not include taxa higher than the family. The volumes are Volume 1 (in two parts), *The Digenetic Trematodes of Vertebrates;* Volume 2, *The Cestodes of Vertebrates;* Volume 3 (in two parts), *The Nematodes of Vertebrates;* Volume 4, *Monogenea and Aspidocotylea;* and Volume 5, *Acanthocephala.*

Lophophorata

Rudwick, M. J. S. **Living and Fossil Brachiopods.** London: Hutchinson, 1970. 199 p. ISBN 0091030803.

A classic guide to the biology and evolution of brachiopods, this little book contains chapters on the anatomy, behavior, and reproduction of living brachiopods as well as their paleontology. Despite the 30-plus years since it was published, it is still one of the best summaries of brachiopod biology.

Ryland, John Stanley. **Bryozoans.** London: Hutchinson, 1970. 175 p. ISBN 0091038707.

Another in Hutchinson's Biological Sciences series of student guides, this handbook is an excellent source of basic information on the biology and classification of bryozoans. The author also discusses fossil bryozoans.

Woollacott, Robert M., and Russel L. Zimmer, eds. **The Biology of Bryozoans.** New York: Academic Press, 1977. 566 p. ISBN 012763150X.

The chapters in this handbook were written by various experts on bryozoan biology and provide detailed coverage of the major aspects of bryozoan biology. In addition to the usual information on development, reproduction, anatomy, behavior, and life histories, chapters cover experimental techniques, population genetics, and phylogenetics.

Tardigrades

Kinchin, Ian M. **The Biology of Tardigrades.** Chapel Hill, NC: Portland Press, 1994. 186 p. $68. ISBN 1855780437.

Tardigrades, or water bears, are an enigmatic phyla of invertebrates. About 750 species are known. They live in aquatic or wet terrestrial habitats, and because they have little-known economic importance, they are seldom studied. The author has gathered together the scattered literature on this group. He discusses systematics, anatomy, reproduction, and ecology, plus the phyla's fascinating ability to suspend metabolic activity. Information on collecting and identifying common species is also provided, along with ideas for further research.

Annelida

Dales, Rodney Phillips. **Annelids.** 2nd ed. London: Hutchinson, 1967. 200 p.

A classic work on the biology and classification of annelids. An appendix lists the classification of annelids to the family level and includes the genera mentioned in the text.

Read, Geoff. **Annelid Worm Biodiversity Resources: Polychaetes, Oligochaetes, Leeches, and Allies.** New Orleans: University of New Orleans, 1996– . URL: http://biodiversity.uno.edu/~worms/annelid.html (Accessed August 25, 2003).

This site includes information on the Sipuncula and Pogonophora as well as annelids.

Rouse, Greg W., and Fredrik Pleijel. **Polychaetes.** New York: Oxford University Press, 2001. 354 p. $175. ISBN 0198506082.

The polychaete worms are a very diverse group of annelids, consisting of about 9,000 species. This survey divides the polychaete groups into 72 chapters, discussing each family or superfamily's morphology and physiology, natural history, and systematics. There are illustrations of representative members of each family as well, and a section of color plates illustrates particularly striking polychaetes. Introductory chapters discuss the importance of the group, plus polychaete systematics and anatomy.

Sawyer, Roy T. **Leech Biology and Behavior.** New York: Oxford University Press, 1986. 3 vol. ISBN 0198573774 (vol. 1); 0198576226 (vol. 2); 0198576234 (vol. 3).

Volume 1 of this treatise covers anatomy, physiology, and behavior; Volume 2 covers feeding biology, ecology, and systematics, and Volume 3 consists of a lengthy bibliography. The author provides a taxonomic synopsis and list of leech species in Volume 2 with references, type species, and other members of the genus. Keys to species can be found in the chapter on zoogeography.

Mollusca

Hughes, Roger N. **A Functional Biology of Marine Gastropods.** Baltimore. Johns Hopkins University Press, 1986. 245 p. ISBN 0801833300.

Like the other volumes in this series, this book concentrates on the aspects of gastropod biology that allow them to feed and reproduce. There is little discussion of anatomy or classification. An appendix provides a classification of the families and genera of the gastropods referred to in the text.

Thiele, Johannes. **Handbook of Systematic Malacology.** Washington, DC: Smithsonian Institution Libraries and the National Science Foundation, 1992–98. 4 vol. in 3.

Thiele was one of the best known systematists of his time, and he did much of the pioneering work on the taxonomy of mollusks. His most famous work was the *Handbuch der systematischen Weichtierkunde,* originally published between 1929 and 1935. This classic was translated into English to allow more people to have access to it. Although some of Thiele's work is out of date, the *Handbook* is still heavily used because it contains extensive anatomical information. The original was published in four sections, which are combined into three volumes in the translation as follows: Part 1, *Loricata; Gastropoda: Prosobranchia;* Part 2, *Gastropoda: Opisthobranchia and Pulmonata;* Part 3, *Scaphopoda, Bivalvia, Cephalopoda;* and Part 4, *Comparative Morphology, Phylogeny, Geographical Distribution.*

Vermeij, Geerat J. **A Natural History of Shells.** Princeton: Princeton University Press, 1993. 207 p. ISBN 069108596X.

The title of this book is a little misleading, because the author is actually writing about how shells are constructed and how they work to protect mollusks from the environment and predators. The focus is on living organisms, although a final section discusses the historical geography and evolution of mollusks. Each chapter has extensive references. There are also many black-and-white and color photographs. This is an interesting complement to *Living Marine Molluscs,* below, which puts less emphasis on the purpose and form of mollusk shells.

Wilbur, Karl M., series ed. **The Mollusca.** New York: Academic Press, 1983–88. 12 vol. Price varies.

This multivolume treatise discusses all major aspects of molluscan biology. Each volume covers a different topic in detail.

Yonge, C.M., and T.E. Thompson. **Living Marine Molluscs.** London: Collins, 1976. 288 p. ISBN 0002190990.

The emphasis in this book is on living mollusks, not just their shells. The authors discuss all aspects of molluscan biology and behavior, including habits and habitats. There are many black-and-white drawings and color photos of both shelled and shell-less mollusks. Although the book is rather old, it is still a good general introduction to the lives of mollusks.

Sipuncula

Cutler, Edward B. **The Sipuncula: Their Systematics, Biology, and Evolution.** Ithaca, NY: Comstock, 1994. 453 p. $91.95. ISBN 0801428432.

This handbook provides an overview of the Sipuncula, a phylum of marine worms. It includes a classification of the phylum, keys, a review of sipunculan biology, and information about the zoogeography and evolution of the worms.

Pseudocoelomates

Anderson, Roy C. **Nematode Parasites of Vertebrates: Their Development and Transmission.** 2nd ed. New York: CABI, 2000. 650 p. $185. ISBN 0851994210.

A companion to *CIH Keys to the Nematode Parasites of Vertebrates,* above, this book summarizes knowledge about the development and transmission of parasitic nematodes. An introductory chapter provides basic information about nematode biology, and subsequent chapters cover each order in detail. Most species that are vertebrate parasites are discussed in detail, and there are lengthy references.

Bird, Alan F., and Jean Bird. **The Structure of Nematodes.** 2nd ed. San Diego: Academic Press, 1991. 316 p. $122.95. ISBN 0120996510.

Gathers together information on the structure and pathology of both free-living and parasitic nematodes. Chapters cover topics such as the nematode egg, growth, reproduction, the various body parts such as muscles and epidermis, and pathology. The reference lists for each chapter are extensive.

Crompton, D. W. T., and Brent B. Nickol, eds. **Biology of the Acanthocephala.** New York: Cambridge University Press, 1985. 519 p. ISBN 0521246741.

A survey of the biology of the spiny-headed worms, updating research done since the publication of Anton Meyer's monograph in Bronn's *Klassen und Ordnungen des Tierreichs* (see chapter 1). The authors cover classification, morphology, physiology, life histories, and population dynamics. There are also biographies and bibliographies for the two major acanthocephalan researchers, Meyer and Harley Van Cleave.

Lee, Donald L., ed. **The Biology of Nematodes.** London: Taylor & Francis, 2002. 635 p. $192. ISBN 0415272114.

Provides detailed, up-to-date information on the biology of both free-living and parasitic nematodes. Topics covered include life cycles, feeding, locomotion, behavior, biological and chemical control, and more. The opening chapter discusses nematode classification and phylogeny and includes a tentative classification to the family level as well as descriptions of the nematode orders. Because the nematode *Caenorhabditis elegans* is one of the most important model organisms for genetics and developmental biology, this volume has a wide audience.

Maggenti, Armand R. **General Nematology.** New York: Springer-Verlag, 1981. 372 p. (Springer Series in Microbiology). $76. ISBN 038790588X.

Provides an introduction to both plant and animal nematodes, including the history of nematology, related phyla, biology, and parasitism on plants, invertebrates, and vertebrates.

Malakhov, V. V. **Nematodes: Structure, Development, Classification, and Phylogeny.** Washington, DC: Smithsonian Institution Press, 1994. 286 p. $25 (paper). ISBN 1560982551; 1560982853 (paper).

Covers the biology and classification of both parasitic and free-living nematodes. The author proposes a new classification of nematodes based on their comparative morphology and embryology. The author also discusses the classification of the other pseudocoelomates. This is a translation of the Russian *Nematody* and contains citations to many Russian articles that are not easily found elsewhere.

Riddle, Donald L., et al., eds. *C. elegans* **II.** Plainview, NY: Cold Spring Harbor Laboratory Press, 1997. 1,222 p. (Cold Spring Harbor Monograph series, no. 33). ISBN 0879694882.

This handbook discusses the biology of *C. elegans* in great detail, providing all the details that researchers who study the development or genetics of this common model organism need. The full text of the volume is also available at no charge for personal use at http://www.ncbi.nlm.nih.gov/books/bv.fcgi?call = bv.View..ShowSection&rid = ce2 as part of the NCBI Bookshelf.

Wharton, David A. **A Functional Biology of Nematodes.** Baltimore: Johns Hopkins University Press, 1986. 192 p. ISBN 0801833590.

Examines the biology of both free-living and parasitic nematodes. The author covers topics such as movement, reproduction, parasitism, life cycles, and physiology. Unlike most other volumes in this series, the volume does not include an appendix with the classification of nematodes.

Wormatlas: A Database of Behavioral and Structural Anatomy of *Caenorhabditis elegans*. 2002– . URL: http://www.wormatlas.org/. Accessed August 25, 2003).

This site provides a number of databases and services for researchers studying *C. elegans,* including a handbook of worm anatomy, cell and neuron identification, a discussion of anatomical methods, a glossary (incomplete at the time of viewing), and links to other sites and literature about this popular nematode.

Echinodermata

Lawrence, John M. **A Functional Biology of Echinoderms.** Baltimore: Johns Hopkins University Press, 1987. 340 p. ISBN 080183547X.

Functional biology refers to the characteristics of organisms that increase fitness through time, principally survival and reproduction. This text provides an overview of the Echinodermata and then discusses feeding, maintenance activities such as locomotion and circulation, and reproduction. The classification of living echinoderms down to the level of the order is covered in an appendix, and of course there is a lengthy list of references.

Mortensen, Theodor. **A Monograph of the Echinoidea.** Copenhagen: C. A. Reitzel, 1928–52. 5 vols. in 17.

This massive set was published shortly after a series of deep sea investigations had greatly expanded knowledge of echinoderms, and it is still the most comprehensive publication on both living and fossil echinoderm species. The author covers the living echinoderms in detail, but most fossil forms are only identified to the genus, not the species. Each part of the series consists of paired volumes, one containing text and the other containing plates.

Nichols, David. **Echinoderms.** Rev. ed. London: Hutchinson, 1966. 200 p.

This small book is still one of the best summaries of the biology of echinoderms to be found. The author discusses each of the five major classes (Crinoidea, Asteroidea, Ophiuroidea, Echinoidea, and Holothuroidea). Further chapters cover echinoderm anatomy and larval forms, plus phylogeny and extinct forms.

Hemichordata

Barrington, E. J. W. **The Biology of Hemichordata and Protochordata.** San Francisco: W. H. Freeman, 1965. 176 p. (University Reviews in Biology).

Provides a summary of the biology of the Hemichordata, Urochordata (tunicates), and Cephalochordata. Although quite old, it is one of the few free-standing volumes covering these interesting organisms. The book has separate chapters on each of the phyla or subphyla and discusses topics such as anatomy, behavior, life histories, and evolution.

Identification Tools

Brusca, Richard C. **Common Intertidal Invertebrates of the Gulf of California.** 2nd ed. Tucson: University of Arizona Press, 1980. 513 p. ISBN 0816506825.

A field manual to 1,300 species of invertebrates found in the Gulf of California, this identification guide contains keys to species plus photographs and illustrations of the marine invertebrates of this region.

Dindal, Daniel L., ed. **Soil Biology Guide.** New York: Wiley, 1990. 1,349 p. ISBN 0471045519.

This fat tome helps identify the invertebrates, from microbes to insects, that are found in North American soils. Each major group (order or family) is covered in a separate chapter. The reproduction, ecology, distribution, sampling and preservation techniques, classification, and identification are covered. There are keys to genus or species, black-and-white illustrations, and an extensive bibliography for each group as well.

Edmondson, W. T., ed. **Fresh-Water Biology.** 2nd ed. New York, Wiley, 1959. 1,248 p.

Updates Henry Baldwin Ward and George Chandler Whipple's manual by the same name, which was the classic work on freshwater plants and animals. It is included here because it covers invertebrates from microbes to insects. The format is the same as Dindal (above), which was in fact designed to complement *Fresh-Water Biology*'s coverage.

Gosliner, Terrence, David W. Behrens, and Gary C. Williams. **Coral Reef Animals of the Indo-Pacific: Animal Life from Africa to Hawaii Exclusive of the Vertebrates.** Monterey, CA: Sea Challengers, 1996. 314 p. $45 (paper). ISBN 0930118219 (paper).

A "scientific field guide" for divers, aquarists, and biologists, this colorful guide identifies 1,150 species of marine invertebrates. There are color photographs, and the descriptions include identification, natural history, and distribution of the animals. One of a large group of similar diver's guides to marine animals.

Guides to the Identification of the Microinvertebrates of the Continental Waters of the World. Leiden: Backhuys, 1992– . Vol. irregular. Price varies. ISSN 0928-2440.

Also known as the "Zooplankton Guides," this series covers the major groups of zooplankton around the world. As of 2003, the series was up to 20 volumes, most covering copepods and rotifers.

Humann, Paul, and Ned Deloach. **Reef Creature Identification: Florida, Caribbean, Bahamas.** 2nd ed., enl. Jacksonville, FL: New World, 2002. 320 p. (Reef Set, vol. 2). $37.95 (paper). ISBN 1878348310 (paper).

Another colorful diver's guide to marine invertebrates, this spiral-bound guide identifies 450 species and features color photographs of the organisms. Companion volumes include *Reef Coral Identification* (below) and *Reef Fish Identification* (see chapter 5).

Kozloff, Eugene N. **Marine Invertebrates of the Pacific Northwest.** Seattle: University of Washington Press, 1987. 511 p. ISBN 0295965304.

Provides keys to the invertebrates of the intertidal and shallow subtidal habitats between Oregon and British Columbia. The manual excludes protozoans, flukes, tapeworms, acanthocephalans, and parasitic nematodes. Each chapter covers a phylum and includes a brief overview, bibliography, key to species, and a list of species. There are numerous black-and-white illustrations and photos.

Meinkoth, Norman August. **National Audubon Society Field Guide to North American Seashore Creatures.** New York: Knopf, 1998. 813 p. (National Audubon Society Field Guide series). $19.95. ISBN 0304519030.

A field guide to 690 species of marine invertebrates found along the Atlantic and Pacific Coasts of North America, featuring color photographs of about 670 species.

Morris, Percy A. **A Field Guide to Pacific Coast Shells, including Shells of Hawaii and the Gulf of California.** 2nd ed. Boston: Houghton Mifflin, 1966. 297 p. (Peterson Field Guide series, no. 6). ISBN 0395183227.

One of the standard field guides for the shells of the Pacific Coast of North America, this guide covers about 945 common species, illustrated with photographs of the shells.

Peckarsky, Barbara L., et al., eds. **Freshwater Macroinvertebrates of Northeastern North America.** Ithaca, NY: Comstock, 1990. 442 p. $32.50 (paper). ISBN 0801420768; ISBN 0801496888 (paper).

The keys in this text cover invertebrates from primarily Pennsylvania, New York, New England, Ontario, Quebec, and New Brunswick, although it is useful outside this area. It includes aquatic insects, crustaceans, water mites, mollusks, and annelids. Each chapter consists of a key to the genera and a checklist to the families and genera covered in the key. There are also a few pages of introduction to the classification and ecology of each taxa. The text is designed for the use of students in aquatic biology courses.

Young, Craig M., ed. **Atlas of Marine Invertebrate Larvae.** San Diego: Academic, 2002. 626 p. $99.95. ISBN 0127731415.

Covers the anatomy of representative larval forms from the 30 invertebrate phyla known to have larvae, including the Urochordata and the Cephalochordata. Each chapter describes the characteristics of the phylum, reproduction, life cycles, anatomy and morphology, and differences between the various classes in the phylum. At the end of each chapter, numerous figures show the life cycles and detailed anatomy of the larvae. Most of the illustrations are photomicrographs, but there are also black-and-white drawings as well. A few color illustrations are found at the end of the text.

Systematic Section

Cnidaria

Humann, Paul. **Reef Coral Identification: Florida, Caribbean, Bahamas: Including Marine Plants.** 2nd ed., enl. Jacksonville, FL: New World Publications, 2002. 278 p. (Reef Set, vol. 3). $34.95. ISBN 1878348329.

A companion to the author's *Reef Creature Identification* (above) and *Reef Fish Identification* (see chapter 5), this colorful field guide identifies 250 species of coral and associated algae found in the region.

Veron, J. E. N. **Corals of Australia and the Indo-Pacific.** Honolulu: University of Hawaii Press, 1993. 644 p. $95. ISBN 0824815041.

Identifies over 1,000 species of corals of this region of the world with information on distribution, abundance, and natural history.

Veron, J. E. N. **Corals of the World.** Townsville MC, Queensland, Australia: Australian Institute of Marine Science, 2000. 3 vol. $160. ISBN 0642322368 (vol. 1); 0642322376 (vol. 2); 0642322384 (vol. 3).

A beautifully illustrated guide to the corals of the world, this set contains color photographs of hundreds of species of coral. Each species account provides general description, similar species, habitat, abundance, range map, references to taxonomic information and identification sources, and several photographs of the coral. In addition to the species accounts, the author provides background information on corals and coral reefs, biogeography, and evolution. There are also keys to genera and species and lists of common names (which are not used in the main text). Although this set is far too large to haul to the beach, the author also lists identification guides that are more portable.

Mollusca

Abbott, R. Tucker. **American Seashells: The Marine Molluska of the Atlantic and Pacific Coasts of North America.** 2nd ed. New York: Van Nostrand Reinhold, 1974. 663 p. ISBN 0442202288.

The standard compilation of the seashells of North America. The author was one of the most highly regarded malacologists and the author of many other guides to mollusks of North America. This guide is intended to help amateurs identify 1,500 common species of the shallow waters of both the Atlantic and Pacific Coasts. Abbott provided an extensive initial section on the natural history of mollusks, followed by a guide to the various classes of mollusks, including cephalopods. There are black-and-white and a few color photos in separate plates, and an extensive guide to the literature.

Abbott, R. Tucker. **Compendium of Landshells: A Color Guide to More Than 2,000 of the World's Terrestrial Shells.** Melbourne, FL: American Malacologists, 1989. 240 p. $21. ISBN 0915826232.

This compendium illustrates about 2,000 species of snails from around the world. It is aimed at amateur shell collectors, so it includes a nice introductory chapter that tells about snail classification and biology, as well as methods of collecting and preserving snail shells. The bulk of the book consists of the color photographs of the species, which are accompanied by a brief description. A final section provides a lengthy bibliography arranged by location and taxonomy. The *Compendium of Seashells,* below, is a companion.

Abbott, R. Tucker, and S. Peter Dance. **Compendium of Seashells: A Color Guide to More Than 4,200 of the World's Marine Shells.** New York: E. P. Dutton, 1982. 411 p. ISBN 0525932690.

A classic guide for amateur shell collectors, this compendium is also often used as a reference for researchers. The shells are generally the most common or desirable ones for collectors. Each is illustrated with a color photograph, often of the type specimen. There are brief descriptions for each species, including common and scientific names, size, distribution, habitat, and abundance. In some cases, the authors also include synonyms if the scientific name is in doubt. They also include an extensive bibliography on the taxonomy of the Mollusca, and indexes to common and scientific names.

Abbott, R. Tucker, and Percy A. Morris. **A Field Guide to Shells: Atlantic and Gulf Coasts and the West Indies.** 4th ed. Boston: Houghton Mifflin, 1995. 350 p. (The Peterson Field Guide series, no. 3). $19 (paper). ISBN 0395697808; 0395697794 (paper); 0618164391 (paper).

A field guide to over 800 species of shells, with color illustrations and information on distribution, habitat, and natural history.

Burch, J. B. **How to Know the Eastern Land Snails: Pictured-Keys for Determining the Land Snails of the United States Occurring East of the Rocky Mountain Divide.** Dubuque, IA: W. C. Brown, 1963. 214 p. (Pictured Key Nature series).

An illustrated key to 390 species of snails found east of the Rockies suitable for students.

Clarke, Arthur Haddleton. **The Freshwater Molluscs of Canada.** Ottawa: National Museum of Natural Sciences, National Museums of Canada, 1981. 446 p. $25. ISBN 0660000229.

Around 180 species of mollusks are listed in this guide. The author provides background information on how and why to collect shells, molluscan classification, and a key to the families of freshwater mollusks before getting to the species accounts. Each species is illustrated with multiple black-and-white photographs, and its description, distribution, and ecology are also provided as well as range maps.

Cummings, Kevin S., and Christine A. Mayer. **Field Guide to Freshwater Mussels of the Midwest.** Champaign: Illinois Natural History Survey, 1992. 194 p. (Illinois Natural History Survey Manual, no. 5). $15.

A fairly technical field guide to 75 species of mussels from the Midwest, many of them endangered or threatened.

Rehder, Harald Alfred. **National Audubon Society Field Guide to North American Seashells.** New York: Knopf, 1981. 894 p. (National Audubon Society Field Guide series). $19.95. ISBN 0394519132.

A photographic field guide covering over 670 species of seashells, with another 200 species mentioned but not illustrated.

Roper, Clyde F.E., Michael J. Sweeney, and Cornelia E. Nauen. **Cephalopods of the World: An Annotated and Illustrated Catalogue of Species of Interest to Fisheries.** Rome: Food and Agricultural Organization of the United Nations, 1984. 277 p. (FAO Species Catalogue, vol. 3). ISBN 9251013829.

This guide identifies the cephalopods of economic importance worldwide. The authors provide general remarks, an illustrated glossary, a key to orders and families, and detailed information on about 200 species of cephalopods. Each species account includes a distribution map, black-and-white illustration, common names in several languages, general remarks, diagnostic features, synonyms, distribution, habitat, size, interest to fisheries, and citations to the literature. There are also appendixes showing cephalopod classification, a list of species by fishing areas, and an extensive bibliography.

Shells Database. URL: http://shell.kwansei.ac.jp/~shell/pic_book/index.html (Accessed August 26, 2003).

A Japanese-English Web database covering 3,865 species of mollusks at the time of viewing. The database can be searched by shell shape, scientific name, or Japanese common name. The mollusks are also listed in taxonomic order so users can browse individual families. The record for each species includes a color photograph, taxonomy, English and Japanese common names, distribution, habitat, notes, and bibliography. The search by shape function is useful for collectors who need to identify a shell; the remainder of the site is oriented more toward researchers.

Platyhelminthes

Cannon, L.R.G. **Turbellaria of the World: A Guide to Families and Genera.** Macintosh and Windows version 1.0. Amsterdam, the Netherlands: ETI Expert Center for Taxonomic Identification and the University of Amsterdam, 1998. 1 CD. (World Biodiversity Database CD-ROM series). $86.95. ISBN 3540145052.

An updated version of the author's 1986 book by the same name. The CD contains a key to 123 families and 57 subfamilies, plus videos of many species, a hyperlinked glossary, information on geographical distribution, references, and more.

Gibson, David I., Arlene Jones, and Rodney A. Bray, eds. **Keys to the Trematoda.** Wallingford, UK: CAB International and the Natural History Museum, 2002–2003. 3 vols. $175 (vol. 1), $150 (vol. 2), $150 (vol. 3). ISBN 0851995470 (vol. 1), 085199587X (vol. 2), 0851995888 (vol. 3).

This set provides a revision of the systematics of the Trematoda along with keys to the level of the genus. The first volume covers the subclasses Aspidogastrea and Digenea while volume two covers the orders Echinostomida and volume three the Plagiorchiida. There are numerous black-and-white illustrations and each family is introduced and described as well as keyed out.

Khalil, L. F., A. Jones, and R. A. Bray, eds. **Keys to the Cestode Parasites of Vertebrates.** Wallingford, UK: CAB International, 1994. 751 p. $195. ISBN 0851988792.

Companion to *CIH Keys to the Nematode Parasites of Vertebrates,* below. The book provides keys allowing the identification of cestode tapeworms to the level of the genus. Each chapter covers a different order or family and contains an introduction and dichotomous keys. For each genus, there is a brief paragraph of diagnosis describing the genera and listing its host, distribution, and the type species. There are numerous line drawings for each chapter as well. A final chapter lists new or invalid generic names, and the editors also provide a glossary and lengthy list of references.

Schell, Stewart C. **How to Know the Trematodes.** Dubuque, IA: W. C. Brown, 1970. 355 p. (Pictured Key Nature series).

A comprehensive illustrated key to the trematodes.

Schmidt, Gerald D. **CRC Handbook of Tapeworm Identification.** Boca Raton, FL: CRC Press, 1986. 675 p. $374. ISBN 084933280X.

Provides keys to the identification of nearly 4,000 species of tapeworms with numerous illustrations of adult tapeworm morphology. The only worldwide key to tapeworm identification in print at the time of writing.

Schmidt, Gerald D. **How to Know the Tapeworms.** Dubuque, IA: W. C. Brown, 1970. 266 p. (Pictured Key Nature series). ISBN 0697048608.

An illustrated key to all genera of tapeworms found around the world.

Echinodermata

Clark, Ailsa McGown, and Maureen E. Downey. **Starfishes of the Atlantic.** New York: Chapman & Hall, 1991. 794 p. (Chapman & Hall Identification Guide, no. 3). $515. ISBN 0412432803.

This technical guide identifies 374 species of starfish found in the Atlantic Ocean. The authors provide tabular keys to the orders, families, and species of starfish. The species accounts list the alternate names, type specimens, description, distribution, and biology. Line drawings and black-and-white photographs of most species are provided in separate sections at the end of the book, along with the lengthy list of references.

Coe, Wesley Roswell. **Starfishes, Serpent Stars, Sea Urchins and Sea Cucumbers of the Northeast.** New York: Dover, 1972. 152 p. ISBN 0486209490.

This little book was originally published in 1912 as *Echinoderms of Connecticut,* no. 19 of the *Bulletin of the Connecticut State Geological and Natural History Survey.* It is a standard handbook, providing keys, black-and-white illustrations and photographs, and background information on the echinoderms of the region and their biology.

Hendler, Gordon, John E. Miller, David L. Pawson, and Porter M. Kier. **Sea Stars, Sea Urchins, and Allies: Echinoderms of Florida and the Caribbean.** Washington, DC: Smithsonian Institution Press, 1995. 390 p. $49.95. ISBN 1560984503.

Most of the species covered in this guide are attractively illustrated with color photographs. It is designed as an identification guide and handbook for amateurs, so the authors provide background information on the shallow-water marine ecosystems in the area, the general features of echinoderms, and how to study and photograph echinoderms. Each class is then covered in detail, and individual species are described in detail. Each species account also includes information on the distribution, habitat, and biology of the echinoderm, and there are also general remarks and references. The brittle stars are difficult to identify so keys to the families are provided. The refer ence list is extensive, and there is also a glossary of terms.

Associations

American Society of Parasitologists. American Society of Parasitology Business Office, P.O. Box 1897, Lawrence, KS 66044-8897. URL: http://asp.unl.edu/ (Accessed August 25, 2003).

International Society of Invertebrate Reproduction. URL: http://sun. science.wayne.edu/~jram/isir.htm (Accessed August 25, 2003).

Society for Invertebrate Pathology. 7413 Six Forks Rd. #114, Raleigh, NC 27615. Phone: 888-486-1505. Fax: 888-684-4682. E-mail: sip@sipweb.org. URL: http://www.sipweb.org/ (Accessed August 25, 2003).

Xerces Society. 4828 SE Hawthorne Blvd. Portland, OR 97215. Phone: 503-232-6639. E-mail: info@xerces.org. URL: http://www.xerces.org/ (Accessed August 25, 2003).

Systematic Section

Mollusks

American Malacological Society. c/o Eugene P. Keferl, Coastal Georgia Community College, 3700 Altama Ave., Brunswick, GA 31520-3644. Phone: 912-262-3089. E-mail: kefer@bc9000.bc.peachnet.edu. URL: http://erato.acnatsci.org/ams/ (Accessed August 25, 2003).

Conchological Society of Great Britain and Ireland. c/o Hon. Membership Secretary Mike Weideli. 35 Bartlemy Road, Newbury, Berks., RG14 6LD, UK. Phone: 01635 42190. E-mail: membership@conchsoc.org. URL: http://www.conchsoc.org/index.htm (Accessed August 25, 2003).

Malacological Society of London. c/o G.B.J. Dussart, Ph.D., Christ Church College, North Holmes Road, Canterbury, Kent, CT1 1QU, UK. URL: http://www.sunderland.ac.uk/MalacSoc/ (Accessed August 25, 2003).

Society for Experimental and Descriptive Malacology (SEDM). PO Box 3037, Ann Arbor, MI 48106. Phone: (734) 764-0470. Fax: (734) 763-4080. E-mail: jbburch@umich.edu

Lophophorates

Society of Nematologists. PO Box 311, Marceline, MO 64658. Phone: 660-376-2939. Fax: 660-376-2939. E-mail: socnema@yahoo.com. URL: http://www.nematologists.org (Accessed August 25, 2003).

Reference

Brusca, Richard C., and Gary J. Brusca. 1990. *Invertebrates*. Sunderland, MA: Sinauer Associates.

3

Arthropods (Including the Spiders, Crustaceans, and Insects)

The arthropods, including the spiders, crustaceans, and insects, are the largest phylum of animals by far. They make up three-fourths of all known species of animals, with at least 123,000 species of spiders and crustaceans and another 751,000 species of insects. There are 350,000 species of beetles alone, and whether or not J. B. S. Haldane actually quipped that the Creator had "an inordinate fondness for beetles," the comment has merit. More species of arthropods are discovered daily, and some experts believe tens of millions of species are waiting to be described. As this chapter was being finished, the discovery of the Mantophasmatodea or Gladiators, an entire new order of insects, was announced (Klass et al., 2002), the first in almost a century. Arthropod taxonomists do not have to worry about running out of work.

The phylum Arthropoda was named for the distinctive jointed appendages, including feet, antennae, and mouthparts, of its members. Other arthropod features include exoskeletons made largely of chitin and segmented bodies. They are a varied phylum and can be found in even the harshest environments. They range in size from the King Crab's 12-foot leg span to microscopic mites and crustaceans. Arthropods are also of considerable economic importance for good and ill. We eat many of the crustaceans, although the insects generally are safe from human consumption (at least on purpose). Instead, the insects eat our food and give us diseases.

The Arthropoda are divided into four main subphyla: extinct Trilobita, Chelicerata, Crustacea, and Uniramia. The Chelicerata include horseshoe crabs, spiders, mites, and scorpions. The Crustacea include barnacles, shrimps, lobsters, crabs, isopods, and many other familiar and unfamiliar animals. The largest subphylum, the Uniramia, includes the millipedes and centipedes as well as the Hexapoda (the "normal" six-legged insects). Because all trilobites are extinct, we do not deal with them in this chapter.

Due to the very large number of books dealing with arthropods, only resources that deal with the arthropod orders of the world and of North American arthropods are covered here. However, selected comprehensive guides from other parts of the world are annotated in the general section of Identification Tools and some other relatively comprehensive handbooks may be found.

Classification of Arthropods (from Daly et al., 1998)

Chelicerata

Xiphosura (Horseshoe Crabs; 5 species)

Arachnida

  Araneae (spiders; 30,000 species)

  Acari (mites and ticks; 15,000–30,000 species)

  Scorpionida (scorpions; 750 species)

Crustacea

Remipedia (few species)

Cephalocarida (9 species)

Branchiopoda (tadpole shrimp; 800 species)

Maxillopoda (barnacles, copepods, others; 18,000 species)

Malacostraca (shrimps, lobsters, crabs, woodlice, others; 20,000 species)

Uniramia

Myriapoda (Millipedes and Centipedes; 13,000 species)

Hexapoda (Insecta)

  Subclass Apterygota

    Protura (proturans; 400 species)

    Collembola (springtails; 6,000 species)

    Diplura (diplurans; 800 species)

    Thysanura (silverfish; 370 species)

    Microcoryphia (bristletails; 350 species)

  Subclass Pterygota

    Ephemeroptera (mayflies; 2,000 species)

Odonata (dragonflies and damselflies; 5,000 species)

Orthoptera (grasshoppers, crickets and katydids; 20,000 species)

Phasmatodea (stick insects; 2,500 species)

Grylloblattodea (16 species)

Dermaptera (earwigs; 1,800 species)

Isoptera (termites; 2,300 species)

Embioptera (webspinners; 200 species)

Plecoptera (stoneflies; 2,000 species)

Zoraptera (angel insects; 30 species)

Psocoptera (booklice; 3,000 species)

Phthiraptera (lice, including the suborders Mallophaga and Anoplura; 3,000 species)

Thysanaptera (thrips; 4,500 species)

Hemiptera (true bugs, cicadas, aphids, including Homoptera; 55,000–82,000 species)

Megaloptera (alderflies; 300 species)

Raphidoptera (snakeflies; 175 species)

Neuroptera (lacewings, antlions, and owlflies; 5,000 species)

Coleoptera (beetles; 300,000–375,000 species)

Strepsiptera (twisted-wing parasites; 525 species)

Mecoptera (scorpionflies and hangingflies; 500 species)

Trichoptera (caddisflies; 7,000 species)

Lepidoptera (butterflies and moths; 112,000 species)

Diptera (flies and mosquitoes; 85,000–98,500 species)

Siphonaptera (fleas; 2,400 species)

Dictyoptera (cockroaches; 4,000 species)

Hymenoptera (wasps, bees, termites; 108,000 species)

Mantodea (mantids; 2,000 species)

Mantophasmatodea (gladiators; 8 species)

Indexes, Abstracts, and Bibliographies

Abstracts of Entomology. Vol. 1– . Philadelphia: BIOSIS, 1970– . Monthly. $643. ISSN 0001-3579.

This index covers all areas of entomology from agronomy and integrated pest management to systematics and genetics. Over 20,000 references are added each year. All references are taken from the *BIOSIS Previews* database (see chapter 1).

Derksen, W., and U. Scheiding. 1963–75. **Index Litteraturae Entomologicae.** Ser. 2, **Die Welt-Literatur über die gesamte Entomologie von 1864 bis 1900.** 5 vol. Berlin: Akademie der Landwirtschaftswissenschaften der Deutschen Demokratischen Republik.

Continues the coverage of the world's entomological literature from Horn and Schenkling's *Index Litteraturae Entomologicae,* below. The set is in alphabetical order by author but also has a subject list by family and a zoogeographical index. Volume 5 contains a list of abbreviated journal titles used in the volume along with their full titles.

Entomology Abstracts. Vol. 1– . Bethesda, MD: Cambridge Scientific Abstracts, 1969– . Monthly. $1,420. ISSN 0013-8924.

Covers all areas of entomology, including basic and applied fields. The index also covers arachnids, myriapods, onychophorans, and terrestrial isopods in addition to insects. About 10,000 records are added per year. Available online and on CD-ROM as part of the *CSA Biological Sciences Database.*

Horn, W., and S. Schenkling. **Index Litteraturae Entomologicae. Die Welt-Literatur über die gesamte Entomologie bis inklusive 1863.** 4 vol. Berlin: Dahlem, 1928–29.

This index covers the literature of entomology from its beginning to 1862. It is in alphabetical order by author, and Volume 4 contains additions and corrections. A revision of Hermann Hagen's *Bibliotheca Entomologica* (1862–63), containing 8,000 additional titles.

Royal Entomological Society of London. **Catalogue of the Library of the Royal Entomological Society of London.** Boston: G. K. Hall, 1980. 5 vol. ISBN 0816103151.

This catalog consists of copies of the card catalog of the Royal Society, which has an excellent collection of rare and obscure materials. It is useful as a citation verification tool.

Systematic Section

Insects

Odonata

Odonatological Abstracts. Vol. 1– . Bilthoven, Netherlands: Societas Internationalis Odonatologica, 1972– .

Indexes the literature of dragonflies. Entries include citations and abstracts. Published as part of *Odonatologica* (see below). Members of the Worldwide Dragonfly Association have access to a database version of the abstracts with their membership.

Dermaptera

Haas, Fabian. **Sakai Literature.** URL: http://134.60.85.50:591/SakaiDB/SakaiN_su.html (Accessed August 25, 2003).

Sakai's massive *Dermapterorum Catalogus* and its continuation, *Forficula,* gather together most of the world literature of the Dermaptera. However, there is no overall index for the 30-plus volumes in the series, so this database was created. It provides author, year, title, and keyword(s) of the articles in the various volumes. At the time of viewing, it was incomplete, containing only records from Volumes 10, 11, 12, 26, 27, 28, 29, 30, and 31 of *Dermapterorum Catalogus* and Volumes 1 to 6 of *Forficula.*

Sakai, Seiroku. **Dermapterorum Catalogus: A Basic Survey for Integrated Taxonomy of the Dermaptera of the World.** Tokyo, Japan: S. Sakai: Ikegami, 1985– .

This massive effort, along with Sakai's *Dermapterorum Catalogus Praeliminaris* (1970–84), catalogs the world literature of the Dermaptera. The volume numbering for the *Dermapterorum Catalogus* continues the numbering from the earlier set.

Isoptera

Ernst, E., and R.L. Araujo, comps. **A Bibliography of Termite Literature, 1966–1978.** New York: Wiley, 1986. 903 p. ISBN 047190466X.

Contains over 3,000 annotated entries on the termites, arranged in alphabetical order by author. There is a junior author index as well as an extensive index to subjects and scientific names. Updates Snyder's *Annotated, Subject-Heading Bibliography of Termites,* below.

Snyder, Thomas Elliott. **Annotated, Subject-Heading Bibliography of Termites, 1350 B.C. to A.D. 1954.** Washington, DC: Smithsonian Institution, 1956. 305 p. (Smithsonian Miscellaneous Collections, vol. 130).

Supplements were published in 1961 and 1968 as Volumes 143(3) and 152(3) of the *Smithsonian Miscellaneous Collections.* Ernst and Araujo (above) bring the literature up to 1978.

Trichoptera

Fischer, F. C. J. **Trichopterorum Catalogus.** Amsterdam: Nederlandsche Entomologische Vereeniging, 1960–73. 16 vol. in 10.

Volumes 1–12 cover the literature of the Trichoptera from 1758 to 1938; Volumes 13–15 are supplements taking the project up to 1958. An index volume was published in 1973. Each volume covers one or more families, and the species are listed in alphabetical order within the genera or subfamilies, which are in systematic order. The author lists about 5,000 papers covering systematics, geographical distribution, physiology, and morphology.

Nimmo, Andrew P. **Bibliographia Trichopterorum: A World Bibliography of Trichoptera (Insecta) with Indexes.** Sofia, Russia: Pensoft, 1996– . vol. (PENSOFT Series Faunistica, no. 5). $55 (vol. 1). ISBN 9546420123 (vol. 1).

This set is intended to update F. C. J. Fischer's *Trichopterorum Catalogus.* It is intended to comprise a four-volume set and covers both the biology and taxonomy of the Trichoptera. To date, only Volume 1 has been published, covering 1961 to 1970. There is a subject index as well as appendixes listing genera and species, journal abbreviations, and an alphabetical list of junior authors.

Hymenoptera

Apicultural Abstracts. Vol. 1– . Cardiff, Wales: International Bee Research Association, 1950– . Quarterly. $295. ISSN 0003-648X.

Indexes the world literature on honeybees and other Apoidea, including biology and behavior as well as beekeeping. Also available on CD-ROM and as part of BeeSearch, a service offered by the International Bee Research Association (IBRA) library.

Porter, Sanford D., and Cesare Baroni Urbani. **FORMIS. A Master Bibliography of Ant Literature.** Gainesville, FL: USDA, ARS, CMAVE, 1999– . URL: http://cmave.usda.ufl.edu/~formis. (Accessed August 25, 2003).

The database is a composite of several ant literature indexes, including *UCD Ant Literature Database, Biblio Fourmis, Baroni Urbani Bibliography,* references from AGRICOLA, and citations from Hölldobler and Wilson's *The Ants* (see under Handbooks). It contained about 30,000 references at the time of viewing. It can be searched on the Web or down-loaded in EndNote format for PCs or Macs.

Zhang, Bin-Cheng. **Index of Economically Important Lepidoptera.** Wallingford, UK: CAB International, 1994. 599 p. $120. ISBN 0851989039.

Based on the ANI, this index covers 6,000 species of Lepidoptera recorded in the last 80 years. Records provide the common and scientific names, host records, geographical records, and references to citations in the *Review of Agricultural Entomology.*

Journals

Advances in Insect Physiology. Vol. 1– . New York: Academic Press, 1963– . Annual. Price varies. ISSN 0065-2806.

This annual series publishes long review articles on any aspect of insect physiology. The individual volumes do not have an overall theme.

African Entomology: Journal of the Entomological Society of Southern Africa. Vol. 1– . Pretoria: Entomological Society of Southern Africa, 1993– . Semiannual. $145. ISSN 1021-3589.

Publishes primarily systematics papers, which must be authored or sponsored by a member of the Entomological Society of Southern Africa.

American Entomologist. Vol. 36– . Lanham, MD: Entomological Society of America, 1990– . Quarterly. $75. ISSN 1046-2821.

This magazine publishes articles of general interest to professional or amateur entomologists. There are several regular columns, including book reviews, research briefs, forums, and obituaries, in addition to the longer articles. Formerly titled *Bulletin of the Entomological Society of America.*

Annals of the Entomological Society of America. Vol. 1– . Lanham, MD: Entomological Society of America, 1908– . Bimonthly. $196. ISSN 0013-8746. Available electronically.

The articles in this journal report on the basic aspects of the biology of arthropods. The articles are arranged into subject areas such as systematics, ecology and population biology, arthropod biology, physiology, morphology, and behavior. Book reviews, letters to the editor, and interpretive articles (Forum section) are also included. Many of the articles are freely available online as PDF files at http://esa.edoc.com/0013-8746/.

Annual Review of Entomology. Vol. 1– . Palo Alto, CA: Annual Reviews Inc., 1956– . Annual. $148. ISSN 0066-4170. Available electronically.

This series publishes authoritative reviews on various topics in entomology. The articles are lengthy and summarize recent research in topics of current interest, so they are an excellent place to get state-of-the-art reviews. There are very lengthy lists of references for each article.

Aquatic Insects: An International Journal of Freshwater Entomology. Vol. 1– . Lisse, Netherlands: Swets and Zeitlinger, 1979– . Quarterly. $418. ISSN 0165-0424. Available electronically.

The journal covers the taxonomy, ecology, and habitats of the many different groups of aquatic insects. There are also occasional book reviews.

Archives of Insect Biochemistry and Physiology. Vol. 1– . New York: Wiley, 1983– . Monthly. $2,250. ISSN 0739-4462. Available electronically.

Published in collaboration with the Entomological Society of America. The journal publishes articles in the areas of insect biochemistry and physiology, especially areas such as endocrinology, development, neurobiology, molecular biology, and nutrition.

Arthropod Structure and Development. Vol. 29– . Kidlington, UK: Elsevier, 2000– . Quarterly. $959. ISSN 0020-7322. Available electronically.

Covers arthropod structural biology, development, and functional morphology, including enigmatic groups such as the Tardigrada and Onchyphora (see chapter 2). As well as research articles, the journal also publishes review articles, short communications, and special issues. Formerly *International Journal of Insect Morphology and Embryology.*

Australian Journal of Entomology. Vol. 1– . Carleton, Australia: Blackwell Science, 1996– . Quarterly. $250. ISSN 1326-6756.

The journal publishes research articles, reviews, notes, theses, and book reviews covering the biology, ecology, taxonomy, and control of insects and arachnids in Australasia. Formerly *Journal of the Australian Entomological Society.*

Bulletin of Entomological Research. Vol. 1– . Wallingford, UK: CAB International, 1910– . Quarterly. $700. ISSN 007-4853.

The emphasis in this journal is on the insects, mites, ticks and other arthropods of economic importance. Some taxonomic papers are accepted.

In addition to the research articles, a forum section includes guest editorials, invited review papers, and short communications on topics of general interest.

Canadian Entomologist. Vol. 1– . Ottawa: Entomological Society of Canada, 1868– . Bimonthly. $180. ISSN 0008-347X.

Publishes original research papers and scientific notes dealing with all facets of entomology. The issues are divided by subject: biodiversity, systematics, morphology and evolution, physiology, biochemistry, development and genetics, and behavior and ecology. Most issues also include broad review articles.

Deutsche Entomologische Zeitschrift. Berlin: Wiley-VCH, 1881– . Biannual. ISSN 1435–1951. Available electronically.

Covers both basic and applied aspects of insect biology, including spiders and mites. The emphasis is on systematics, fauntistics, biology, zoogeography, morphology, and ecology.

Ecological Entomology. Vol. 1– . Osney Mead, UK: Blackwell Science, 1976– . Quarterly. $610. ISSN 0307-6946. Available electronically.

The journal publishes original research articles dealing with insect ecology. There are also occasional reviews, descriptive papers, short communications, and opinion pieces. Formerly *Transactions of the Royal Entomological Society of London.*

Entomologia Experimentalis et Applicata. Vol. 1– . Dordrecht: Kluwer Academic Publishers, 1958– . Monthly. $1,434. ISSN 0013-8703. Available electronically.

The journal is published for the Nederlandse Entomologische Vereniging. It covers experimental biology and ecology of insects and other land arthropods, including research on integrated insect control and the relationship between insects and their host plants. The journal publishes original research articles, short communications, and book reviews.

Entomological News. Vol. 1– . Philadelphia: American Entomological Society, 1889– . Bimonthly. $20. ISSN 0013-872X.

Provides rapid publication of short articles on taxonomy, systematics, morphology, physiology, ecology, behavior, and similar aspects of insect life and related terrestrial arthropods, with manuscripts submitted by members receiving the highest priority.

Entomological Review. Vol. 1– . New York: Scripta Technica, 1957– . Quarterly. $3,130. ISSN 0013-8738.

This translation journal contains translations of papers from the Russian *Entomologicheskoe Obozrenie*. Topics covered include all aspects of theoretical and applied entomology.

Environmental Entomology. Vol. 1– . Lanham, MD: Entomological Society of America, 1972– . Bimonthly. $210. ISSN 0046-225X. Available electronically.

The journal publishes original research papers covering the interaction of insects with all aspects of their environment. Each issue is divided by subject, into physiological and chemical ecology, community and ecosystem ecology, population ecology, pest management and sampling, and biological control. The journal also publishes letters to the editor, interpretive articles, and book reviews. Many of the articles in each issue are freely available online as PDF files at http://esa.edoc.com/0046-225X/.

European Journal of Entomology. Vol. 90– . Ceské Budejovice, Czech Republic: Institute of Entomology, Czech Academy of Sciences and the Czech Entomological Society, 1993– . Quarterly. $180. ISSN 1210-5759.

An international journal covering all aspects of general, experimental, systematic, and applied entomology. Articles are published in English. The journal also publishes occasional symposia proceedings, which are available separately. Also titled *Ceskoslovenská Spolecnost Entomologická*. Formerly *Acta Entomologica Bohemoslovaca*.

Florida Entomologist. Vol. 1– . Lutz: Florida Entomological Society, 1920– . Quarterly. $50. ISSN 0015-4040. Available electronically.

Published by the Florida Entomological Society. Covers all areas in entomology, although at least one author must be a member of the Florida Entomological Society. The journal publishes research articles, short scientific notes, book reviews, and the occasional symposium proceedings. *Florida Entomologist* was one of the first journals available on the Internet, and it is still available at no charge at http://www.fcla.edu/FlaEnt/. All issues back to 1917 (when it was titled the *Florida Buggist*) are available. Authors may also choose to add supplementary files to the online version of their articles.

Insect Biochemistry and Molecular Biology. Vol. 1– . Kidlington, UK: Pergamon, 1971– . 8/yr. $1,786. ISSN 0965-1748. Available electronically.

Publishes original research articles, rapid communications, and reviews in the fields of insect biochemistry and insect molecular biology. Formerly *Insect Biochemistry.*

Insectes Sociaux: International Journal for the Study of Social Arthropods. Vol. 1– . Basel: Birkhauser Verlag, 1992– . Quarterly. $511. ISSN 0020-1812. Available electronically.

Publishes original research papers, short communications, and reviews on all aspects of the biology and evolution of social insects. The official journal for the International Union for the Study of Social Insects.

Insect Molecular Biology. Vol. 1– . Osney Mead, UK: Blackwell Science, 1992– . Quarterly. $710. ISSN 0962-1075. Available electronically.

Publishes original research articles on the structure, function, mapping, organization, expression, and evolution of insect genomes. It covers fundamental and applied aspects of insect molecular biology, including medical and agricultural aspects. In addition to the research articles, the journal also publishes brief communications and occasional review papers. Published for the Royal Entomological Society.

Journal of Agricultural and Urban Entomology. Vol. 16– . Clemson: South Carolina Entomological Society, 1999– . Quarterly. $50. ISSN 1523-5475.

The emphasis in this journal is on applied entomology, although some basic research topics are also covered. Topics of interest include arthropods that impact humans, livestock, and wildlife in agricultural and urban settings. Formerly *Journal of Agricultural Entomology.*

Journal of Applied Entomology. Vol. 1– . Berlin: Blackwell Wissenschafts Verlag GmbH, 1914– . 10/yr. $943. ISSN 0931-2048 (print). Available electronically.

Publishes original research articles on insects related to agriculture, forestry, biomedical areas, food, and feed storage. The articles are published in English, German, and French, although abstracts are in English. There are a few book reviews in most issues. Formerly *Zeitschrift für Angewandte Entomologie.*

Journal of Economic Entomology. Vol. 1– . Lanham, MD: Entomological Society of America, 1908– . Bimonthly. $234. ISSN 0022-0493. Available electronically.

Publishes articles on the economic significance of insects. They are divided by subject into sections such as apiculture and social insects; insecticide resistance and resistance management; ecology and behavior; sampling and biostatistics; and horticultural entomology. Many of the articles in each issue are freely available online as PDF files at http:// esa.edoc.com/0022-0493/.

Journal of Entomological Science. Vol. 20– . Tifton: Georgia Entomological Society, 1985– . Quarterly. $50. ISSN 0749-8004.

Publishes articles and brief notes and covers subjects such as systematics, biological control, crop protection, behavior, physiology, and medical and veterinary entomology. Formerly *Journal of the Georgia Entomological Society.*

Journal of Insect Behavior. Vol. 1– . New York: Kluwer/Plenum, 1988– . Bimonthly. $567. ISSN 0892-7553. Available electronically.

Publishes original research articles and short critical reviews on all aspects of the behavior of insects and other terrestrial arthropods.

Journal of Insect Physiology. Vol. 1– . Kidlington, UK: Pergamon, 1957– . $1,959. ISSN 0022-1910. Available electronically.

Publishes research articles and occasional reviews on all aspects of insect physiology, including articles on the physiology of other arthropods if they are of broad interest. Topics covered by the journal include endocrinology, pheromones, neurobiology, physiological pharmacology, nutrition, homeostasis, reproduction, and behavior.

Journal of Insect Science. Vol. 1– . Tucson: University of Arizona Library, 2001– . ISSN 1536-2442. Available electronically.

Publishes articles on all aspects of the biology of insects and other arthropods. This online-only journal was created as an alternative to expensive commercial publications. It is available at no charge on the Web at http://insectscience.org/. Articles are published as available, rather than being grouped together in issues. Thirteen articles were published in the journal's first year of publication.

Journal of Medical Entomology. Vol. 1– . Lanham, MD: Entomological Society of America, 1964– . Bimonthly. $196. ISSN 0022-2585. Available electronically.

Publishes articles, short communications, rapid communications, forum articles, and book reviews in all aspects of medical entomology and medical acarology. Many of the articles in each issue are freely available online as PDF files at http://esa.edoc.com/0022-2585/.

Medical and Veterinary Entomology. Vol. 1– . Osney Mead, UK: Blackwell Science, 1987– . Quarterly. $460. ISSN 0269-283X. Available electronically.

Covers all aspects of the biology and control of insects, ticks, mites and other arthropods of medical and veterinary importance. Topics of interest include vector biology, parasitology, behavior, biosystematics, ecology, distribution, and control methods.

Oriental Insects: An International Journal of Taxonomy and Zoogeography of Insects and Other Land Arthropods of the Old World Tropics. Vol. 1– . Gainesville, FL: Associated Publishers, 1968– . Annual. $65. ISSN 0030-5316.

Covers original research and reviews on the taxonomy, ecology, zoogeography, and evolution of insects and other land arthropods of the Old World Tropics. The emphasis is on taxonomic revisions.

The Pan-Pacific Entomologist. Vol.– . San Francisco: Pacific Coast Entomological Society, July 1924– . Quarterly. $40. ISSN 0031-0603.

Publishes papers on all aspects of the biosystematics of insects and closely related arthropods. Topics of interest include taxonomy, biology, behavior, ecology, life history, biogeography, and distribution.

Physiological Entomology. Vol. 1– . Osney Mead, UK: Blackwell Science, 1976– . Quarterly. $422. ISSN 0307-6962. Available electronically.

Publishes articles dealing with the behavior of insects and other arthropods, with emphasis on physiological and experimental approaches. Topics of interest include experimental analysis of behavior, behavioral physiology and biochemistry, neurobiology, general physiology, and circadian rhythms. Formerly *Journal of Entomology, Series A: Physiological and Behaviour.* Published for the Royal Entomological Society.

Systematic Entomology. Vol. 1– . Osney Mead, UK: Blackwell Science, 1976– . Quarterly. $538. ISSN 0307-6970. Available electronically.

Publishes original research articles dealing with insect taxonomy and systematics, with emphasis on comprehensive or revisionary studies, and on work with a biological or zoogeographical relevance. Formerly *Journal of Entomology, Series B: Taxonomy and Systematics.* Published for the Royal Entomological Society.

Transactions of the American Entomological Society. Vol. 17– . Philadelphia: American Entomological Society at the Academy of Natural Sciences, 1890– . $20. ISSN 0002-8320.

Publishes papers of moderate length on taxonomic, morphological, and ecological studies. Formerly *Transactions of the American Entomological Society and Proceedings of the Entomological Section of the Academy of Natural Sciences.*

Systematic Section

Arachnida

Acarologia. Vol. 1– . Paris: Acarologia, 1959– . Quarterly. $143.61. ISSN 0044-586X.

Publishes research articles covering all aspects of the biology and systematics of mites and ticks, including basic and applied studies and the occasional review article. The journal's Web site at http://alor. univ-montp3.fr/acrlg/Acrlg800/AcrlgEN/Prncplen.htm also includes links to other acarological sites.

Experimental and Applied Acarology. Vol. 1– . London: Kluwer, 1985– . Monthly. $1,234. ISSN 0168-8162. Available electronically.

Also covering basic and applied acarology, this journal places more emphasis on control of mites and ticks and tick/host interactions than *Acarologia,* but it also covers basic biology and systematics.

Journal of Arachnology. Vol. 1– . New York: American Arachnological Society, 1973– . 3 times/yr. $125. ISSN 0160-8202.

Publishes feature articles and short communications in all areas of arachnology, including spider biology and systematics. The journal also publishes the proceedings of the International Congress of Arachnology. Starting with 1999, the society began publishing the journal online at no charge on a trial basis. Full text of volumes from 1999 to the present plus a few earlier volumes are available at http://www.americanarachnology. org/JOA_online.html.

Crustacea

Crustaceana. Vol. 1– . Leiden: E.J. Brill, 1960– . Bimonthly. $540. ISSN 0011-216X. Available electronically.

Publishes in all areas of crustacean research, including taxonomy, ecology, physiology, and paleontology. In addition to the research articles, the journal also publishes book reviews, meeting announcements, and "News and Notes."

Journal of Crustacean Biology. Vol. 1– . Lawrence, KS: Allen Press, 1981– . Quarterly. $145. ISSN 0278-0372. Available electronically.

Publishes papers dealing with any aspect of crustacean biology, plus obituaries, notices of business transacted at meetings of the Crustacean Society, book reviews, and announcements. Papers are published in English but may include abstracts in other languages.

Insecta

Odonata

International Journal of Odonatology: Official Organ of the Worldwide Dragonfly Association. Vol. 1– . Leiden, The Netherlands: Backhuys, 1998– . Biannual. ISSN 1388-7890.

Covers all areas of odonatology from paleontology to anatomy, publishing both research articles and short notes.

Notulae Odonatologicae. Vol. 1– . Bilthoven, The Netherlands: Published by Ursus Scientific for the International Odonatological Foundation, Societas Internationalis Odonatologica, 1978– . Semiannual. ISSN 0166-6584.

This companion to *Odonatologica* contains short papers covering faunistics, field observations, and breeding and laboratory records. The journal also publishes book reviews.

Odonatologica. Vol. 1– . Bilthoven: URSUS Scientific Publishers, 1972– . Quarterly. $143.76. ISSN 0375-0183.

Publishes original papers dealing with any area of dragonfly and damselfly study. Each issue also includes the *Odonatological Abstracts* section, which gathers citations and abstracts of papers dealing with odonatology. The official journal of Societas Internationalis Odonatologica (SIO).

Orthoptera

Journal of Orthoptera Research: JOR. Vol. 1– . Philadelphia: Orthopterists' Society, 1992– . Semiannual. $25. ISSN 1082-6467.

Publishes articles and short notes covering all aspects of orthoptera biology and systematics. The journal also publishes the proceedings of the triennial International Conference on Orthopteroid Insects. Tables of contents and a few full-text articles are available at the journal's Web site at http://140.247.119.145/OrthSoc/jor_index.htm.

Coleoptera

Coleopterists Bulletin. Vol. 1– . Natchez, MS: Coleopterists Society, 1947– . Quarterly. $50. ISSN 0010-065X.

The journal publishes articles and brief notes covering both systematics and natural history of the Coleoptera. Short notices and book reviews are also published on occasion.

Lepidoptera

Journal of the Lepidopterists' Society. Vol. 1– . Los Angeles: Lepidopterists' Society, 1947– . Quarterly. $60. ISSN 0024-0966.

Articles, profiles, general notes, technical comments, book reviews, obituaries, and feature photographs dealing with all aspects of Lepidoptera study are published in the journal.

Diptera

Journal of the American Mosquito Control Association. Vol. 1– . Lake Charles, LA: American Mosquito Control Association, 1985– . Quarterly. $110. ISSN 8756-971X.

Publishes papers dealing with mosquito and vector biology and control Formerly *Mosquito News;* absorbed *Mosquito Systematics*

Hymenoptera

Apidologie. Vol. 1– . Paris: EDP Sciences, 1970– . Bimonthly. $305. ISSN 0044-8435. Available electronically.

Publishes articles and research notes on the biology of the members of the superfamily Apoidea, including both basic and applied studies. The main topics of interest include behavior, ecology, pollination, genetics, physiology, toxicology, and pathology of bees. Some systematics articles are also accepted. Articles are published in English, French, and German, with abstracts in the other two languages.

Bee World. Vol. 1– . Gerrards Cross, UK: International Bee Research Association, 1919– . Quarterly. $85. ISSN 0005-772X.

Provides research and review articles, editorials, news, and special features for researchers and beekeepers.

Journal of Apicultural Research. Vol. 1– . Cardiff, UK: International Bee Research Association (IBRA) , 1962– . $225. ISSN 0021-8839.

Publishes research papers, notes, and commentaries dealing with the biology, ecology, natural history, and culture of bees and other members of the Apoidea superfamily.

Journal of Hymenoptera Research. Vol. 1– . Washington, DC: International Society of Hymenopterists, 1992– . Semiannual. $60. ISSN 1070-9428.

Publishes articles dealing with the biology, behavior, ecology, systematics, taxonomy, genetics, and morphology of the Hymenoptera. The society also publishes Special Publications; the first, *Manual of the New World Genera of the Family Braconidae,* was published in 1997.

Guides to the Literature

Arachnology Home Page: The Arachnological Hub of the World Wide Web. 1995– . URL: http://www.arachnology.org (Accessed August 25, 2003).

This site contains over 2,000 links arranged by order or subject. The links include sites from around the world in several different languages and are appropriate for both amateurs and arachnologists.

Bishop, Jason, and Lou Bjostad. **Colorado State University Entomology.** Fort Collins: Colorado State University, 1994– . URL: http://www.colostate.edu/Depts/Entomology/ (Accessed August 25, 2003).

According to the Web site, this was the first entomology site in the world, in existence since February 1994. The site provides an extensive list of sources in a number of categories, such as jobs, universities, publications, favorite readings, images, and films.

British Museum (Natural History). **List of Serial Publications in the Libraries of the Departments of Zoology and Entomology.** London: Trustees of the British Museum (Natural History), 1967. 281 p.

A good source for citation verification for entomological periodicals. Each entry includes abbreviations for the title. The book covers reports, publications of organizations, multivolume faunas, and multivolume reports of expeditions as well as the usual periodical literature.

Gilbert, Pamela, and Chris J. Hamilton. **Entomology: A Guide to Information Sources.** 2nd ed. London: Mansell, 1990. 259 p. $130. ISBN 0720120527.

This guide provides extensive coverage of the literature of entomology, including information on entomological collections, suppliers, and sources of illustrations, as well as the usual primary and secondary literature, indexes, and societies. It is arranged by type of literature rather than by subject within entomology.

Hammack, Gloria M. **The Serial Literature of Entomology: A Descriptive Guide.** College Park, MD: Entomological Society of America, 1970. 85 p.

A survey and analysis of the serial literature of entomology, this volume lists and describes 762 entomological periodicals, both current at the time and ceased. The entries include title, address of publisher, description of contents, language of articles and abstracts, frequency, years of publication, indexes covering the title, average number of articles per year and percentage dealing with entomology, cost, and circulation figures. There are language and geographical indexes as well.

NC State AgNIC Systematic Entomology: A Guide to Online Insect Systematic Resources. URL: http://www.lib.ncsu.edu/agnic/sys_ entomology/index_txt.html (Accessed August 25, 2003).

The results of collaboration between North Carolina State University Libraries and the North Carolina State Department of Entomology, this site provides access to research and practical resources on the identification, classification, nomenclature, and evolution of insects and related arthropods. Links are organized into several categories, including North Carolina Resources, Educational Resources, Catalogues, Checklists, and Phylogenies, People and Places, Identification and Research Tools, and Electronic Publications. The site is an excellent source of information.

Majka, Christopher. **Electronic Resources on Lepidoptera: Butterflies and Moths.** 1996– . URL: http://www.chebucto.ns.ca/Environment/ NHR/lepidoptera.html (Accessed August 25, 2003).

This directory provides an extensive series of links dealing with Lepidoptera. The links are arranged alphabetically, by subject and by geographical region, and include both popular and research-oriented sites.

Samuelson, Al, and Neal Evenhuis. **Insect and Spider Collections of the World.** URL: http://hbs.bishopmuseum.org/codens/codens-r-us.html (Accessed August 25, 2003).

Based on R. H. Arnett, G. A. Samuelson, and G. M. Nishida, *The Insect and Spider Collections of the World,* 2nd ed. The database can be searched by coden, location, or name, and collections with Web sites are linked.

Van Dyke, John, and L. B. Bjostad. **The Entomology Index of Internet Resources.** Ames: Iowa State University. URL: http://www.ent.iastate. edu/list/ (Accessed August 25, 2003).

This excellent directory is arranged by subjects such as beekeeping, insect sounds, and pesticides and resource types such as bibliographies and newsgroups.

Biographies and Histories

Essig, E. O. **A History of Entomology.** New York: Macmillan, 1931. 1,029 p.

Discusses the history of entomology in the United States, in particular the western states. Essig takes a truly long-range view of history, starting with prehistoric entomology (primarily fossils from the La Brea tar pits) and continuing with the relationship of California Native Americans with insects. Other chapters cover California entomology, biological control, insecticides, entomological legislation, and biographies of about 150 entomologists.

Gaedike, Reinhard. "Berichtigungen und Ergänzungen zu P. Gilbert: **A Compendium of the Biographical Literature on Deceased Entomologists.**" Beitrage zur Entomologie 35(2): 369–407, 1985.

Updates and provides corrections for Gilbert's *Compendium,* below. About 1,900 new and corrected entries are listed in the same format, with name, dates, and additional biographical notes.

Gaedike, Reinhard. **Collectiones entomologicae (1961–1994).** Berlin: Akademie Verlag, 1995. 83 p. (Nova supplementa entomologica, vol. 6).

Continues Horn's *Collectiones entomologicae,* below, with additions and corrections.

Gilbert, Pamela. **A Compendium of the Biographical Literature on Deceased Entomologists.** London: British Museum (Natural History), 1977. 455 p. (Publication of the British Museum [Natural History], no. 786). $79. ISBN 0565007866.

The compendium contains references to about 7,500 deceased entomologists up to the end of 1975. Entries provide birth and death dates, obituaries or other biographical notes, and bibliographies where available. The work is updated by Gaedike's *Berichtigungen und Ergänzungen zu P. Gilbert* (above).

Horn, Walther. **Collectiones entomologicae: Eine Kompendium über den Verbleib entomologischer Sammlungen der Welt bis 1960.** Berlin: Akademie der Landwirtschaftswissenschaften der Deutschen Demokratischen Republik, 1990. 2 vol. ISBN: 3744000672.

Provides information about entomological collectors from around the world, including birth and death dates for the collectors, where they were active and what groups they were active in, and the present location of their collections.

Mallis, Arnold. **American Entomologists.** New Brunswick, NJ: Rutgers University Press, 1971. 549 p. ISBN 0813506867.

Contains biographies of over 200 deceased American entomologists. Nearly all of the entries include portraits, and the emphasis in the biographies is on the lives of the entomologists, not their scientific accomplishments. After initial chapters featuring early entomologists from the United States and Canada, the remaining chapters are arranged by the order of insect studied (e.g., butterflies or beetles).

Salmon, Michael A., Peter Marren, and Basil Harley. **The Aurelian Legacy: British Butterflies and Their Collectors.** Berkeley: University of California Press, 2000. 432 p. $35. ISBN 0520229630.

A lavishly illustrated history of butterfly collectors in Britain, this book provides a brief history of butterfly collecting, biographies of 101 amateur lepidopterists from 1550 to the late twentieth century, and notes on 35 historically interesting butterfly species. There are also two appendixes, one listing the British and Irish butterflies with their past and present common names and the other listing entomological societies, publications, and significant events plus an extensive bibliography. The book, full of details on the lives of the often eccentric natural historians, contains many portraits of the collectors as well as reprints of lovely butterfly illustrations.

Schmitt, Michael, Heike Hübner, and Reinhard Gaedike. **Nomina auctorum: Auflösung von Abkürzungen taxonomischer Autoren-Namen.** Berlin: Wiley-VCH, 1998. 189 p. (Nova supplementa entomologica, Heft 11). ISSN 0948-6038. URL: http://www.wiley-vch.de/berlin/journals/nse/contents/1998_11.html (Accessed August 25, 2003).

According to the International Code on Zoological Nomenclature, zoologists should cite the original author who described a species or genus without abbreviating the name, but in past years names were often abbreviated. Volume 1 of this set lists 4,687 abbreviations and gives the full names of the authors; Volume 2 lists 3,533 authors with birth and death dates along with the abbreviations used for their names and their taxonomic specialties. The Web site contains the full text of the printed volumes.

Smith, Ray F., Thomas E. Mittler, and Carroll N. Smith, eds. **History of Entomology.** Palo Alto, CA: Annual Reviews, 1973. 517 p. ISBN 0824321017.

Unlike most of the other entomological histories listed in this section, this book takes a worldwide view of the history of entomology, including chapters on entomology in East Asia, the Middle East, and Europe from antiquity to modern times. Other chapters discuss the history of various subdisciplines such as phylogeny, morphology, and agricultural entomology. The volume was a supplement to the *Annual Review of Entomology.* Many other volumes of the *Annual Review* also include historical chapters, including chapters on the roles of Darwin and Linnaeus and biographies of entomologists such as Fabricius and John Ray.

Sorensen, Willis Conner. **Brethren of the Net: American Entomology, 1840–1880.** Tuscaloosa: University of Alabama Press, 1995. 357 p. (History of American Science and Technology series). $59.95. ISBN 0817307559.

This scholarly history discusses the emergence of North American entomology from the province of amateurs to a science of its own. The author discusses several specific events that helped shape entomology such as the Rocky Mountain locust plague of the 1870s as well as discussing the general characteristics of the entomological community. The emphasis is on history, not biography.

Dictionaries and Encyclopedias

Feltwell, John. **The Encyclopedia of Butterflies.** New York: Prentice Hall General Reference, 1993. 288 p. ISBN 0671868284.

More than 1,000 species of butterflies are illustrated in color in this attractive encyclopedia. The encyclopedia takes a systematic approach to presenting data, with each family introduced briefly and then representative or well-known species from each genus illustrated and described. Icons in each species description show which family it belongs to, its biogeographical region, size, and conservation status.

Gordh, G., and D.H. Headrick. **A Dictionary of Entomology.** Wallingford, UK: CAB International, 2001. 1,032 p. $140. ISBN 0851992919.

Covers 35,000 terms from all subdisciplines of entomology, including the origin, etymology, and definition of each term. In addition to subject terms, the dictionary includes the common names of insects from North America and Australia, names of insect families, and names of prominent North American entomologists plus citations to their biographies.

Harbach, Ralph E., and Kenneth L. Knight. **Taxonomists' Glossary of Mosquito Anatomy.** Marlton, NJ: Plexus, 1980. 415 p. ISBN 0937548006.

As the title suggests, this heavily illustrated glossary is designed for the use of taxonomists and covers the arcane vocabulary of dipteran anatomy in detail. It is arranged by life cycle stage (adult, egg, larva, and pupa), with a final section on vestiture (the surface of the mosquito and its structures).

O Toole, Christopher, ed. **The New Encyclopedia of Insects and their Allies.** Oxford: Oxford University Press, 2002. 240 p. $41. ISBN 0198525052.

This one-volume encyclopedia provides an excellent introduction to the arthropods of the world, including myriapods, insects, and arachnids. The entries are by taxonomic groups and include information on systematics and behavior. There are numerous excellent photographs and line drawings. The encyclopedia is designed for the general public. The first edition was published as *The Encyclopedia of Insects.*

Resh, Vincent H., and Ring Cardé, eds. **Encyclopedia of Insects.** London: Academic Press, 2002. 1,300 p. $99.95. ISBN 0125869908.

Contains over 300 articles on various topics dealing with entomology, including the arachnids. Each of the 30 or so insect orders, including the newly discovered Mantophasmatodea, is discussed in detail along with essays covering other topics such as beekeeping, chitin, digestion, and principles of nomenclature. Each article includes a brief bibliography for further reading and cross-references.

de la Torre-Bueno, J.R., et al. **The Torre-Bueno Glossary of Entomology.** rev. ed. New York: New York Entomological Society in cooperation with the American Museum of Natural History, 1989. 840 p. ISBN 0913424137.

This is a revised and expanded edition of Torre-Bueno's 1937 *Glossary of Entomology,* and includes George S. Tulloch's *Supplement A* (1960). The terms covered include systematic, descriptive, and general terms. The editors have also included an extensive list of references. A portion of the glossary dealing with social insects is available at the American Museum of Natural History's Social Insects Web site, at http://research.amnh.org/entomology/social%5Finsects/siglossary.html.

Tuxen, Søren Ludvig, ed. **Taxonomist's Glossary of Genitalia in Insects.** 2nd ed., rev. and enl. Copenhagen: Munksgaard, 1970. 359 p.

A specialized illustrated glossary designed to assist taxonomists in describing insect genitalia, which often form an important part of identifying or describing insect species.

Wootton, Anthony. **Insects of the World.** New York: Facts on File, 1984. 224 p. $29.95; $17.95 (paper). ISBN 0871969912; 0713723661 (paper).

A colorful general survey of insect biology covering classification, anatomy, life history, behavior, and other entomology topics. Examples are taken from insects around the world.

Wrobel, M. **Elsevier's Dictionary of Butterflies and Moths, in Latin, English, German, French, and Italian.** New York: Elsevier Science, 2000. 278 p. $131. ISBN 0444504338.

Contains 4,185 names of super- and subfamilies, families, genera, and species of Lepidoptera found in Europe, North America, South Africa, New Zealand, and Australia. Names used in French-speaking Canada are also included. The main part of the dictionary lists names alphabetically by scientific name with relevant English, German, French, and Italian common names. Separate indexes list common names in each language.

Wrobel, M. **Elsevier's Dictionary of Entomology: In Latin, English, German, French and Italian.** New York: Elsevier Science, 2001. 374 p. ISBN 04444503927.

The dictionary contains 5,500 orders, families, genera, and species of insects, spiders, and other invertebrates found in Europe, North America, South Africa, New Zealand, and Australia. Names used in French-speaking Canada are also included.

Textbooks

Blum, Murray S., ed. **Fundamentals of Insect Physiology.** New York: Wiley, 1985. 598 p. $225. ISBN 0471054682.

An advanced textbook for upper-level undergraduate or graduate students, this text covers all major areas in insect physiology. There are numerous black-and-white illustrations.

Borror, Donald J, Charles A. Triplehorn, and Norman F. Johnson. **An Introduction to the Study of Insects.** 6th ed. Philadelphia: Saunders College, 1989. 875 p. $97.50. ISBN 0030253977.

A standard for many years, this textbook provides students with information on the biology, behavior, ecology, and classification of insects. Although the emphasis is on the Hexapoda, there are chapters on other arthropods as well. Most of the text consists of an order-by-order discussion of the major insect groups. There are illustrated keys for all orders and families of insects in North America and some subfamilies and information on collecting and preserving insects.

Chapman, R. F. **The Insects: Structure and Function.** 4th ed. New York: Cambridge University Press, 1998. 770 p. $58 (paper). ISBN 0521570484; 0521578906 (paper).

Unlike most entomology texts, this book covers insect morphology and physiology by system, rather than in a systematic arrangement. There is a taxonomic index to facilitate locating discussion of particular insect groups, and of course each chapter contains extensive references.

Daly, Howell V., John T. Doyen, and Alexander H. Purcell, III. **Introduction to Insect Biology and Diversity.** 2nd ed. New York: Oxford University Press, 1998. 680 p. $89.95. ISBN 0195100336.

This text is intended to be used in general entomology courses. It is in three sections covering insect biology, ecology and diversity. About half the book is taxonomy, with keys to over 400 common North American insect families scattered throughout.

Davies, R. G. **Outlines of Entomology.** 7th ed. New York: Chapman & Hall, 1988. 408 p. $46.95 (paper). ISBN 0412266709; 0412266806 (paper).

An enlarged edition of A. D. Imms's *Outlines of Entomology.* The text covers insect biology, ecology, and classification as well as a section on injurious insects.

Division of Entomology, Commonwealth Scientific and Industrial Research Organization. **The Insects of Australia: A Textbook for Students and Research Workers.** 2nd ed. Ithaca, NY: Cornell University Press, 1991. 2 vol. $265. ISBN 0801426693 (set).

This major textbook has value far exceeding its useful description of the insects of Australia. The sections introducing each order are frequently cited for their general description of the order and its systematics. The illustrations are also valuable, as is the key to all hexapod orders and selected related arthropod groups (pp. 24–32).

Elzinga, Richard J. **Fundamentals of Entomology.** 4th ed. Upper Saddle River, NJ: Prentice Hall, 1997. 475 p. ISBN 0135080371.

The bulk of this introductory text covers the anatomy, biology, ecology, and behavior of insects, although classification is covered. The chapter on classification includes a key to the orders of insects commonly found in collections, plus keys to suborders or families of the larger orders. The author also discusses insect pest management and techniques for making an insect collection.

Huffaker, Carl B., and Andrew P. Gutierrez, eds. **Ecological Entomology.** 2nd ed. New York: Wiley, 1999. 756 p. $150. ISBN 047124483X.

Intended as a reference for researchers and a text for upper-level classes. It covers insect ecology at a more advanced level than Gullan and

Cranston, below, and has less taxonomic information. Basic insect biology and ecological adaptations are covered, as well as insect population control and pest management. Each chapter has extensive references.

Gullan, Penny J., and Peter S. Cranston. **The Insects: An Outline of Entomology.** 2nd ed. Osney Mead, UK: Blackwell Science, 2000. 496 p. $73.95 (paper). ISBN 0632053437 (paper).

Rather than following an order-by-order taxonomic arrangement, this text is organized by subject, discussing aspects of insect ecology and behavior with each order discussed in appropriate places throughout (e.g., bees and termites in the chapter on social behavior). The book includes information on methods in entomology, and an index provides an illustrated guide to insect orders from Protura to Strepsiptera.

Klowden, Marc J. **Physiological Systems in Insects.** San Diego: Academic, 2002. 415 p. $59.95 (paper). ISBN 0124162649 (paper).

This textbook discusses insect physiology with emphasis on the ecological consequences of the various systems. Each chapter covers a different system such as the integumental system or communication systems. The list of references at the end of each chapter are arranged by broad subject area rather than grouped together.

McGavin, George. **Essential Entomology: An Order-by-Order Introduction.** New York: Oxford University Press, 2001. 318 p. $35 (paper). ISBN 0198500025 (paper).

A survey of the insect orders, this text begins with an overview of insect anatomy and physiology and concludes with an introduction to entomological fieldwork. The central portion covers each order of insects. The chapters have a text box with basic information and key features, then describe the order. There are black-and-white illustrations in each chapter and key readings.

Richards, O. W., and R. G. Davies. **Imms' General Textbook of Entomology.** 10th ed. New York: Wiley, 1977. 2 vol. ISBN 0470001224 (vol. 1); 0470989963 (vol. 1, paper); 0470991232 (vol. 2).

This classic text goes into great detail. Volume 1 covers anatomy, physiology, and development; Volume 2 discusses the classification and phylogeny of insect orders.

Romoser, William S., and John G. Stoffolano, Jr. **The Science of Entomology.** 3rd ed. Boston: WCB McGraw-Hill, 1998. 605 p. $62.50. ISBN 0697228487.

A general introduction to entomology designed both as a textbook and reference. An initial chapter offers a good introduction to scientific research and the literature of entomology. The remainder of the text is divided into five broad sections: Structure and Function, Insects and Their Environment, Unity and Diversity, Applied Entomology, and The Modern Interface. The emphasis is on insect biology rather than functioning as a survey of the insects, but it also includes keys to the major orders of insects.

Snodgrass, R. E. **Principles of Insect Morphology.** New York: McGraw-Hill, 1935. 667 p. (McGraw-Hill publications in the zoological sciences).

A classic, this textbook was reprinted by Cornell University Press in 1993. It is still one of the best sources of information on insect morphology. Morphology is of great importance to insect taxonomists because classification is often based on minute details of morphology.

Williams, D. Dudley, and Blair W. Feltmate. **Aquatic Insects.** Wallingford, UK: CAB International, 1992. 358 p. ISBN 0851987826 (paper).

Covers a variety of aspects of the study of aquatic insects. The authors discuss the aquatic insect orders and provide keys to the orders of pupae as well as nymphs, larvae, and adults. They also discuss the ecology, adaptations, and population biology of aquatic insects as well as their relationships with humans and experimental design for ecological studies of aquatic insects.

Checklists and Classification Schemes

ANI-CD (Arthropod Name Index on CD-ROM). Wallingford, UK: CAB International, 19?– . Annual. $899. ISSN 1359-5415.

The index contains preferred terms, synonyms, common names, taxonomic positions, and important bibliographic references for arthropods of economic importance going back to 1913. The database, which contains about 110,000 records, is based on CAB's internal authority file for insect names. Both Pittaway and Wood, below, are excerpted from the ANI.

Committee on Common Names of Insects. **Common Names of Insects and Related Organisms.** 4th ed. Lanham, MD: Entomological Society of America, 1997. 232 p. $45. ISBN 0938522647.

This list provides official common names of 2,046 insects from the United States. There are four sections: insects listed by common name, insects listed by scientific name, a hierarchical listing of names, and a final section listing vernacular equivalents for higher taxonomic groups. The list is updated on the society's Web page at http://www.entsoc.org/pubs/ publish/commname.html.

Opler, Paul A., coordinator. **Insects and Related Arthropods of North America.** Jamestown, ND: Northern Prairie Wildlife Research Center Home Page, 1999. URL: http://www.npwrc.usgs.gov/resource/1999/ insect/insect.htm. (Accessed August 25, 2003).

This site provides access to checklists of insects found at various parks, refuges, and management units within North America. At the time of viewing, only a few lists were provided, but more are expected. Separate lists are provided for Lepidoptera and dragonflies.

Pittaway, A. R. **Arthropods of Medical and Veterinary Importance: A Checklist of Preferred Names and Allied Terms.** Wallingford, UK: CAB International, 1991. 178 p. $50 (paper). ISBN 0851987419 (paper).

This list provides the preferred scientific names of arthropods of importance in human and veterinary medicine, including harmful arthropods, natural enemies, parasites, and intermediate hosts. Scientific names are listed by genus, with higher taxa listed for each genus and approved name for each species. The list is based on the card file used by CAB in preparing the *Review of Medical and Veterinary Entomology,* now available as *ANI-CD* (above).

Systematic Section

Arachnida

American Arachnological Society, Spiders of North America Check-list Committee. **Spiders of North America (North of Mexico).** URL: http://kaston.transy.edu/spiderlist/index.html (Accessed August 25, 2003).

Based on Platnick's *Advances in Spider Taxonomy1992–1995* (see below), this site provides a list of valid names for the spiders of North America north of Mexico. Names are listed in alphabetical order within each family. The entries include synonymy and the states where the species are known to occur. The site also includes modern names for the spiders listed in three well-known older works: Kaston's *Spiders of Connecticut,* Kaston's *How to Know the Spiders,* and Emerton's *Common Spiders of the United States* (see entries under Identification Tools, below).

Stockwell, Scott A. 1996. **Classification of the Class Scorpionida.** URL: http://wrbu.si.edu/www/stockwell/classification/classification.html (Accessed August 25, 2003).

This site is based on the author's 1989 Ph. D. dissertation, *Revision of the Phylogeny and Higher Classification of Scorpions (Chelicerata).* The author also provides links to other scorpion sites.

Crustacea

Kensley, Brian, Marilyn Schotte, and Steve Schilling. **World List of Marine, Freshwater and Terrestrial Isopod Crustaceans.** Washington, DC: Smithsonian Institution, 1996. URL: http://www.nmnh.si.edu/iz/ isopod/ (Accessed August 25, 2003).

The taxonomy of the isopods is in a state of confusion, so this list is intended as a rough guide to the correct nomenclature. The list includes information on the classification, type locality, habitat/depth, original genus, and remarks for each taxon and can be searched or browsed. An extensive bibliography is also provided. As of the date of accession, 10,184 names were included in the list.

Martin, Joel W., and George E. Davis. **An Updated Classification of the Recent Crustacea.** Los Angeles: Natural History Museum of Los Angeles, 2001. 124 p. (Science series, Natural History Museum of Los Angeles County, no. 39). ISBN 1891276271.

Updates the classification system laid out by Bowman and Abele in *Biology of Crustaceans,* below. The book is designed for both experienced taxonomists and students, so it contains extensive introductory material on nomenclature, molecular systematics, larval morphology, the fossil record, and much more. The authors also provide a lengthy rationale for their decisions, and an appendix lists comments and opinions by other crustacean taxonomists. Another useful appendix lists other crustacean resources, including journals and newsletters, Web sites, listservs, and museums with crustacean holdings on the Web.

Williams, Austin B., et al., eds. **Common and Scientific Names of Aquatic Invertebrates from the United States and Canada: Decapod Crustaceans.** Bethesda, MD: American Fisheries Society, 1989. 77 p. (American Fisheries Society Special Publication, no. 17). $25 (paper). ISBN 0913235628; 0913235490 (paper).

Provides a checklist of species and recommends common names for North American decapod crustaceans. All 1,614 freshwater species of North America north of Mexico are included, and each entry lists the scientific name, broad distribution information, and common name where established. The index includes both scientific and common names, and there are also color photographs of 12 common species of shrimps and crabs.

Insects

Belton, E.M., and D.C. Eidt. **Common Names of Insects in Canada (revised 1999).** Entomological Society of Canada, 1999. URL: http://esc-sec.org/menu.htm (Accesssed August 25, 2003).

This list is based on Paul Benoit's *Nomenclatura Insectorum Canadensium* (5th ed.). The updated list is only available electronically, either on the Web or as a DOS zip file. English and French common names are included for each species, as well as scientific names and order and family names.

A Checklist of the Insects of Subsaharan Africa. Washington, DC: National Museum of Natural History, Department of Systematic Biology, Entomology, 2000– . URL: http://entomology.si.edu/Entomology/Subsahara/index.html. (Accessed August 25, 2003).

This database is designed as an authoritative record of the over 10,000 species of insects known to occur in Subsaharan Africa. It is both printable and searchable by genus and species names. The site also includes a "Summary of Key Literature on Identification of Afrotropical Insects and Spiders."

Nomina Insecta Nearctica: A Check List of the Insects of North America. Rockville, MD: Entomological Information Services, 1996–97, 4 vols, plus CD ROM. URL: http://www.nearctica.com/nomina/nomina.htm (Accessed August 25, 2003).

This set provides a directory of scientific names applied to the insects of North America, including synonyms, homonyms, unavailable names, and misspellings. It is intended as a preliminary checklist. The CD-ROM consists of a database divided into three groups of tables: family names, generic names, and species names. The associated Web site provides a classification of the North American insects covered in the print volumes that serves as a table of contents to the individual checklists.

Myriapoda

Hoffman, Richard L. **Checklist of the Millipedes of North and Middle America.** Martinsville: Virginia Museum of Natural History, 1999. 584 p. (Special Publication of the Virginia Museum of Natural History, no. 8). $50. ISBN 1884549128.

Summarizes the known species of millipedes for the Americas north of Colombia and Trinidad, a total of 2,167 species. Each entry lists the original description, changes in status, location of type specimens, distribution information, and references to published maps. The author also provides citations to more general taxonomic keys, revisions, descriptions, and other materials for the higher level taxa.

Apterygota

Bellinger, P. F., K. A. Christiansen, and F. Janssens. 1996–2001. **Checklist of the Collembola of the World.** URL: http://www.collembola.org. (Accessed August 25, 2003).

The site includes a great deal of information on the world's Collembola, including a bibliography, glossary of morphological terms, image gallery, classification, list of genera, list of keys to genera, and much more.

Mari Mutt, José A., and Peter F. Bellinger. **A Catalog of the Neotropical Collembola, including Nearctic Areas of Mexico.** Gainesville, FL: Sandhill Crane Press, 1990. 237 p. (Flora & Fauna Handbook, no. 5). $89.95. ISBN 1877743003.

Presents a complete list of species of neotropical Collembola reported up to August 1, 1989. Entries are in systematic order above the level of the genus and alphabetical within each genus. The entries contain the name of the species, the name of the author, the geographical distribution, synonymy, and references to reports of distribution, description, and biology of each species. The authors also provide a lengthy bibliography and an alphabetical index, which is useful for finding synonyms.

Salmon, John T. **An Index to the Collembola.** Wellington, 1964. 3 vol. (Bulletin of the Royal Society of New Zealand, no. 7).

The intent of this work was to present a complete index to the genera and species of Collembola from around the world. It is in three parts, a bibliography, a classification of the Collembola with keys to the families and genera, and a systematic index. The checklist is arranged systematically with references arranged chronologically.

Ephemeroptera

Hubbard, Michael D. **Mayflies of the World: A Catalog of the Family and Genus of Group Names: (Insecta: Ephemeroptera).** Gainesville, FL: Sandhill Crane, 1990. 119 p. (Flora & Fauna Handbook, no. 8). $79.95. ISBN 1877743062.

Covers family-group and genus-group names for recent and fossil mayflies from around the world. It is in four parts: a hierarchical classification, an alphabetical list of family groups, an alphabetical list of genus groups, and full references. The catalog lists 371 valid genera.

Mayfly Central. West Lafayette, IN: Department of Entomology, Purdue University. URL: http://www.entm.purdue.edu/entomology/research/ mayfly/mayfly.html. (Accessed August 25, 2003).

The two main resources available at this site at the time of viewing were *The Mayflies of North America* and *The Mayflies of Central America,* two species lists maintained by researchers at Mayfly Central.

Odonata

Dragonfly Society of the Americas. **The Odonata of North America.** 1998– . URL: http://www.ups.edu/biology/museum/NAdragons.html (Accessed August 25, 2003).

This list is both a current North American checklist and a list of standard common names. The common names were originally established in 1978 and revised over the years by the members of the Common Names Committee of the society.

Garrison, Rosser W. **A Synonymic List of the New World Odonata.** (June 25, 2001 Version). URL: http://www.ups.edu/biology/museum/ NewWorldOD.html (Accessed August 25, 2003).

This page updates Garrison's "A synonymic list of the New World Odonata" published in *Argia* 3(2): 1–30, 1991.

Schorr, Martin, Martin Lindeboom, and Dennis Paulson. **List of Odonata of the World.** (July 28, 2003 Version). URL: http://www.ups.edu/ biology/museum/worldodonates.html (Accessed August 25, 2003).

An attempt to list all valid species of Odonata. It includes the author and year of description for all genera and species, plus synonyms for almost all North American, South American, Australian, and African species. At the time of viewing, synonyms for Eurasian species were still incomplete.

Updates D. Allen Davies and Pamela Tobin's *The Dragonflies of the World: A Systematic List of the Extant Species of Odonata.*

Plecoptera

Stark, Bill P. 1998. **North American Stonefly List.** URL: http://www.mc.edu/campus/users/stark/Sfly0102.htm (February 16, 2001 version). (Accessed August 25, 2003).

The list contains 628 species of stoneflies found in North America. It is in systematic order and includes the state and provinces where each species is found.

Hemiptera

Eastop, Victor Frank, and D. Hille Ris Lambers. **Survey of the World's Aphids.** The Hague: Junk, 1976. 573 p. ISBN 906193561X.

Provides a list of described species and genera of aphids, plus synonyms. The authors also attempted to revise and standardize aphid classification. There are two parts: Aphid Genera of the World with Their Species, and Index by Species-Group Names and Infra-Subspecific Names.

Maw, H. E. L., R. G. Foottit, and K. G. A. Hamilton. **Checklist of the Hemiptera of Canada and Alaska.** Ottawa: NRC Research Press, 2000. 220 p. $39.95. ISBN 0660181657 (paper).

The catalog lists over 3,900 species of Hemiptera and Homoptera that occur in Canada and Alaska. It is arranged taxonomically, and each superfamily and family have a brief introduction that provides a list of identification tools, bibliographies, common names in English and French, pest status, and general description. Within each genus, the individual species are listed with common name in English and French and distribution.

Yépez, Fernándo Francisco. **Neotropical Cicadellidae.** Maracay, Venezuela: Museo del Instituto Zoología Agrícola. URL: http://www.miza-fpolar.info.ve/cicadellidae/index.php. (Accessed August 28, 2003).

The site presents information on the neotropical leafhoppers. At the time of viewing, the site included species lists for the 662 species of neotropical leafhoppers, along with distribution, synonymy, and a few photographs. In Spanish and English.

Coleoptera

Arnett, Ross H., Jr., comp. and ed. **Checklist of the Beetles of North and Central America and the West Indies.** Gainesville, FL: Flora and Fauna Publications, 1983. 10 vol. in 7. ISBN 0916846211.

Updates the *Checklist of the Beetles of Canada, United States, Mexico, Central America, and the West Indies,* published in the late 1970s. This loose-leaf set includes all the beetle families of the world, arranged by family. The families of Coleoptera that are not found in North and Central America are listed in their phylogenetic position with only brief information. The checklist provides citations to original descriptions and distribution information. The final volume of the set contains an extensive bibliography.

Blackwelder, Richard E., comp. **Checklist of the Coleopterous Insects of Mexico, Central America, the West Indies, and South America.** Washington, DC: U.S. Government Printing Office, 1944–57. 6 pts. (Bulletin of the United States National Museum, no. 185, pts. 1–6).

Covers 50,000 species of beetles found from Mexico to Tierra del Fuego. The checklist takes up Parts 1–5 and is arranged systematically. The entries provide authors, synonyms, and location for each name. Part 6 contains the bibliography (current to 1946), corrigenda, and index of genera and higher taxa. Still the only checklist to all of South and Central America.

Bousquet, Yves, ed. **Checklist of Beetles of Canada and Alaska.** Ottawa: Agriculture Canada, 1991. 430 p. (Publication, Agriculture Canada, 1861/E). ISBN 0660137674.

This checklist covers all species and subspecies of beetles found in Canada and Alaska. Species names are arranged alphabetically within the genera, and include synonyms, distribution by province or region, and references to keys. Also available on the Web at http://res.agr.ca/brd/beetles/english/html/bhome_e.html.

Families and Subfamilies of Coleoptera. Coleopterists Society. URL: http://www.coleopsoc.org/colelist.shtml (Accessed August 25, 2003).

This site lists the higher-order taxonomy of the Coleoptera. It is based on J.F. Lawrence and A.F. Newton, Jr.'s "Families and subfamilies of Coleoptera (with selected genera, notes, references and data on family-group names)," pp. 779–1006 in *Biology, Phylogeny, and Classification of Coleoptera: Papers Celebrating the 80th Birthday of Roy A. Crowson,* 1995.

Mecoptera

Penny, Norman D. **World Checklist of Extant Mecoptera Species.** California Academy of Sciences, 1997. URL: http://www.calacademy.org/research/entomology/Entomology_Resources/mecoptera/index.htm (Accessed August 25, 2003).

Provides an updated list of the world species of Mecoptera with references. Most species are listed with author and date of description and distribution. There are also a few photographs.

Trichoptera

Trichoptera Checklist Coordinating Committee, International Symposia on Trichoptera. **Trichoptera World Checklist.** URL: http://entweb. clemson.edu/database/trichopt/. (Accessed August 25, 2003).

Includes taxonomic hierarchy and searchable database of the names of living and fossil Trichoptera. The database can be searched by taxon/synonym, type country, and biogeographic regions, and records also list biogeographic region and notes.

Lepidoptera

Hodges, Ronald W., et al., eds. **Check List of the Lepidoptera of America North of Mexico: Including Greenland.** Washington, DC: The Wedge Entomological Research Foundation, 1983. 284 p. $20. ISBN 0860960161.

The checklist includes synonyms, homonyms, and other systematic information as well as original author. They cover 11,233 valid species. The editors provide introductory information on the classification of North American Lepidoptera and an extensive index.

Miller, Jacqueline Y., ed. **Common Names of North American Butterflies.** Washington, DC: Smithsonian Institution Press, 1992. 177 p. ISBN 1560981229.

This slim little volume provides preferred and alternate common names for the butterflies of North America north of Mexico, including Hawaii.

Miller, Lee D., and F. Martin Brown. **A Catalogue/Checklist of the Butterflies of America, North of Mexico.** Los Angeles: Lepidopterist's Society, 1981. 280 p. (Memoirs of the Lepidopterists' Society, no. 2). ISBN 0930282035.

The catalog covers 241 genera and 763 species arranged in taxonomic order. The author of the name and original description are listed as well as references to subsequent updates. The catalog also lists the type species, synonyms, and geographical distribution. A *Supplement to A Catalogue/ Checklist of the Butterflies of America, North of Mexico* was prepared in 1989 by Clifford D. Ferris and features nomenclatural changes since the original publication, corrects some errors, and brings the checklist in alignment with the 1985 revision of the *International Code of Zoological Nomenclature.*

Nye, I. W. B., ed. **The Generic Names of Moths of the World.** London: British Museum (Natural History), 1975–91. 6 vol. (Publication of the British Museum [Natural History], no. 770).

Attempts to provide a complete catalog of all genus-group names for moths of the world. Each volume covers a superfamily. Within the families, the genus-group names are listed in alphabetical order, with homonyms and synonyms grouped chronologically under the valid name along with the type species, type locality, and citations to original description and revisions. Volumes 1 and 2 cover the Noctuoidea; Volume 3, Geometroidea; Volume 4, Bombycoidea, Castnioidea, Cossoidea, Sesioidea, Sphingoidea, Zygaenoidea; Volume 5, Pyralidoidea; and Volume 6, Microlepidoptera.

Diptera

Knight, Kenneth L., and Alan Stone. **A Catalog of the Mosquitoes of the World (Diptera: Culicidae).** 2nd ed. College Park, MD: Entomological Society of America, 1977. 611 p. (Publications of the Thomas Say Foundation, vol. 6).

The catalog lists the basic information for the known species of Diptera to 1973. Entries include authors' names, distribution, citation, stages described, type locality and depository, homonymy, and systematic status.

Sabrosky, Curtis W., F. Christian Thompson, and N. L. Evenhuis. **Family-Group Names in Diptera: An Annotated Catalog.** Leiden, The Netherlands: Published for North American Dipterists' Society by Backhuys, 1999. 576 p. (Myia, vol. 10). $107. ISBN 9057820269.

In four parts, this catalog contains a listing of the type genera for each family, an annotated catalog of family-group names, a supplemental list including group names not based on generic names, and a bibliography. The catalog covers both extinct and living species. The annotated catalog includes notes on the nomenclature and citations.

Soós, Á., and L. Papp, eds. **Catalogue of Palaearctic Diptera.** New York: Elsevier, 1984– . vol. ISBN 0444996001 (set).

A comprehensive checklist to the Diptera of Europe, Asia north of the Himalayas, North Africa, and part of Arabia. Each volume covers two families, and the entries list synonyms, citations to original descriptions, type location, and distribution.

Stone, Alan et al., eds. **A Catalog of the Diptera of America North of Mexico.** Washington, DC: U.S. Government Printing Office, 1965. 1,696 p. (Agricultural Handbook, U.S. Department of Agriculture, no. 276).

The catalog covers 1,971 valid genera and 16,130 valid species recognized up to 1962 and includes general distribution information.

Thompson, F.C., ed. **Biosystematic Database of World Diptera.** Washington, DC: Systematic Entomology Laboratory, ARS, USDA, Honolulu, Hawaii; B. Bishop Museum, 1998. URL: http://www.sel.barc.usda.gov/diptera/biosys.htm (Accessed August 25, 2003).

The database provides names and information about world Diptera. It consists of four major parts: a nomenclator listing valid and invalid names, the species database (under construction) providing information such as distribution, biological associates, and economic importance, a reference database, and a selection of tools such as a directory of dipterologists and historical information (also under construction). The site also provides an outline of the family-level classification used in the database.

Siphonaptera

Lewis, Robert Earl, and Joanne H. Lewis. **A Catalogue of Invalid or Questionable Genus-Group and Species-Group Names in the Siphonaptera (Insecta).** Königstein, Germany: Költz Scientific Books, 1989. 263 p. (Theses Zoologicae, vol. 11). $95. ISBN 3874293025.

Lists the invalid names used for fleas. A typical entry includes the original citation, location where the original specimens were found, notes, location of type specimens, and accepted name. Appendixes list bird and mammal hosts, journal abbreviations, and a glossary.

Hymenoptera

Bolton, Barry. **A New General Catalogue of the Ants of the World.** Cambridge, MA: Harvard University Press, 1995. 504 p. $153. ISBN 067461514X.

This catalog lists all taxonomic names, valid and invalid, applied to fossil and living ants worldwide. It is in three major parts: Catalogue of Family-Group Taxa, Catalogue of Genus-Group Taxa, and Catalogue of Species-Group Taxa. There is also a brief Checklist of Fossil Taxa and extensive references. This is the first attempt at cataloging the worldwide ant species since the publication of *Genera Insectorum,* below.

Dalla Torre, K.W. von. **Catalogus Hymenopterorum: Hucusque Descriptorum Systematicus et Synonymicus.** Lipsiae: G. Engelmann, 1892–1902. 10 vol.

A classic catalog of the world hymenoptera, this series is in taxonomic order. Within each genus, species are listed alphabetically with citation to first description and distribution information. The source or meaning of the generic names is also given.

Ferrière, Charles, Jacobus van der Vecht, and Roy D. Shenefelt, eds. **Hymenopterorum Catalogus.** Nova editio. Gravenhage, The Netherlands: W. Junk, 1965–85. 17 vol.

Updates Hans Hedicke's *Hymenopterorum Catalogus.* The original work was published by taxa, whereas the new edition covers small families worldwide and regional studies for some of the larger families. For each higher taxa, the name, references to revisions and catalogs, and general notes are provided; for genera and species, the name, original author and citation, type species, synonymy, keys and revisions, and distribution are listed.

Krombein, Karl V., et al., eds. **Catalog of Hymenoptera in America North of Mexico.** Washington, DC: Smithsonian Institution Press, 1979. 3 vol.

This catalog is an update of C. F. W. Musebeck's *Hymenoptera of America North of Mexico, Synoptic Catalog* from 1951 including the first and second supplements. The set consists of Volume 1, *Symphyta and Apocrita (Parasitica)*; Volume 2, *Apocrita (Aculeata);* and Volume 3, *Indexes.*

Yu, Dicky S. **A Catalogue of World Ichneumonidae (Hymenoptera).** Gainesville, FL: American Entomological Institute, 1997. 2 vol. (Memoirs of the American Entomological Institute, vol. 58, pt. 1–2). $180. ISBN 1887988025 (set).

The catalog updates dalla Torre, above, covering the literature from Linnaeus to the 1995 volume of *Zoological Record.* It covers 21,805 valid species and 36,179 names. The catalog is arranged systematically, and each entry includes original author, distribution, references, and synonyms. Part 1 covers the subfamilies Acaenitinae to Ophioninae, and Part 2 covers subfamilies Orthocentrinae to Xoridinae.

Mantophasmatodea

Zompro, Oliver. **Mantophasmatodea: Gladiators.** URL: http://www.mantophasmatodea.de/index.html (Accessed August 25, 2003).

Zompro is one of the original discoverers of this new order of insects. This Web site includes a bibliography and species list as well as information on keeping these insects in captivity.

Handbooks

Manton, S. M. **The Arthropoda: Habits, Functional, Morphology, and Evolution.** Oxford, UK: Clarendon Press, 1977. 527 p. ISBN 019857391X.

Although old, this is still an excellent overview of the Arthropoda, from trilobites to insects. The evolution, anatomy, and behavior of arthropods are covered in detail, and there are many excellent black-and-white illustrations.

Systematic Section

Xiphosura

Sekiguchi, Koichi, ed. **Biology of Horseshoe Crabs.** Tokyo: Science House, 1988. 428 p. ISBN 4915572250.

This handbook gathers together information on the taxonomy, distribution, ecology, morphology, development, and biochemistry of the four known species of horseshoe crabs. Books on horseshoe crabs are often restricted to discussion of the North American *Limulus,* but the three species from Southeastern Asia are also discussed here.

Arachnida

Bonnet, Pierre. **Bibliographia Araneorum.** Toulouse, France: Frères Douladoure, 1945–61. 3 vol. in 7.

Covers the spider species described up to 1939. It is in French. The main part of the catalog is in alphabetical order by genera. Separate volumes contain an introduction and bibliography as well as an index. Roewer's *Katalog der Araneae,* below, is similar but arranged by family.

Brignoli, Paolo Marcello. **A Catalogue of the Araneae Described between 1940 and 1981.** Manchester: Manchester University Press in association with the British Arachnological Society, 1983. 755 p. ISBN 0719008565.

Updates Roewer's *Katalog der Araneae* and Bonnet's *Bibliographia Araneorum,* and is itself updated by Platnick's various *Advances in Spider Taxonomy* supplements. It lists all the genera of spiders described after 1940 for most families and after 1954 for the remainder. Unlike Bonnet's work, the *Catalogue* is arranged systematically. It contains about 7,000 species in 96 families and excludes fossil species.

Brownell, Philip, and Gary Polis, eds. **Scorpion Biology and Research.** New York: Oxford University Press, 2001. 431 p. $110. ISBN 0195084349.

This volume covers a number of topics in scorpion biology, including morphology, ecology, biogeography, and paleontology. There is a taxonomic index.

Fet, Victor, et al. **Catalog of the Scorpions of the World (1758–1998).** New York: New York Entomological Society, 2000. 690 p. $55. ISBN 0913424242.

Both living and fossil scorpions are included in this catalog, a total of 1,259 species. They are listed in systematic order, and each entry lists the original author, the type species, references to descriptions, distribution, and notes.

Foelix, Rainer F. **Biology of Spiders.** 2nd ed. New York: Oxford University Press, 1996. 330 p. $40 (paper). ISBN 0195095936; 0195095944 (paper).

A general overview of spider biology, covering everything from anatomy and metabolism to web spinning and prey capture; also includes phylogeny of spiders.

Gertsch, Willis John. **American Spiders.** 2nd ed. New York: Van Nostrand Reinhold, 1979. 274 p. ISBN 0442226497.

One of the best overviews of the natural history, morphology, and distribution of North American spiders. The author presents extensive information on the often little-known habits of spiders, starting with a general introduction and descriptions of behaviors such as web spinning and courtship, then discusses the various types of spiders. He also discusses the medical and economic importance of spiders, and offers an overview of spider evolution and the American spider fauna. Although not intended as an identification tool, there are many black-and-white and colored photographs of common spider species and their webs.

Hammen, L. van der. **An Introduction to Comparative Arachnology.** The Hague, The Netherlands: SPB Academic, 1989. 576 p. $206.50. ISBN 9051030231.

The author describes this book as a "general survey of personal insights" rather than as a handbook, but it is as comprehensive and detailed as any handbook. It is in two general parts: a general part, discussing the morphology, reproduction, development, and classification of arachnids, and a systematic section. The morphology and internal anatomy of each order is described in detail, as well as reproduction and development.

Krantz, G. W. **A Manual of Acarology.** 2nd ed. Corvallis: Oregon State University Book Stores, 1978. 509 p. ISBN 0882460641.

Covers the biology and systematics of the mites and ticks with emphasis on systematics. Each account includes basic information on the biology of the group. There are many illustrations and keys to genera.

Platnick, Norman I. **Advances in Spider Taxonomy, 1981–1987: A Supplement to Brignoli's A Catalogue of the Araneae Described between 1940 and 1981.** Manchester, UK: Manchester University Press in association with the British Arachnological Society, 1989. 673 p. ISBN 0719027829.

As the title suggests, this and subsequent volumes update Brignoli's *Catalogue.* The supplement is also arranged systematically, and includes descriptions of new taxa, synonymies of previously described taxa, and taxonomically useful references to previously described taxa. About 105 families are covered. Other supplemental volumes were published in 1993 and 1997 bringing the work up to 1995. Further updates are found on Platnick's Web site, below.

Platnick, N. I. **The World Spider Catalog, Version 2.5.** New York: American Museum of Natural History, 2002. URL: http://research.amnh.org/entomology/spiders/catalog81-87/index.html. (Accessed August 25, 2003).

This site, an electronic version of Brignoli's *Catalogue of the Araneae* and Platnick's three-volume *Advances in Spider Taxonomy* supplements, will update the printed works.

Polis, Gary A., ed. **The Biology of Scorpions.** Stanford, CA: Stanford University Press, 1990. 587 p. $99.50. ISBN 0804712492.

Several authors contributed to this overview of scorpion biology and systematics. The section on systematics includes keys to genera of living scorpions plus information on their biogeography as well as discussing the evolution of the order. Other chapters cover topics such as life history, morphology, ecology, venoms, and field and laboratory methods for studying scorpions. An interesting addition is the chapter on scorpions in history and folklore. There is also an appendix listing synonyms for genera or species, and a very extensive bibliography.

Preston-Mafham, Rod, and Ken Preston-Mafham. **Spiders of the World.** New York: Facts on File, 1984. 190 p. $32.95. ISBN 0871969963.

This beautifully illustrated survey of the spiders of the world is suitable for students and the general public. The authors discuss spider anatomy, behavior, and life history using interesting spider species from around the world as examples. An appendix lists the spider families from around the world, and of course there is a lengthy bibliography as well.

Roewer, Carl Friedrich. **Katalog der Araneae.** Bremen: Natura, 1942–54. 2 vol. in 3.

Along with Bonnet (above), this is one of the classic arachnalogical catalogs. It is arranged by family and covers the relevant literature from 1758 to either 1940 or 1954, depending on the family.

Sonenshine, Daniel E. **Biology of Ticks.** New York: Oxford University Press, 1991–93. 2 vol. ISBN 0195059107 (vol. 1); 0195084314 (vol. 2).

A detailed guide to the biology of ticks. Volume 1 covers the systematics, life cycles, morphology, physiology, and biochemistry of ticks; Volume 2 covers the ecology of nidicolous and non-nidicolous ticks (those living in shelters and those living in the open), host/parasite interactions, the role of ticks in disease transmission, and tick control. An appendix dealing with techniques for studying ticks is also included in Volume 2.

Walter, David Evans, and Heather Coreen Proctor. **Mites: Ecology, Evolution and Behaviour.** Wallingford, UK: CABI, 1999. 322 p. $95. ISBN 0851993753.

Mites are very important economically, and this book covers basic information on their life cycles, feeding and reproductive behavior, host associations, evolution, and other topics. There is also a survey of mite systematics.

Crustacea

Barnard, J. Laurens, and C. M. Barnard. **Freshwater Amphipoda of the World.** Mt. Vernon, VA: Hayfield Associates, 1983. 2 vol.

Volume 1 of this set covers evolutionary patterns; Volume 2 provides a handbook and bibliography of the world amphipods. The handbook volume includes phyletic and geographical keys, nomenclature, and illustrations of major characters for diagnosis.

Bliss, Dorothy E., ed. **Biology of Crustacea.** New York: Academic Press, 1982–85. 10 vol. Price varies.

This set covers all areas of crustacean biology, including systematics, embryology, neurobiology, anatomy and physiology, ecology, and economic aspects.

Burggren, Warren W., and Brian R. McMahon, eds. **Biology of the Land Crabs.** New York: Cambridge University Press, 1988. 479 p. ISBN 0521306906.

Summarizes the known aspects of the biology of land crabs. The authors cover evolution and systematics as well as anatomy, physiology, ecology, and behavior. An appendix describes the natural histories of selected land crabs.

Crustacean Issues. Rotterdam: Balkema, 1983– . ISSN 0168-6356. Price varies.

A series of volumes covering various topics in crustacean biology and taxonomy such as crustacean phylogeny and biogeography, growth, invasive species, and aspects of crustacean biology.

Lowry, J. K., Les Watling, and Matz Berggren, eds. **Crustacea.net: An Information Retrieval System for Crustaceans of the World.** Sydney: Australian Museum, 1999– . URL: http://www.crustacea.net (Accessed August 25, 2003).

This site provides a variety of information on the crustaceans of the world, including keys, morphological descriptions, glossaries of morphological terminology, current family level lists, and links to other crustacean sites.

Schram, Frederick R. **Crustacea.** New York: Oxford University Press, 1986. 606 p. $110. ISBN 0195037421.

The author provides an overview of the natural history and evolution of the Crustacea. After introductory chapters describing the phylum and its relationship with other arthropod phyla, the remainder of the book is dedicated to an order-by-order discussion of the morphology, natural history, evolution, and taxonomy of crustaceans. Final chapters discuss enigmatic fossil larvae, crustacean phylogeny, and evolutionary patterns.

Warner, G. F. **The Biology of Crabs.** New York: Van Nostrand, 1977. 202 p. ISBN 0442292058.

An overview of the biology of primarily true crabs (Brachyura), although hermit crabs (Anomura) are also included. The author discusses anatomy, locomotion, sensory organs, biological rhythms, ecology, food, social behavior, evolution, and crabs and humans.

Williams, Austin B. **Shrimps, Lobsters, and Crabs of the Atlantic Coast of the Eastern United States, Maine to Florida.** Washington, DC: Smithsonian Institution Press, 1984. 550 p. ISBN 0874749603.

Covers the identification, description, distribution, life history, and ecology of the decapod crustaceans of the Atlantic Coast of the United States. Each species account includes original author, recognition characteristics, size, color, habitat, type locality, range, and remarks. There are keys to species and black-and-white illustrations as well. It is a revised edition of the author's *Marine Decapod Crustaceans of the Carolinas* from 1965.

Insects

Burrows, Malcolm. **The Neurobiology of an Insect Brain.** New York: Oxford University Press, 1996. 682 p. ISBN 0198523440.

Burrows covers all aspects of locust neurobiology, including anatomy, development, neurotransmitters, and control of movements. Insects are important study organisms for neurobiologists because they have simple brains with relatively few neurons; locusts are studied not only for their economic importance but because they are easily kept in the lab. The glossary and list of references are extensive.

Dent, D. R., and M. P. Walton, eds. **Methods in Ecological and Agricultural Entomology.** Wallingford, UK: CAB International, 1997. 387 p. $70 (paper). ISBN 0851991319; 0851991327 (paper).

Covers both experimental and analytical methods used to study insects, including sampling and rearing insects, methods for studying population, migration, pollination, natural enemies, and other topics, and molecular and biochemical methods.

Hennig, Willi. **Insect Phylogeny.** New York: Wiley, 1981. 514 p. ISBN 0471278483.

A classic work on the phylogeny of insects, this is a translation and revision of the author's 1969 *Die Stammesgeschichte der Insekten.* Hennig provides an overall introduction, outlines the known locations for fossil insect discoveries, and presents a detailed discussion of the phylogeny of the insect families and orders. The translated version presents Hennig's original text with revisions made by other experts at the end of each section.

Hermann, Henry R., ed. **Social Insects.** New York: Academic Press, 1978–82. 4 vol.

A treatise covering the sociobiology of social insects, including bees, wasps, ants, termites, and arachnids. The first volume discusses theoretical issues, the second covers behavioral phenomena exhibited by social and eusocial insects, and the final two volumes discuss the behavior of the various groups of social insects.

Hinton, H. E. **Biology of Insect Eggs.** New York: Pergamon Press, 1981. 3 vol. $494. ISBN 0080215394 (set).

Covers all areas relating to the biology of insect eggs. Volume 1 offers general topics (parental care, oviposition, etc.); Volume 2 covers each insect order. The final volume provides references, species, author, and subject indexes, and a bibliography.

Hogue, Charles L. **Latin American Insects and Entomology.** Berkeley: University of California Press, 1993. 536 p. $95. ISBN 0520078497.

This book could be included among the identification materials as well. It consists of an extensive introductory section covering the history and present state of entomology in Central and South America and a discussion of general entomology followed by accounts of selected families and orders. An extensive section lists sources for further information such as Latin American journals, institutions, insect collections, and other resources. The intended audience includes both amateurs and professional entomologists.

Imes, Rick. **The Practical Entomologist.** New York: Simon & Schuster, 1992. 160 p. $27.95; $16.00 (paper). ISBN 0671746960; 0671746952 (paper).

This is a handy guide for amateur entomologists. It includes information on capturing and keeping live insects, making an insect collection, tips on insect photography, and chapters on each major order of insects.

Kerkut, Gerald A., and Lawrence I. Gilbert, eds. **Comprehensive Insect Physiology, Biochemistry, and Pharmacology.** New York: Pergamon Press, 1985. 13 vol. $3,803.25. ISBN 0080268501 (set).

This massive set contains 200 articles written by 220 researchers, and refers to 5,000 species of insects. It is designed for both practitioners and students. Topics covered include all areas of insect physiology, behavior, biochemistry, pharmacology, and control. Each article contains extensive references and numerous illustrations. The final volume contains species, author, and subject indexes.

King, Robert C., and Hiromu Akai, eds. **Insect Ultrastructure.** New York: Plenum Press, 1982–84. 2 vol. $199.50 (vol. 1), $231.50 (vol. 2). ISBN 0306409232 (vol. 1); 0306415453 (vol. 2).

The treatise provides reviews of selected topics in insect ultrastructure, in the broad categories of gamete ultrastructure, developing cells, and the differentiation and functioning of specialized tissues and organs. Another section deals with cells in pathological states such as tumors or invaded by protozoan parasites.

Lehane, M. J. **Biology of Blood-Sucking Insects.** London: HarperCollins Academic, 1991. 288 p. $41.95; $36.95. ISBN 0044154000; 0044154104.

Covers the biology of the blood-sucking members of the Phtheraptera, Hemiptera, Siphonaptera, and Diptera. The author discusses the evolution, feeding preferences, methods of locating hosts, ingestion and management of the blood meal, host/insect interactions, and transmission of parasites.

Metcalf, Robert L., and Robert A. Metcalf. **Destructive and Useful Insects: Their Habits and Control.** New York: McGraw-Hill, 1993. var. pagings. ISBN 0070416923.

A classic introduction and survey of economic entomology, this volume was designed as a reference and textbook for undergraduates and nonscientists. The authors provide extensive background on insect morphology, development, classification, and control as well as discussing over 600 species of North American insects. The species accounts include keys, life histories, and further references to pests arranged by type of plant or animal attacked such as cotton or domestic animals.

Methven, Kathleen R., et al. **How to Collect and Preserve Insects.** Champaign: Illinois Natural History Survey, 1995. 76 p. $6 (paper). (Illinois Natural History Survey Special Publication, no. 17).

This guide for amateur entomologists provides detailed information on making an insect collection, including capturing and preserving insects, keeping proper records, and identifying species. A bibliography and list of supply companies are also included. The spiral-bound format makes it easy to use in the lab or field.

Papaj, Daniel R., and Alcinda C. Lewis, eds. **Insect Learning: Ecological and Evolutionary Perspectives.** New York: Chapman & Hall, 1993. 412 p. $140.50. ISBN 0412025612.

A multiauthored review of learning in both social and nonsocial insects. Includes applications for pest control.

Price, Peter W. **Insect Ecology.** 3rd ed. New York: Wiley, 1997. 874 p. $160. ISBN 0471161845.

A comprehensive treatise covering the major trends in insect ecology. It is in four broad sections: an introduction, trophic relationships, populations, and communities and distributions. There are extensive references to the original literature.

Schauff, M. E., ed. **Collecting and Preserving Insects and Mites: Techniques and Tools.** Washington, DC: National Museum of Natural History. URL: http://www.sel.barc.usda.gov/selhome/collpres/collpres.htm (Accessed August 25, 2003).

An updated version of USDA Miscellaneous Publication 1443, this manual provides methods for collecting and preserving insects. Designed for both amateurs and professional entomologists, it covers trapping, rearing, preserving, mounting, labeling, and shipping specimens.

Wilson, Edward Osborne. **The Insect Societies.** Cambridge, MA: Belknap Press, 1971. 548 p. $26.95 (paper). ISBN 0674454901; 0674454952 (paper).

Wilson is well known for his work on social insects, and this is a classic summary of insect sociobiology. Wilson discusses sociality in the various orders (social wasps, ants, social bees, termites, and presocial insects), then covers various types of behavior such as communication, control of nest mates, and symbioses. A very detailed synopsis of insect behavior.

Wytsman, Philogene, ed. **Genera Insectorum.** Brussels: Chez M. P. Wytsman, 1902–71. 218 fasc.

A classic source for insect systematic studies. Each fascicle covers one group of insects worldwide. Each genus is described and usually illustrated with line drawings, followed by a list of known species with references to the original description. There are also separate plates illustrating selected species. The language varies depending on the author's native tongue. Indexes were prepared by L. H. Townsend in 1937 (*Revista de Entomologica,* 7 [2–3]: 217–30) and Amy L. Paster in 1987 (*Genera Insectorum Index*).

Apterygota

Hopkin, Stephen P. **Biology of the Springtails (Insecta: Collembola).** New York: Oxford University Press, 1997. 330 p. $135. ISBN 0198540841.

The only recent comprehensive work on the biology of the Collembola. The springtails are common terrestrial arthropods, although relatively little work has been done on them. The author discusses the evolution and systematics, morphology and anatomy, ecology, reproduction, and ecotoxicology of the Collembola, among other subjects. He also discusses the literature of the Collembola and includes a 2,500-entry bibliography concentrating on publications after 1964. Appendixes list the world genera of Collembola, regional checklists, and laboratory and field studies on the effects of chemicals on Collembola.

Myriapoda

Hopkin, Stephen P., and Helen J. Read. **The Biology of Millipedes.** New York: Oxford University Press, 1992. 233 p. $95. ISBN 0198576994.

The only recent introduction to the biology of the millipedes. The author discusses a variety of topics from evolution to reproduction to ecology. The extensive bibliography contains about 750 items.

Lewis, J. G. E. **The Biology of Centipedes.** New York: Cambridge University Press, 1981. 476 p. ISBN 0521234131.

Gathers together information on the biology of the Chilopoda. The author covers all areas of biology and includes three chapters on the taxonomy and classification of the Chilopoda. There are numerous illustrations and a lengthy bibliography.

Ephemeroptera

Kondratieff, Boris C., coord. **Mayflies of the United States.** Jamestown, ND: Northern Prairie Wildlife Research Center Home Page, 2000. URL: http://www.npwrc.usgs.gov/resource/distr/insects/mfly/mflyusa.htm. (Version June 26, 2002). (Accessed August 25, 2003).

One of several similar sites from the Northern Prairie Wildlife Research Center, this site provides distribution maps, checklists, links to other sites, and references to the distribution of Ephemeroptera in the United States.

Kondratieff, Boris C., and Richard W. Baumann, coords. **Stoneflies of the United States.** Jamestown, ND: Northern Prairie Wildlife Research Center Home Page, 2000. URL: http://www.npwrc.usgs.gov/resource/distr/insects/sfly/sflyusa.htm. (Version June 26, 2002). (Accessed August 25, 2003).

A sibling to the mayfly site listed above, containing the same types of information for the Plecoptera of the United States.

Needham, James G., Jay R. Traver, and Yin-chi Hsu. **The Biology of Mayflies: With a Systematic Account of North American Species.** Ithaca, NY: Comstock, 1935. 759 p.

The taxonomic portion of this book has been updated, but the book also covers the biology of mayflies in detail, hence its presence in this section.

Permanent Committee of the International Conferences on Ephemeroptera. **Ephemeroptera Galactica: The Ephemeropterists' Home Page.** URL: http://www.famu.org/mayfly/index.asp (Accessed August 25, 2003).

This site is the official page for the Permanent Committee of the International Conferences on Ephemeroptera. It lists news, publications, catalogs, other links, and directories. Many faunal and systematic lists are provided for mayflies around the world.

Odonata

Corbet, Philip S. **Dragonflies: Behavior and Ecology of Odonata.** Ithaca, NY: Comstock, 1999. 829 p. $115. ISBN 0801425921.

This massive text covers topics such as habitat selection, behavior of eggs and sublarvae, larvae, and adults as well as ecological topics and the relationships between dragonflies and humans. There are extensive references, plus author, species, and subject indexes.

Kondratieff, B.C. **Dragonflies and Damselflies (Odonata) of the United States.** Jamestown, ND: Northern Prairie Wildlife Research Center, 2000. (Version June 26, 2002). URL: http://www.npwrc.usgs.gov/resource/distr/insects/dfly/dflyusa.htm (Accessed August 25, 2003).

This extensive site provides information on all of the Odonata of the United States, including distribution maps, photographs, checklists, links to other sites, and references.

Silsby, Jill. **Dragonflies of the World.** Washington, DC: Smithsonian Institution Press, 2001. 216 p. $39.95. ISBN 1560989599.

This colorful guide is aimed at both amateurs and researchers and illustrates at least one species from each of the 73 dragonfly and damselfly subfamilies. It covers the life cycle, behavior, ecology, and habitats of dragonflies around the world as well as evolution, conservation, and artificial rearing. There is an extensive systematic section in which each family and subfamily is described and illustrated, along with its distribution and brief mention of its ecology. An appendix lists 20 dragonfly societies from around the world.

Orthoptera

Beier, Max, ed. **Orthopterorum Catalogus.** Gravenhage, The Netherlands: Junk, 1968-77. 17 vol.

The catalog covers the taxonomic literature of the Orthoptera up to 1974. The entries are in systematic order. For well-studied taxa, the editor lists publication types such as nomenclature, monographs and catalogs, regional faunas and lists, fossils, biology, cytology, economic impact, utility, and literary works as well as the usual descriptions. Numbers 1–2 were first published in 1938–39. Publication was then suspended until 1962, starting with Part 3; the revised edition of Parts 1 and 2 was published in 1964.

Chapman, R. F., and A. Joern, eds. **Biology of Grasshoppers.** New York: Wiley, 1990. 563 p. $275. ISBN 0471609013.

This volume takes an organismal approach to the biology of grasshoppers and discusses their chemoreception, feeding, thermoregulation, locomotion, chemical communication, population dynamics, and diseases.

Gangwere, S. K., M. C. Muralirangan, and M. Muralirangan. **The Bionomics of Grasshoppers, Katydids, and Their Kin.** New York: CAB International, 1997. 529 p. $170. ISBN 0851991416.

Covers a range of topics in the biology of the Orthoptera, including systematics, distribution (both fossil and recent species), habits and behavior, and control and conservation. There is an extensive introduction.

Jones, Jack Colvard. **The Anatomy of the Grasshopper.** (Romalea microptera). Springfield, IL: Charles C. Thomas, 1981. 281 p. ISBN 0398041261 (spiral).

A dissection manual for the large grasshopper *Romalea.*

Otte, Daniel, and Piotr Naskrecki. 1997. **Orthoptera Species Online.** (Version 2). URL: http://140.247.119.145/Orthoptera (Accessed August 25, 2003).

The Orthoptera Species File (OSF) is a taxonomic database of the world's orthopteroid insects. It contains full synonymic and taxonomic information for over 25,000 species and genera. At the time of viewing, Version 2 (using SQL Server) did not contain the images or sound recordings found in Version 1 but did include corrections. The site also includes a searchable database of entomologists working on the Orthoptera and links to other Orthoptera sites.

Naskrecki, Piotr, and Otte, Daniel. **An Illustrated Catalog of Orthoptera.** Philadelphia: Orthopterists' Society at the Academy of Natural Sciences of Philadelphia, Department of Entomology, 1999– . CD-ROM. $95 (vol. 1). ISBN 1929014007 (vol. 1).

So far, only Volume 1 of this series has been published, covering the Tettigonioidea (katydids or bush-crickets).

Preston-Mafham, Ken, and Rod Preston-Mafham. **Grasshoppers and Mantids of the World.** New York: Facts on File, 1990. 192 p. $32.95. ISBN 0816022984.

An overview of the biology of grasshoppers and mantids, this book is illustrated by colorful photographs of orthopterids from around the world. Chapters cover classification, behavior, distribution, enemies, and interactions with humans.

Dermaptera

Steinmann, Heinrich. **World Catalogue of Dermaptera.** Boston: Kluwer, 1989. 933 p. (Series Entomologica, vol. 43). $699. ISBN 0792300963.

Based on systematic revisions for *Das Tierreich,* this catalog lists over 2,000 taxa of Dermaptera. The taxa are listed in systematic order above the level of the genus and alphabetically by genus and species. Each taxa has information on the original author, citations to valid names, year of original description, citation to the original description, and type specimen data. Valid taxa also include selected citations to the international literature covering matters such as revisions of the taxa or redescriptions. Systematic and alphabetical indexes are also included.

Isoptera

Constantino, Reginaldo. **Online Termite Database.** Departamento de Zoologia, Universidade de Brasília. URL: http://www.unb.br/ib/zoo/docente/constant/catal/catnew.html (Accessed August 25, 2003).

This taxonomic database is complete for the Nearctic and Neotropical regions, with data based on the author's "Catalog of the Living Termites of the New World," which was published in *Arquivos de Zoologia (São Paulo)* 35(2): 135–231 (1998). It has been expanded to include a nearly complete list of genera and species of the world, although the information on the New World species is more complete. The data included for each species include full synonymic and taxonomic information, illustrations, distribution maps, pest status, bibliography, and type depositories.

Krishna, Kumar, and Frances M. Weesner, eds. **Biology of Termites.** New York, Academic, 1969–70. 2 vol. ISBN 0124263011.

This two-volume set covers the biology of termites in detail. Volume 1 includes chapters on a variety of topics such as anatomy, social behavior, caste differentiation, and biochemical studies. Most of the chapters in Volume 2 cover the taxonomy and biogeography of termites, although this volume also discusses termite control.

Snyder, Thomas Elliott. **Catalog of the Termites (Isoptera) of the World.** Washington, DC: Smithsonian Institution, 1949. 490 p. (Smithsonian Miscellaneous Collections, vol. 112).

The catalog covers both fossil and extant species and is arranged systematically. Data provided for each taxa includes the author's name and year published. For generic names, the type species is also provided, and for species, it includes lists of illustrations, distribution, and location of type specimens. The catalog also includes an index and separate bibliographies for fossil and living species.

Termites: Urban Entomology Program. Toronto: Urban Entomology Program, University of Toronto, 1998. URL: http://www.utoronto.ca/ forest/termite/termite.htm (Accessed August 25, 2003).

This site is part of the University of Toronto's Urban Entomology Program's Web site. The termite site provides information on termite biology, taxonomy, phylogeny, distribution of northern termites, termite control, images, and keys as well as a wealth of miscellaneous information and links.

Zoraptera

Hubbard, Michael D. **Zoraptera Database.** Florida A&M University. URL: http://www.famu.org/zoraptera/index.html (Accessed August 25, 2003).

This site contains a catalog of the 30 or so species of Zoraptera, current to about 1990, and a general bibliography as well as a general introduction and links to other Zorapteran sites.

Thysanoptera

Jacot-Guillarmod, Charles Frederic. **Catalogue of the Thysanoptera of the World.** Grahamstown, South Africa: Cape Provincial Museum at the Albany Museum, 1970–71. 2 vol. (Annals of the Cape Provincial Museums of Natural History, vol. 7, pt. 1 and 2).

A first attempt at a catalog of the Thysanoptera of the world, this catalog includes all valid and invalid names and lists all references for each name. For each genus and species, the type species are given, along with distribution and habitat.

Lewis, Trevor. **Thrips: Their Biology, Ecology and Economic Importance.** New York: Academic Press, 1973. 349 p. ISBN 0124471609.

Presents information on the biology of thrips. It is in four sections, covering biology, techniques for laboratory and field studies, ecology, and economic importance. There are several appendixes of use to taxonomists, including a guide to catalogs and regional faunas and a list of thrips with their authors, synonyms, and common names. Other appendixes cover methods for mounting and preserving thrips, the predators, parasites, and prey of thrips, and insecticides used against thrips.

Hemiptera

Aukema, Berend, and Christian Rieger. **Catalogue of the Heteroptera of the Palaearctic Region.** Amsterdam: Netherlands Entomological Society, 1995– . 5 vol. ISBN 9071912124.

The Heteroptera are treated as a suborder of the Hemiptera in this catalog. Each of the infraorders and families covered in the book contains introductory text with a listing of the most important references. Each entry includes citation to original description, distribution, references, and often general notes. An introductory chapter in Volume 1 lists the most important literature on the Heteroptera, including catalogs for the Palearctic region.

Dixon, A. F. G. **Biology of Aphids.** London: Edward Arnold, 1973. 58 p. (Institute of Biology's Studies in Biology, no. 44).

This slim volume provides an overview of aphid biology for students. Topics covered include life cycles, hosts, migration, predators and parasites, aphids and plant viruses, and regulation of aphid numbers.

Dolling, W. R. **The Hemiptera.** New York: Oxford University Press, 1991. 274 p. ISBN 0198540167.

Although this survey of Hemipteran and Heteropteran biology and systematics concentrates on the British Hemiptera, it has much broader applicability. The author discusses the usual topics such as symbiotic relationships, dispersal, and morphology. The second half of the book concentrates on classification, including a discussion of the British Hemiptera as a sample of the world fauna, a key to suborders of British Hemiptera, and techniques for collecting and preserving Hemiptera. About half of the book comprises chapters on each of the three suborders, Heteroptera, Auchenorryncha, and Sternorrhycha.

Henry, Thomas J., and Richard C. Froeschner. **Catalog of the Heteroptera, or True Bugs, of Canada and the Continental United States.** New York: E. J. Brill, 1988. 958 p. $79. ISBN 091684644X.

This catalog was designed to list each species of Heteroptera in North America as it was originally described. Each family is described and illustrated and there are citations to reports of the ecology and biology of the family. General distribution information is also provided, and there is an extensive bibliography.

Horváth, G., general ed.; H. M. Parshley, managing ed. **General Catalogue of the Hemiptera.** Northhampton, MA: Smith College, 1927–71. 8 fasc.

The original eight fascicles of this catalog covered the literature of the Hemiptera. Each fascicle covered a family, with species listed in alphabetical order within each genus. Citations, in chronological order, also include the location dealt with in regional articles. Starting in 1962, supplements were published in the series under the title *General Catalogue of the Homoptera,* most written by Z. P. Metcalf.

McGavin, George. **Bugs of the World.** New York: Facts on File, 1993. 192 p. $32.95. ISBN 0816027374.

Like the other volumes in this series, this book provides a nice overview of insect biology. There are beautiful color photographs illustrating bugs from around the world, and easy-to-understand discussions of morphology, classification, behavior, diseases and enemies, and the relationship of bugs with humans. The author also discusses how to collect bugs for the amateur.

Miller, Norman Cecil Egerton. **The Biology of the Heteroptera.** 2nd ed., rev. Hampton, UK: E. W. Classey, 1971. 206 p. ISBN 0900848456.

This survey of Heteropteran biology is in two parts, a general account of the Heteroptera and a family-by-family description of their biology and distribution. There are several black-and-white photographs illustrating typical bugs as well as numerous drawings.

Minks, A. K., and P. Harrewijn, eds. **Aphids: Their Biology, Natural Enemies, and Control.** New York: Elsevier, 1987–89. 3 vol. $296.50 (vol. A). ISBN 0444426302 (vol. A)

This set provides detailed information on the biology and control of aphids. Volume A covers biology, including morphology, systematics, anatomy and physiology, ecology, and evolution; Volume B covers techniques and natural enemies; Volume C covers damage and control.

Mound, L. A., and S. H. Halsey. **Whitefly of the World: A Systematic Catalogue of the Aleyrodidae (Homoptera) with Host Plant and Natural Enemy Data.** New York: Wiley, 1978. 340 p. ISBN 0471996343.

Lists 1,156 species of whiteflies. The genera and species are listed alphabetically within each subfamily, and the original author and reference are given for both genera and species. For species, the locality, host plants, and depository are provided as well as synonyms. The authors also provide a summary of nomenclatural changes established in the catalog and systematic lists of whitefly natural enemies and host plants.

Nault, L.R., and J.G. Rodriguez. **The Leafhoppers and Planthoppers.** New York: Wiley, 1985. 500 p. $275. ISBN 0471806110.

The material in this handbook was based on a symposium of the Entomological Society of America in 1983. Chapters cover the systematics, morphology, behavior, nutrition, population dynamics, parasites, and pathogens of the insects, plus leafhoppers and planthoppers as pests.

Scalenet: A Database of the Scale Insects of the World. Beltsville, MD: U.S. Department of Agriculture, Systematic Entomology Laboratory, 1997– .   URL: http://www.sel.barc.usda.gov/scalenet/scalenet.htm. (Accessed August 25, 2003).

The site covers the scale insects (Coccoidea) worldwide. The site covers classification, nomenclatural history, distribution, hosts, and references to the literature. At the time of viewing, data were available for about 25 families, with plans to expand the site to cover the remaining 3 families in the near future. Users can also find general information about scale insects, links to other sites, a glossary, and even poetry about scale insects.

Schaefer, Carl W., and Antônio Ricardo Panizzi, eds. **Heteroptera of Economic Importance.** Boca Raton, FL: CRC Press, 2000. 828 p. $129.95. ISBN 0849306957.

This handbook summarizes the literature covering the biology and control of economically important bugs. Each chapter covers a different taxon, and most follow a standard format. They provide a general statement of the importance of the group, discuss the distribution, biology, damage done, and control of important species. There are extensive references for each chapter.

Schuh, Randall T. **Plant Bugs of the World (Insecta, Heteroptera, Miridae): Systematic Catalog, Distributions, Host List, and Bibliography.** New York: New York Entomological Society, 1995. 1,329 p. ISBN 0913424153.

As the title suggests, this massive work covers higher classification, taxonomy, nomenclature, hosts, and literature of the Miridae.

Schuh, Randall T., and James Alexander Slater. **True Bugs of the World (Hemiptera: Heteroptera): Classification and Natural History.** Ithaca, NY: Comstock, 1995. 336 p. $99.50. ISBN 0801420660.

This survey provides general background on the classification and natural history of the Heteroptera as well as a catalog to the subfamily level. The introductory material includes information on Heteroptera researchers, techniques for studying bugs, morphology, and a hierarchical classification to the subfamily level.

Coleoptera

Arnett, Ross H., and M. C. Thomas, eds. **American Beetles.** Boca Raton, FL: CRC Press, 2001–02. 2 vol. $139.95 (vol. 1); $139.95 (vol. 2). ISBN 0849319250 (vol. 1); 0849309549 (vol. 2).

Updates Arnett's classic *Beetles of the United States,* covering all of the beetles of North America north of Mexico. Volume 1 includes an introduction, outline of beetle classification, and species accounts for the suborders Archostemata, Myxophaga, Adephaga, and Polyphaga: Staphyliniformia, and Volume 2 covers the remaining beetles and contains keys to families. Each family is described in detail and information on habits and habitat, status of classification, and distribution are included. Identification is to the genus only, and brief generic accounts cover distribution, number of species, and habitat.

Baptist, Vratislav R. E. M. J. **Coleoptera Home Page.** Sydney: University of Sydney. URL: http://www.coleoptera.org/ (Accessed August 25, 2003).

Gathers a variety of information of interest to coleopterists, including taxonomic databases, bibliographies, control information, and a wide variety of miscellaneous tips and Web sites. Amateurs and students will find much of interest as well, such as photographs, cartoons, biggest and smallest species, and more.

Booth, R. G., M. L. Cox, and R. B. Madge. **Coleoptera.** London: International Institute of Entomology, Natural History Museum, 1990. 384 p. (IIE Guides to Insects of Importance to Man, 3). ISBN 0851986781 (spiral).

Developed for a course on applied taxonomy, this identification guide covers the larger and/or most economically important beetle families of the world. An introductory chapter covers beetle biology and economic importance, as well as how to collect and mount beetles. An illustrated key helps users identify beetles to families, which are then discussed in more detail. The family descriptions include a detailed description, biology, and distribution. Typical or important species or genera are often included in the family description. A separate chapter covers beetle larvae.

Crowson, R. A. **The Biology of the Coleoptera.** New York: Academic Press, 1981. 802 p. ISBN 0121960501.

This book surveys the biology of the beetles, including examining the morphology, physiology, adult and larval behavior, ecology, distribution, and evolution of beetles. The author also provides a classification of beetle families as used in the book, and of course there is an extensive list of references.

Lepidoptera

Aurivillius, Chr., et al., eds. **Lepidopterorum Catalogus.** Berlin: W. Junk, 1911–39. 93 parts.

This extensive catalog was published in systematic order, with species names listed alphabetically within each genus. For each name, the first author and reference are listed, along with other references and distribution information. Parts 85 and 87 were never published.

Eaton, John L. **Lepidopteran Anatomy.** New York: Wiley, 1988. 257 p. (Wiley-Interscience Series in Insect Morphology). $275. ISBN 0471058629.

Provides a detailed discussion of the anatomy of the Lepidoptera, from eggs to adults. There are many labeled line drawings detailing muscles and organs.

Ferguson, Douglas C., et al., coord. **Moths of North America.** Jamestown, ND: Northern Prairie Wildlife Research Center, 1999. (Version December 30, 2002). URL: http://www.npwrc.usgs.gov/resource/distr/lepid/moths/mothsusa.htm. (Accessed August 26, 2003).

One of several similar sites covering the distribution and identification of plants and animals of the United States, this site contains distribution maps, species accounts, and photographs for the moths of the United States and northern Mexico. Canadian moths will be added in the future. There are also checklists for counties in the United States and states in Mexico, links to other butterfly resources, and FAQs.

Heppner, John B., ed. **Lepidopterorum Catalogus: New Series.** Gainesville, FL: Association for Tropical Lepidoptera in cooperation with Scientific Publishers, 1989– . Vol. price varies.

This set is designed to update the original *Lepidopterorum Catalogus,* with plans for 124 fascicles, one each for the 124 families of butterflies around the world. As of 2003, about 20 fascicles had been published out of sequence.

The Moths of America North of Mexico, including Greenland. London: E. W. Classey. 1971–99. 27 fasc.

This long-running series provides a detailed catalog of the moths of North America. Each fascicle covers a different family. The editors provide general information on the family such as life history, characteristics, immature stages, and classification. The bulk of each volume consists of keys and species accounts with citations to original descriptions, synonymy, and descriptions of the moths and their biology. Some volumes include range maps and/or black-and-white illustrations. All volumes have color plates in the back.

Opler, Paul A., Harry Pavulaan, and Ray E. Stanford, coord. **Butterflies of North America.** Jamestown, ND: Northern Prairie Wildlife Research Center Home Page, 1995. (Version 30 DEC 2002). URL: http://www.npwrc.usgs.gov/resource/distr/lepid/bflyusa/bflyusa.htm. (Accessed August 25, 2003).

A companion to Ferguson's *Moths of North America* Web page, above, containing the same types of information.

Sbordoni, Valerio, and Saverio Forestiero. **Butterflies of the World.** Buffalo, NY: Firefly Books, 1998. 312 p. $45. ISBN 1552092100.

This colorful book provides a nice popular introduction to the Lepidoptera. There are chapters covering the life cycle, evolution, systematics, behavior, demography, ecology, and distribution of butterflies around the world. The authors also provide an extensive survey of butterfly families, with typical or well-known species illustrated in color. The book is a translation of *Mondo delle Farfalle.*

Scoble, M. J. **The Lepidoptera: Form, Function, and Diversity.** New York: Oxford University Press, 1992. 404 p. (Natural History Museum Publications). ISBN 0198540310.

Covers the anatomy, ecology and economic importance, and systematics of the Lepidoptera in considerable detail. The systematic portion is a guide to the diversity of the Lepidoptera and covers butterflies down to the family or subfamily level. Each taxonomic level is briefly described and citations given to revisions. The adults, immature forms, and biology of the families or subfamilies are described as well, and phylogenetic relationships are listed for most.

Seitz, Adalbert. **The Macrolepidoptera of the World: A Systematic Account of All the Known Macrolepidoptera.** Stuttgart, Germany: F. Lehmann, 1906–33. 16 vol.

The standard work on the Macrolepidoptera of the world, this massive set took decades to finish. It is in two major divisions, consisting of the butterflies of the Palearctic region and "Fauna Exotica" (the rest of the world). The set is also available in the original German as *Die Gross-schmetterlinge der Erde* and in a partial French translation.

Vane-Wright, Richard Irwin, and Phillip Ronald Ackery. **The Biology of Butterflies.** Orlando: Published for the Royal Entomological Society by Academic Press, 1984. 429 p. (Symposium of the Royal Entomological Society of London, no. 11). $157. ISBN 0127137505.

Based on papers read at the 11th Symposium of the Royal Entomological Society of London, this volume covers systematics, populations and communities, food, predation, genetic variation, mate selection and communication, migration, and conservation of butterflies.

Winter, Dave. **Basic Techniques for Observing and Studying Moths and Butterflies.** Los Angeles: Lepidopterists' Society, 2000. 444 p. (Memoirs of the Lepidopterists' Society, no. 5). $44. ISBN 0930282078.

Designed for the beginning entomologist or committed amateur, this handbook covers the methods for studying the Lepidoptera, including photography, recording data, identifying moths and butterflies, butterfly gardening, rearing Lepidoptera, collecting and preserving specimens, and so on.

Diptera

Ashburner, M., and E. Novitski, eds. **The Genetics and Biology of Drosophila.** New York: Academic Press, 1976–86. Vol. 1a–3e.

This series contains review articles from a variety of experts covering numerous aspects of *Drosophila* genetics and biology, including taxonomy, ecology, parasites, population genetics, molecular genetics, and behavior. Volume 3a includes a catalog of the 2,558 species of mosquitoes identified up to 1980, which is updated in the final chapter of Volume 3e.

Bächli, Gerhard. **TaxoDros: The Database on Taxonomy of Drosophilidae.** URL: http://taxodros.unizh.ch/ (Accessed August 25, 2003).

Based on the Drosophila Taxonomy Database maintained by the author since 1975, this searchable database contains information on the classification, descriptions, and biodiversity of Drosophila and related fruitflies. There is also a searchable database of references.

Clements, A. N. **The Biology of Mosquitoes.** Oxon: CABI, 1992– . 3 vol. $190 (vol. 1); $175 (vol. 2). ISBN 0851993745 (vol. 1); 0851993133 (vol. 2)

This massive set covers the biology of mosquitoes in depth. Volume 1 covers development, nutrition, and reproduction; Volume 2 covers sensory reception and behavior. Volume 3 is due in 2004 and will cover dormancy, survival, speciation, and evolution. The set is a revised edition of *The Physiology of Mosquitoes* (1963).

Griffiths, Graham C.D., ed. **Flies of the Nearctic Region.** Stuttgart: E. Schweizerbart, 1980– . Vol. price varies.

Designed as a companion to Lindner's *Die Fliegen der palaearktischen Region,* this ongoing series provides descriptions of adults, pupae, and larvae, life histories, and distribution for each species. There are keys and black-and-white illustrations as well. Volume 1 covers the history of Nearctic Diptera research.

McAlpine, J.F., et al., coord. **Manual of Nearctic Diptera.** Ottawa: Research Branch, Agriculture Canada, 1981–89. 3 vol. (Monograph of the Research Branch, Agriculture Canada, nos. 27, 28, and 32). $52. ISBN 0660107317.

This manual covers 108 families and 2,150 genera of North American Diptera. The first two volumes cover the anatomy, terminology, and identification of the families and genera of the Diptera of North America north of Mexico, including keys to families and genera. The third volume contains three chapters discussing the cladistic phylogeny of the Diptera.

Siphonaptera

Medvedev, Sergei G., and Valentin Vashchonok. **Fleas (Siphonaptera).** St. Petersburg, Russia: Zoological Institute, Russian Academy of Sciences. URL: http://www.zin.ru/Animalia/Siphonaptera/index.htm (Accessed August 25, 2003).

This site provides information on the biology, ecology, morphology, distribution, taxonomy, hosts, and control of fleas. The creators of the site also provide images, references to the literature, links to other Web pages, and more.

Dictyoptera

Atkinson, Thomas H., Philip G. Koehler, and R. S. Patterson. **Catalog and Atlas of the Cockroaches (Dictyoptera) of North America North of Mexico.** Lanham, MD: Entomological Society of America, 1991. 85 p. (Miscellaneous Publications of the Entomological Society of America, no. 78).

Covers 69 species of native and introduced cockroaches found in North America. Each species account includes synonyms, ecological summary, distribution, and references. Most species accounts also include a range map.

Bell, William J., and K. G. Adiyodi, eds. **The American Cockroach.** New York: Chapman & Hall, 1982. 529 p. $85. ISBN 0412161400.

Although this book emphasizes the biology of the American cockroach (*Periplaneta americana*), the lab rat of the insect world, other species are covered as well. The book updates both Cornwell and Guthrie and Tindall, below.

Cornwell, P. B. **The Cockroach.** London: Hutchinson, 1968–76. 2 vol. ISBN 0090886704.

The first volume of this set discusses cockroaches in the lab and as pests; Volume 2 covers roach control and insecticides. In Volume 1, the author discusses classification, the most common species, anatomy, physiology, development, movement, disease, and other topics. The second volume, aimed at pest control specialists, discusses a variety of insecticides, their method of action, and other topics dealing with cockroaches as pests.

Guthrie, D. M., and A. R. Tindall. **The Biology of the Cockroach.** New York: St. Martin's Press, 1968. 408 p.

The topics covered in this text are similar to those covered in Volume 1 of Cornwell, above. The authors concentrate on *Periplaneta americana, Blatta orientalis,* and *Blattella germanica,* the most commonly studied species.

Roth, Louis M., and Edwin R. Willis. **The Biotic Associations of Cockroaches.** Washington, DC: Smithsonian Institution, 1960. 470 p. (Smithsonian Miscellaneous Collections, vol. 141).

This compilation gathers together all the known research on the ecology of cockroaches, both pest and nonpest species, around the world. Chapters discuss ecological relationships of cockroaches in various environments, mutualism, other organisms associated with cockroaches, and more.

Hymenoptera

Agosti, Donat, and Norman Johnson. **Antbase.** American Museum of Natural History. URL: http://research.amnh.org/entomology/social _insects/.

Antbase was created to provide free information on Hymenoptera. The center of the site is an updated list of species names, currently containing 11,006 species of ants. This "Hymenoptera Name Server" provides valid names, initial description, synonyms, and links to the "Hymenoptera On-Line" database. The database provides access to other information, such as images, citations, maps, online keys, links to databases such as GenBank, and more. Other resources available from AntBase include the FORMIS ant bibliography (see Indexes, above), the IUCN Red List for ants, the Ant Image database from Japan, and general information about ants. The site is the first of several planned to cover other social insects such as social wasps, bees, and termites.

Evans, Howard Ensign, and Mary Jane West Eberhard. **The Wasps.** Ann Arbor: University of Michigan Press, 1970. 265 p. ISBN 0472001183; 0472050184.

This small book provides a concise synopsis of the biology of wasps. The authors cover the natural history of wasps, the nesting behavior of solitary wasps, the social behavior of the social wasps, and the biotic relationships of wasps.

Gauld, Ian, and Barry Bolton, eds. **The Hymenoptera.** New York: Oxford University Press, 1988. 332 p. ISBN 0198585217.

The emphasis in this book is on the British Hymenoptera, but the discussions of the biology, economic importance, morphology, classification, and evolution of the order are of much broader interest, as is the section on how to study Hymenoptera. There is a key to the families of Hymenoptera found in Britain and descriptions of British families of Hymenoptera.

Hölldobler, Bert, and Edward Osborne Wilson. **The Ants.** Cambridge, MA: Belknap Press of Harvard University Press, 1990. 732 p. $95. ISBN 0674040759.

This oversized work summarizes ant taxonomy, biology, and behavior. The authors provide a wealth of data on ants and their world.

Michener, Charles D. **The Bees of the World.** Baltimore: Johns Hopkins University Press, 2000. 913 p. $160. ISBN 0801861330.

A comprehensive treatment of 1,200 genera containing 16,000 species of bees from around the world. It is in four sections, covering bee biology, evolution, taxonomy, and systematics. The bulk of the book consists of the systematic section, which has keys to the subgeneric level as well as generic descriptions covering distribution, natural history, number of species, and general notes. There are a number of black-and-white illustrations and photographs, plus a few color photos.

O'Neill, Kevin M. **Solitary Wasps: Behavior and Natural History.** Ithaca, NY: Comstock, 2001. 406 p. (Cornell Series in Arthropod Biology). $39.95. ISBN 0801437210.

Wasps are fascinating subjects for behavioral studies, and this book gathers together old and new studies on the solitary wasps. After a brief chapter on wasp classification, the author goes on to discuss the foraging behavior, nests, natural enemies, mating strategies, thermoregulation, and the evolution of parental strategies. Appendixes list the superfamilies, families, and subfamilies of solitary wasps and the wasp genera mentioned in the book.

Winston, Mark L. **The Biology of the Honey Bee.** Cambridge, MA: Harvard University Press, 1987. 281 p. $53. ISBN 0674074084.

Provides an overview of the biology and social behavior of honeybees. The topics covered include evolution, anatomy, development, nest architecture, age related activities of worker bees, the chemical world of bees, communication, collection of food, reproduction, and the biology of temperate and tropical bees.

Identification Tools

Arnett, Ross H., Jr. **American Insects: A Handbook of the Insects of America North of Mexico.** Gainesville, FL: Sandhill Crane Press, 1993. 850 p. ISBN 1877743194.

A synopsis of the insects of North America. The handbook contains keys to the generic level, and descriptions of orders, families, and some subfamilies as well as representative species. In addition, there is introductory material on insect biology, systematics, and preparation of specimens. Over 22,000 species are described. An authoritative work; there is nothing else quite as comprehensive for North American insects. Reprint of the 1985 edition.

Bland, Roger G., and H.E. Jaques. **How to Know the Insects.** 3rd ed. Dubuque, IA: W.C. Brown, 1978. 409 p. (Pictured Key Nature Series). $25.80. ISBN 0697047539; 0697047520.
    An illustrated key to the families of insects found in North America. The guide also includes information on collecting and studying insects.

Borror, Donald J., and Richard E. White. **A Field Guide to Insects of America North of Mexico.** Boston: Houghton Mifflin, 1970. (Peterson Field Guide series, 19). 404 p. ISBN 0395074363; 0395185238 (paper).
    The field guide covers 579 families representing all of the insect orders. Large and conspicuous insects are identified to species, but most inconspicuous or difficult insects are just identified to family (flies, for instance). The standard insect field guide for North America.

Brues, Charles T., A.L. Melander, and Frank M. Carpenter. **Classification of Insects: Keys to the Living and Extinct Families of Insects, and to the Living Families of Other Terrestrial Arthropods.** 2nd ed., rev. Cambridge, UK: The Museum, 1954. 917 p. (Bulletin of the Museum of Comparative Zoology, vol. 108).
    The keys provided in this comprehensive volume cover all the living and extinct families of insects and terrestrial arthropods in the world. It was designed as a guide for students, and the keys include many illustrations of whole insects as well as an extensive bibliography for each family. The keys to recent insects, recent arthropods, and extinct insects are separate.

Burgess, N.R.H., and G.O. Cowan. **A Colour Atlas of Medical Entomology.** New York: Chapman & Hall, 1993. 152 p. $225.50. ISBN 0412323400.
    This is an identification guide to insects of medical importance, mainly of the tropics. The atlas includes many photographs of the insects, their habitats, and the diseases caused by them. In addition, the authors provide information on the life cycle, habits, and medical problems caused by each species.

Chinery, Michael. **Collins Guide to the Insects of Britain and Western Europe.** London: Collins, 1986. 320 p. ISBN 0002191709; 0002191377 (paper).

Although currently out of print, this field guide covers more species of insects than most of its competitors with over 2,000 species described and 778 common species illustrated. It includes keys to species.

Chinery, Michael. **Insects of Britain and Northern Europe.** 3rd ed. London: HarperCollins, 1986. 320 p. (Collins Field Guide Series). $29.95. ISBN 0002199181.

One of the classic field guides to the insects of Europe, this guide illustrates 778 species. An introductory section discusses insects in general, followed by the main description section. It is arranged by order and each section contains keys to species and descriptions.

Chu, Hung-fu. **How to Know the Immature Insects.** 2nd ed. Dubuque, IA: W. C. Brown, 1992. (Pictured Key Nature Series). ISBN 0697048063 (paper).

This guide provides illustrated keys to the larvae of about 400 families of insects worldwide.

Dindal, Daniel L., ed. **Soil Biology Guide.** New York: Wiley, 1990. 1,349 p. ISBN 0471045519.

See chapter 2 for full annotation. The guide provides keys to the major groups of soil arthropods as well as other invertebrates, including keys and black-and-white illustrations.

Edmondson, W. T., ed. **Fresh-Water Biology.** 2nd ed. New York, Wiley, 1959. 1,248 p.

See chapter 2 for full annotation. The manual provides keys to the major groups of freshwater arthropods as well as other invertebrates, including keys and black-and-white illustrations.

Gibbons, Bob. **Field Guide to the Insects of Britain and Northern Europe.** Marlborough, Wiltshire, UK: Crowood, 1995. 320 p. $24.95 (paper). ISBN 185223895X; 1852239379 (paper).

A detailed field guide to over 1,500 species of insects, this guide features color photographs and includes illustrations of galls, nests, and other insect-related objects.

Goddard, Jerome. **Physician's Guide to Arthropods of Medical Importance.** 3rd ed. Boca Raton, FL: CRC Press, 1999. 440 p. $169.95. ISBN 0849311861.

This guide covers the identification of insects, mites, scorpions, and spiders of public health importance. It is designed to assist doctors and other medical entomologists in identifying and diagnosing arthropods and the injuries they cause.

The Insects and Arachnids of Canada. Pt. 1– . Ottawa: Agriculture Canada, 1977– . Irregular. ISSN 0706–7313.

A complete listing of all insects and arachnids of Canada and the adjacent states. Part 1 consists of a guide to collecting and preserving insects. The remaining volumes feature keys to species.

Lane, Richard P., and Roger W. Crosskey, eds. **Medical Insects and Arachnids.** New York: Chapman & Hall, 1993. 744 p. $199.95. ISBN 0412400006.

An identification guide for medically important insects and arachnids. Each chapter covers a major group and includes information not only on identification, but also distribution, control, biology, medical importance, and collecting specimens. The insects covered include Diptera, cockroaches, bedbugs, lice, fleas, arachnids, and other minor pest groups.

Lehmkuhl, Dennis M. **How to Know the Aquatic Insects.** Dubuque, IA: W.C. Brown, 1979. 168 p. (Pictured Key Nature Series). $33.75 (paper). ISBN 0697047679 (paper).

This guide contains keys to the families and distinctive genera of aquatic insects of North America north of Mexico. The author also includes extensive introductory information on aquatic insect ecology and morphology, their role as indicator organisms, and how to collect aquatic insects.

Merritt, Richard W., and Kenneth W. Cummins, eds. **An Introduction to the Aquatic Insects of North America.** 3rd ed. Dubuque, IA: Kendall/Hunt, 1996. 862 p. ISBN 0840375883 (spiral bound); 0787217611.

An identification guide to the aquatic insects, this book includes keys for each order, usually to the level of the genus. The text covers general biology, phylogeny, and classification of aquatic insects and then provides an order-by-order guide to the insects. Each order is introduced and described in general, and then keys lead to the identification of genera, which may be illustrated but are not described.

Milne, Lorus, and Margery Milne. **The Audubon Society Field Guide to North American Insects and Spiders.** New York: Knopf, 1980. (Audubon Society Field Guide Series). 959 p. $19.95. ISBN 0394507630.

This is the only major field guide to include a few arachnids. It covers 600 species from the major orders, including some caterpillars, and is illustrated with color photos.

New, T. R. **Name That Insect: A Guide to the Insects of Southeastern Australia.** Melbourne: Oxford University Press, 1996. 194 p. $19.95 (paper). ISBN 0195537823 (paper).

A comprehensive guide to the orders of insects found in Australia, this guide keys the insects to order but only selected species of the most common orders are described.

Nilsson, Anders N., ed. **Aquatic Insects of North Europe: A Taxonomic Handbook.** Stenstrup, Denmark: Apollo Books, 1996–97. 2 vol. ISBN 8788757072 (set); 8788757099 (vol. 1); 8788757153 (vol. 2).

The handbook covers those insect families with aquatic representatives. The keys were designed to identify both larvae and adults to genera. There is a table listing Danish, Norwegian, Swedish, Finnish, and English common names for the higher taxa covered in the book. Each order is discussed in a separate chapter, with an overview, illustrations, and keys to larvae and adults. Some groups are keyed to the species level, and there are references and a checklist for each chapter as well.

Stehr, Frederick W., ed. **Immature Insects.** Dubuque, IA: Kendall/Hunt, 1987–91. 2 vol. $199.95 (vol. 1). ISBN 0840337027 (vol. 1); 0840346395 (vol. 2).

Designed to serve as identification guide and textbook, this set includes keys, tables of features, and extended literature references. Covers mainly North American insects. Chu, above, offers a less expensive and more portable alternative.

Zimmerman, Elwood Curtin. **Insects of Hawaii: A Manual of the Insects of the Hawaiian Islands, including an Enumeration of the Species and Notes on Their Origin, Distribution, Hosts, Parasites, etc.** Honolulu: University of Hawaii Press, 1948– . vol. $35 (vol. 1), $50 (vol. 16, pt. 1). ISBN 082482427X (vol. 1, reprint); 0824823567 (vol. 16, pt. 1).

A classic handbook to the insects of Hawaii and other Pacific islands with extensive information on natural history. The catalog has keys to families and species, black-and-white illustrations, and information on the synonyms, common name, distribution, food, and parasites along with general notes for the better-known species. Each volume contains a checklist, bibliography, and index to scientific names. Volume 1, containing introductory material on the geological history and its effects on the development of endemic species of the islands, has recently been reprinted. The set is currently up to Volume 16, Part 1 (2000), covering part of the Coleoptera.

Systematic Section

Arachnida

Emerton, James H. **The Common Spiders of the United States.** New York: Dover, 1961. 227 p.

Although the nomenclature is rather outdated, this guide about 200 spiders of the eastern and central United States is still one of the standards, and one of the few spider identification guides for this region. A key to the common groups of spiders refers users to the appropriate pages in the book, where they will find black-and-white drawings and photographs of spiders and their webs plus descriptions and information on the biology and distribution of the spiders. The American Arachnological Society's *Spiders of North America* Web site provides modern names for Emerton's spiders.

Kaston, Benjamin J. **How to Know the Spiders.** 3rd ed. Dubuque, IA: W.C. Brown, 1978. 272 p. (Pictured Key Nature Series). $41.55 (paper). ISBN 0697048985 (paper).

Contains keys for 271 species of spiders from North America. Identification to species may require microscope and/or hand lens. See the American Arachnological Society's *Spiders of North America* Web site (above) for modern names of the spiders discussed in the key.

McDaniel, Burruss. **How to Know the Mites and Ticks.** Dubuque, IA: W.C. Brown, 1979. 335 p. (Pictured Key Nature Series). ISBN 0697047563; 0697047571 (paper).

This illustrated key covers about 400 species of North American mites and ticks, but because many species are widely distributed, the key is useful elsewhere as well.

Crustacea

Fitzpatrick, Joseph F. **How to Know the Freshwater Crustacea.** Dubuque, IA: W.C. Brown, 1983. 227 p. (Pictured Key Nature Series). $31.25 (paper). ISBN 0697047830 (paper).

An illustrated key to most of the genera of freshwater Crustacea found in the Americas.

Holthuis, L. B. **Marine Lobsters of the World: An Annotated and Illustrated Catalogue of Species of Interest to Fisheries Known to Date.** Rome: Food and Agriculture Organization of the United Nations, 1991. 292 p. (FAO Fisheries Synopsis, no. 125, vol. 13; FAO Species Catalogue, vol. 13). $55. ISBN 9251030278.

The catalog contains all species known to be consumed by humans, used for bait, or considered to be of potential commercial value. It both identifies and provides basic data on species of interest. There are keys and black-and-white illustrations to facilitate identification. The catalog is arranged in systematic order, and each species account includes synonyms, common names, citations to the literature, distribution, habitat, size, interest to fisheries, and remarks. There is also a list of species found in the major marine fishing areas, references, and alphabetical indexes to scientific and common names.

Holthuis, L. B. **Shrimps and Prawns of the World: An Annotated Catalogue of Species of Interest to Fisheries.** Rome: Food and Agriculture Organization of the United Nations, 1980. 271 p. (FAO Fisheries Synopsis, no. 125, vol. 1; FAO Species Catalogue, vol. 1). ISBN 9251008965.

See the description for *Marine Lobsters of the World,* above.

Schultz, George A. **How to Know the Marine Isopod Crustaceans.** Dubuque, IA: W.C. Brown, 1969. 359 p. (Pictured Key Nature Series). ISBN 6970186'40.

Designed for both amateurs and professionals, this illustrated key identifies all 174 genera and most of the 444 species of marine isopods from North America.

Insects

Apterygota

Tuxen, Søren Ludvig. **The Protura: A Revision of the Species of the World, with Keys for Determination.** Paris: Hermann, 1964. 360 p.

(Problèmes d'écologie; Cahiers de Géobiologie et d'écologie. Actualités Scientifiques et Industrielles, 1311).

Provides a catalog of the 208 described species of Protura. The introduction describes the morphology, development, and ecology of the Protura. The bulk of the work identifies and describes the species. The descriptions are very detailed and include illustrations of body parts, and there are keys to species.

Ephemeroptera

Edmunds, George F., Jr., Steven L. Jensen, and Lewis Berner. **The Mayflies of North and Central America.** Minneapolis: University of Minnesota Press, 1976. 330 p. ISBN 0816607591.

Provides keys to the genera of the mayflies of North and Central America. The authors provide general discussion of the methods for rearing, collecting, and preserving mayflies, plus an overview of mayfly systematics. There are separate illustrated keys to mayfly nymphs and adults. For each genus, the authors summarize nymphal and adult characteristics, habitat and habits, life history, mating flights, taxonomy, and distribution.

Odonata

Harvey, Alan W. **Generic Key to Adult North American Dragonflies.** Statesboro: Georgia Southern University. URL: http://www.bio.gasou. edu/bio-home/Harvey/dragonkey.html (Accessed August 25, 2003).

Key to 63 genera of adult dragonflies. It can be used online with illustrations of features or printed. It is based on Needham and Westfall's 1955 classic, *A Manual of the Dragonflies of North America (Anisoptera)* (see above for the second edition). Harvey's key includes page numbers referring to the first edition of Needham and Westfall.

Needham, James G., Minter J. Westfall, Jr., and Michael L. May. **Dragonflies of North America.** Rev. ed. Gainesville, FL: Scientific Publishers, 2000. 939 p. $125. ISBN 0945417942.

This massive work is a revised edition of Needham and Westfall's *A Manual of the Dragonflies of North America (Anisoptera)* from 1955. This new edition covers North America as far south as northern Mexico and the Greater Antilles. Introductory material describes the order, including adult and larval forms, and keys. Each species account includes references, size, description, black-and-white photographs or illustrations, distribution, and times of the year found.

Walker, Edmund Murten. M. **The Odonata of Canada and Alaska.** Toronto: University of Toronto Press, 1953–75.

Volume 3 of this set was completed, after Walker's death, by Philip S. Corbet. This guide to the dragonflies and damselflies of Canada includes a general overview of the morphology and life histories of the Odonata and goes on to provide detailed species accounts for all species found in the region. There are keys to families, genera, and species as well, and each species account includes descriptions of males, females, and nymphs, plus habitat and range, distribution, field notes, and illustrations. Volume 1 covers the Zygoptera; the remaining volumes discuss the Anisoptera.

Orthoptera

Helfer, Jacques R. **How to Know the Grasshoppers, Crickets, Cockroaches, and Their Allies.** Dover ed. New York: Dover, 1987. 363 p. ISBN 0486253953 (paper).

This classic identification guide was first published in 1953 and updated and expanded in 1987. It includes a key to species and covers all of the Orthoptera of North America.

Otte, Daniel. **The North American Grasshoppers.** Cambridge, MA: Harvard University Press, 1981– . $90.50 (vol. 1); $95.00 (vol. 2). ISBN 0674626605 (vol. 1); 0674626613 (vol. 2).

This identification manual provides illustrated keys to the families and genera of the grasshoppers of North America. The species accounts list the taxonomy, distribution, recognition, variation, habitat, behavior, life cycle, and references for each species, along with range map and black-and-white illustrations. The set was intended to be in three parts, Volume 1, *Acrididae: Gomphocerinae and Acridinae;* Volume 2, *Acrididae: Oedipodinae;* and Volume 3, Melanoplinae, Romaleinae, and other smaller groups. Only the first two volumes have been published.

Walker, Thomas J., and Thomas E. Moore. **Singing Insects of North America.** Gainesville: University of Florida, 2000– . URL: http://buzz.ifas.ufl.edu/index.htm. (Accessed August 25, 2003).

When completed, this site will provide images, sounds, descriptions, and other information to assist users in identifying the crickets, katydids, and cicadas of North America. There are keys to families and subfamilies, genera, and species to assist identification as well as checklists, distribution maps, and more. The site was still under construction at the time of viewing, but was already quite extensive.

Isoptera

Weesner, Frances M. **The Termites of the United States: A Handbook.** Elizabeth, NJ: National Pest Control Association, 1965. 67 p.

The handbook provides background information about termites and termite colonies as well as keys and detailed descriptions of the North American species. After one chapter describing the classification and identification of termites in the United States, the remainder take a geographical orientation, dividing the United States into five broad geographical areas. Although the book was published by the National Pest Control Association, the emphasis throughout is on identification, not control.

Plecoptera

Stark, Bill P., Stanley W. Szczytko, and C. Riley Nelson. **American Stoneflies: A Photographic Guide to the Plecoptera.** Columbus, OH: Caddis Press, 1998. 126 p. ISBN 0966798201.

There are about 600 species of North American stoneflies, many of which are illustrated in this guide. The authors provide background information on the stoneflies and their biology and classification as well as the identification guide. A pictorial key to families of both adult and nymphal stoneflies sends users to the appropriate family. Within each family, genera and species are described and selected species illustrated. The text also lists more detailed keys for specific groups, and because stoneflies are an important source of trout food, the authors discuss artificial flies based on stoneflies as well.

Stewart, Kenneth W., and Bill P. Stark. **The Nymphs of North American Stonefly Genera (Plecoptera).** Hyattsville, MD: Entomological Society of America, 1988. 460 p. (Thomas Say Foundation Series, vol. 12). ISBN 0938522337.

This guide describes the morphology and biology of 99 genera of stonefly nymphs, all of the genera described up to 1987. The generic accounts include distribution, type species, previous descriptions, morphology, biology, and distribution plus black-and-white illustrations of the nymphs.

Psocoptera

Mockford, Edward L. **North American Psocoptera (Insecta).** Gainesville, FL: Sandhill Crane Press, 1993. 455 p. (Flora and Fauna Handbook, no. 10). $139.95. ISBN 1877743127.

Covers the booklice of North America north of Mexico, both native and introduced. The author provides a general introduction to the biology and classification of the Psocoptera. The remainder of the book is divided into chapters corresponding to the three suborders (Trogiomorpha, Troctomorpha, and Psocomorpha). Each chapter contains illustrated keys to families and genera. The entries for higher-order groups (genus and above) include authors, diagnosis, type, and a list of North American genera or species. The species accounts include author, recognition features, relationships to other species, and distribution and habitat.

Pthiraptera

Kim, Ke Chung, Harry D. Pratt, and Chester J. Stojanovich. **The Sucking Lice of North America: An Illustrated Manual for Identification.** University Park: Pennsylvania State University Press, 1986. 241 p. ISBN 0271003952.

This manual covers the order Anoplura, the blood-sucking lice, and treats 76 species in 19 genera. After introductory chapters discussing topics such as collecting, morphology, immature stages, and public health importance, the remainder of the book provides identification of the North American species. Each genus is listed with original description, type species, diagnosis, hosts, and remarks, and the species accounts include the same information plus biology, distribution, and taxonomic notes. There are illustrations of each species as well as illustrated keys.

Thysanoptera

Mound, L. A., and Geoffrey Kibby. **Thysanoptera: An Identification Guide.** 2nd ed. New York: CAB International, 1998. 70 p. $40. ISBN 0851992110.

Contains illustrated keys to the economically important thrips of the world. It is an updated version of a volume in the CIE Guide to Insects of Importance to Man series.

Hemiptera

Slater, James A., and Richard M. Baranowski. **How to Know the True Bugs (Hemiptera-Homoptera).** Dubuque, IA: W. C. Brown, 1978. 256 p. (Pictured Key Nature Series). ISBN 0697048934; 0697048942 (paper).

Contains illustrated keys to 750 common species of North American bugs.

Coleoptera

Arnett, Ross H., N. M. Downie, and H. E. Jaques. **How to Know the Beetles.** 2nd ed. Dubuque, IA: W.C. Brown, 1980. 416 p. (Pictured Key Nature Series). $25.80. ISBN 0697047768.

An illustrated key to 1,500 species of beetles from North America, covering all families found in the region.

White, Richard E. **A Field Guide to the Beetles of North America.** Boston: Houghton Mifflin, 1983. (Peterson Field Guide Series, no. 29). 368 p. ISBN 0395318084; 0395339537 (paper).

This guide covers 600 beetle species and has black-and-white and color illustrations. It is the only popular field guide to the beetles of North America.

Trichoptera

Wiggins, Glenn B. **Larvae of the North American Caddisfly Genera (Trichoptera).** 2nd ed. Toronto: University of Toronto Press, 1996. 457 p. $120. ISBN 0802027237.

This guide identifies caddisfly larvae to the genus. The records for each genus include distribution, morphology, the type of shelter constructed by the larvae, biology, and remarks. There are black-and-white illustrations and keys to genera.

Lepidoptera

Braby, Michael F. **Butterflies of Australia: Their Identification, Biology and Distribution.** Collingwood, Victoria: CSIRO Publishing, 2000. 2 vol. $141. ISBN 0643065911; 0643064923 (vol. 1); 0643064931 (vol. 2).

This oversized set has two purposes: to provide a manual for the identification of Australian butterflies and to summarize the knowledge about the species. It is designed for the use of butterfly collectors and breeders, students, and entomologists. There is a checklist of the butterfly species of Australia and introductory materials for students and amateurs, plus species accounts arranged in systematic order. The species accounts include black-and-white photographs of male and female specimens, range maps, description of standard and variant specimens, similar species, immature species, larval food plants, life cycle, distribution, and major references. There are also color plates in the back of each volume illustrating selected adults, caterpillars, and eggs.

Coote, Lonny D. **CITES Identification Guide—Butterflies: Guide to the Identification of Butterfly Species Controlled under the Convention on International Trade in Endangered Species of Wild Fauna and Flora.** Ottawa: Environment Canada, 2000. 204 p. ISBN 0660615622.

Covers 45 species of the family Papillionidae that are covered by the Convention on International Trade in Endangered Species (CITES). In English, French, and Spanish. The full text of this identification guide can be found at http://www.cws-scf.ec.gc.ca/enforce/pdf/Butterfly/CITES_Butterfly_Guide.pdf.

Covell, Charles V., Jr. **A Field Guide to the Moths of Eastern North America.** Boston: Houghton Mifflin, 1984. (Peterson Field Guide Series, no. 30). 496 p. ISBN 0395361001.

A classic field guide to 1,300 species of eastern moths. There are color and black-and-white illustrations.

D'Abrera, Bernard. **Butterflies of the World.** Melbourne: Lansdowne Editions in association with E. W. Classey, 1980– . Vol. price varies.

This oversized (33 cm) set is intended as an aid to identification of the world's butterflies. There are several subsections: *Butterflies of the Afrotropical Region, Butterflies of the Australian Region, Butterflies of the Holarctic Region, Butterflies of the Neotropical Region,* and *Butterflies of the Oriental Region.* The volumes consist of plates of color photographs of butterflies of the various regions, with accepted names, citation to the original description, geographical range, and notes for each species. About 15 volumes have been published to date.

Ehrlich, Paul R. **How to Know the Butterflies: Illustrated Keys for Determining to Species All Butterflies Found in North America, North of Mexico, with Notes on Their Distribution, Habits, and Larval Food, and Suggestions for Collecting and Studying Them.** Dubuque, IA: W. C. Brown, 1961. 262 p. (Pictured Key Nature Series).

An illustrated key to the butterflies of North America. As the title suggests, it also includes information on studying butterflies. Many larvae and pupae are illustrated, as well as adult butterflies.

Glassberg, Jeffrey. **Butterflies through Binoculars: The East.** New York: Oxford University Press, 1999. 242 p. $18.95 (paper). ISBN 0195106687 (paper).

Like its companion volume to the butterflies of the west (below), this field guide features clear, gorgeous photographs of butterflies along with distribution maps and detailed identification information plus information on the abundance, habitat, food plants, and other comments. It covers over 300 species of southeastern Canada and the eastern United States.

Glassberg, Jeffrey. **Butterflies through Binoculars: The West.** New York: Oxford University Press, 2001. 374 p. $19.95 (paper). ISBN 0195106695 (paper).

A companion to the author's guide covering the butterflies of the east, with similar detailed information on the identification and natural history of the butterflies of the region.

Holloway, J. D., J. D. Bradley, and D. J. Carter. **Lepidoptera.** Wallingford, UK: CAB International Institute of Entomology, 1987. 262 p. (CIE Guides to Insects of Importance to Man, no. 1). ISBN 0851986056.

Designed for a practical introductory course for applied entomologists, this identification guide facilitates the identification of economically important Lepidoptera to the family or subfamily level. It contains illustrated keys and descriptions of the families.

Layberry, Ross A., Peter W. Hall, and J. Donald Lafontaine. **The Butterflies of Canada.** Toronto: Published in association with NRC Research Press, Canada Institute for Scientific and Technical Information by University of Toronto Press, 1998. 280 p. $35 (paper). ISBN 0851986056; 0802078818 (paper).

This book is designed as an identification guide and summary of the state of knowledge of Canadian butterflies. It includes chapters on butterfly distributions and conservation, photography, butterfly gardening, and the history of the study of butterflies in Canada. The bulk of the book consists of species accounts arranged in systematic order. Each account includes black-and-white photographs, diagnosis, subspecies, distribution, range map, similar species, early stages, abundance, flight season, habits, and remarks. The authors also provide a checklist of Canadian butterflies and color plates showing adult and larval forms of the more common species.

Opler, Paul A. **A Field Guide to Eastern Butterflies.** 2nd ed. Boston: Houghton Mifflin, 1998. (Peterson Field Guide Series, 4). 486 p. ISBN 0395364523 (paper).

This field guide covers 524 species. The first edition, by Alexander Klots, was titled *A Field Guide to Butterflies East of the Great Plains,* 1951.

Opler, Paul A. **A Field Guide to Western Butterflies.** 2nd ed. Boston: Houghton Mifflin, 1998. (Peterson Field Guide Series, no. 33). 528 p. $32; $24 (paper) ISBN 0395791529; 0395791510 (paper).

A companion to Opler's *A Field Guide to Eastern Butterflies,* this field guide covers 590 species. It is a revised edition of Tilden and Smith's *A Field Guide to Western Butterflies.*

Pyle, Robert Michael. **The Audubon Society Field Guide to North American Butterflies.** New York: Knopf, 1981. (Audubon Society Field Guide Series). 916 p. $19. ISBN 0394519140.

Unlike the Peterson Field Guides listed above, this Audubon guide contains color photographs rather than drawings. It identifies 600 species of butterflies from both eastern and western states.

Diptera

Thompson, F. Christian, ed. **Fruit Fly Expert Identification System and Systematic Information Database: A Resource for Identification and Information on Fruit Flies and Maggots, with Information on Their Classification, Distribution and Documentation.** Leiden, The Netherlands: Backhuys for the North American Dipterists' Society, 1998. 524 p. plus 1 CD-ROM. (Myia, vol. 9). ISBN 9057820137.

This book plus CD-ROM set provides a wide variety of information on the identification and systematics of the fruit flies. The CD-ROM contains the full text of the book in PDF format plus an expert system for identifying the flies. The program allows users to select character data to identify species, much like a key, but in any order. The print volume is a catalog of the fruit flies of the world, not an identification tool. The authors provide a survey of the state of knowledge about fruit fly systematics, a systematic list of names, and an extensive bibliography.

Hymenoptera

Bolton, Barry. **Identification Guide to the Ant Genera of the World.** Cambridge, MA: Harvard University Press, 1994. 222 p. $85. ISBN 0674442806.

This oversized guide provides keys to the 296 extant genera of ants found around the world. Each subfamily is presented in a separate chapter, with information on the diagnosis of workers, separate keys to genera for each biogeographical region, taxonomic references, and numerous electron microscope photographs of representative specimens. The author also lists faunistic studies of ants, an illustrated glossary, a bibliography, and a combined index and checklist.

Goulet, Henri, and John T. Huber, eds. **Hymenoptera of the World: An Identification Guide to Families.** Ottawa: Centre for Land and Biological Resources Research, 1993. 668 p. (Publication of Agriculture Canada, no. 1894/E). $58.95. ISBN 0660149338.

The keys in this guide were created by specialists and are designed to work on Hymenoptera from all parts of the world. Initial chapters provide general information on the Hymenoptera and their morphology, including a very useful illustrated glossary. There is also a chapter describing how to use the keys. These introductory chapters are followed by a key to the superfamilies, and then eleven keys for the superfamilies keying specimens to the level of the family. Each key has numerous illustrations ranging from whole flies to body parts.

Michener, Charles D., Ronald J. McGinley, and Bryan N. Danforth. **The Bee Genera of North and Central America.** Washington, DC: Smithsonian Institution Press, 1994. 209 p. $45. ISBN 156098256X.

A key to the 169 species of bees found north of the Colombia-Panama border, with parallel text in English and Spanish. There are numerous line drawings and photographs, and the introduction includes information on collecting and preserving specimens as well as terminology used in the keys.

Associations

American Entomological Society. Academy of Natural Sciences of Philadelphia, 1900 Race St., Philadelphia, PA 19103. E-mail: aes@say.acnatsci.org. URL: http://www.acnatsci.org/hosted/aes/ (Accessed August 25, 2003).

Entomological Society of America. 9301 Annapolis Rd, Lanham, MD 20706-3115. E-mail: info@entsoc.org. URL: http://www.entsoc.org/ (Accessed August 25, 2003).

Entomological Society of Canada/Société d'Entomologie du Canada. 393 Winston Ave., Ottawa, ON K2A 1Y8 CANADA. E-mail: entsoc.can@ sympatico.ca. URL: http://esc-sec.org/ (Accessed August 25, 2003).

International Centre for Insect Physiology and Ecology (ICIPE). P.O. Box 30772, Nairobi, Kenya. E-mail: directorgeneral@icipe.org. URL: http:// www.icipe.org (Accessed August 25, 2003).

Royal Entomological Society. 41 Queen's Gate, London SW7 5HR UK. URL: http://www.royensoc.co.uk/ (Accessed August 25, 2003).

Systematic Section

Crustacea

Crustacean Society. Business Office, The Crustacean Society, P.O. Box 1897, Lawrence, KS 66044-8897. Phone: (785) 843-1221. URL: http://www.vims.edu/tcs/ (Accessed August 25, 2003).

Arachnida

American Arachnological Society. c/o Dr. Norman I. Platnick, American Museum of Natural History, Central Park West at 79th St., New York, NY 10024-5192. E-mail: 72737.3624@compuserve.com. URL: http://www. americanarachnology.org/ (Accessed August 25, 2003).

British Arachnological Society. c/o Dr Helen J. Read, Secretary, 2, Egypt Wood Cottages, Egypt Lane, Farnham Common, Bucks. SL2 3LE. E-mail: secretary@britishspiders.org.uk. URL: http://www.britishspiders. org.uk/index.html (Accessed August 25, 2003).

International Society of Arachnology. c/o Dr. Jason A. Dunlop, Museum fur Naturkunde, Humboldt Universite zu Berlin, Invalidenstrase 43, Berlin 10115, Germany. E-mail: Jason.Dunlop@rz.hu-berlin.de. URL: http://www.arachnology.org/ (Accessed August 25, 2003).

Odonata

Dragonfly Society of the Americas. c/o T. Donnelly 2091 Partridge Lane, Binghamton, NY 13903. E-mail: tdonnel@binghampton.edu. URL: http://www.afn.org/~iori/dsaintro.html (Accessed August 25, 2003). Formerly Dragonfly Society of America.

Orthoptera

Orthopterist's Society. c/o Dr. Jeffrey A. Lockwood, Department of Renewable Resources (Entomology), University of Wyoming, Laramie, WY 82071-3354. E-mail: lockwood@uwyo.edu. URL: http://140.247. 119.145/OS_Homepage/ (Accessed August 25, 2003). Formerly the Pan American Acridological Society.

Isoptera

International Isoptera Society. c/o R.H. Scheffrahn, Wood-Destroying Insects Unit, Ft. Lauderdale Research & Education Center, University of Florida, 3205 College Ave., Ft. Lauderdale, FL 33314. E-mail: rhsc@gnv.ifas.ufl.edu. URL: http://www.cals.cornell.edu/dept/bionb/isoptera/ homepage.html (Accessed August 25, 2003).

Hemiptera

International Heteropterists' Society. URL: http://entomology.si.edu/IHS/ home.lasso (Accessed August 25, 2003).

Neuroptera

International Association of Neuropterology. c/o Wieland Röhricht, "Eckardthaus," Neue Promenade 5, D-15377 Buckow (Märkische Schweiz), Germany. E-mail: wieland@roehricht.de. URL: http://www. neuropterology.org/oian.html (Accessed August 25, 2003).

Coleoptera

Coleopterist's Society. c/o Terry Seero at COFA-PPO, 3294 Meadowview Road, Sacramento, CA 95832-1448. URL: http://www.coleopsoc.org/ (Accessed August 25, 2003).

Lepidoptera

Lepidopterists' Society. c/o Ernest H. Williams, Department of Biology, Hamilton College, Clinton, NY 13323. URL: http://alpha.furman.edu/ ~snyder/snyder/lep (Accessed August 25, 2003).

Diptera

American Mosquito Control Association. c/o Pamela Toups, 2200 E. Prien Lake Road, Lake Charles, LA 70601. URL: http://www.mosquito.org/ (Accessed August 25, 2003).

Hymenoptera

International Bee Research Association (IBRA). 18 North Road, Cardiff, S. Glam, CF1 3DY UK. E-mail: ibra@cardiff.ac.uk. URL: http://www. ibra.org.uk/index.html (Accessed August 25, 2003).

The International Society of Hymenopterists. c/o John Huber, Biological Resources Program/ECORC, Agriculture Canada-Research Branch, KW Neatby Building. CEF. Ottawa, ON KIA 0C6 CANADA. E-mail: huberj@ncccot.agr.ca. URL: http://iris.biosci.ohio-state.edu/ish/ (Accessed February 19, 2003).

International Union for the Study of Social Insects. c/o Dr. M. D. Breed, EPO Biology, University of Colorado, Campus Box 334, Boulder, CO 80309. URL: http://iussi.bees.net/ (Accessed August 25, 2003).

References

Daly, Howell V., John T. Doyen, and Alexander H. Purcell, III. 1998. *Introduction to Insect Biology and Diversity.* 2nd ed. New York: Oxford University Press.

Klass, Klaus-D., Oliver Zompro, Niels P. Kristensen, and Joachim Adis. 2002. Mantophasmatodea: A new insect order with extant members in the afrotropics. *Science* 296 (5572): 1456–1459.

4

Vertebrates

Our own phylum, the Chordata, consists of about 43,000 species compared to nearly a million species and 35 to 40 phyla of invertebrates. There are three major divisions of the phylum: the Cephalachordata, the Urochordata, and the Vertebrata. The Cephalochordata and the Urochordata are often grouped as the Protochordata. At some point in their life cycles, all chordates have pharyngeal slits, a dorsal nerve cord, a notocord (a cartilagenous rod supporting the nerve cord), and a postanal tail. Some of these features are seen only in embryos in the so-called higher vertebrates. There are only about 25 species of cephalochordates (Amphioxus and other lancelets) and 2,000 species of urochordates (also known as tunicates or sea squirts). The Hemichordata are often included with the Protochordata, but more recent texts list it as a separate phylum, and in this book the phylum has been treated in chapter 2 on invertebrates.

The other chordate subphylum is the Vertebrata. All vertebrates possess a vertebral column or backbone with a nerve cord running through its middle. This vertebral column may be made of cartilage (lampreys, sharks, and rays) or bone (higher fishes, amphibians, reptiles, birds, and mammals). One division of the vertebrates sometimes used is the Tetrapods, or four-legged vertebrates (amphibians, reptiles, birds, and mammals). The term is most often used in paleontology.

Much more research has been done on vertebrates than invertebrates, perhaps because vertebrates tend to be larger and more visible than invertebrates. Of course, our own status as a vertebrate may explain some of our

173

interest as well. However, most of the resources describing this research are located in the subsequent chapters dealing with each individual vertebrate class. This chapter lists resources that cover the protochordates, general works on the vertebrates in general, and books covering more than one vertebrate class.

Indexes, Abstracts, and Bibliographies

Blackwelder, Richard E. **Guide to the Taxonomic Literature of Vertebrates.** Ames: Iowa State University Press, 1972. 259 p. ISBN 0813816300.

Unlike Wood, below, this bibliographical guide lists resources systematically rather than by author. It covers both books and journal articles, including bibliographies, glossaries, checklists, regional faunas, and so on. Within each major taxa are subheadings for geographical region and families.

References on Endangered, Threatened, and Recently Extinct Vertebrates and Sources for Additional Information. Smithsonian Institution. URL: http://www.si.edu/resource/faq/nmnh/endsp.htm (Accessed August 25, 2003).

This site provides an extensive bibliography of literature covering endangered, threatened, and extinct species. It is divided into several sections, covering general works, regional literature, information on the various groups of vertebrates, popular magazines that cover the topic, and sources of information from governmental bodies and societies. Although many of the books and magazines emphasize endangered species from North America, the coverage is worldwide.

Wood, Casey A. **An Introduction to the Literature of Vertebrate Zoology.** New York: Arno Press, 1974. 643 p. $45.95. ISBN 0405057725.

An invaluable retrospective bibliographical reference. Several introductory chapters cover the history and types of the zoological literature, covering topics such as Beginnings of Zoological Records, Medieval Writers on Zoology, Travelogues of Explorers, Oriental Literature, and Literature of Zoogeography. The bulk of the work consists of an annotated catalog of the holdings of several libraries at McGill University in Montreal up to 1930, listed alphabetically by author. Originally published by Oxford University Press in 1931.

Journals

Copeia. Vol. 1– . New York: American Society of Ichthyologists and Herpetologists, 1913– . Quarterly. $100. ISSN 0045-8511. Available online.

Publishes results of original research performed by members in which fish, amphibians, or reptiles are utilized as study organisms. Includes research articles, short communications, historical perspectives, book reviews, obituaries, and news items.

Dictionaries and Encyclopedias

Gotch, A. F. **Latin Names Explained: A Guide to the Scientific Classification of Reptiles, Birds and Mammals.** New York: Facts on File, 1996. 714 p. $60.50. ISBN 0816033773.

This dictionary translates scientific names into English and provides the reason why the name was chosen by the original author. Many of the accounts also include distribution and tidbits of information about the species or higher taxa. An initial section discusses classification and nomenclature in general, followed by separate sections on the reptiles, birds, and mammals. There are separate indexes for English and scientific names for the three groups as well as a table transliterating the Greek alphabet.

Jacobs, George J. **Dictionary of Vertebrate Zoology, English-Russian/Russian-English: Emphasizing Anatomy, Amphibians, and Reptiles.** Washington, DC: Smithsonian Institution Press, 1978. 48 p. ISBN 0874745519.

Although this dictionary covers a range of topics as described in the title, it is strongest in herpetology. It is in two sections, English-Russian and Russian-English. Russian common names are translated into the scientific name, rather than into English. In addition to anatomical terms, the dictionary includes scientific names, genera, and families of amphibians and reptiles.

Whitfield, Philip. **The Simon and Schuster Encyclopedia of Animals: A Visual Who's Who of the World's Creatures.** New York: Simon & Schuster Editions, 1998. 616 p. $50. ISBN 0684852373.

Despite the title, this encyclopedia covers only the vertebrates. It is designed for younger readers but provides a nice overview for readers of all ages. It is arranged by systematic order from mammals to fishes rather than alphabetically, and family accounts include representative species accounts with illustrations, cladograms, and descriptions.

Textbooks

Butler, Ann B., and William Hodos. **Comparative Vertebrate Neuroanatomy: Evolution and Adaptation.** New York: Wiley-Liss, 1996. 514 p. $130. ISBN 0471888893.

This text is designed for advanced neuroscience students. It covers comparative neuronatomy on a system-by-system basis. Part 1 discusses evolution and organization of the central nervous system; the remaining sections cover the various parts (spinal cord, midbrain, diencephalon, and telencephalon). Each chapter concludes with a summary, a short list of further readings, and a longer list of additional references.

Hairston, Nelson G. **Vertebrate Zoology: An Experimental Field Approach.** New York: Cambridge University Press, 1994. 280 p. ISBN 0521417031; 0521427126 (paper).

Emphasizes experimental and field zoology, rather than descriptive taxonomy. The author provides a survey of vertebrate classification, ecology, and behavior. He makes suggestions for experimental studies as well as imparting facts.

Hildebrand, Milton. **Analysis of Vertebrate Structure.** 5th ed. New York: Wiley, 2001. 635 p. $106.50. ISBN 0471295051.

Covers the evolutionary and functional morphology of vertebrates. The initial chapters provide a survey of the vertebrate classes. Part 2 covers the phylogeny and ontogeny of various structures, and Part 3 discusses the adaptation of the structures. An appendix describes how to make anatomical preparations.

Kardong, Kenneth V. **Vertebrates: Comparative Anatomy, Function, Evolution.** 3rd ed. Boston: McGraw-Hill, 2002. 762 p. $116.80. ISBN 0072909560.

A survey of the animal kingdom designed for undergraduate courses. The text emphasizes the function and evolution of vertebrates. Four appendixes list vector algebra, the international system of units, common Greek and Latin terms used in anatomy, and the classification of chordates. Each chapter includes a bibliography and links to the book's Web site at http://www.mhhe.com/biosci/pae/zoology/kardong. Some of the Web material is only available to purchasers of the text, but the collection of Web links is available to all.

Kent, George C., and Robert K. Carr. **Comparative Anatomy of the Vertebrates.** 9th ed. Boston: McGraw-Hill, 2001. 524 p. $112.55. ISBN 0073038695.

A survey of vertebrate anatomy designed for biology majors and premed students, this text is arranged by system or body part. Introductory chapters cover evolution, protochordates, extinct forms, and morphogenesis; later chapters discuss each body part or system. There are numerous illustrations, but this is not a dissection guide. Each chapter concludes with a summary, critical thinking questions, selected readings, and Web resources. The Web sites do not have URLs listed in the book, but the publisher provides a freely accessible site at http://www.mhhe.com/biosci/pae/zoology/kentcarr/links.html that contains links and updates the items listed in the book.

Liem, Karel F., et al. **Functional Anatomy of the Vertebrates: An Evolutionary Perspective.** 3rd ed. Fort Worth: Harcourt College Publishers, 2000. 703 p. $97.95. ISBN 0030223695.

This text assumes basic knowledge of biology. It discusses anatomy in a functional context, rather than a systematic one, so the various systems (support and movement, sense organs and the brain, and metabolism and reproduction) are discussed across the various groups. An introductory chapter covers phylogeny and evolution of vertebrates. Each chapter begins with an outline and ends with a summary and references.

Linzey, Donald W. **Vertebrate Biology.** Boston: McGraw-Hill, 2001. 530 p. $105.45. ISBN 0697363872.

This survey of vertebrate biology covers the systematics, evolution, zoogeography, biology, behavior, ecology, and conservation of vertebrates. In addition to chapters covering each of these subjects, the author includes chapters covering each major class (early chordates, fishes, amphibians, reptiles, and mammals). Each chapter concludes with review questions, supplemental readings, and relevant Web sites. The Web sites do not have URLs listed in the book, but the publisher provides a freely accessible site at http://www.mhhe.com/catalogs/sem/zoology/index.mhtml?file=/catalogs/0697363872&newcat=yes that contains links and updates the items listed in the book.

McGowan, Christopher. **A Practical Guide to Vertebrate Mechanics.** New York: Cambridge University Press, 1999. 301 p. $110; $42 (paper). ISBN 0521571944; 0521576733 (paper).

According to the back cover, "This text can be considered an engineering text for biologists," an accurate description. It is designed for use in a laboratory course, so each chapter provides an introduction to the material covered followed by one or more experiments. Topics covered include elasticity, material strength, how things break, bone as a composite material, friction, muscles, locomotion, and more.

Pough, F. Harvey, Christine M. Janis, and John B. Heiser. **Vertebrate Life.** 6th ed. Upper Saddle River, NJ: Prentice Hall, 2002. 699 p. $100. ISBN 0130412481.

This survey text discusses the biology of vertebrates, using cladistics to provide an evolutionary framework to form a context for studies of the behavior, ecology, and physiology of vertebrates. The text includes information on extinct vertebrates such as the mammal-like reptiles and dinosaurs as well as living forms. The publisher's site promised a companion Web site, but it was not available at the time of viewing (August 27, 2003).

Radinsky, Leonard B. **The Evolution of Vertebrate Design.** Chicago: University of Chicago Press, 1987. 188 p. $15 (paper). ISBN 0226702367 (paper).

An introduction to vertebrate evolution, paleontology, vertebrate biology, and functional, comparative anatomy, with emphasis on explaining the functional significance of changes in anatomy.

Romer, Alfred Sherwood, and Thomas Sturges Parsons. **The Vertebrate Body.** 6th ed. Philadelphia: Saunders, 1986. 679 p. ISBN 0030584469.

The classic vertebrate comparative anatomy textbook, Romer's text discusses vertebrate evolution and taxonomy and development as well as anatomy. Each system (musculature, circulatory system, body cavities, etc.) is compared in detail across the vertebrate classes. An appendix provides a synoptic classification of the chordates, and users can also find a list of scientific terminology and Latin and Greek word parts used in anatomy.

Wake, Marvalee H., ed. **Hyman's Comparative Vertebrate Anatomy.** 3rd ed. Chicago: University of Chicago Press, 1992. 788 p. $45. ISBN 0226870138.

A revised edition of the second edition of Libbie Hyman's classic *Comparative Vertebrate Anatomy,* this text is similar to Romer's *The Vertebrate Body* (above). It provides an extensive introduction to the classification and development of vertebrates, although unlike Romer, it also includes the Hemichordata and the lower chordates. The bulk of the book is a system-by-system discussion of vertebrate anatomy, with separate sections within each chapter discussing early vertebrates, Elasmobranchs (usually the dogfish shark), bony fishes, amphibians (typically *Necturus*), reptiles (turtles), birds (the pigeon), and mammals (cat or rabbit).

Willson, Mary F. **Vertebrate Natural History.** Philadelphia: Saunders College, 1984. 621 p. $115.95. ISBN 0030618045.

Discusses the natural history of vertebrates, including their relations with the physical environment, relations with other species, and social and reproductive patterns, arranged by topic rather than by taxon.

Young, J.Z. **The Life of Vertebrates.** 3rd ed. Oxford, UK: Clarendon Press, 1981. 645 p. ISBN 0198571720; 0198571739 (paper).

This text covers the anatomy, physiology, and evolution of the vertebrates and takes a systematic approach. After an initial chapter covering evolution in general, the remainder of the text discusses Amphioxus, Agnatha, Chondricthyes, Otsteichthyes, Amphibia, Reptilia, Aves, and Mammalia. The mammals are covered in more detail than the other groups, with separate chapters on the major orders. The author also discusses general issues in the adaptation of vertebrates to the various major lifestyles (life in the water, on land, and in the air).

Checklists and Classification Schemes

Banks, Richard C., Roy W. McDiarmid, and Alfred L. Gardner. **Checklist of Vertebrates of the United States, the U.S. Territories, and Canada.** Washington, DC: U.S. Department of the Interior, Fish and Wildlife Service, 1987. 79 p. (Resource Publication of the U.S. Fish and Wildlife Service, no. 166).

This pamphlet covers the amphibians, reptiles, birds, and mammals of North America, plus Hawaii and the U.S. territories in the Caribbean Sea and the Pacific Ocean. The checklist covers migratory, invasive, and recently extinct species, and each entry lists scientific and common names, author and date of original description, and conservation status.

Handbooks

Barrington, E. J. W. **The Biology of Hemichordata and Protochordata.** Edinburgh: Oliver and Boyd, 1965. 176 p.

The protochordates such as Amphioxus and the tunicates possess a notochord and other organs that place them within the phylum Chordata, but they lack a vertebral column. This little guide discusses the biology, life histories, and evolution of the Hemichordata, Urochordata, and Cephalochordata.

Benton, M. J., ed. **The Phylogeny and Classification of the Tetrapods.** New York: Oxford University Press, 1988. 2 vol. (The Systematics Association Special Volume, no. 35a and 35b). ISBN 0198577052 (vol. 1); 0198577125 (vol. 2).

The results of an international symposium, "The Phylogeny and Classification of the Tetrapods," held in 1987, this set covers the higher-level classification of amphibians, reptiles, birds, and mammals. The mammals are covered in Volume 2; the other classes are discussed in the first volume. The authors discuss both well-established cladograms as well as disputed areas.

Carey, James R., and Debra S. Judge. **Longevity Records: Life Spans of Mammals, Birds, Amphibians, Reptiles, and Fish.** Odense, Denmark: Odense University Press, 2000. 241 p. (Monographs on Population Aging, no. 8). $23.50. ISBN 8778385393.

Contains nearly 4,100 longevity records for 3,054 vertebrate species or subspecies. The authors have compiled the records from a variety of sources ranging from *Grzimek's Animal Life Encyclopedia* (see chapter 1) to journal articles. The book is divided into chapters dealing with each class. The orders are briefly described, and the data on longevity is provided in a lengthy table for each class. The table lists order/family, genus/species, common name, longevity for wild and captive animals, sex if known, and references.

Davis, David E., ed. **CRC Handbook of Census Methods for Terrestrial Vertebrates.** Boca Raton, FL: CRC Press, 1982. 397 p. $319.95. ISBN 0849329701.

Brief descriptions of census methods for about 130 species of vertebrates are included, plus a few nonterrestrial species such as coastal whales and manatees where the census methods are useful for other species. There is a separate chapter on calculations and statistics.

Kardong, Kenneth V., and Edward J. Zalisko. **Comparative Vertebrate Anatomy: A Laboratory Dissection Guide.** 3rd ed. Boston: McGraw-Hill, 2002. 211 p. $72.45. ISBN 0072909579.

Covers cat, shark, salamander, and lamprey dissection. It can be used with any anatomy text but is primarily designed for use with Kardong's *Vertebrates: Comparative Anatomy, Function, Evolution* and Kent's *Comparative Anatomy of the Vertebrates,* below. Like those books, it is arranged by anatomical system rather than by organism.

McNab, Brian Keith. **The Physiological Ecology of Vertebrates: A View from Energetics.** Ithaca, NY: Cornell University Press, 2002. 576 p. $75. ISBN 0801439132.

Physiological ecology integrates the physiology and behavior of organisms with the physical conditions of their environments. This treatise surveys the current state of awareness of the field. It is organized by system, including thermal exchange with the environment, material exchange with the environment, ecological energetics, and a final section summarizing the consequences of physiological ecology (thermal limits to the distribution of birds, for example). There are over 3,100 references as well.

Thompson, William L., Gary C. White, and Charles Gowan. **Monitoring Vertebrate Populations.** San Diego: Academic Press, 1998. 365 p. $77.95. ISBN 0126889600.

This handbook is designed for biological and resource managers who need to monitor vertebrate numbers in a particular area with a limited budget and relatively little statistical training, such as conservation officers or park rangers. In addition to general survey techniques, the authors also provide information on surveying different types of vertebrates. Each chapter lists some recommendations and provides a dichotomous key to enumeration methods to help users decide which method to use.

Wischnitzer, Saul. **Atlas and Dissection Guide for Comparative Anatomy.** 5th ed. New York: W. H. Freeman, 1993. 284 p. $48.64. ISBN 0716723743.

Arranged by organism, this laboratory manual covers the anatomy of protochordates, the lamprey, the dogfish shark, the mud puppy *Necturus,* and the cat. The section on the cat includes information on the sheep heart, eye, and brain. These organs are often substituted or used to supplement cat dissection because they are large and easily obtained.

Identification Tools

Blair, W. Frank, et al. **Vertebrates of the United States.** 2nd ed. New York: McGraw-Hill, 1968. 616 p.

The manual covers fishes, amphibians, reptiles, birds, and mammals of the United States with keys to genera and species of each group. The species accounts include identification characters and distribution information, and there are many illustrations and black-and-white photographs.

Boschung, Herbert T., David K. Caldwell, Melba C. Caldwell, Daniel W. Gotshall, and James D. Williams. **The Audubon Society Field Guide to North American Fishes, Whales, and Dolphins.** New York: Knopf, 1983. 848 p. (Audubon Society Field Guide series). $19. ISBN 0394534050.

A photographic guide to 521 species of marine vertebrates from both the Atlantic and Pacific Coasts of North America, with description plus information on habitat, range, and behavior. Another 400 species are briefly discussed.

Reader's Digest North American Wildlife. Mammals, Reptiles, and Amphibians. New York: Reader's Digest, 1998. 191 p. $16.95. ISBN 0762100354.

This field guide, which covers 230 species of mammals, 300 species of reptiles, and 200 species of amphibians, is excerpted from the *Reader's Digest North American Wildlife* (described in chapter 1). It provides color illustrations and range maps for the animals.

Shirihai, Hadoram. **The Complete Guide to Antarctic Wildlife: Birds and Marine Mammals of the Antarctic Continent and the Southern Ocean.** Princeton, NJ: Princeton University Press, 2002. 510 p. $49.50. ISBN 0691114145.

A single-volume guide to the wildlife of Antarctica and the surrounding islands and ocean, this guide provides species accounts, natural history information, and information for visitors for the breeding birds and marine mammals of the region. There are numerous maps and color photographs.

Association

Society of Vertebrate Paleontology. 60 Revere Dr., Ste. 500, Northbrook, IL 60062. Phone: 847-480-9282, Fax: 847-480-9282, E-mail: svp@vertpaleo. org. URL: http://www.vertpaleo.org/. (Accessed August 25, 2003).

5

Fishes

The fishes are a large group: there are about 25,000 species, or about half the described species of vertebrates. About 40% of all fish species occur in fresh water. We certainly have not discovered all species of fishes, whether freshwater or marine. The 16-foot-long megamouth shark (*Megachasma pelagios*) was discovered near Hawaii in 1976. The discovery of the coelacanth (*Latimeria chalumnae*) in 1938 was probably *the* new species discovery of the century, but the coelacanth story did not end there. A new species (*Latimeria menadoensis*) from Indonesia was found in 1998, 60 years after the original coelacanth was discovered in South Africa. And of course, there are certainly many deep-sea fishes waiting to be described.

The organisms we traditionally call "fish" actually represent a very taxonomically diverse group of animals, from the hagfishes to the bony fishes. The cladistic arrangement of fishes is very complex, because the hagfishes, lampreys, sharks, lobe-finned fishes, and ray-finned fishes are all in very different clades. Hagfishes lack a bony skeleton and even a braincase, whereas lampreys have braincases but also lack a skeleton and jaws. Sharks and rays add a cartilaginous skeleton and are famous for their jaws, and the bony fishes add a mineralized skeleton. The ray-finned fishes such as perch or tuna are the largest group of fishes; the lobe-finned fishes such as the coelacanth and lungfishes include the ancestors of the tetrapods (amphibians, reptiles, birds, and mammals). In this chapter, however, we follow the traditional grouping of fishes into three groups: lampreys and hagfishes, sharks and rays, and bony fishes.

183

There is general confusion about the plural of the word *fish*. Properly speaking, multiple individuals of the same species are referred to as "fish," and the plural of fish of differing species is *fishes*. Thus a school of tuna contains many fish, and tuna are one of the many species of predatory fishes.

Classification of Fishes (from Nelson, 1994)

Hyperoartia

Myxiniformes (hagfishes; 43 species)

Petromyzontiformes (lampreys; 41 species)

Chondrichthyes

Holocephali (chimaeras; 31 species)

Elasmobranchii (sharks and rays, 780 species)

Osteichthyes

Sarcopterygii (coelacanth and lungfishes; 7 species)

Actinopterygii (ray-finned fishes; 23,500 species)

Indexes, Abstracts, and Bibliographies

Dean, B. **A Bibliography of Fishes.** New York: American Museum of Natural History, 1916–23. 3 vol.

Based on the author's personal files, this bibliography provides indexes to the literature of fishes arranged by author, title, pre-Linnean publications, voyages and expeditions, periodicals, and subjects from 1758. It was continued in 1968 and 1969 under the title *Dean Bibliography of Fishes* by the American Museum of Natural History and was then incorporated into *Zoological Record* as part of the Pisces section.

Fish & Fisheries Worldwide. Baltimore: National Information Services Corp., 1992– . Quarterly. CD-ROM.

This CD-ROM contains citations from several databases, including *FISHLIT* (1985–present), *Fisheries Review* (1971–present), *Fishing Industry Research Institute (FIRI) Database* from Cape Town, South Africa, *Fish Database* (1960–present) from the Fish and Wildlife Reference Service, and *Castell's Nutrition References* (1970–present), among others.

Journals

Copeia. See entry in chapter 4.

Environmental Biology of Fishes. Vol. 1– . Dordrecht: Kluwer Academic, 1976– . Monthly. $1,499. ISSN 0378-1909. Available electronically.

Publishes original research articles on ecology, life history, epigenetics, behavior, physiology, morphology, systematics, and evolution of marine and freshwater fishes. The journal also occasionally publishes brief communications, editorials, rapid communications, essays, reviews, book reviews, and other article types.

Fish Physiology and Biochemistry. Vol. 1– . Kluwer, 1986– . 8/yr. $594. ISSN 0920-1742. Available electronically.

Publishes research articles on all aspects of the physiology and biochemistry of fishes. In addition to full papers, the journal also publishes brief communications, rapid communications, unsolicited and invited reviews, and editorial comments and announcements.

Ichthyological Research. Vol. 43– . Springer, 1996– . Quarterly. $248. ISSN 1341-8998. Available electronically.

The journal primarily publishes descriptive or experimental research on all aspects of fish biology, including taxonomy, systematics, evolution, biogeography, ecology, ethology, genetics, morphology, and physiology. It is an official journal of the Ichthyological Society of Japan, formerly titled *Gyoruigaku zasshi.*

Journal of Fish Biology. Vol. 1– . London: Academic Press, 1969– . Monthly. $1,802.86. ISSN 0022-1112. Available electronically.

The journal publishes research articles on all aspects of freshwater and marine fish and fisheries research including taxonomy. One topical review article is published per issue, and papers from the Annual Symposium of the Fisheries Society of the British Isles are published in a supplementary issue.

Journal of Ichthyology. Vol. 10– . Silver Spring, MD: Scripta, 1970– . Irregular. $2,690. ISSN 0032-9452.

Translation of the Russian *Voprosy Ikhtiologii.* Formerly *Problems of Ichthyology.*

Reviews in Fish Biology and Fisheries. Vol. 1– . Kluwer, 1991– . Quarterly. $518. ISSN 0960-3166. Available electronically.

This review journal publishes review articles on fish biology, including evolutionary biology, zoogeography, taxonomy, ecology, and various aspects of fisheries. It also publishes details of selected papers given at recent conferences, book reviews, and correspondence.

Transactions of the American Fisheries Society. Vol. 29– . Bethesda, MD: American Fisheries Society, 1900– . Bimonthly. ISSN 0002-8487. Available online.

Publishes research articles covering basic and applied research dealing with fish and fisheries. Formerly *Proceedings of the American Fisheries Society.* The journal is available to libraries only as part of a package including *North American Journal of Fisheries Management, North American Journal of Aquaculture,* and *Journal of Aquatic Animal Health.*

Guides to the Literature

Jackson, Keith L. **Ichthyology Web Resources.** 2000. URL: http://www2. biology.ualberta.ca/jackson.hp/IWR/index.php. (Accessed August 25, 2003).

This excellent site lists ichthyology resources of scientific and educational value. The sites are arranged by subject, including areas such as anatomy, behavior, biodiversity, taxonomy, techniques, and educational resources. There are also lists of associations, journals, directories, museums, and more.

Tisserand, Cecil T. **Elasmoworld.** URL: http://www.elasmoworld.org/main.html. (Accessed August 25, 2003).

Contains a variety of material dealing with sharks and their relatives, including a 4,000-item searchable bibliography, the directory for the American Elasmobranch Society (see Associations, below), extensive information about the biology of elasmobranchs, links to other sites, and much more.

Biographies and Histories

Cuvier, Georges. **Historical Portrait of the Progress of Ichthyology: From its Origins to Our Own Time.** Baltimore: Johns Hopkins University Press, 1995. 366 p. (Foundations of Natural History). $85. ISBN 0801849144.

Originally written in 1828 as part of Cuvier's *Histoire Naturelle des Poissons,* this is one of the most important and complete descriptions of the history of the science of ichthyology. It covers the period from the Egyptians to Cuvier's own time in chronological order and contains many illustrations. Cuvier discusses natural historians, collectors, explorers, and illustrators. A separate chapter talks about the development of museum and private collections. Both Günther and Jordan, below, owe a lot to Cuvier's work.

Günther, Albert C. L. G. **An Introduction to the Study of Fishes.** New York: Hafner, 1963. 720 p.

Günther was an important ichthyologist in the late nineteenth century, and this classic textbook includes a history of ichthyology. His emphasis is more on biography than Jordan's (below), and he includes a list of major expeditions, faunas, and important anatomical works. The text was originally published in 1880.

Jordan, David Starr. **A Guide to the Study of Fishes.** New York: Henry Holt, 1905. 2 vol.

Jordan was one of the most important American ichthyologists in his time, and this textbook provides a summary of the state of knowledge at the beginning of the twentieth century. In addition, chapter 22 is a history of ichthyology emphasizing the eighteenth and nineteenth centuries. There are several portraits of famous ichthyologists, including Dr. Jordan himself, although the emphasis is on the research rather than biographies of individuals.

Dictionaries and Encyclopedias

Commission of the European Communities. **Multilingual Illustrated Dictionary of Aquatic Animals and Plants.** 2nd ed. Oxford, UK: Fishing News Books, 1998. 548 p. $95. ISBN 0852382405; 9282818861.

Covers 1,532 species of fish, crustaceans, mollusks, seaweeds, and fishery products, providing scientific and family names plus common names in eleven European languages.

Jackson, Keith L. **Dictionary of Ichthyology-Related Terms.** 2000– . URL: http://www2.biology.ualberta.ca/jackson.hp/IWR/Dictionary/index. php (Accessed August 25, 2003).

This dictionary, part of the *Ichthyology World Resources* site listed under Guides to the Literature, has hyperlinked definitions to a number of terms used in ichthyology. Many of the terms relate to fish anatomy or taxonomy.

Negedly, Robert. **Elsevier's Dictionary of Fishery, Processing, Fish, and Shellfish Names of the World in Five Languages, English, French, Spanish, German, and Latin.** New York: Elsevier, 1990. 623 p. $201. ISBN 0444880399.

Covers terms in fishing methods, fishing vessels, fish processing, fish products, fishery biology, ichthyology, and both scientific and common names of crustaceans, mollusks, and marine mammals. Appendixes provide a table of catch units and a list of abbreviations of fishery institutions and other terms. The main section is in alphabetical order in English, and there are indexes to French, Spanish, German, and Latin.

Organisation for Economic Co-operation and Development. **Multilingual Dictionary of Fish and Fish Products.** 4th ed. Cambridge, MA: Fishing News Books, 1995. 352 p. $62. ISBN 0852382162.

Covering over 1,200 species or fish products, this dictionary provides definitions in 18 European languages.

Paxton, John R., and William N. Eschmeyer, eds. **Encyclopedia of Fishes.** 2nd ed. San Diego: Academic Press, 1998. 240 p. (Natural World Series). $39.95. ISBN 0125476655.

This colorful encyclopedia provides a description of the major families of fishes. There is an introductory section with information on the classification, evolution, adaptations, and behavior of fishes, plus a discussion of endangered species. The remainder of the encyclopedia covers the orders of fishes, starting with the Agnatha. Each chapter contains many color photographs and illustrations, and there are distribution maps and a boxed "Key Facts" section listing the number of species, the smallest and largest members of the order, and conservation status.

Rojo, Alfonso L. **Dictionary of Evolutionary Fish Osteology.** Boca Raton: CRC Press, 1991. 273 p. $84.95. ISBN 0849342147.

The dictionary covers 375 terms, primarily the names of the bones of fish. The terms are arranged alphabetically in English, and definitions are also in English with the name translated into French, German, Latin, Russian, and Spanish. There are numerous illustrations, an extensive bibliography, and indexes in each language.

Sterba, Günther. **Freshwater Fishes of the World.** Rev. ed. Hong Kong: TFH, 1973. 2 vol. $390. ISBN 0785500561.

Although long out of print, this encyclopedia still provides a useful survey of about 1,300 species of aquarium fishes, including many species not normally thought of as aquarium fishes. Each species account includes author, distribution, description, and care. It is a translation of *Süsswasserfische aus aller Welt.*

Wheeler, Alwyne C. **The World Encyclopedia of Fishes.** London: Macdonald and Queen Anne Press, 1985. 368 p. ISBN 0356107159.

This encyclopedia includes numerous color plates in addition to line drawings. It is in two sections, one containing color plates arranged by family and a dictionary section listing fish species by scientific name. The species accounts include information on common name, distribution, size, diet, and so on. Common names are cross-referenced to the scientific name. Nelson, above, only lists families and subfamilies.

Textbooks

Bond, Carl E. **Biology of Fishes.** 2nd ed. Fort Worth: Saunders College, 1996. 750 p. $92.95. ISBN 0030703425.

A basic textbook covering the biology of fishes, including the jawless hagfishes and lampreys. The text is in four parts, discussing introductory material, evolution and diversity, biology, and ecology. The evolution and diversity section provides a detailed discussion of the families of fishes down to the level of the suborder.

Bone, Q., N. B. Marshall, and J. H. S. Blaxter. **Biology of Fishes.** 2nd ed. New York: Chapman & Hall, 1994. 288 p. $59.95 (paper). ISBN 075140022X; 0412741407 (paper).

More advanced than Bond, above, this textbook discusses all aspects of fish biology. Fish diversity and habitats are covered in two short chapters, and the bulk of the book discusses locomotion, buoyancy, physiology, reproduction, sensory and nervous systems, behavior, and fisheries.

Diana, James S. **Biology and Ecology of Fishes.** Carmel, IN: Biological Sciences Press, a Division of Cooper Publishing Group, 1995. 441 p. $45. ISBN 1884125247.

Designed for use in upper undergraduate and graduate courses in fisheries biology or fish ecology, this text emphasizes fish ecology rather than biology or classification. The author discusses general ecological subjects such as predator/prey relations and reproductive strategies as well as specific aquatic ecosystems.

Evans, David H., ed. **Physiology of Fishes.** 2nd ed. Boca Raton: CRC Press, 1998. 519 p. (Marine Science series). $119.95. ISBN 0849384273.

This text, which provides a review of fish physiology, is designed for both students and researchers. It is in four broad sections, covering locomotion and energetics, gas exchange and cardiovascular physiology, homeostasis, and neurobiology. There are systematic and general indexes.

Helfman, Gene S., Bruce B. Collette, and Douglas E. Facey. **The Diversity of Fishes.** Malden, MA: Blackwell Science, 1997. 528 p. $82.95. ISBN 0865422567.

Covers both fish biology and taxonomy. The text, designed for both upper-level undergraduate and graduate students, is in six parts: introduction, form and function, taxonomy and evolution, habitats, behavior and ecology, and conservation.

Moyle, Peter B. **Fish: An Enthusiast's Guide.** Berkeley: University of California Press, 1993. 272 p. ISBN 0520079779.

A popular guide to fish biology. The author covers biology, anatomy, diversity, and ecology of North American fish. There are separate chapters on each major marine and freshwater ecosystem such as lakes, streams, and reservoirs.

Moyle, Peter B., and Joseph J. Cech, Jr. **Fishes: An Introduction to Ichthyology.** 4th ed. Upper Saddle River, NJ: Prentice Hall, 2000. 612 p. $92. ISBN 0130112828.

An undergraduate text for fish biology courses in five parts: introduction, structure and form, systematics, zoogeography, and ecology. The emphasis is on the biology and ecology of the fishes, not systematics.

Checklists and Classification Schemes

2002 Seafood List. Center for Food Safety and Applied Nutrition, U.S. Food and Drug Administration. URL: http://vm.cfsan.fda.gov/~frf/seaintro.html. (Accessed August 25, 2003).

This site lists acceptable market names for imported and domestically available seafood as well as scientific names, common names, and known vernacular or regional names. It updates the print edition of *The Seafood List: FDA's Guide to Acceptable Market Names for Seafood Sold in Interstate Commerce* published by the U.S. Government Printing Office in 1993, which is out of print.

Berg, L. S. **Classification of Fishes both Recent and Fossil.** Ann Arbor: J. W. Edwards, 1947. 88–517 p. $135.80. ISBN 0598529403.

A reprint and translation from the Russian of Berg's original text, this classic work on fish taxonomy is still being cited. It was originally published in the journal *Akademiia nauk SSSR. Trudy Zoologicheskogo instituta,* vol. 5, part 2 in 1940.

Common and Scientific Names of Fishes from the United States and Canada. 5th ed. C. Richard Robins et al., eds. Bethesda, MD: American Fisheries Society, 1991. 183 p. (American Fisheries Society, no. 20). $43; $34 (paper). ISBN 0913235709; 0913235695 (paper).

Previous editions published as *A List of Common and Scientific Names of Fishes*... The list provides approved common names for the fishes of North America. It contains scientific and common names, occurrence, references for first description, and appendixes on exotics and hybrid fishes.

Jordan, David Starr. **The Genera of Fishes and a Classification of Fishes.** Stanford, CA: Stanford University Press, 1963. 800 p. $100. ISBN 0804702012.

A reprint of Jordan's classic works, *The Genera of Fishes* (1917–20) and *A Classification of Fishes* (1923). The catalog was an attempt to identify all generic names of fishes and stabilize their nomenclature. Unlike most catalogs, Jordan takes a chronological approach, covering different time periods in each part and listing all the names proposed by major ichthyologists in their individual works. The *Classification of Fishes* was an attempt to list all generic names and list them in their proper families. Although both books are outdated and should be used with care, they are still frequently cited.

Jordan, David Starr, Barton Warren Evermann, and Howard Walton Clark. **A Check List of the Fishes and Fishlike Vertebrates of North and Middle America, North of Venezuela and Colombia.** Ashton, MD: Lundberg, 1962. 670 p.

Originally printed as the U.S. Bureau of Fisheries Document 1055 in 1930, this classic checklist covers 4,139 valid species from lancelets to teleosts. The accounts include authors, synonymy, common names, and distribution.

Luca, Florenza de. **Taxonomic Authority List: Aquatic Sciences and Fisheries Information System.** Rome, Italy: Food and Agriculture Organization of the United Nations, 1988. 465 p. (Casfis Reference Series, no. 8). $55. ISBN 9251027722.

The list contains over 10,000 terms, in systematic and alphabetical lists, with the date and original author of the term. Created by the Aquatic Sciences and Fisheries Information System for use in preparing the *FAO Yearbook of Fishery Statistics* and the *Aquatic Sciences and Fisheries Abstracts.*

Robins, C. Richard, and Reeve M. Bailey. **World Fishes Important to North Americans: Exclusive of Species from the Continental Waters of the United States and Canada.** Bethesda, MD: American Fisheries Society, 1991. 243 p. (American Fisheries Society Special Publication, no. 21). $47; $39 (paper). ISBN 0913235547; 0913235539 (paper).

This list provides standard common names for economically important species of fishes. Each entry contains the common and scientific names, alternate common names, reason for considering the species important, range and habitat, and remarks.

Systematic Section

Chondrichthyes

Compagno, Leonard J. V. **Sharks of the World: An Annotated and Illustrated Catalogue of Shark Species Known to Date.** New York: United Nations Development Programme, 1984. 2 vol. (FAO Fisheries Synopsis, no. 125, vol. 4, pt. 1 and 2; FAO Species Catalogue, vol. 4, pt. 1 and 2).

One of the standard catalogs of the sharks, this is part of the series of FAO species catalogs intended to describe fish of economic importance. As in the other volumes in the series, the author provides keys and detailed species accounts. See the series annotation for full description.

Mould, Brian. **A Classification of the Recent Elasmobranchii.** 1997. URL: http://ibis.nott.ac.uk/elasmobranch.html. (Accessed August 25, 2003).

This site provides access to the PDF file of the author's classification of the sharks and rays. The publication lists scientific names, type localities, and distributional ranges of the living sharks and rays of the world.

Osteichthyes

Gosline, William A. **Functional Morphology and Classification of Teleostean Fishes.** Honolulu: University Press of Hawaii, 1971. 208 p. ISBN 0870223003.

The author proposes using functional morphological characteristics to classify fish families. The book is in two parts, one providing an overview of the morphological characteristics the author feels are useful in classifying fish and the other listing his classification system. The orders and families are described in detail.

Handbooks

Berra, Tim M. **An Atlas of Distribution of the Freshwater Fish Families of the World.** Lincoln: University of Nebraska Press, 1981. 197 p. ISBN 0803214111; 0803260598 (paper).

Designed as a supplement to courses in ichthyology and biogeography, this atlas contains maps showing the worldwide distribution of freshwater fish families, including a few families of marine fishes that may be found in coastal rivers. Each family account includes the map, a line drawing of a representative member of the family, natural history or taxonomy notes, and references. Appendixes list the principal rivers and lakes of the world, provide a geological time chart, and list some popular magazine articles and identification guides.

Cailliet, Gregor M., Milton S. Love, and Alfred W. Ebeling. **Fishes: A Field and Laboratory Manual on Their Structure, Identification, and Natural History.** Belmont, CA: Wadsworth, 1986. 194 p. ISBN 0534055567 (paper).

Includes laboratory exercises and methods for studying the various aspects of ichthyology, such as dissecting and identifying fish in the lab and capture methods in the field.

Chapman & Hall Fish and Fisheries Series. Vol. 1– . Boston: Kluwer Academic, 1990– . Irregular. Price varies.

This series covers a variety of subjects in fish biology and fisheries. Up to 2002, 23 volumes have been published in such areas as fish behavior, bioenergetics, genetics, and ecology. Some volumes cover a specific group of fish such as pike or electric fishes.

Eschmeyer, William N. **Catalog of Fishes.** San Francisco: California Academy of Sciences, 1998. 3 vol. plus CD-ROM. $150. ISBN 0940228475.

This catalog lists genera in alphabetical order with name, author, date, type specimen, remarks, and status. Separate sections list names by class and provide literature cited. Updates the author's *Catalog of the Genera of Recent Fishes,* published in 1990. Available on the Web at http://www.calacademy.org/research/ichthyology/catalog/. The online version includes all species, genera, and references, along with the classification, introduction, and list of museum abbreviations from the print version, but excludes the appendixes and other material.

FAO Species Catalogue. Vol. 1– . Rome: Food and Agriculture Organization of the United Nations, 1980– . (FAO Fisheries Synopsis, vol. 125). Irregular. Price varies.

This series within a series covers the major groups of fishes and marine invertebrates of economic importance. They are in a standard format, with each species account providing an illustration, distribution map, synonyms, approved common names, description, habitat, size, fisheries importance, and references. There are keys as well. The format is similar to the FAO Species Identification Guides for Fishery Purposes series (see the Identification Tools section, below), which takes a geographical rather than systematic approach. Families covered to date include sharks, clupeoid fishes (herrings and relatives), fusiliers, emperorfish, gadiiforms, nempterids, snake mackerels, groupers, pearl perches, and ophidiiforms.

Froese, R., and D. Pauly, eds. **FishBase: A Global Information System on Fishes.** Makati City, Philippines: FishBase, 2002– . URL: http://www.fishbase.org/home.htm. (Accessed August 25, 2003).

FishBase is a relational database containing data on almost all known species of fishes. It can be searched on the Web but is also available as four CD-ROMs for $95. Each species account summarizes information on classification, size, habitat, description, biology, fisheries importance and status, and references, and contains links to more detailed information on everything from allele frequencies to vision. The *FishBase* site also has a utility allowing fish watchers to link observations to the *FishBase* records, a forum, useful links, and more fish-related information.

Harder, Wilhelm. **Anatomy of Fishes.** Stuttgart: Schweizerbart, 1975. 2 vol. $154. ISBN 3510650670 (set).

This set provides a detailed description of the anatomy of fishes, with emphasis on the Osteichthyes. The Agnatha are excluded altogether. The first volume contains text; the figures and plates were published in the second volume.

Hoar, W. S., and D. J. Randall, eds. **Fish Physiology.** Vol. 1– . New York: Academic Press, 1969– . Irregular. Price varies.

Each volume in this ongoing series covers different aspects of fish physiology, such as the gills, locomotion, reproduction, and so on. There are author, systematic, and subject indexes in each volume. The set is currently up to Volume 20, *Nitrogen Excretion.*

Hochachka, Peter W., and T. P. Mommsen, eds. **Biochemistry and Molecular Biology of Fishes.** New York: Elsevier, 1991–95. 5 vol. ISBN 0444891854 (set).

This treatise gathers together the scattered literature on the molecular biology and biochemistry of fishes for both students and researchers.

Kocher, Thomas D., and Carol A. Stepien, eds. **Molecular Systematics of Fishes.** San Diego: Academic Press, 1997. 314 p. $93.95. ISBN 0124175406.

The first volume to discuss the results of DNA sequencing and its application in the systematics of fishes, this book covers a variety of topics. The authors discuss the phylogeny of several fish groups such as cichlids, blennies, and sharks as well as basic topics such as the rate of base substitution in fishes, major histocompatibility complex genes, and molecular clocks.

Lindberg, G. U. **Fishes of the World: A Key to Families and a Checklist.** New York: Wiley, 1974. 545 p. ISBN 0470535652.

Translated from the original Russian, this is a classic survey of fish biodiversity. It contains a checklist of all of the fish families, plus illustrated keys to families and orders. The checklist includes published sources and commercial orders. The book also includes a very extensive bibliography arranged by broad subject (systematics, general, and regional) and indexes to scientific and common names in European languages, Russian, and Chinese and Japanese.

Migdalski, Edward C., and George S. Fichter. **The Fresh and Salt Water Fishes of the World.** New York: Knopf, 1976. 316 p. ISBN 0394492390.

A colorful survey of the fishes of the world designed for the general public, this book covers the families of fishes of the world. Each family is described and the natural history of typical or interesting species discussed. Excellent color illustrations of selected species mingle with the family descriptions. The authors have also provided saltwater and freshwater record fishes for the anglers.

Nelson, Joseph S. **Fishes of the World.** 3rd ed. New York: Wiley, 1994. 600 p. $199. ISBN 0471547131.

Provides a systematic overview of the fishes of the world. The author provides a brief overview of fish biology, diversity, classification, and biogeography. The remainder of the book is a systematic description of fish orders, families, and subfamilies, including a brief description of the urochordates and cephalochordates. Most of the descriptions include a line drawing of a typical member, description, citation to major publications, distribution, and occasionally genera or species. An appendix serves as a checklist and classification scheme, and there are also very extensive references. The distribution maps found in the second edition have been removed, however.

Ontogeny and Systematics of Fishes. New York: American Society of Ichthyologists and Herpetologists, 1984. 760 p. (Special Publication of the American Society of Ichthyologists and Herpetologists, no. 1).

This handbook is based on an international symposium in honor of Elbert Halvor Ahlstrom, held in 1983. The papers discuss the relationship between the early life history and systematics in fishes. There are introductory chapters discussing techniques as well as more specific chapters covering many of the major families or orders. The systematic discussions include illustrations of developmental stages of various species, a discussion of the known aspects of the development of the group, and how this relates to taxonomy.

Schreck, Carl B., and Peter B. Moyle, eds. **Methods for Fish Biology.** Bethesda, MD: American Fisheries Society, 1990. 684 p. $64. ISBN 091323558X.

This manual provides techniques for taxonomic, biological, and behavioral studies of fishes. It also includes information on histology and surgery and on keeping fish in captivity.

Stiassny, Melanie L. J., Lynne R. Parenti, and G. David Johnson, eds. **Interrelationships of Fishes.** San Diego: Academic, 1996. 496 p. $122.95. ISBN 0126709505 (paper).

Updates the volume by the same name published in 1973 as a supplement to the *Zoological Journal of the Linnean Society.* Each chapter discusses the phylogenetic relationships of a particular group of fishes. The morphological characteristics of the species are emphasized. Cladograms and classification or nomenclatural recommendations are given for each group, and most chapters also list the specimens examined, data matrix, and characters used in constructing the cladogram.

Systematic Section

Agnatha

Hardisty, M. W. **Biology of the Cyclostomes.** London: Chapman & Hall, 1979. 428 p. ISBN 0412141205.

Summarizes known aspects of the biology of hagfishes and lampreys. The author, one of the editors of the series discussed below, covers distribution and lifestyles, relationships with other vertebrates, ecology, respiration, anatomy, physiology, and biochemistry of this little-studied group.

Hardisty, M. W., and I. C. Potter, eds. **The Biology of Lampreys.** New York: Academic Press, 1971–82. 4 vol. in 5. $209 (vol. 4b). ISBN 0123248019 (vol. 1); 0123248248 (vol. 4b).

This series attempts to cover all aspects of the biology of lampreys. Volume 1 contains review articles on taxonomy, fossil record, general biology, ecology, and other subjects, and the remaining three volumes discuss more specialized physiological and anatomical topics. Some of the chapters in the final volume update material discussed in earlier volumes.

Jørgensen, Jørgen Mørup, et al., eds. **The Biology of Hagfishes.** New York: Chapman & Hall, 1998. 578 p. $234.50. ISBN 0412785307.

Updates the classic *The Biology of Myxine* by A. Brodal and Ragnar Fänge with chapters on the evolution, development, anatomy, and physiology of hagfishes.

Chondrichthyes

Ashley, Laurence M., and Robert B. Chiasson. **Laboratory Anatomy of the Shark.** 5th ed. Dubuque, IA: W.C. Brown, 1988. 84 p. (Laboratory Anatomy series). $47.60. ISBN 0697051218.

An atlas of shark anatomy featuring line drawings of anatomical features.

Hamlett, William C., ed. **Sharks, Skates, and Rays: The Biology of Elasmobranch Fishes.** Baltimore: Johns Hopkins University Press, 1999. 515 p. $129.95. ISBN 0801860482.

Covering all aspects of the biology of the Chondrichthyes, this treatise updates Dr. Frank Daniel's *The Elasmobranch Fishes*. Chapters cover systematics, anatomy, and physiology, and there is also a checklist of the living species.

Springer, Victor Gruschka, and Joy P. Gold. **Sharks in Question: The Smithsonian Answer Book.** Washington, DC: Smithsonian Institution Press, 1989. 187 p. $24.95. ISBN 0874748771 (paper).

A popular guide to the most frequently asked questions about sharks, this book covers questions such as "Do sharks get sick?" as well as shark attacks and other questions about shark biology. The authors also provide general information about shark classification and well-known or interesting shark species. Appendixes provide an outline of shark classification and selected common and scientific names.

Osteichthyes

All Catfish Species Inventory. Philadelphia: Academy of Natural Sciences, 2002. URL: http://clade.acnatsci.org/allcatfish/ (Accessed August 25, 2003).

A project designed to facilitate the description and dissemination of information about catfish species. Over 2,700 species are currently known, and the authors estimate another 1,750 are waiting to be discovered. The site includes a catfish gallery, information on catfish specimen repositories, a bibliography, news and announcements, and more.

Axelrod, Herbert R. **The Most Complete Colored Lexicon of Cichlids: Every Known Cichlid Illustrated in Color.** 2nd ed. Neptune, NJ: TFH, 1996. 864 p. $100. ISBN 0793800269.

Cichlids are a large and important family of fishes. They include the commercially valuable tilapia as well as many popular aquarium fishes such as angelfish and discus. This massive volume features color photographs or illustrations of all 1,500 known species of cichlids along with notes on their behavior, reproduction, and value. The book is arranged by region, with genera listed alphabetically within each location.

Bemis, William E., Warren W. Burggren, and Norman E. Kemp, eds. **The Biology and Evolution of Lungfishes: A Centennial Supplement to the** *Journal of Morphology.* New York: A.R. Liss, 1987. 383 p. ISBN 0845142259.

The articles published in this volume are based on the proceedings of a symposium in 1984. It covers a wide range of topics in lungfish biology, including a list of lungfish species, a 2,200-item bibliography of lungfishes covering the years 1811 to 1985, paleontology and systematics, and the biology of lungfishes.

Chiasson, Robert B., and William Radke. **Laboratory Anatomy of the Perch.** 4th ed. Boston: WCB McGraw-Hill, 1991. 93 p. (Laboratory Anatomy series). $47.60. ISBN 0697049396.

A standard atlas of the anatomy of a typical fish, the perch.

Géry, Jacques. **Characoids of the World.** Neptune City, NJ: TFH, 1977. 672 p. ISBN 0876664583.

Designed for both aquarists and zoologists, this book surveys the characoids, an order of fish that includes tetras, piranhas, and other popular aquarium fishes. They are found in Africa and South America. The author provides keys to species and a detailed account of their systematics, as well as color photographs of the species most likely to be found in aquaria.

Horn, Michael H., Karen L.M. Martin, and Michael A. Chotkowski, eds. **Intertidal Fishes: Life in Two Worlds.** San Diego: Academic Press, 1999. 399 p. $81.95. ISBN 0123560403.

Intertidal fishes live at the interface between the air and water, which presents them with interesting challenges and opportunities. This text describes methods for studying intertidal fishes and describes their physiology, behavior, reproduction, and communities. It also covers the systematics, biogeography, and evolution of intertidal fishes and provides an annotated list of species.

Moller, Peter. **Electric Fishes: History and Behavior.** New York: Chapman & Hall, 1995. 584 p. (Chapman & Hall Fish and Fisheries series, no. 17). $253. ISBN 0412373807.

A survey of the electric fishes, this book covers the history of the study of electric fishes, the behavior of weakly and strongly discharging species, the electric sensorimotor system in electric fishes, and the taxonomy, zoogeography, and ecology of this interesting group of fish. In addition to his extensive list of references, the author also provides an appendix highlighting some of the major reviews on electric fishes.

Musick, John A., Michael N. Bruton, and Eugene K. Balon, eds. **The Biology of *Latimeria chalumnae* and Evolution of Coelacanths.** Boston: Kluwer Academic, 1991. 446 p. (Developments in Environmental Biology of Fishes, no. 12). $283.00; $160.50 (paper). ISBN 0792312244; 0792312899 (paper).

Several groups of scientists cooperated to prepare this volume, intended for publication on the 50th anniversary of the original description of the species in 1939. The topics covered in the volume range from systematics and evolution to biology to conservation of the coelacanth. The volume also includes an inventory of all known specimens plus bibliographies of fossil and living coelacanths, a chronology of the study of *Latimeria,* and numerous drawings of coelacanths done by everyone from students to professional artists. Reprinted from *Environmental Biology of Fishes* 32 (1–4), 1991.

Steene, Roger C., Gerald R. Allen, and Hans A. Baensch. **Butterfly and Angelfishes of the World.** New York: Wiley, 1978–80. 2 vol. ISBN 0471047376 (vol. 1); 0471056189 (vol. 2).

Volume 1 of this set covers the Chaetodontidae of Australia and New Guinea; Volume 2 covers the western part of New Guinea. The volumes are lavishly illustrated with color photographs of the fish, and each species account includes description, behavior, food, distribution, and often tips for aquarists.

Geographical Section

North America

Allen, M. James, and Gary B. Smith. **Atlas and Zoogeography of Common Fishes in the Bering Sea and Northeastern Pacific.** Seattle: U.S. Department of Commerce, National Oceanic and Atmospheric Administration, National Marine Fisheries Service, 1988. 151 p. (NOAA Technical Report NMFS, no. 66).

Covers 124 common species of fishes from the northeastern Pacific. The geographical range of the fishes is based on catch records over a 30-year period. Each species account includes a distribution map with depth information, brief survey of the literature reporting on distributions, survey data, and conclusions on the species' zoogeography, life zone, range, and depth.

Böhlke, James E., and Charles C. G. Chaplin. **Fishes of the Bahamas and Adjacent Tropical Waters.** 2nd ed. Austin: University of Texas Press, 1993. 771 p. $135. ISBN 0292707924.

Originally published in 1968, this catalog describes the fishes found to depths of about 100 feet and includes keys and descriptions.

Carlander, Kenneth D. **Handbook of Freshwater Fishery Biology.** 3rd ed. Ames: Iowa State University Press, 1969–97. 3 vol. $59.99 (vol. 3). ISBN 0813806704 (vol. 2); 0813807093; 0813829992 (vol. 3).

This handbook summarizes data on the life histories of North American freshwater fishes, including range and habitat, reproduction data, food habits, age at maturity, growth, length/weight, and condition data. Volume 1 is the third edition of data on fishes exclusive of the Perciformes, Volume 2 is the first edition on Centrarchid fishes, and Volume 3 is the first edition on Ichthyopercid and percid fishes.

Hocutt, Charles H., and E. O. Wiley, eds. **The Zoogeography of North American Freshwater Fishes.** New York: Wiley, 1986. 866 p. ISBN 0471864196.

An analysis of the data presented by Lee et al. in their *Atlas of North American Freshwater Fishes* (below), this book summarizes the zoogeography of the fish of North America. It is arranged by geographical region because the phylogenetic relationships of the fishes was not well understood at the time.

Hubbs, Carl L., and Karl Frank Lagler. **Fishes of the Great Lakes Region.** Ann Arbor: University of Michigan Press, 1964. 213 p. Reprint.

A classic regional study covering the Great Lakes and their tributaries. It was originally published in 1954 as Bulletin 26 of the Cranbrook Institute of Science. The handbook lists 234 species in 13 orders and provides an illustrated key to the family level, plus keys to species of adults and larvae (as needed). Each family is described in general, and brief species accounts provide information on the distribution and habitat of the fish. There are also color plates for 44 species as well as black-and-white photographs and line drawings. The book is designed for both students and researchers, so the introduction describes the fish fauna of the region and gives methods of collecting, studying, and identifying fish.

Jordan, David Starr, and Barton Warren Evermann. **The Fishes of North and Middle America: A Descriptive Catalogue of the Species of Fish-Like Vertebrates Found in the Waters of North America, North of the Isthmus of Panama.** Washington, DC: U.S. Government Printing Office, 1896–1900. 4 vol. (Bulletin of the United States National Museum, no. 47).

This classic catalog, now outdated in its details, is still one of the most comprehensive works on the fishes of North and Central America. It also covers the West Indies, the Caribbean Sea, and the Galápagos as well as marine species found north of the Equator. The accounts include synonymy, description, distribution, and citations. Volume 3 includes a key to families, a glossary, and an index for the first three volumes; Volume 4 contains addenda, plus plates illustrating about 900 species of fish. The set was reprinted in 1963 by TFH Publications.

Lee, David S., et al. **Atlas of North American Freshwater Fishes.** Raleigh: North Carolina State Museum of Natural History, 1980. 854 p. ISBN 0917134036.

Provides distribution information on the freshwater fishes of the United States and Canada. Each species account contains information on the biology of the fish, its systematics, distribution, and habitat. There are also black-and-white illustrations and distribution maps. A supplement was published in 1983.

Mayden, Richard L., ed. **Systematics, Historical Ecology, and North American Freshwater Fishes.** Stanford, CA: Stanford University Press, 1992. 969 p. $105. ISBN 0804721629.

This volume is designed to provide a holistic examination of the value of using phylogenetic information to examine the biology and ecology of fishes. Topics include general discussion of phylogeny and fishes, the phylogenetic relationships of North American fishes, morphology and genetics, ecology and evolution, and speciation and biogeography.

McEachran, John D., and Janice D. Fechhelm. **Fishes of the Gulf of Mexico.** Austin: University of Texas Press, 1998– . vol. $125 (vol. 1). ISBN 0292752067 (vol. 1).

Unlike Hoese, below, this set gathers together information on the fishes of the entire Gulf of Mexico, covering 44 orders. There are keys to families, genera, and species, and each species account provides a description of the species with a black-and-white illustration, along with information on the distribution, habitat, and food sources along with references. The set will be in two volumes. The first volume covers the Myxiniformes to Gasterosteiformes.

Scott, W. B., and M. G. Scott. **Atlantic Fishes of Canada.** Toronto: University of Toronto Press, 1988. 731 p. (Canadian Bulletin of Fisheries and Aquatic Sciences, no. 219). $54. ISBN 0802057128.

Replaces *Fishes of the Atlantic Coast of Canada,* published in 1966. The text provides detailed species accounts for all the fishes found from northern Labrador south to the United States. A checklist and keys are also provided. The species accounts include information on the biology, distribution, fisheries importance, description, systematic notes, and common names. The species are also illustrated by drawings or black-and-white photographs.

Sigler, William F., and John W. Sigler. **Fishes of the Great Basin: A Natural History.** Reno: University of Nevada Press, 1987. 425 p. (Max C. Fleischmann Series in Great Basin Natural History). $49.95. ISBN 0874171164.

Another very useful regional fauna, this guide covers primarily Nevada and adjoining portions of California, Oregon, and Utah. The authors provide chapters introducing the region and its fishes, plus an illustrated key to species as well as detailed species accounts of approximately 90 species of fish found in the region. The species accounts include extensive information on the natural history of the fish, including importance, range, description, size, limiting factors, food, habitat, and conservation. There are black-and-white illustrations for each species as well as a few color plates.

Tee-Van, John, et al., eds. **Fishes of the Western North Atlantic.** New Haven: Sears Foundation for Marine Research, Yale University, 1948–89. 9 vol. (Sears Foundation for Marine Research, Memoir, no. 1).

This set synthesizes information on the fishes of the western half of the North Atlantic from Hudson Bay to the Amazon River. The set covers lancelets and Agnatha as well as Chondrychthyes and Osteichthyes. The accounts include information on the biology, nomenclature, range, distinctive characters, and references.

Tomelleri, Joseph R., and Mark E. Eberle. **Fishes of the Central United States.** Lawrence: University Press of Kansas, 1990. 226 p. $35.00; $17.95 (paper). ISBN 070060457X; 0700604588 (paper).

Covers 120 species of fish found from Montana to Wisconsin in the north and eastern New Mexico to Mississippi in the south. Species of importance to anglers are covered in greater depth. Each species account lists common names, the derivation of the scientific name, distribution, size, status, and general notes on their ecology and feeding, many of them of interest to anglers. The first author provided excellent color illustrations of each fish species.

Africa

Daget, J., J.-P. Gosse, and D. F. E. Thys van den Audenaerde, eds. **Checklist of the Freshwater Fishes of Africa, Cloffa.** Paris: ORSTOM, 1984–86. 3 vol. ISBN 2871770026 (vol. 2), 2871770034 (vol. 3).

The checklist covers 993 species of fish found in continental Africa as well as the nearby islands such as Madagascar and Mauritius.

Dor, Menahem. **CLOFRES: Checklist of the Fishes of the Red Sea.** Jerusalem: Israel Academy of Sciences and Humanities, 1984. 437 p. (Publications of the Israel Academy of Sciences and Humanities, Section of Sciences). ISBN 9652080616.

One of a series of similar fish checklists, this volume covers all species recorded in the Red Sea, a total of about 1,000 species. In addition to recording the original description and citations to information on the distribution of each species, the checklist includes the museum holding each type specimen. The bibliography includes all publications dealing with the fishes of the Red Sea, including systematics, zoogeography, ecology, and biology.

Goren, Menachem, and Menaham Dor. **An Updated Checklist of the Fishes of the Red Sea: CLOFRES II.** Jerusalem: Israel Academy of Sciences and Humanities, 1994. 120 p. ISBN 9652081140.

Updates Dor's original *CLOFRES* volume, above.

Randall, John E. **Coastal Fishes of Oman.** Honolulu: University of Hawaii Press, 1995. 439 p. $65. ISBN 0824818083.

Like the other regional fish guides published by the University of Hawaii Press, this book provides high-quality color photographs of the 930 species of fishes it covers. Oman is on the eastern edge of the Arabian Peninsula, and the guide covers both the fishes of the Gulf of Oman and the portion of the Arabian Sea that borders Oman. Each species account includes illustration and description, typically including detailed diagnostic features plus more general information on distribution.

Smith, Margaret Mary, and Phillip C. Heemstra, eds. **Smith's Sea Fishes.** 6th ed. New York: Springer-Verlag, 1986. 1,047 p. $279. ISBN 0387168516.

First published in 1949, this massive tome identifies the 2,200 species of fishes known to occur off the shores of southern Africa between Namibia on the west coast and Mozambique on the east. The book is in several sections, including an introduction to fishes, classification, and the region. This is followed by the main systematic section, which contains the species accounts and keys. Each species is illustrated and has a brief technical description and distribution and habitat information. There is also a separate section with color plates and a reference section with a key using fin spines, glossary, bibliography, and indexes to scientific, English, and Afrikaans common names.

Antarctica

Eastman, Joseph T. **Antarctic Fish Biology: Evolution in a Unique Environment.** San Diego: Academic Press, 1993. 322 p. $102. ISBN 0122281403.

Covers the biology of the fishes found in the Antarctic Ocean, especially the endemic notothenoids. The book is in three parts, discussing the past and present environment, the taxonomy and zoogeography of the modern fish fauna, and adaptations found in Antarctic fishes.

Gon, O., and Phillip C. Heemstra, eds. **Fishes of the Southern Ocean.** Grahamstown, South Africa: J. L. B. Smith Institute of Ichthyology, 1990. 462 p. ISBN 0868102113.

This catalog of the fishes of the Antarctic Ocean includes a more extensive discussion of the biology, exploitation, and origin of the Antarctic fish fauna than Miller's later volume, below. The species accounts include keys to genera and species, illustration of the whole fish and an otolith, map, diagnosis, distribution, and remarks.

Miller, Richard Gordon, Philip A. Hastings, and Josette Gourley. **History and Atlas of the Fishes of the Antarctic Ocean.** Carson City, NV: Foresta Institute for Ocean and Mountain Studies, 1993. 792 p. $162. ISBN 0963443607.

A combination history of Antarctic ichthyology and catalog of Antarctic fishes, this volume summarizes the state of our knowledge of this region of the world. The catalog section includes keys to species, and each species account includes illustrations, maps, description, identification tips, remarks, size, distribution, depth, biology, and notes. The historical section discusses the geology and biology of the Antarctic Ocean as well as the history of various expeditions to the Antarctic from the famous to the obscure. It includes many photographs of explorer/ichthyologists and the region.

Asia

Jayaram, K.C. **The Freshwater Fishes of the Indian Region.** Delhi: Narendra, 1999. 551 p. ISBN 8185375542.

This handbook covers 852 species of freshwater fishes of the Indian subcontinent. The author provides background information and descriptions of each order and family of fishes, along with keys to families, genera, and species. Each species account includes citations, diagnostic features, and distribution. There are numerous black-and-white illustrations.

Masuda, H., et al., eds. **The Fishes of the Japanese Archipelago.** Tokyo: Tokai University Press, 1984. 2 vol. ISBN 4486050541.

Including over 3,200 species of freshwater and marine fishes found within 200 miles of Japan, this handbook illustrates and describes the fish of the region. The species accounts include name, author, Japanese common name, description, and distribution. The English names of families and subfamilies are usually included as well. The first volume of the set contains the text; the second contains plates, most of them color photographs.

Nichols, J.T. **The Fresh-Water Fishes of China.** New York: American Museum of Natural History, 1943. 322 p. (Central Asiatic Expeditions of the American Museum of Natural History. Natural History of Central Asia, vol. 9).

Based on the collections made during the Asiatic expeditions in the 1920s and 1930s, this book provides a general report on the American Museum of Natural History's collections and reviews the fishes of China. It covers about 550 species of fishes, with keys to species, some color plates, and species accounts.

Talwar, P. K., and Arun G. Jhingran. **Inland Fishes of India and Adjacent Countries.** New Delhi: Oxford and IBH, 1991. 2 vol. ISBN 8120406397 (set).

This catalog covers about 700 species of fishes. The systematic section provides an illustration of each species, plus citation to the original description, English and local common names, distinctive characteristics, distribution, and fishery information. There is also a checklist and keys to species.

Australasia

Allen, Gerald R. **Freshwater Fishes of Australia.** Neptune City, NJ: THF, 1989. 240 p. ISBN 0866229361.

A colorful guide to the fishes of Australia, this book is arranged by family. Each species account contains common and scientific name, first author, synonymy, description, distribution, habitat, and size, plus range map. There is also an illustrated key to families, and the book includes a list of threatened species and a gazetteer.

Allen, Gerald R. **Marine Fishes of Tropical Australia and South-East Asia.** 3rd ed., rev. Perth: Western Australian Museum, 1997. 292 p. $30. ISBN 0730983633.

An expanded version of the author's *Marine Fishes of North-Western Australia,* this volume identifies about 1,600 species of reef and shore fishes from northern Australia, Malaysia, Indonesia, Philippines, New Guinea, and Solomon Islands, along with some deep water species of interest to anglers. Each brief description covers habitat, distribution, size, and indicates the family.

Kuiter, Rudolf H. **Coastal Fishes of South-Eastern Australia.** Honolulu: University of Hawaii Press, 1993. 437 p. $60. ISBN 0824815238.

Another of the excellent regional guides published by the University of Hawaii Press, this guide covers the fishes found along the coast of south-eastern Australia from northern New South Wales to western Victoria.

There is a pictorial guide to families, and each species account consists of a paragraph describing the species, its range, size, and habitat. Most descriptions are illustrated by high-quality color photographs.

McDowall, R. M. **New Zealand Freshwater Fishes: A Natural History and Guide.** Rev. ed. Birkenhead, Auckland: Heinemann Reed, 1990. 553 p. ISBN 0790000229.

Designed for both scientists and interested laypeople, this book surveys the 50 species of fish found in New Zealand, including 20 introduced species. There are distribution maps and black-and-white drawings of most of the species as well as numerous color photographs. Each species account includes a detailed description covering size, color, and distinguishing characteristics, distribution, taxonomic notes, and biology.

Randall, John E., Gerald R. Allen, and Roger C. Steene. **Fishes of the Great Barrier Reef and Coral Sea.** Rev. and enl. ed. Honolulu: University of Hawaii Press, 1997. 557 p. $85. ISBN 0824818954.

A colorful guide to the fishes of the Great Barrier Reef, this book identifies over 1,200 species of fishes a diver is likely to see. There is a pictorial guide to families, and each species account consists of a paragraph describing the species, its range, size, and habitat. Most descriptions are illustrated by high-quality color photographs.

Central and South America

Allen, Gerald R., and D. Ross Robertson. **Fishes of the Tropical Eastern Pacific.** Honolulu: University of Hawaii Press, 1994. 332 p. $85. ISBN 0824816757.

A colorful guide to the shore fishes of the area from the central Gulf of California to Ecuador, this book identifies the species of fishes that a diver is most likely to see or that are of economic importance. There is a pictorial guide to families, and each species account consists of a paragraph describing the species, its range, size, and habitat. Most descriptions are illustrated by high-quality color photographs.

Grove, Jack S., and Robert J. Lavenberg. **The Fishes of the Galápagos Islands.** Stanford, CA: Stanford University Press, 1997. 863 p. $130. ISBN 0804722897.

This guide to the fishes of the Galápagos includes an illustrated guide to identifying the families of fish plus detailed species accounts covering the

natural history, description, habitats, and range of the fishes. Most species
are illustrated.

**Inter-Institutional Database of Fish Biodiversity in the Neotropics
(NEODAT II).** URL: http://www.neodat.org/. (Accessed August 25, 2003).

The Inter-Institutional Database of Fish Biodiversity in the Neotropics
(NEODAT II) is a database containing systematic and geographical data
on Neotropical freshwater fish specimens deposited in 24 natural history
collections. The searchable database includes distribution maps and references to original descriptions and systematic revisions. The site also
houses an image gallery and a Rare Literature section with electronic versions of several rare ichthyological works and some original descriptions.

Malabarba, Luiz R. **Phylogeny and Classification of Neotropical Fishes.**
Porto Alegre, Brazil: EDIPUCRS, 1998. 603 p. ISBN 8574300357.

The results of a symposium held in 1997, this volume contains the latest research on the phylogeny and classification of the fishes of Central
and South America. There are overviews for the Characiformes, Characi-
dae, Siluriformes, Gymnotiformes, Atherinopsidae, Cyprinodontiformes,
and Cichlidae as well as more narrowly focused papers on these groups.

Europe

Holcík, Juraj, ed. **The Freshwater Fishes of Europe.** Wiesbaden, Germany: AULA-Verlag, 1986– . Vol. price varies.

This series is more than a catalog of the fishes of Europe. It describes all
species of fishes found in Europe and covers their taxonomy, morphology,
ecology, and relations to humans. Volume 9 covers the threatened fishes of
Europe; the remaining volumes cover the various families. The volumes
provide a detailed discussion of the biology of the families and then contain detailed species accounts listing synonyms, holotypes, etymology,
detailed description, subspecies, hybrids, distribution, ecology, and more,
with extensive references. Nine volumes are planned and have been published out of sequence. To date, Volumes 1-1, 1-2, 2, 5-1, 5-3, and 9 have
been published.

Hureau, J.-C. **Fishes of the North-Eastern Atlantic and the Mediterranean.** Paris; Amsterdam: UNESCO; Springer Electronic Media, 1995. 1
CD-ROM disc plus booklet. (World Biodiversity Database). $180. ISBN
3540141952 (Windows); 3540141960 (Macintosh).

This CD covers 1,265 species of fish in this region and includes an illustrated interactive key, color photos and illustrations, and distribution maps for each species. The disk also includes an extensive glossary and lengthy bibliography.

Hureau, J.-C., and Th. Monod, eds. **Check-list of the Fishes of the North-Eastern Atlantic and of the Mediterranean (Clofnam) with Supplement 1978.** Paris: UNESCO, 1979. 2 vol. ISBN 9230017620 (set).

The checklist is designed as a preliminary survey of the fishes of the Atlantic and Mediterranean. The species accounts include synonyms, illustrations, common names, and information on the eggs, otoliths, and habitats of the species treated.

Mater, S., M. Kaya, and M. Bilecenoglu. **Checklist of Marine Fishes of Turkey (CLOMFOT).** 2000– . URL: http://bornova.ege.edu.tr/~mbilecen/index.html (Accessed August 25, 2003).

This site covers 417 species of fishes found in the Black Sea, Sea of Marmara, Aegean Sea, and the Mediterranean Sea. The species accounts include common Turkish name, distribution, habitat, length, and commercial importance. Available in PDF and html versions.

Quéro, J.C., et al., eds. **Check-list of the Fishes of the Eastern Tropical Atlantic: Clofeta.** Paris: European Ichthyological Union: UNESCO, 1990. 3 vol. ISBN 9230026204.

This checklist covers the eastern Atlantic from the coast of Morocco south to 23 degrees. It is intended as a basic reference for the 1,572 species of fishes of the region. The individual records include first description and notes on distribution.

Wheeler, Alwyne C. **The Fishes of the British Isles and North-West Europe.** London: Macmillan, 1969. 613 p. ISBN 0333059557.

Includes freshwater and marine fishes. The guide includes an illustrated key to fish families as well as keys to species within each family. Most species are illustrated by black-and-white drawings, but there are some color illustrations as well. The species accounts include common names in the major European languages, identification, biology, and distribution.

Whitehead, P.J.P., et al., eds. **Fishes of the North-Eastern Atlantic and the Mediterranean.** Paris: UNESCO, 1984– . 3 vol. ISBN 9230022152 (vol. 1).

This fauna covers the marine fishes of Europe and the Mediterranean. It covers about 1,250 species of fishes, all of which are illustrated and keyed. The species accounts list first description, synonyms, common names, description, habitat, food, reproduction, and distribution. There are distribution maps for most species as well. The set is written in English, but the introduction and notes are in French and English. The French title is *Poissons de l'Atlantique du Nord-est et de la Méditerranée.*

Pacific Ocean

Burgess, Warren, and Herbert R. Axelrod. **Pacific Marine Fishes.** 2nd ed. Neptune City, NJ: TGH, 1973–85. 9 vol.

Although dated, this set provides color photographs of most of the marine fishes in the Pacific Ocean. It is designed for the use of aquarists, divers, and dealers as well as ichthyologists. The descriptions of the families are written in nontechnical language and include information on behavior and suitability for aquarium use as well.

Tinker, Spencer Wilkie. **Fishes of Hawaii: A Handbook of the Marine Fishes of Hawaii and the Central Pacific Ocean.** Honolulu: Hawaiian Service, 1978. 532 p. $29.95 (paper). ISBN 0930492021; 0930492145 (paper).

This handbook covers both the shallow and deep water fishes of the central Pacific. It was written for students and the general public. The species accounts include a general description of the fish, along with the distribution and depth range. Most species are illustrated with either a nontechnical illustration or photograph, although there are a few color plates. An appendix lists additional species that were missed in the main text or had just been discovered.

Identification Tools

CITES Identification Guide—Sturgeons and Paddlefish: Guide to the Identification of Sturgeon Species Controlled under the Convention on International Trade in Endangered Species of Wild Fauna and Flora. Ottawa: Environment Canada, 2001. Various p. ISBN 0660616416.

This spiral-bound identification guide, written in English, French, and Spanish, is designed to help customs officers identify the 24 species of sturgeons that are covered under the CITES convention. It is in several sections, a visual key to the species of sturgeons, illustrations of the most easily recognized species (and cans of caviar), illustrations of very similar species, and a table summarizing the characteristics of each species. Also available in PDF format at http://www.cws-scf.ec.gc.ca/enforce/pdf/ Sturgeon/CITES_Sturgeons_Guide.pdf.

FAO Species Identification Field Guides for Fishery Purposes. Rome: Food and Agriculture Organization of the United Nations, 1993– . Price varies.

The guides in this series are designed to help identify fishes and other aquatic animals that are or could be used for fisheries. They cover areas such as Sri Lanka, the Mekong Delta, the Pacific Ocean, and regions in Africa.

Frimodt, Claus. **Multilingual Illustrated Guide to the World's Commercial Coldwater Fish.** Cambridge, MA: Fishing News Books, 1995. 244 p. $72. ISBN 0852382138.

Features two-page spreads identifying and illustrating 170 species of commercially important cold-water fishes. Each entry includes scientific name and family plus common names in up to 13 languages, length and weight, description including economic importance, and information on the nutritional value of the species. There are also color illustrations for each species.

Frimodt, Claus. **Multilingual Illustrated Guide to the World's Commercial Warmwater Fish.** Cambridge, MA: Fishing News Books, 1995. 215 p. $72. ISBN 0852382146.

Similar in format to the cold-water fish guide described above, this guide contains information on over 150 species of commercially important fishes.

Regulatory Fish Encyclopedia (RFE). Center for Food Safety and Applied Nutrition, U.S. Food and Drug Administration (FDA). URL: http://vm.cfsan.fda.gov/~frf/rfe0.html. (Accessed August 25, 2003).

The encyclopedia is a compilation of data in several formats that assists with the accurate identification of fish species. The data included for each species includes high-resolution images, description, and chemical taxonomic information. The database can be browsed by common name, market name, scientific name, or family.

Ueberschär, Bernd. **LarvalBase: A Global Information System on Fish Larvae.** Kiel, Germany: Institute for Marine Research, 1999– . URL: http://www.larvalbase.org/background_1.htm. (Accessed August 25, 2003).

This database is a companion to *FishBase,* which does not contain information on larval fish. *LarvalBase* is an integrated system providing data on fish eggs and larvae, including identification and rearing. It is designed to improve aquaculture, and at the time of viewing it covered 1,850 species. The database can be searched or browsed by scientific name, and the data for each species includes identification, hatchery and rearing information, and links to *FishBase.* Photographs of some larvae are also available on a separate page.

Geographical Section

North America

Eschmeyer, William N., and Earl S. Herald. **A Field Guide to Pacific Coast Fishes of North America: From the Gulf of Alaska to Baja California.** Boston: Houghton Mifflin, 1983. 336 p. (Peterson Field Guide series, no. 28). $19 (paper). ISBN 061800212X (paper).

Identifies over 500 species of fish found along the Pacific Coast in waters shallower than 650 feet. Some deep-sea fish are included as well. The guide is arranged in systematic order with color and black-and-white illustrations of the fish in a separate section.

Hoese, H. Dickson. **Fishes of the Gulf of Mexico, Texas, Louisiana, and Adjacent Waters.** 2nd ed. College Station: Texas A&M University Press, 1998. 422 p. (W. L. Moody, Jr. Natural History Series, no. 22). $34.95. ISBN 0890967377.

An identification guide to the fishes of the Texas and Louisiana coasts, this guide has keys to genera and species and about 500 color photographs of fishes. The concise species accounts include description, abundance, and distribution.

Humann, Paul. **Reef Fish Identification: Florida, Caribbean, Bahamas.** 3rd ed., enl. Jacksonville, FL: New World, 2002. 481 p. (Reef Set, vol. 1). $39.95. ISBN 1878348302.

A colorful guide to the reef fishes of the region, identifying 600 species arranged by appearance rather than by family. This edition includes information on the reef fishes of Brazil as well as the Caribbean. Other volumes

in the three-volume set are also of interest to divers, including reef creatures (invertebrates) and corals (see chapter 2).

Page, Lawrence M., and Brooks M. Burr. **A Field Guide to Freshwater
Fishes: North America North of Mexico.** Boston: Houghton Mifflin,
1991. 432 p. (Peterson Field Guide series, no. 42). $19 (paper). ISBN
061800212X (paper).

One of the highly regarded Peterson Field Guides, this comprehensive
guide provides identification, range, habitat, and similar species information for each species. There are color and black-and-white illustrations and
range maps.

Robins, C. Richard, and G. Carleton Ray. **A Field Guide to Atlantic
Coast Fishes of North America.** Boston: Houghton Mifflin, 1986. 354 p.
(Peterson Field Guide series, no. 32). $20.95; $14.95 (paper). ISBN
0395318521; 0395391989 (paper).

A comprehensive field guide to over 1,000 species of marine fishes
found along the Atlantic Coast of North America, including the Gulf
Coast. The brief species accounts include identification, range, and habitat. There are color and black-and-white illustrations, but no range maps.

Smith, C. Lavett. **National Audubon Society Field Guide to Tropical
Marine Fishes of the Caribbean, the Gulf of Mexico, Florida, the
Bahamas, and Bermuda.** New York: Knopf, 1997. 720 p. (National
Audubon Society Field Guide series). $19.95. ISBN 067944601X.

A photographic field guide to the fishes of this popular region, this
guide covers 400 species in detail and mentions another 800. The fishes
are arranged by body type rather than by family.

Africa

Debelius, Helmut. **Red Sea Reef Guide: Egypt, Israel, Jordan, Sudan,
Saudi Arabia, Yemen, Arabian Peninsula (Oman, UAE, Bahrain).**
Frankfurt, Germany: IKAN, 1998. 321 p. $53. ISBN 3931702979.

Covers over 1,000 species of fish found in the Red Sea region. The
descriptions include information on depth and habitat for each species.
Illustrated with color photographs.

Skelton, Paul H. **A Complete Guide to the Freshwater Fishes of Southern Africa.** New ed. Cape Town: Struik, 2001. 395 p. ISBN 1868726436.

Covers the fishes of Namibia, Zambia, Zimbabwe, Botswana, and South Africa. The author provides extensive background information on fish biology and classification as well as the history of ichthyology in southern Africa in addition to the usual species accounts. There is an illustrated key to families as well as keys to species within each family. The species accounts include illustrations, distribution map, and description, biology, uses, conservation status, and notes. Common names are in English and Afrikaans.

Asia

Leis, Jeffrey M., and Brooke M. Carson-Ewart, eds. **The Larvae of Indo-Pacific Coastal Fishes: An Identification Guide to Marine Fish Larvae.** Boston: Brill, 2000. 850 p. (Fauna Malesiana Handbooks, no. 2). $261. ISBN 9004115773.

Hatchling fish often look very different from their adult forms, so identifying them can be difficult. This guide is designed to facilitate identification of larval fish of the Indo-Pacific region and to document their specializations and ontogeny as an aid to phylogenetic analysis. There is an illustrated key to major groups. The larvae are often identified only to the level of family or genus, but each account includes information on the spawning mode, development at hatching, larval morphology, pigmentation, and similar families.

Leis, Jeffrey M., and D. S. Rennis. **The Larvae of Indo-Pacific Coral Reef Fishes.** Honolulu: University of Hawaii Press, 1984. 269 p. ISBN 0824809106.

Similar in design and intent to *The Larvae of Indo-Pacific Coastal Fishes* (above), this guide covers the larvae of coral reef fishes of the western Indo-Pacific region as far east as Hawaii and Easter Island. The larvae are identified only to family, and the accounts contain the same information found in the coastal fish book.

Lieske, Ewald, and Robert Myers. **Coral Reef Fishes: Indo-Pacific and Caribbean.** Rev. ed. Princeton, NJ: Princeton University Press, 2002. 400 p. $24.95. (Princeton Pocket Guides). ISBN 0691089957.

This field guide covers over 2,000 species of fishes found in the coral reef regions of the Caribbean and Indo-Pacific Oceans. About 80% of the species are from the Indo-Pacific region, reflecting the greater diversity and size of this region. The guide also includes an introduction covering the origin, evolution, and zoogeography of coral reefs.

Europe

Lythgoe, J. N. **Fishes of the Sea: The North Atlantic and Mediterranean.** Cambridge, MA: MIT Press, 1992. 256 p. $45. ISBN 026212162X.

An identification guide to the fishes of the region, this book uses color photographs of fish in their native habitat as well as line drawings to facilitate identification. The region covered extends north of the Chesapeake Bay in the west and Gibraltar in the east, including the Mediterranean Sea. The book is in systematic order and lacks keys. Each species description includes distribution, detailed description, size, habitat, and often brief notes on natural history. Most species are illustrated either by a photograph or line drawing.

Miller, Peter J. **Fish of Britain and Europe.** London: HarperCollins, 1997. 288 p. (Collins Pocket Guide). $26.75. ISBN 0002199459 (paper).

Covers both freshwater and saltwater species from the North Atlantic to the Mediterranean, and from Ireland to the Danube basin. There are color illustrations to 753 species and a visual key to families.

Pacific Islands

Hoover, John P. **Hawaii's Fishes: A Guide for Snorkelers, Divers, and Aquarists.** Honolulu: Mutual, 1993. 178 p. $18.95 (paper). ISBN 1566470013 (paper).

A colorful photographic guide to 230 species of fishes found throughout the Hawaiian Islands. Common names are given in English and Hawaiian, and an appendix lists invalid scientific names.

Myers, Robert F. **Micronesian Reef Fishes: A Comprehensive Guide to the Coral Reef Fishes of Micronesia.** 3rd ed., rev. and enl. Barrigada, Territory of Guam: Coral Graphics; distributed by Sea Challengers, 1999. 330 p. ISBN 0962156450.

As the title suggests, this is a comprehensive guide to 1,400 species of reef fishes of the Pacific. It contains keys and checklists by island group as well as the usual descriptions and photographs.

Randall, John E. **Shore Fishes of Hawaii.** Vida, OR: Natural World Press, 1996. 216 p. $19.95 (paper). ISBN 0939560224 (paper).

The author has written a number of excellent books about fishes. This guide covers 340 species found off of Hawaii and features color photographs. The volume also includes a checklist of species and lists common names in both English and Hawaiian.

Associations

American Elasmobranch Society. c/o Rebeka Rand Merson. E-mail: rmerson@whoi.edu. URL: http://www.flmnh.ufl.edu/fish/organizations/aes/abst85.htm. (Accessed August 25, 2003).

American Fisheries Society. 5410 Grosvenor Lane, Suite 110, Bethesda, MD 20814. Phone: 301-897-8616. Fax: 301-897-8096. E-mail: main@fisheries.org. URL: http://www.fisheries.org. (Accessed August 25, 2003).

American Society of Ichthyologists and Herpetologists. Grice Marine Laboratory, University of Charleston, 205 Fort Johnson Rd., Charleston, SC 29412. Phone: 843-406-4017. E-mail: asih@mail.utexas.edu. URL: http://199.245.200.110/. (Accessed August 25, 2003).

European Ichthyological Society (EIS). CP 57, CH-2952 Cornol, Switzerland. Phone: 41 32 4622259. Fax: 41 32 4622259. URL: http://www.nrm.se/ve/pisces/eis/. (Accessed August 25, 2003).

Neotropical Ichthyological Association. E-mail: nia-net-request@inpa.gov.br. URL: http://www.mct.pucrs.br/lab/museu/nia/. (Accessed August 25, 2003).

Reference

Nelson, Joseph S. 1994. *Fishes of the World.* 3rd ed. New York: Wiley.

6

Amphibians and Reptiles

There are about 5,500 described species of amphibians and 8,050 species of reptiles. Herpetology is the study of both amphibians and reptiles, and the two groups have been studied together since the beginning of modern systematics. Linnaeus combined the two groups in the "Amphibia" along with the sharks, which were included because they had "arbitrary lungs" and a single-chambered heart as do both reptiles and amphibians. Linnaeus divided the Amphibia by form into the Reptiles (turtles, crocodiles, lizards, salamanders, and frogs), Serpentes (snakes, caecilians, and amphisbaenians), and Nantes (sharks and rays). However, modern systematics now puts the three groups in very different clades. "Herp" or "herpetile" are often used as abbreviated terms referring to both amphibians and reptiles, and they are occasionally used that way in the present chapter. Besides classifying herps in his peculiar way, Linnaeus suffered from the common dislike of his Amphibia, using terms like "terrible and vile animals" having a "ghastly color," "foul skin," and a "squalid habitat" (Kitchell and Dundee, 1994, pp. 5–6).

Amphibians, as they are now defined, include three major groups: Anura (frogs and toads), Caudata (salamanders), and Caecilia (legless amphibians that resemble worms or snakes). "Amphibian" means "double life," a reference to the fact that amphibians, unlike amniotes such as reptiles, birds, and mammals, must lay their eggs in water even though they may live their adult lives on land. Because amphibians have soft, porous skins and are in close contact with their environment, they are particularly sus-

219

ceptible to environmental toxicants. Some species have dramatically declined in recent years, and some, such as the beautiful Golden Toad *Bufo periglenes* of Costa Rica, have even gone extinct. A number of reasons have been proposed for this dramatic decline, including pesticides, UV radiation, climate change, and habitat loss.

Reptiles include Testudines (turtles), Amphisbaenia (worm lizards), Sauria (lizards), Serpentes (snakes), Crocodylia, and Rhynchocephalia (tuataras). Lizards, snakes, and amphisbaenids are all part of the Squamata, but the three groups are divided here. Turtles are anapsids, with only one opening on each side of the skull; all other reptiles, birds, and mammals are diapsids, having two openings in the skull. Reptiles lay eggs on land, although some species are ovoviviparous, meaning the egg develops within the mother and young are born live.

Amphibians (species counts from http://research.amnh.org/herpetology/amphibia/asw_summary.html)

Salientia/Anura (frogs and toads; 4,837 species)

Caudata (salamanders and newts; 502 species)

Gymnophiona (caecelians; 165 species)

Reptiles (species counts from http://www.embl-heidelberg.de/~uetz/db-info/SpeciesStat.html)

Testudines (turtles; 302 species)

Squamata

    Amphisbaenia (worm lizards; 160 species)

    Sauria (lizards; 4,675 species)

    Serpentes (snakes; 2,940 species)

Crocodylia (crocodiles; 23 species)

Rhynchocephalia (tuataras; 2 species)

Indexes, Abstracts, and Bibliographies

Smith, Charles H. **HERPFAUN.** Heidelberg, Germany: EMBL, 1993. URL: http://www.embl-heidelberg.de/~uetz/db-info/HERPFAUN.html (Accessed August 25, 2003).

This bibliography contains over 2,000 references dealing with the geographical distribution of reptiles and amphibians worldwide. It includes a variety of document types, including faunal monographs, checklists, determination keys, taxonomic revisions, bibliographies, conservation status reports, field guides, and so on. The database can be searched by higher taxon and by geographical location and can be downloaded either as a text file, an hqx file, or a zipped text file.

Journals

Amphibia-Reptilia. Vol. 1– . Leiden, The Netherlands: E. J. Brill, Aug. 1980– . Quarterly. $307. ISSN 0173-5373. Available electronically.

Publication of the Societas Europaea Herpetologica (SEH). Publishes research articles in all areas of herpetology, short papers on new methods or research areas, book reviews, and news of the SEH.

Chelonian Conservation and Biology: International Journal of Turtle and Tortoise Research. Vol. 1, no. 1– . Lunenburg, MA: Chelonian Research Foundation, Nov. 1993– . Irregular. $100/vol. (4 issues). ISSN 1071-8443.

Publishes articles, notes, commentaries, research reports on projects funded by the Linneaus Fund, and other features covering all aspects of turtle biology and conservation, including marine, freshwater, and terrestrial turtles and tortoises. Some issues cover a single topic such as hawksbill turtles. The journal publishes about two issues per year.

Contemporary Herpetology. No.1– . Hammond, LA: Contemporary Herpetology, 1998– . ISSN 1094-2246. URL: http://dataserver.calacademy. org/herpetology/herpdocs/ (Accessed August 25, 2003). Only available electronically.

An electronic journal publishing articles on all aspects of herpetology, including ecology, ethology, systematics, conservation biology, and physiology. CH will also publish monographs, points of view, and faunistic surveys of poorly known areas.

Herpetologica. Vol. 1– . Johnson City, TN: Herpetologists' League, 1936– . Quarterly. ISSN 0018-0831.

Publishes papers, essays, and book reviews covering the biology of amphibians and reptiles. Annual supplements published as *Herpetological Monographs* (see below).

The Herpetological Journal. Vol. 1, no. 1– . London: British Herpetological Society, 1985– . Semiannual. Free with membership. ISSN 0268-
0130.

Publishes articles, reviews, mini-reviews, short notes, the Forum (for
controversial topics), and book reviews in a wide range of reptile and
amphibian biology. Formerly *British Journal of Herpetology.*

Herpetological Monographs. No. 1– . Johnson City, TN: Herpetologists' League, 1982– . Annual. ISSN 0733-1347.

An annual supplement to *Herpetologica,* above; publishes longer
research articles, syntheses, and special symposia.

Herpetological Review. Vol. 1– . St. Louis, MO: Society for the Study of
Amphibians and Reptiles, 1967– . Quarterly. ISSN 0018-084X.

An organ for news and opinion for members of the Society for the
Study of Amphibians and Reptiles. In addition to news items, the journal
publishes short notes on captive breeding, limited natural history observations, geographical range extensions, and essays. A companion to *Journal
of Herpetology,* below.

Journal of Herpetology. Vol. 1– . St. Louis, MO: Society for the Study of
Amphibians and Reptiles, 1968– . Quarterly. ISSN 0022-1511. Available
electronically.

Publishes articles on the biology of amphibians and reptiles, with
emphasis on behavior, biochemistry, conservation, ecology, evolution,
morphology, physiology, and systematics.

Guides to the Literature

Center for North American Herpetology. URL: http://www.naherpetology.
org/index.asp (Accessed August 25, 2003).

The Center for North American Herpetology (CNAH) is a nonprofit
organization dedicated to promoting education about and conservation of
amphibians and reptiles. Its Web site, subtitled "The Academic Portal to
North American Herpetology," lives up to its billing. It provides many
links to herpetology sites, including North American sites arranged by taxonomic group, lists of societies and collections, directories, information
on careers and jobs, links to *Standard Common and Current Scientific
Names for North American Amphibians, Turtles, Reptiles, and Crocodilians,* 5th ed., and much more.

Biographies and Histories

Adler, Kraig, ed. **Contributions to the History of Herpetology.** Oxford, OH: SSAR, 1989. 202 p. (Contributions to Herpetology, no. 5). ISBN 0916984192.

Along with biographies of past herpetologists, this collection includes an index of authors of taxonomic names and a list of the academic lineages of doctoral degrees (i.e., who studied with whom).

Dictionaries and Encyclopedias

Cogger, Harold G., Richard George Zweifel, and David Kirshner. **Encyclopedia of Reptiles and Amphibians.** 2nd ed. San Diego: Academic Press, 1998. 240 p. (AP Natural World). $39.95. ISBN 0121785602.

Very similar to Halliday and Adler's encyclopedia, below, this book also contains extensive information on the natural history and biology of amphibians and reptiles, plus descriptions of orders and families.

Gotch, A. F. **Latin Names Explained: A Guide to the Scientific Classification of Reptiles, Birds and Mammals.**

See chapter 4 for a full annotation. Explains the source of Latin terms used in reptile scientific names.

Halliday, T. R., and K. Adler, eds. **The Encyclopedia of Reptiles and Amphibians.** New York: Facts on File, 1986. 143 p. $29.95. ISBN 0816013594.

This encyclopedia contains extended descriptions of each of the amphibian and reptile orders, plus briefer entries for each family. A separate section provides distribution and classification information for the families in addition to listing well-known or representative species. There are many color photographs and illustrations of representative species from around the world.

Halliday, T. R., and K. Adler, eds. **Firefly Encyclopedia of Reptiles and Amphibians.** Toronto: Firefly Books, 2002. 240 p. $40. ISBN 1552976130.

A student's encyclopedia to reptiles and amphibians, this colorful text surveys the world's amphibians and reptiles. The book is separated into two sections, one for each group. Each section begins with a general description of the class and its biology, then discusses the orders in more detail, going down to the family level. There are many articles on topics such as the mechanics of frog locomotion, adaptation to desert conditions, and others, in addition to the systematic section.

Peters, James Arthur. **Dictionary of Herpetology: A Brief and Meaningful Definition of Words and Terms Used in Herpetology.** New York: Hafner, 1964. 392 p.

Most of the terms in this classic dictionary deal with descriptive morphology, although terms from other fields such as physiology and collecting techniques can also be found. Many of the definitions include information on the authorities who popularized the term. Although the dictionary is out of date, it is still useful for its coverage of morphological terms.

Wareham, David C. **The Reptile and Amphibian Keeper's Dictionary: An A-Z of Herpetology.** New York: Distributed in the United States by Sterling, 1993. 248 p. ISBN 0713723181.

Although designed for the use of amateur herpetologists, this dictionary has a broader use for professionals as well. It defines 2,000 terms dealing with amphibians and reptiles that a herpetologist is likely to encounter, including terms from reptile anatomy, physiology, and taxonomy, as well as biographies of well-known herpetologists and herpetological slang. There are some illustrations as well.

Textbooks

Cloudsley-Thompson, J. L. **The Diversity of Amphibians and Reptiles: An Introduction.** New York: Springer, 1999. 254 p. $89. ISBN 3540650563.

Discusses the biology and adaptations of amphibians and reptiles, including fossil forms, in nontechnical terms. The emphasis is on the variety of adaptations that herps demonstrate, including locomotion, reproduction, temperature regulation, and more. The author also discusses the evolution and classification of herps and their relationships with humans.

Duellman, William Edward, and Linda Trueb. **Biology of Amphibians.** New York: McGraw-Hill, 1986. 670 p. ISBN 0070179778.

A classic textbook. The emphasis is on amphibian biology rather than diversity, but it does include chapters on evolution, phylogeny, biogeography, and classification to the level of the genus.

Grenard, Steve. **Medical Herpetology.** Pottsville, PA: Reptile and Amphibian Magazine, 1994. 139 p. $19.95. ISBN 0964103206 (paper).

Covers human medicine in relation to herpetology, especially venomous or poisonous herps, zoonoses transmitted by herps, and drugs or medical treatments derived from herps. The major taxa are covered in separate chapters.

Pough, F. Harvey, et al. **Herpetology.** 2nd ed. Upper Saddle River, NJ: Prentice Hall, 2001. 612 p. $91. ISBN 0130307955.

A basic textbook for students; in four main sections covering classification and evolution, physiology, behavior and ecology, and conservation. The classification section is divided into two chapters, one on amphibians and one on reptiles. Each family and its distribution is then described and further readings provided.

Zug, George R., Laurie J. Vitt, and Janalee P. Caldwell. **Herpetology: An Introductory Biology of Amphibians and Reptiles.** 2nd ed. San Diego: Academic, 2001. 630 p. $69.95. ISBN 012782622X.

A basic textbook covering the biology and systematics of amphibians and reptiles. The systematic section includes distribution maps and color photographs.

Checklists and Classification Schemes

Beltz, Ellin. **Names of the Reptiles and Amphibians of North America.** 2002. URL: http://ebeltz.net/herps/etyhome.html (Accessed August 25, 2003).

Provides a checklist of scientific and common names of North American herps, including translations of scientific names, a biographical appendix listing individuals who had species named after them, citations to original descriptions, and a glossary of mythological terms used in herp nomenclature.

Cope, E. D. **Check-List of North American Batrachia and Reptilia: With a Systematic List of the Higher Groups, and an Essay on Geographical Distribution.** Washington, DC: U.S. Government Printing Office, 1875. 104 p. (Smithsonian Miscellaneous Collections, vol. 13, no. 1; Publication of the Smithsonian Institution, no. 292).

For each of the 358 species listed in this checklist, the author provides scientific name, citations to the literature, and geographical distribution. Cope also includes an essay on the geographical distribution of the North American amphibians and reptiles and a bibliography.

Crother, Brian I. **Scientific and Standard English Names of Amphibians and Reptiles of North America North of Mexico: With Comments Regarding Confidence in Our Understanding.** St. Louis, MO: Society for the Study of Amphibians and Reptiles, 2001. 82 p. (Herpetological Circular, no. 29). $11. ISBN 0916984540.

Formerly published as *Standard Common and Current Scientific Names for North American Amphibians and Reptiles.* The guide provides information on forming acceptable common names, and it includes references to the literature used in creating the list. The bulk of the list consists of an alphabetical list of genera within each order with notes, common names, and scientific names. An html version of the book is available at the society's Web page, http://www.herplit.com/SSAR/circulars/HC29/names.html, along with a PDF version at http://www.ku.edu/~ssar/pdf/crother.pdf.

Frank, Norman, and Erica Ramus. **A Complete Guide to Scientific and Common Names of Reptiles and Amphibians of the World.** Pottsville, PA: NG Publishers, 1995. 377 p. $19.95. ISBN 0964103230.

This list contains standard common names for over 12,000 species of herps. It is arranged taxonomically, with indexes to genera, species, and common names.

Kitchell, Kenneth, Jr., and Harold A. Dundee. **A Trilogy on the Herpetology of Linnaeus's Systema Naturae X.** Washington, DC: Smithsonian Herpetological Service, 1994. 61 p.

Provides a translation of the herpetological section of *Systema Naturae,* along with current scientific names for the herps listed by Linnaeus and the literature cited by Linnaeus.

Liner, Ernest A. **Scientific and Common Names for the Amphibians and Reptiles of Mexico in English and Spanish = Nombres Científicos y Comunes en Inglés y Español de los Anfibios y los Reptiles de México.** St. Louis, MO: Society for the Study of Amphibians and Reptiles, 1994. 113 p. (Herpetological Circular, no. 23). $12. ISBN 091698432X.

Lists scientific names for Mexican amphibians and reptiles, along with common names used by local people and standard English common names (some invented by the author).

Logier, E. B. S., and G. C. Toner. **Check List of the Amphibians and Reptiles of Canada and Alaska.** 2nd ed. Toronto: The Royal Ontario Museum, 1961. 92 p. (Royal Ontario Museum, Life Sciences Division. Contribution, no. 53).

A revision of the museum's Contribution no. 41, this checklist provides range maps as well as original author, common name, range, and Canadian and Alaskan locality records. The authors also provide an extensive bibliography, but there is no index.

Loveridge, Arthur. **Check List of the Reptiles and Amphibians of East Africa (Uganda; Kenya; Tanganyika; Zanzibar).** Cambridge, MA: Museum of Comparative Zoology, 1957. [151]-362 p. (Bulletin of the Museum of Comparative Zoology, vol. 117, no. 2).

This checklist covers 527 species of herps found in East Africa. It is arranged in systematic order and has an extensive list of synonyms for each species and genus. The entries also include range, original author, and a selective list of references.

Schmidt, Karl Patterson. **A Check List of North American Amphibians and Reptiles.** 6th ed. Chicago: American Society of Ichthyologists and Herpetologists, 1953. 280 p.

Arranged in systematic order, this checklist provides scientific name, original author, references to the literature, range, and common name for each species or subspecies. It is based in part on Cope's *Check-List* (above).

Systematic Section

Amphibians

Gorham, Stanley W. **Checklist of World Amphibians up to January 1, 1970 = Liste des Amphibiens du Monde D'après L'état du 1er Janvier 1970.** Saint John: New Brunswick Museum, 1974. 172 p.

This checklist is arranged in systematic order. For each genus and species, the scientific name, first author and date of naming, and synonyms are listed as well as the continental distribution for many species. The checklist also includes a selective list of taxonomic references. There is an index to families but not to lower taxa. The introductory material is in English and French, although the body of the checklist is only in English.

Northern Prairie Wildlife Research Center. **Checklist of Amphibian Species and Identification Guide: An Online Guide for the Identification of Amphibians in North America North of Mexico.** (Version September 30, 2002). Jamestown, ND: Northern Prairie Wildlife Research Center Home Page, 1997. URL: http://www.npwrc.usgs.gov/narcam/idguide/. (Accessed August 25, 2003).

This site provides a browseable checklist of all amphibian species and subspecies currently recognized in North America north of Mexico. Salamanders, newts, frogs, and toads are briefly described in their adult phase; many entries include photos and range maps showing where a species is found. There is also an annotated list of amphibian and reptile identification Web sites.

Reptiles

King, F. Wayne, and Russell L. Burke, eds. **Crocodilian, Tuatara, and Turtle Species of the World: A Taxonomic and Geographic Reference.** Washington, DC: Association of Systematics Collections, 1989. 216 p. ISBN 0942924150.

The checklist includes a bibliography of publications written by Archie Carr, who had recently died, as well as a checklist covering 271 species of nonsquamata reptiles arranged taxonomically. Each entry includes synonymy, type species and location, distribution, and comments. There are some black-and-white illustrations. An updated version is also available on the Web at http://www.flmnh.ufl.edu/natsci/herpetology/turtcroclist/.

Uetz, Peter. **The EMBL Reptile Database.** Heidelberg, Germany: EMBL Heidelberg, 1995. URL. http://www.embl-heidelberg.de/~uetz/Living Reptiles.html (Accessed August 25, 2003).

Intended to provide classification information on all species of living reptiles, this database is updated about every three months and contains listings of synonyms, subspecies, family, distribution, comments, and references for each species of reptile. The site also includes links to other reptile sites, information on keeping reptiles as pets, a list of references used to create the database, and more. The database will include distribution maps and descriptions in the future. At the time of visiting, only families were described, although some species accounts included links to photographs.

Turtles

Iverson, John B., A. Jon Kimerling, and A. Ross Kiester. **EMYSystem.** Corvallis: Terra Incognita Laboratory, Oregon State University, 2000. URL: http://emys.geo.orst.edu/ (Accessed August 25, 2003).

The site is a continuation of Iverson's *A Revised Checklist with Distribution Maps of the Turtles of the World,* which included distribution maps and keys as well as taxonomic and nomenclatural information. Entries cover synonymy, common name, holotype, type location, distribution, subspecies, comments, and phylogenies where available. In addition to the information found in the book, the site provides links to resources for turtle conservation and an identification resource that was under construction at the time of viewing. The database can be browsed by scientific or common name or searched.

Márquez M., René. **Sea Turtles of the World: An Annotated and Illustrated Catalogue of Sea Turtle Species Known to Date.** Rome: Food and Agriculture Organization of the United Nations, 1990. 81 p. (FAO Fisheries Synopsis, no. 125, vol. 11; FAO Species Catalogue, vol. 11). $21. ISBN 9251028915.

Follows the format of other volumes in this series (see chapter 5 for full annotation). Eight sea turtle species are covered, and the species accounts include detailed information on each species' natural history, fisheries importance, and numerous local common names.

Welch, Kenneth R.G. **Turtles, Tortoises, and Terrapins: A Checklist.** Taunton, UK: R & A Research and Information Limited, 1994. 79 p. ISBN 1859130305.

Similar in format to the author's other checklists, listing distribution information and names.

Lizards

Estes, Richard, and Gregory Pregill, eds. **Phylogenetic Relationships of the Lizard Families: Essays Commemorating Charles L. Camp.** Stanford, CA: Stanford University Press, 1988. 631 p. $96. ISBN 0804714355.

Camp published the first modern classification of squamates, *Classification of Lizards,* in 1923. This volume reproduces papers from a symposium on lizard phylogeny held in 1982 in Camp's honor. Chapters cover the phylogeny of extinct lepidosauromorphs as well as living species of lizards.

Welch, Kenneth R. G. **Lizards of the World: A Checklist.** Taunton, UK: R & A Research and Information, 1994– . vol. ISBN 1859130224 (vol. 1); 1859130259 (vol. 5).

One of a series of similar checklists, this set is planned for six volumes. Each covers a different family or families of lizards and provides names, distribution, and authors for the species covered.

Snakes

Harding, Keith A., and Kenneth R.G. Welch. **Venomous Snakes of the World: A Checklist.** New York: Pergamon, 1980. 188 p. ISBN 0080254950.

This checklist is in two parts, the first covering the nomenclature of venomous species and the second providing geographical fauna lists for the world. The authors also include taxonomic references, bibliography, and author and subject indexes.

McDiarmid, Roy W., Jonathan A. Campbell, and T'Shaka A. Touré. **Snake Species of the World: A Taxonomic and Geographic Reference.** Washington, DC: Herpetologists' League, 1999–   vol. ISBN 1893777014 (vol. 1); 1893777006 (set).

This set is designed as a three-volume set. Volume 1 is a checklist to the snake species of the world and includes names, type specimens, local names, distribution, and comments. The volume was accepted as the standard reference to snake nomenclature by CITES.

Underwood, Garth. **A Contribution to the Classification of Snakes.** London: British Museum (Natural History), 1967. 179 p. (Publications of the British Museum [Natural History], no. 653).

Surveys the anatomy of snakes in detail and relates these anatomical features to each infraorder, family, and subfamily. The author also provides a summary of his proposal for snake systematics along with the diagnostic feature for each group.

Welch, Kenneth R. G. **Snakes of the World: A Checklist.** England: R & A Research and Information, distributed by KCM Books, 1994– . vol. ISBN 1859130224 (vol. 1); 1859130232 (vol. 2).

Volume 1 of this series covers venomous snakes; Volume 2 covers boas, pythons, shield-tails, and worm snakes. Volume 3, in preparation, will cover the Colubrid snakes. Distribution information is given for each species, and a few also include rarity.

Williams, Kenneth L., and V. Wallach. **Snakes of the World.** Malabar, FL: Krieger, 1989– vol. $15.75 (vol. 1). ISBN 0894642154 (vol. 1).

Volume 1 (the only volume published to date) provides a synopsis of snake generic and subgeneric names of living and extinct snakes.

Crocodiles

Britton, Adam. **Crocodilian Species List.** URL: http://www.flmnh.ufl. edu/natsci/herpetology/brittoncrocs/csl.html (Accessed August 25, 2003).

This site provides detailed species accounts for all 23 species of crocodilians, including photographs, distribution maps, conservation status, and natural history. The site also discusses crocodilian classification, communication, captive care, and much more information about crocodilian evolution and biology.

Handbooks

Catalogue of American Amphibians and Reptiles. New York: American Museum of Natural History for the Society for the Study of Amphibians and Reptiles, 1971– . $20.

This publication consists of a series of individual two- to five-page species accounts. As of 2002, about 760 accounts had been published in loose-leaf format. Each entry lists previous references, description, illustrations, distribution, fossil record, remarks, etymology, and comments. A list of recently published accounts can be found at http://www.herplit. com/contents/Catalogue.html.

Murphy, James B., Kraig Adler, and Joseph T. Collins, eds. **Captive Management and Conservation of Amphibians and Reptiles.** Ithaca, NY: Society for the Study of Amphibians and Reptiles, 1994. 408 p. (Contributions to Herpetology, vol. 11). $58. ISBN 0916984338.

The articles in this book were taken from a 1991 symposium and cover a range of topics. Although general issues such as nutrition and reproductive biology of herps are covered, the emphasis is not on caring for individual species but rather on conservation, model programs, and other research areas. The volume is dedicated to Roger Conant and includes biographical information on this well-known herpetologist.

Systematic Section

Amphibians

Amphibiaweb: An Information System for Amphibian Conservation Biology. Berkeley: Museum of Vertebrate Zoology, University of California, Berkeley, 2000. URL: http://elib.cs.berkeley.edu/aw/. (Accessed August 25, 2003).

This database provides detailed taxonomic and conservation information on all 5,000 species of amphibians of the world. It includes taxonomic information taken from Frost's *Amphibian Species of the World* (below). At the time of viewing, coverage was spotty as some pages contained only taxonomic information and links to museum collections. Other pages were more complete, with photographs, descriptions, life history, distribution, and references. The site also includes information on the decline in amphibian populations worldwide.

Feder, Martin E., and Warren W. Burggren, eds. **Environmental Physiology of the Amphibians.** Chicago: University of Chicago Press, 1992. 646 p. $160; $55 (paper). ISBN 0226239438; 0226239446 (paper).

The topics covered in this handbook include control systems, exchange of gases, energetics and locomotion, and development and reproduction.

Frost, Darrel R. **Amphibian Species of the World: An Online Reference.** New York: American Museum of Natural History, 2002. Version 2.21 (July 15, 2002). URL: http://research.amnh.org/herpetology/amphibia/index.html. (Accessed August 25, 2003).

This site provides scientific name, authority, year of publication, type species and location, English common name, distribution, and status for all species of amphibians. It updates the author's *Amphibian Species of the World: A Taxonomic and Geographical Reference,* published in 1985. Users can search by taxonomic or geographical name or browse by taxonomic hierarchy.

Heatwole, Harold, ed. **Amphibian Biology.** Chipping Norton, NSW: Surrey Beatty & Sons, 1994–   vol. $95. ISBN 0949324531 (set).

This multivolume treatise is modeled after Gans's *Biology of the Reptilia,* below. To date four volumes have been published, covering the integument, social behavior, sensory perception, and paleontology. Volume 5, *Osteology,* should be published at the end of 2003.

Heyer, W. Ronald et al., eds. **Measuring and Monitoring Biological Diversity: Standard Methods for Amphibians.** Washington, DC: Smithsonian Press, 1994. 364 p. (Biological Diversity Handbook series). $26.95 (paper). ISBN 1560982705; 1560982845 (paper).

Covers standard methods for monitoring amphibian diversity, from planning a study through data analysis. Appendixes discuss handling live amphibians, marking individuals, recording frog calls, preparing specimens, collecting tissues, and vendors selling equipment for amphibian studies. The book discusses a number of techniques from species inventories, setting up artificial habitats, estimating population size, and more.

Hofrichter, Robert, ed. **Amphibians: The World of Frogs, Toads, Salamanders and Newts.** Buffalo, NY: Firefly Books, 2000. 264 p. $49.95. ISBN 155209541X.

This oversized, colorful survey of the amphibian world was originally published in Germany, so it has a European emphasis. That said, it is an excellent source of information on amphibian biology, systematics, and ecology and has much more information on caecilians than most amphibian surveys. An appendix lists all amphibian species and genera known as of the end of 1997.

Moore, John Alexander, ed. **Physiology of the Amphibia.** New York: Academic, 1964–76. 3 vol. ISBN 0124554032 (vol. 3).

This classic treatise covers many topics in amphibian physiology, including metabolism, reproduction, metamorphosis, and more.

Stebbins, Robert C., and Nathan W. Cohen. **A Natural History of Amphibians.** Princeton, NJ: Princeton University Press, 1995. 316 p. ISBN 0691032815.

This book provides a general discussion of amphibian natural history for the interested nonspecialist. The authors discuss anatomy, physiology, behavior, declining populations, and human interactions with amphibians.

Frogs

Chiasson, Robert B., and Raymond A. Underhill. **Laboratory Anatomy of the Frog and Toad.** 6th ed. Dubuque, IA: W.C. Brown, 1994. 72 p. (Laboratory Anatomy series). ISBN 0697123138.

A popular dissection manuals for frogs, arranged by system.

Deuchar, Elizabeth M. **Xenopus: The South African Clawed Frog.** New York: Wiley, 1975. 246 p. ISBN 0471209627.

Xenopus is one of the most popular research subjects for work in embryology and developmental biology because it is easy to care for, breeds around the year, and produces large numbers of eggs at a time. This classic text covers the taxonomy, anatomy, physiology, and development of this frog.

Mattison, Christopher. **Frogs and Toads of the World.** New York: Facts on File, 1987. 191 p. ISBN 081601602X.

Unlike other volumes in this series, this handbook emphasizes the biology of the 3,500 species of frogs and toads, rather than providing a survey of the families of anurans. Chapters cover anatomy, physiology, antipredation techniques, reproduction, life histories, and more. A final chapter outlines the families of anurans.

McDiarmid, Roy W., and Ronald Altig, eds. **Tadpoles: The Biology of Anuran Larvae.** Chicago: University of Chicago Press, 1999. 444 p. $70. ISBN 0226557626.

This oversized handbook includes discussions of techniques, anatomy, development, physiology, behavior, evolution, and diversity of tadpoles.

Wingerd, Bruce D. **Frog Dissection Manual.** Baltimore: Johns Hopkins University Press, 1988. $13.95 (paper). ISBN 0801836018 (paper).

Another popular frog dissection manual.

Salamanders

Chiasson, Robert B. **Laboratory Anatomy of Necturus.** 3rd ed. Dubuque, IA: W. C. Brown, 1976. 62 p. ISBN 0697046230.

Covers the anatomy of the aquatic salamander *Necturus maculosus.*

Gilbert, Stephen G. **Pictorial Anatomy of the Necturus.** Seattle: University of Washington Press, 1973. 47 p.

Another popular dissection guide to the salamander *Necturus.*

Caecilians

Herndon, Rebecca, and Seth Morris. **Caecilians Web Site.** URL: http://www.caecilian.org/ (Accessed August 25, 2003).

It is difficult to find information about caecilians (also known as rubber eels or black eels in the aquarium trade). This site provides basic information about caecilians, including taxonomy, a bibliography, care in captivity, images, and video clips.

Taylor, Edward Harrison. **The Caecilians of the World: A Taxonomic Review.** Lawrence: University of Kansas Press, 1968. 848 p.

This catalog covers about 125 species of caecilians. The author provides an extensive introduction covering the history of caecilian research, locations where unknown caecilian species might be found, and information on the higher taxa. The amount of information on each species varies, but generally includes synonymy, diagnosis, description, range, and remarks. There are often several photographs or drawings of preserved specimens, including X rays.

Reptiles

Gans, Carl, ed. **Biology of the Reptilia.** New York: Academic Press, 1969–98. 19 vol. Price varies.

Each volume in this classic treatise covers a particular topic such as morphology or physiology. The articles are designed to summarize the state of knowledge in reptilian biology and contain numerous illustrations and extensive references. Volume 1 contains a chapter discussing the origin of reptiles, but all other chapters deal with living reptiles rather than fossils. Later volumes were published by Wiley, Liss, the University of Chicago Press, and the Society for the Study of Amphibians and Reptiles.

Turtles

Alderton, David. **Turtles and Tortoises of the World.** New York: Facts on File, 1988. 191 p. $32.95. ISBN 0816017336.

One of the several excellent Facts on File encyclopedias, this one covers the biology and classification of chelonians around the world. The author provides extensive background information on interactions with humans, anatomy, reproduction, and evolution of turtles. This introductory section is followed by descriptions of each turtle family. There are distribution maps and color photographs of representative species as well as text discussing the natural history, range, and descriptions of family members. An appendix provides a systematic list of turtle species, including English common names.

Ashley, Laurence M., and Carl Petterson. **Laboratory Anatomy of the Turtle.** Dubuque, IA: W.C. Brown, 1962. 48 leaves. (Laboratory Anatomy series). $39.06. ISBN 069704601X.

A dissection manual for a generalized turtle (species not defined).

Ernst, Carl H., R. G. M. Altenburg, and Roger William Barbour. **Turtles of the World.** Amsterdam, The Netherlands: Expert-Center for Taxonomic Identification, 2000. 1 CD. (World Biodiversity Database CD-ROM series). $149. ISBN 3540145478 (Windows version 1.2); 3540145486 (Macintosh version 1.0).

This CD-ROM updates Ernst and Barbour's classic *Turtles of the World.* Users can browse through the taxonomical hierarchy, map geographical distributions, and use an interactive key for identifying species. Each species account includes background information, multiple color photographs, identification, distribution, geographical variation, habitat, natural history, and conservation status. ETI also has a "microsite" containing general information on turtles taken from the CD at http://www.eti.uva.nl/Turtles/Turtles.html. The taxonomic information from the CD can also be searched at ETI's World Biodiversity Database site at http://www.eti.uva.nl/Database/WBD.html.

Ernst, Carl H., and Roger W. Barbour. **Turtles of the World.** Washington, DC: Smithsonian Institution Press, 1989. 313 p. ISBN 0874744148.

Discusses 257 species of turtles. Keys to families, genera, and species; species accounts include description, distribution, habitat, and natural history; most species are illustrated by black-and-white photographs.

Ferri, Vincenzo. **Tortoises and Turtles.** Willowdale, ON: Firefly Books, 2002. 255 p. $24.95. ISBN 1552096319 (paper).

A nice little beginner's guide to turtles, this colorful book provides species accounts for 190 turtles and tortoises. Initial chapters cover the biology, evolution, classification, and conservation of turtles; the bulk of the work contains species accounts. The author also provides a bibliography, glossary, and list of Web sites and associations for further information.

Lutz, Peter L., and John A. Musick, eds. **The Biology of Sea Turtles.** Boca Raton, FL: CRC Press, 1997. 432 p. (Marine Science series). $99.95. ISBN 0849384222.

In addition to chapters covering the biology, molecular evolution, and conservation of sea turtles, this text also covers sea turtle phylogeny and systematics.

Obst, Fritz Jürgen. **Turtles, Tortoises, and Terrapins.** New York: St. Martin's Press, 1986. 231 p. ISBN 0312823622.

This overview covers turtle phylogeny, distribution, anatomy, and cultural history. Although he does include a systematic classification of turtles to the subfamily, the discussion hinges more on ecosystems than on classification.

Orenstein, Ronald I. **Turtles, Tortoises and Terrapins: Survivors in Armor.** Buffalo, NY: Firefly Books, 2001. 308 p. $45. ISBN 155209605X.

Surveys turtle classification and biology. There is an extensive discussion of turtle evolution, biodiversity, conservation, and biology focusing on the unique requirements of living within a box. As with other books of this ilk, there are many attractive color photographs and interesting tidbits.

Pritchard, Peter Charles Howard. **Encyclopedia of Turtles.** Neptune, NJ: TFH, 1979. 895 p. ISBN 0876669186.

This encyclopedia is arranged in taxonomic order and includes keys to families and genera of turtles, a checklist, and alphabetical list of genera as well as species accounts and background information on turtle biology and conservation. Each chapter includes a short bibliography for further reading.

Lizards

Mattison, Christopher. **Lizards of the World.** New York: Facts on File, 1989. 192 p. $32.95. ISBN 0816019002.

Similar in format to other volumes in this series, this book provides an overview of lizard biology and classification for general audiences, including information on keeping lizards in captivity. Each family is described, the number of species included, distribution, and the natural history of typical members is discussed. There are many attractive color photographs as well.

Rogner, Manfred. **Lizards.** Malabar, FL: Krieger, 1997. 2 vol. $99.50. ISBN 0894649728 (set).

This set covers the care of captive lizards in detail, but it is of value to more than just pet owners and zookeepers. The species accounts include distribution, description, habitat, and lifestyle in the wild as well as husbandry and reproduction of captive specimens for about 550 species. Volume 1 provides an introduction and covers geckoes to iguanas; Volume 2 covers the other lizards, including tuataras and crocodilians.

Steel, Rodney. **Living Dragons: A Natural History of the World's Monitor Lizards.** Sanibel Island, FL: Ralph Curtis Books, 1996. 160 p. $39.50. ISBN 0883590409.

This survey of the monitor lizards of the world covers the species by geographical region rather than by taxonomic relationship. After describing the region's monitor fauna, each species and its natural history is described. The author also includes a chapter on the extinct mosasaurs and provides a list of synonyms used in monitor lizard classification.

Snakes

Bauchot, Roland, ed. **Snakes: A Natural History.** New York: Sterling, 1994. 220 p. $39.95. ISBN 0806906545.

Originally published in French, this oversized volume surveys the natural history of snakes of the world. It is intended as an introduction to snakes for the general public, and although the evolution and taxonomy of snakes are covered, the emphasis is on snake biology, ecology, and relationship to humans. There is extensive discussion of snake venoms, and the numerous photographs and drawings complement the text.

Brazaitis, Peter, and Myrna E. Watanabe. **Snakes of the World.** New York: Crescent Books, 1992. 176 p. ISBN 0517023261.

A colorful survey of snakes and snake biology, this book covers snake evolution, classification, anatomy, natural history, venoms, and interactions with humans. The many color photographs show snakes from around the world, and a separate "Gallery of Snakes" provides color photographs of typical snakes from each family along with a brief species account. The authors also provide appendixes listing zoos from around the world with significant snake collections, herpetology societies, and recommended books.

Dunson, William A., ed. **The Biology of Sea Snakes.** Baltimore: University Park Press, 1975. 530 p. ISBN 0839108192.

Chapters in this handbook cover the natural history of primarily Australian sea snakes, plus ecological relationships, physiology, and venom.

Ernst, Carl H., and George R. Zug. **Snakes in Question: The Smithsonian Answer Book.** Washington, DC: Smithsonian Institution Press, 1996. 203 p. $49.00; $24.95 (paper). ISBN 1560986484; 1560986492 (paper).

Organized in question-and-answer format, this handy book answers the most common questions about snake biology, folklore, snakebite, snakes and humans, and more. Appendixes describe the classification of snakes, body sizes, locomotion speeds, reproduction, and herpetological associations. There are also bibliographies and a glossary.

Greene, Harry W. **Snakes: The Evolution of Mystery in Nature.** Berkeley: University of California Press, 1997. 351 p. $55. ISBN 0520200144.

A well-written survey of the snake world, illustrated with gorgeous photographs of snakes from around the world. The book is in three sections, one covering the natural history of snakes, one discussing the various orders of snakes, and a final summary section covering evolution, biogeography, and snakes and humans. An appendix provides more information on systematics and phylogeny.

Mattison, Christopher. **The Encyclopedia of Snakes.** New York: Facts on File, 1995. 256 p. $44. ISBN 0816030723.

A colorful overview of snake biology and systematics, written for undergraduates or the general public, this encyclopedia provides a nice entry point for snake research. About two-thirds of the text involves snake biology, with the final third of the book consisting of a family-by-family account of snake systematics. Each entry contains a general description, information on the family in captivity, brief descriptions of the genera, distribution maps, and a short reference list. There are numerous attractive color photographs throughout.

Mehrtens, John M. **Living Snakes of the World in Color.** New York: Sterling, 1987. 480 p. $65. ISBN 080696460X.

This encyclopedia provides an overview of the 3,000 species of snakes around the world. About 500 are illustrated and described, with notes on their habitat, range, natural history, and care in captivity. There is a glossary and indexes, but no bibliography.

Stafford, Peter J. **Snakes.** Washington, DC: Smithsonian Institution Press in association with the Natural History Museum, London, 2000. 112 p. $16.95. ISBN 1560989971 (paper).

This survey of the snakes is aimed at a general audience. The author briefly describes snake anatomy and natural history, then surveys the main snake families and subfamilies. There are many color photographs, and brief lists of books, Web sites, and herpetological associations around the world for further information.

Crocodiles

Alderton, David. **Crocodiles and Alligators of the World.** New York: Facts on File, 1991. 190 p. $32.95. ISBN 0816022976.

Similar to the other encyclopedias in this series. Because there are only about 20 species of living crocodilians, the author has room to discuss each species in detail and to provide extensive general discussion of crocodilians and humans plus crocodilian anatomy, reproduction, and evolution.

Chiasson, Robert B. **Laboratory Anatomy of the Alligator.** Dubuque, IA: W. C. Brown, 1962. 56 p. (Laboratory Anatomy series).

A dissection manual for the alligator.

Grenard, Steve. **Handbook of Alligators and Crocodiles.** Malabar, FL: R. E. Krieger, 1991. 210 p. $49.50. ISBN 0894644351.

Provides extensive information on the alligators and crocodiles. In addition to general information on crocodilian classification, biology, and conservation status, the handbook contains detailed species accounts of alligators, crocodiles, and gavials and an extensive bibliography. The author also provides an illustrated identification key based on the appearance of the top of the heads of crocodilians.

Ross, Charles A., ed. **Crocodiles and Alligators.** New York: Facts on File, 1989. 240 p. $35. ISBN 0816021740.

An oversized general introduction to the crocodiles and alligators of the world, suitable for the general public. There are chapters on evolution and biology, behavior and ecology, and crocodilians and humans. The authors also provide a checklist of living crocodilians.

Geographical Section

North America

Bishop, Sherman C. **Handbook of Salamanders: The Salamanders of the United States, of Canada, and of Lower California.** Ithaca, NY: Comstock, 1994. 555 p. (Comstock Classic Handbooks). $46.50 (paper). ISBN 0801482135 (paper).

This classic handbook was originally published in 1943. Bishop provides general information on salamanders and their study as well as keys, distribution maps, and detailed descriptions of 126 species. They are illustrated with black-and-white photographs.

Ernst, Carl H., and Roger W. Barbour. **Snakes of Eastern North America.** Fairfax, VA: George Mason University Press, 1989. 282 p. $108. ISBN 0913969249.

Covers the natural history and identification of the 58 species of snakes found east of the Mississippi River. Each species account covers identification, karyotype, fossil record, distribution, geographical variation, confusing species, habitat, behavior, reproduction, longevity, food, predators, population size, and remarks. Distribution maps and black-and-white photographs accompany each species account, and there are color photographs for most species as well. The authors also include a key to adult snakes and a bibliography listing all papers on the ecology, ethology, and systematics of eastern snakes published after 1956.

Ernst, Carl H., Roger W. Barbour, and Jeffrey E. Lovich. **Turtles of the United States and Canada.** Washington, DC: Smithsonian Institution Press, 1994. 578 p. $60. ISBN 1560983469.

Updates Ernst and Barbour's *Turtles of the United States* from 1972. Each species account discusses recognition, karyotype, fossil record, distribution, confusing species, and natural history of the North American species. Each record includes a distribution map and one or more black-and-white photographs; there are also color photographs and a key to species.

Petranka, James W. **Salamanders of the United States and Canada.** Washington, DC: Smithsonian Institution Press, 1998. 587 p. $65. ISBN 1560988282.

This handbook replaces Sherman Bishop's classic *Handbook of Salamanders,* above. It contains information on identifying North American salamanders and keys to both adult and larval salamanders, as well as species accounts. The accounts include identification, systematics, distribution, and a detailed description of the natural history of the salamander species. There are photographs and range maps for each species as well.

Smith, Hobart Muir. **Handbook of Lizards: Lizards of the United States and of Canada.** Ithaca, NY: Comstock, 1995. 557 p. (Comstock Classic Handbooks). $46.50. ISBN 0801482364.

A classic handbook first published in 1946. In addition to detailed species accounts of 136 species, the handbook provides background information, keys, distribution maps, and a list of lizard species recorded in each state.

Wright, Albert Hazen, and Anna Allen Wright. **Handbook of Frogs and Toads of the United States and Canada.** 3rd ed. Ithaca, NY: Comstock, 1995. 640 p. (Comstock Classic Handbooks). $47.50. ISBN 0801482321.

This handbook is a reprint of the classic published in 1949, covering the identification and classification of the anurans of North America. There are keys to species, black-and-white photographs, and distribution maps for each species, and the species accounts include multiple common names, range, habitat, description, voice, breeding, and general notes. There are also "synopses" (i.e., keys) to eggs and tadpoles.

Wright, Albert Hazen, and Anna Allen Wright. **Handbook of Snakes of the United States and Canada.** Ithaca, NY: Comstock, 1994. 2 vol. (Comstock Classic Handbooks). $79.95. ISBN 0801482143.

This classic handbook was first published in 1957 and represents the standard resource for information on the snakes of North America. There are keys to species, black-and-white photographs, and line drawings. Each species account includes multiple common names, range, distinctive characteristics, habitat, and natural history as well as a brief bibliography. A list of important North American snake references appeared in Volume 2, and the complete bibliography was published in 1962 in a third volume by the Society for the Study of Amphibians and Reptiles (reprinted 1969; $18).

Africa

Channing, A. **Amphibians of Central and Southern Africa.** Ithaca, NY: Comstock, 2001. 470 p. (Comstock Books in Herpetology). $49.95. ISBN 0801438659.

Covers the natural history of the 200 frog species and 2 caecilians of the southern third of Africa (no salamanders live in the region). There are keys to both adults and tadpoles, and each species account includes local common names, description, distribution and habitat, voice, breeding, tadpoles, and notes as well as a distribution map. Most species are illustrated by color photographs, and a separate section describes and identifies tadpoles.

Schleich, Hans-Hermann, Werner Kästle, and Klaus Kabisch. **Amphibians and Reptiles of North Africa: Biology, Systematics, Field Guide.** Koenigstein, Germany: Koeltz Scientific Books, 1996. 630 p. ISBN 3874293777.

One of the very few books that cover the herpetology of Morocco, Algeria, Tunisia, and Libya. There is also limited coverage of Egyptian species. Initial chapters describe the geography and ecology of northern African amphibians and reptiles; the bulk of the book consists of species accounts. The species accounts provide etymology of the scientific name, common names in English, French, German, and Arabic, description, ecology, and behavior, reproduction, range, and references. There are also keys to adult and juvenile forms and color photographs of most species. Species that are only found in Egypt are not included in this section, but they are listed and keyed in an appendix.

Welch, Kenneth R. G. **Herpetology of Africa: A Checklist and Bibliography of the Orders Amphisbaenia, Sauria, and Serpentes.** Malabar, FL: R. E. Krieger, 1982. 293 p. ISBN 0898744288.

This checklist was intended to help standardize names of African amphibians and reptiles. Each entry includes references. The checklist concludes with a bibliography and indexes to genera and species.

Asia

Chao, Erh-mi, Kraig Adler, and John E. Simmons. **Herpetology of China.** Oxford, OH: Society for the Study of Amphibians and Reptiles in cooperation with the Chinese Society for the Study of Amphibians and Reptiles, 1993. 522 p. (Contributions to Herpetology, no. 10). $60. ISBN 0916984281.

Provides a survey of the state of herpetology in China. In addition to a checklist to the amphibians and reptiles of China, Tibet, and Hong Kong, the book contains a section on the history of herpetology in China, keys, and color photographs of some species. The annotated checklist includes names, type specimens, ranges, and notes for each species.

Daniel, J.C. **The Book of Indian Reptiles.** Bombay: Bombay Natural History Society, 1983. 141 p.

This handbook provides information on the natural history of the reptiles of India. Each species account includes local names, identification, habitat and status, habits, food, reproduction, voice, and miscellaneous notes.

Welch, Kenneth R. G. **Snakes of the Orient: A Checklist.** Malabar, FL: R. E. Krieger, 1988. 183 p. $28.50. ISBN 0894642030.

Similar in format to the author's *Herpetology of Africa,* above. It covers the area from Pakistan east to China as well as Australasia. The entries include synonymy, type location, and distribution; a separate bibliography is arranged by location.

Australasia

Rooij, Nelly de. **The Reptiles of the Indo-Australian Archipelago.** Leiden: E. J. Brill, 1915–17. 2 vol.

This handbook covers the reptiles of the area formerly known as the Dutch East Indies, including Sumatra, Borneo, Timor, and New Guinea. Each species account includes scientific name, first author, description, and distribution. Many of the species are illustrated, and there are lists of species showing their distribution throughout the archipelago. Volume 1 covers the Lacertilia, Chelonia, and Emydosauria; Volume 2 covers the Ophidia.

Central and South America

Campbell, Jonathan A., and William W. Lamar. **The Venomous Reptiles of Latin America.** Ithaca, NY: Comstock, 1989. 425 p. $75. ISBN 0801420598.

This catalog includes information on snakebite treatment, including a bibliography and list of antivenom producers, in addition to the regional and species accounts of venomous reptiles. The regional accounts include keys to venomous snakes in each country from Mexico south. The species accounts include the poisonous gila monster and beaded lizard of the United States and Mexico. The species accounts include distribution map, local names, habitat, description, similar species, remarks, and references. A final chapter covers the mimics of venomous snakes, especially false coral snakes.

Duellman, William Edward. **The Hylid Frogs of Middle America.** Lawrence: University of Kansas, 1970. 2 vol. (Monograph of the Museum of Natural History, the University of Kansas, no. 1).

A monograph of the tree frogs of Central America from Mexico to Panama. The author presents detailed information on the tree frogs, including synonymy, diagnosis, description of adults and tadpoles, mating calls, natural history, remarks, etymology, and distribution.

Freiberg, Marcos A. **Snakes of South America.** Neptune, NJ: TFH, 1982. 189 p. ISBN 0876669127.

About 500 species of snakes are known from South America, and this volume provides a survey of this poorly known fauna. There are many photographs illustrating about 75 common species, as well as a checklist, key to genera, more detailed descriptions of 50 common species, and introductory material covering the biology and classification of South American snakes. Much of the data presented in the volume is based on Peters's *Catalogue of the Neotropical Squamata,* below.

Harding, Keith A. **Catalogue of New World Amphibians.** New York: Pergamon, 1983. 406 p. ISBN 0080288995.

Contains two sections, a checklist in systematic order and faunal lists by region. The area covered includes the Americas and the Hawaiian Islands. The author also provides a list of synonyms in alphabetical order as well as extensive references and author and subject indexes.

Köhler, Gunther. **Reptilien und Amphibien Mittleamerikas.** Offenbach, Germany: Herpeton, 2000– . Vol. 34.80 euros (vol. 2). ISBN 3980621405 (vol. 1); 3980621456 (vol. 2).

Planned for three volumes, this set is designed to help travelers identify the amphibians and reptiles of Central America from southern Mexico to Panama. It is written in German and provides keys, color photographs, and general descriptions. Volume 1 covers the crocodiles, lizards, and turtles; Volume 2 covers snakes. Volume 3, not yet published at the time of writing, will cover the amphibians.

Peters, James Arthur, et al. **Catalogue of the Neotropical Squamata.** Rev. ed. Washington, DC: Smithsonian Institution Press, 1986. 2 vol. in 1. ISBN 0874747570.

A reprint of Volume 297 of the *United States National Museum Bulletin* from 1970, this catalog lists all the known snakes and lizards of the neotropics. It includes some new material and notes the reliability of the data provided. Each entry contains the citation to the original description, the type locality, and distribution. There are keys to well-known genera, and for lesser-known groups matrixes are provided to assist identification. Volume 1 covers snakes, and Volume 2 covers lizards and amphisbaenians.

Villa, Jaime, Larry David Wilson, and Jerry D. Johnson. **Middle American Herpetology: A Bibliographic Checklist.** Columbia: University of Missouri Press, 1988. 131 p. ISBN 0826206654.

Synthesizes the herpetological literature for Central America, containing a species list, citations to major works, and information on distribution. The

782 species accounts include references to the key literature, illustrations, and distribution information. The authors also provide a list of useful regional keys and color photographs for about 100 species of herps.

Europe

Böhme, Wolfgang, and N.B. Anan'eva, eds. **Handbuch der Reptilien und Amphibien Europas.** Wiesbaden, Germany: Akademische Verlagsgesellschaft, 1981– 6 vol. in 8.

This set discusses the herps of Europe in great depth, covering identification, distribution, geographical variation, ecology, reproduction, and more. Each species account also includes distribution maps and illustrations, most of skulls or details of scale patterns. The series is written in German. Volumes 1 through 4 are in systematic order; Volume 5 (although not so noted) consists of the *Nomina herpetofaunae Europaeae* (common names), and Volume 6 covers the reptiles of the Canary Islands and Madeira. A supplement published in 1981, *Threatened Amphibians and Reptiles in Europe,* discusses the reasons for the decline in these species and provides species accounts for 61 species of threatened and endangered species.

Griffiths, Richard A. **Newts and Salamanders of Europe.** San Diego: Academic, 1996. 188 p. $55.95. ISBN 012303955X.

Covers the biology, ecology, behavior, and conservation of the salamanders of Europe. The final chapter provides species accounts for the 32 species found in the western Palearctic region. Each account includes distribution map, description, habitat, natural history, eggs and larvae, and references.

Welch, Kenneth R.G. **Herpetology of Europe and Southwest Asia: A Checklist and Bibliography of the Orders Amphisbaenia, Sauria and Serpentes.** Malabar, FL: R.E. Krieger, 1983. 135 p. ISBN 0898745330.

Each family is listed in separate chapters. Information given for each species includes author's name and date, geographical distribution, and citations. A separate bibliography provides the cited literature, and there is also an index to scientific names of species and subspecies.

Identification Tools

CITES Identification Guide—Crocodilians: Guide to the Identification of Crocodilian Species Controlled under the Convention on

International Trade in Endangered Species of Wild Fauna and Flora. Ottawa: Environment Canada, 1995. 1 vol. (various pagings). ISBN 0662619579.

A guide to the identification of 21 species of crocodilians. The multilingual guide has keys to adult specimens and hides. Species accounts provide a black-and-white illustration, distribution map, CITES status, and type of trade in body parts. The full text of the guide is also available in html format at URL: http://www.flmnh.ufl.edu/natsci/herpetology/CITEScroc/default.htm.

CITES Identification Guide—Turtles and Tortoises: Guide to the Identification of Turtles and Tortoises Species Controlled under the Convention on International Trade in Endangered Species of Wild Fauna And Flora. Ottawa: Environment Canada, 1999. 1 vol. (various pagings). ISBN 0662641698.

Covers turtle species protected by CITES or likely to be mistaken for protected species, plus some common commercial species. Similar in format to the crocodilian guide above. In English, French, and Spanish. Full text of the guide is available in PDF format at URL: http://www.cws-scf.ec.gc.ca/enforce/pdf/Turtle/CITES_Turtle_Guide.pdf.

Coborn, John. **The Atlas of Snakes of the World.** Neptune City, NJ: TFH, 1991. 591 p. $129.95. ISBN 0866227490.

This oversized guide to snakes provides information on captive care for each genus of snakes throughout the world. Following introductory chapters on evolution and classification of snakes, snake housing and general care in captivity, and reproduction, the book covers each snake family in detail. Species accounts include information on distribution, natural history, identification, and captive care of the snakes. There are excellent color photographs of most species.

Geographical Section

North America

Altig, Ronald, Roy W. McDiarmid, Kimberly A. Nichols, and Paul C. Ustach. **Tadpoles of the United States and Canada: A Tutorial and Key.** Patuxent, MS: Patuxent Wildlife Research Center. URL: http://www.pwrc.usgs.gov/tadpole/ (Accessed August 25, 2003).

A key to the tadpoles of North America, this site does not use the usual dichotomous key system. Instead, users first key the specimen to the family level. Within each family are separate sections for groups of characteristics such as range, coloration, labial tooth row formula, and others. The authors plan to publish this key and similar ones for other larval amphibians in book format (date not given).

Ballinger, Royce E., and John D. Lynch. **How to Know the Amphibians and Reptiles.** Dubuque, IA: W.C. Brown, 1983. 229 p. (Pictured Key Nature Series). $41.55 (paper). ISBN 0697047865 (paper).
    An illustrated key to North American amphibians and reptiles. The volume includes a separate key to larval amphibians.

Behler, John L., and F. Wayne King. **National Audubon Society Field Guide to North American Reptiles and Amphibians.** New York: Knopf, 1998. 743 p. (National Audubon Society Field Guide series). $19.95. ISBN 0394508246.
    A photographic field guide to 400 species of herps. The species accounts include natural history and distribution maps, and poisonous or dangerous species are noted.

Conant, Roger, and Joseph T. Collins. **A Field Guide to Reptiles and Amphibians: Eastern and Central North America.** 3rd ed., enl. Boston: Houghton Mifflin, 1998. 616 p. (Peterson Field Guide series, no. 12). $20 (paper). ISBN 0395904528 (paper).
    One of the standard field guides to North American amphibians and reptiles, this guide covers 575 species and contains color and black-and-white illustrations. The guide also provides information on capturing and keeping amphibians and reptiles as pets.

Cook, Francis R. **Introduction to Canadian Amphibians and Reptiles.** Ottawa: National Museum of Natural Sciences: National Museums of Canada, 1984. 200 p. ISBN 0660107554 (paper).
    Provides basic introductory information on the herps of Canada such as classification, characteristics, and care as pets in addition to a field guide for identifying species. The species accounts include a black and white illustration as well as range map and description.

Harding, James H. **Amphibians and Reptiles of the Great Lakes Region.** Ann Arbor: University of Michigan Press, 1997. 378 p. (Great Lakes Environment). $21.95 (paper). ISBN 0472096281; 0472066285 (paper).
    An identification guide and reference for amateurs and professionals, this guide covers the herpetofauna of the Great Lakes Basin, the area surround-

ing the lakes. An introductory section provides information on the classification, ecology, and conservation of the area's herps, followed by detailed species accounts and a section listing resources such as recordings of vocalizations, herpetological associations, regulatory agencies, and references. Each species account includes a color photograph, distribution map, description, confusing species, status, natural history, and conservation.

Nussbaum, Ronald A., Edmund D. Brodie, and Robert M. Storm. **Amphibians and Reptiles of the Pacific Northwest.** Moscow: University Press of Idaho, 1983. 332 p. (Northwest Naturalist Books). $24.95 (paper). ISBN 0893010863 (paper).

Covers 62 species of herps found in British Columbia, Idaho, Oregon, and Washington. The species accounts include extensive information on the natural history of each species, and there are black-and-white photographs, range maps, and references for each account as well. The authors also provide keys to each group, and there are also some color photographs.

Powell, Robert, Joseph T. Collins, and Errol D. Hooper, Jr. **A Key to Amphibians and Reptiles of the Continental United States and Canada.** Lawrence: University Press of Kansas, 1998. 131 p. $17.95. ISBN 0700609296 (paper).

The key is designed for use in herpetology courses and covers only adult specimens. Students are referred to Stebbins's and Conant's Peterson field guides (see this section) and to the *Catalogue of American Amphibians and Reptiles* (in the Handbooks section) for more information on each species. There are many drawings and a glossary to help students.

Stebbins, Robert C. **A Field Guide to Western Reptiles and Amphibians.** 2nd ed., rev. Boston: Houghton Mifflin, 1985. 336 p. (Peterson Field Guide series, no. 16). ISBN 0395082110; 0395382548; 039538253X (paper); 0395194210 (paper).

Covers all the herps of western North America. There are keys to adults, eggs, and larvae as well as species accounts with information on identification, similar species, range, subspecies, remarks, and color illustrations.

Africa

Branch, Bill. **Field Guide to Snakes and Other Reptiles of Southern Africa.** 3rd ed., rev. Sanibel Island, FL: Ralph Curtis Books, 1998. 399 p. $32.50. ISBN 0883590425.

This guide describes and illustrates the wide variety of reptiles found in southern Africa. The author provides background information on reptile observation and collection as well as the ecology of southern Africa and keys to species. The species accounts include identification, biology and breeding, habitat, and range. The color photographs illustrating most species are in a separate section.

Henkel, Friedrich-Wilhelm, and Wolfgang Schmidt. **Amphibians and Reptiles of Madagascar, the Mascarenes, the Seychelles, and the Comoros Islands.** 1st English ed. Malabar, FL: Krieger, 1998. 311 p. $72.50. ISBN 1575240149.

This natural history guide covers 240 species of herps found on the islands of the Indian Ocean. The guide features color photographs and includes background information, description, life histories, and care in captivity for each species.

Schleich, Hans-Hermann, Werner Kastle, and Klaus Kabisch. **Amphibians and Reptiles of North Africa: Biology, Systematics, Field Guide.** Koenigstein, Germany: Koeltz Scientific, 1996. 630 p. $126. ISBN 3874293777.

One of the few resources dealing with this region, this guide covers 100 species of the Maghreb states of Morocco, Algeria, Tunisia, and part of Libya. The guide includes keys, common names in several languages, and extensive information on the natural history of the animals.

Spawls, Stephen, Kim Howell, Robert Drewes, and James Ashe. **A Field Guide to the Reptiles of East Africa: Kenya, Tanzania, Uganda, Rwanda and Burundi.** San Diego: Academic, 2002. 543 p. (AP Natural World). $49.95. ISBN 0126564701.

Provides descriptions and distribution maps for all species of reptiles known to occur in East Africa. Most are illustrated with a color photograph, and the descriptions also summarize what is known of the natural history of the species. There are also keys to species and appendixes providing information on snakebite, local names of some of the most common reptiles, a gazetteer, a glossary, and references.

Australasia

Cogger, Harold G. **Reptiles and Amphibians of Australia.** 6th ed. Sanibel Island, FL: Ralph Curtis Books, 2000. 808 p. $110. ISBN 0883590484.

A hefty identification guide to the herps of Australia, this highly regarded manual provides a checklist and background information on the nomenclature, conservation, and study of Australian herps, in addition to identification. The species accounts include brief descriptions, distribution information, and habitat as well as range maps and color photographs. An appendix covers changes in taxonomy and nomenclature since the previous edition in 1992, and the author also provides a glossary and an extensive list of references.

Central and South America

Campbell, Jonathan A. **Amphibians and Reptiles of Northern Guatemala, the Yucatán, and Belize.** Norman: University of Oklahoma Press, 1998. 380 p. (Animal Natural History Series, vol. 4). $39.95 (paper). ISBN 0806130644 (paper).

Intended for the use of nonherpetologists, this guide covers the 160 species of herps of the Petén region of northern Guatemala and adjacent regions, including Tikal National Park. Color photographs in the middle of the book illustrate each species, and the species accounts include common names in English and Spanish, description, natural history, distribution, and remarks. The author includes a number of personal observations and anecdotes about studying herps in the region. Appendixes provide dichotomous keys to the various groups and in both English and Spanish.

Lee, Julian C. **A Field Guide to the Amphibians and Reptiles of the Maya World: The Lowlands of Mexico, Northern Guatemala, and Belize.** Ithaca, NY: Comstock, 2000. 402 p. $59.95; $35.00 (paper). ISBN 0801436249; 0801485878 (paper).

A comprehensive guide to the herps of the region, this guide features color photographs and detailed species accounts, including resources for further reading. All tadpoles are illustrated as well as adult specimens.

Murphy, John C. **Amphibians and Reptiles of Trinidad and Tobago.** Malabar, FL: Krieger, 1997. 245 p. $72.50. ISBN 089464971X.

A detailed guide to all 129 species and subspecies found on the islands. The author provides detailed information about each species, along with color photographs, distribution maps, and keys.

Europe

Arnold, Nicholas. **Reptiles and Amphibians of Britain and Europe.** 2nd ed. London: HarperCollins, 2002. 288 p. $35. ISBN 0691114137.

A comprehensive guide to the 198 species of the herps of Europe, including an identification section on the eggs and larvae of amphibians such as frogs and newts.

Leviton, Alan E., Steven C. Anderson, Kraig Adler, and Sherman A. Minton. **Handbook to Middle East Amphibians and Reptiles.** S.l.: Society for the Study of Amphibians and Reptiles, 1992. 252 p. (Contributions to Herpetology, no. 8). $30. ISBN 0916984230.

This handbook covers 148 species and subspecies found in the region from the Turkish border south to the Arabian peninsula, including Bahrain, Qatar, and the United Arab Emirates, and parts of Iraq, Iran, and Saudi Arabia. This area has not been extensively studied, so the handbook is designed as an interim guide representing what is known. The handbook is primarily an identification guide but also contains information on the venomous snakes of the Middle East and snakebite symptoms and treatment. An appendix covers field techniques for collecting and preserving herps.

Pacific Islands

McKeown, Sean. **A Field Guide to Reptiles and Amphibians in the Hawaiian Islands.** Los Osos, CA: Diamond Head, 1996. 172 p. $15.95 (paper). ISBN 0965073106 (paper).

Covers all 33 species found in the Hawaiian Islands, with detailed information on natural history and care in captivity.

Associations

American Society of Ichthyologists and Herpetologists. Grice Marine Laboratory, University of Charleston, 205 Fort Johnson Rd., Charleston, SC 29412. Phone: 843 406 4017. E-mail: asih@mail.utexas.edu. URL: http://199.245.200.110/ (Accessed August 25, 2003).

British Herpetological Society. c/o The Zoological Society of London, Regent's Park, London, NW1 4RY, UK. E-mail: info@thebhs.org. URL: http://www.thebhs.org/ (Accessed August 25, 2003).

Herpetologists' League. Biological Sciences Box 4050, Emporia State University, Emporia, KS 66801-4050. Phone: 316-341-5606. E-mail: sievert1@esumail.emporia.edu. URL: http://www.inhs.uiuc.edu/cbd/HL/HL.html (Accessed August 25, 2003).

Societas Europaea Herpetologica (SEH). c/o M. R. K. Lambert, Natural Resources Institute, Central Avenue, Chatham Maritime, Kent ME4 4TB, UK. E-mail: Lambertmrk@aol.com. URL: http://www.gli.cas.cz/SEH/ (Accessed August 25, 2003).

Society for the Study of Amphibians and Reptiles. Biology Dept., St. Louis University, 3507 Laclede Ave., St. Louis, MO 63103-2010. Phone: 314-977-3916. Fax: 314-977-3658. E-mail: ssar@slu. URL: http://www. ssarherps.org/ (Accessed August 25, 2003).

Reference

Kitchell, Kenneth, Jr., and Harold A. Dundee. 1994. Translation and annotation of the amphibian and reptile section of *Systema Naturae X*. In *A Trilogy on the Herpetology of Linnaeus's Systema Naturae X*. Washington, DC: Smithsonian Herpetological Service.

7

Birds

Birds are a highly successful group of animals with about 9,700 species around the world. Birds are warm blooded, lay eggs, have bills and feathers, and they are distinguished by their many specializations for flight such as light hollow bones and a unique breathing system. These specializations are found even in birds such as ostriches that have lost the ability to fly. Most taxonomists now agree that birds are descended from the theropod dinosaurs, although a significant minority still hold out for a crocodilian ancestor. Avian taxonomy underwent a major upheaval in the 1990s when Charles Sibley and Burt Monroe published a revised classification based on DNA-DNA hybridization in their *Distribution and Taxonomy of Birds of the World*. The details of the new system are still being debated, but most of the changes have been accepted and many newer publications follow the Sibley-Monroe system.

Birds hold a special fascination for many people. The vast number of birders, as the more dedicated bird watchers prefer to be called, have had a greater effect on the study of ornithology than have amateurs in other fields. The National Audubon Society's annual Christmas Bird Count in North America is probably one of the best-known efforts by amateurs and has been the model for other census efforts. In addition, the growing sophistication of birders has led to the publication of a number of detailed identification/taxonomic guides to bird families, which are of value to ornithologists as well as birders. Many of these are annotated here.

Classification of Birds (from Monroe & Sibley, 1993; species counts from Gill, 1995)

Eoaves (the ratites and tinamous)

Struthioniformes (ostriches, rheas, and cassowaries; 10 species)

Tinamiformes (tinamous; 47 species)

Neoaves (all other modern birds)

Craciformes (guans and megapodes; 69 species)

Galliformes (domestic fowl and game birds; 214 species)

Anseriformes (ducks, geese, and swans; 161 species)

Turniciformes (buttonquail; 17 species)

Piciformes (woodpeckers, toucans, and relatives; 355 species)

Galbuliformes (jacamars; 51 species)

Bucerotiformes (hornbills; 56 species)

Upupiformes (hoopoes and scimitarbills; 10 species)

Trogoniformes (trogons and quetzal; 39 species)

Coraciiformes (rollers, kingfishers, hornbills, etc.; 152 species)

Coliiformes (mousebirds; 6 species)

Cuculiformes (cuckoos and hoatzin; 143 species)

Psittaciformes (parrots; 358 species)

Apodiformes (swifts; 103 species)

Trochiliformes (hummingbirds; 319 species)

Musophagiformes (turacos; 23 species)

Strigiformes (owls, nighthawks, frogmouths; 291 species)

Columbiformes (doves and pigeons; 313 species)

Gruiformes (cranes, hemipodes, gallinules; 196 species)

Ciconiiformes (herons, shorebirds, seabirds, hawks, loons, penguins, etc.; 1,027 species)

Passeriformes (songbirds and perching birds; 5,076 species)

Indexes, Abstracts, and Bibliographies

Coues, Elliott. **American Ornithological Bibliography.** New York: Arno Press, 1974. 1,066 p. (Natural Sciences in America). ISBN 0405057040.

A reprint of the second and third installments of Coues's *American Ornithological Bibliography,* originally published as *Bulletin of the U.S. Geological and Geographical Survey of the Territories,* vol. 5, no. 2, pp. 239–330, and no. 4, pp. 521–1066. The second installment covers faunal publications for Latin America and the West Indies; the third and longer installment lists publications dealing with avian taxonomy. The first installment, which is not reprinted in this volume, is from the *Miscellaneous Publications of the U.S. Geological and Geographical Survey of the Territories,* no. 11, and consists of a list of faunal publications relating to North American ornithology. Coues also prepared a fourth installment, which was a list of faunal publications relating to British birds, published in the *Proceedings of the United States National Museum,* vol. 2 (1880).

Recent Ornithological Literature (ROL). 1986– . Washington, DC: American Ornithologists' Union, British Ornithologists' Union, and Royal Australasian Ornithologists' Union. Quarterly. URL: http://www.nmnh.si. edu/BIRDNET/ROL/index.html (Accessed August 26, 2003).

A supplement to the ornithological journals *The Auk, The Emu,* and *Ibis,* ROL was formerly a print publication available for free with a subscription to any of the journals. Since 1999 it has been published only on the Web as a browseable list of issues or searchable database, both going back to October 1997 at the time of viewing. ROL covers about 900 journals worldwide, plus dissertations, conference proceedings, and similar resources. The bibliography is organized by broad subject categories such as systematics, morphology, identification, or distribution, and it includes information on new and renamed journals.

Strong, R.M. **A Bibliography of Birds: With Special Reference to Anatomy, Behavior, Biochemistry, Embryology, Pathology, Physiology, Genetics, Ecology, Aviculture, Economic Ornithology, Poultry Culture, Evolution, and Related Subjects.** (Publications of the Field Museum of Natural History, vol. 25). Chicago: Field Museum of Natural History, 1939–59.

This bibliography provides a comprehensive coverage of the world literature of ornithology up to 1926, although there are some references later than that year. It is in alphabetical order by author with a subject and finding index.

Zimmer, John Todd. **Catalogue of the Edward E. Ayer Ornithological Library.** Chicago: Field Museum of Natural History, 1926. (Fieldiana

Zoology, vol. 16; Publications, vol. 239–240). Reprint, New York: Arno Press, 1974. 706 p. $47.95. ISBN 0405057733.

An annotated catalog of the books donated to the ornithological library at the Field Museum by Ayer, plus other then-current ornithological works. It is arranged in alphabetical order by author, then chronologically rather than alphabetically. There are no subject or title indexes. The catalog is useful for verifying old and obscure materials.

Journals

Ardea. Vol. 1– . Groningen: Netherlands Ornithologists' Union, 1912– . Semiannual. $61.42. ISSN 0373-2266.

Publishes articles in English dealing with the ecology, biogeography, and evolution of birds as well as book reviews, short notes, essays, and reports of meetings. The official journal of the Netherlands Ornithologists' Union.

Auk: A Quarterly Journal of Ornithology. Vol. 1– . Lawrence, KS: American Ornithologists' Union, 1884– . Quarterly. $70. ISSN 0004-8038. Available electronically.

The most highly regarded journal in ornithology, *Auk* publishes articles on all aspects of ornithology, including systematics, ecology, and behavior. The journal also publishes perspectives, overviews, short communications, book reviews, obituaries, and a history column. The journal of the American Ornithologists' Union.

Bird Study. Vol. 1– . Thetford, UK: British Trust for Ornithology, 1954– . 3/yr. $140. ISSN 0006-3657.

Publishes articles on aspects of field ornithology of interest to both amateurs and professionals. The official journal of the British Trust for Ornithology.

The Condor: An International Journal of Avian Biology. Vol. 1– . Lawrence, KS: Allen Press, 1899– . Quarterly. $115. ISSN 0010-5422. Available electronically.

Publishes articles, short communications, book reviews, and news dealing with the biology of wild birds. At the time of viewing (August 26, 2003), full text of the entire back run of the journal from 1899 through 2000 was available at the Cooper Ornithological Society's Web site at http://elibrary.unm.edu/Condor/, and current issues were available by sub-scription only. The journal of the Cooper Ornithological Society.

Current Ornithology. Vol. 1– . New York: Kluwer, 1983– . Irregular. ISSN 0742-390X.
A serial journal publishing review articles on all topics of avian biology, from molecular biology to ecology. Behavioral and ecological topics pre-dominate in the most recent volumes.

Emu. Vol. 1– . Melbourne, Australia: CSIRO, 1901– . Quarterly. $190. ISSN 0158-4197. Available electronically.
Publishes articles on all aspects of ornithology, including conservation and applied ornithology, with emphasis on the birds of Australasia. New species are frequently listed. Selected articles are available at no charge for personal use at the journal's Web site (http://www.publish.csiro.au/journals/emu/index.cfm), but most require a subscription or per article fee. The journal of the Royal Australasian Ornithologists Union.

Ibis. Vol. 1– . Osney Mead, UK: Blackwell Scientific, 1859– . Quarterly. $306. ISSN 0019-0019. Available electronically.
Publishes papers, reviews, and short communications on all aspects of ornithology with emphasis on systematics, behavior, and ecology. Some articles are available only as online publications but are also listed in the print table of contents. Selected articles are available for free at the jour-nal's Web site at http://www.ibis.ac.uk/. The journal of the British Ornithologists' Union.

Journal für Ornithologie. Vol. 1– . Berlin: Blackwell Wissenschafts-Verlag, 1853– . Quarterly. 372 euros. ISSN 0021-8375. Available elec-tronically.
Publishes articles, reviews, short communications, letters to the editor, and society news on all aspects of ornithology, especially European birds. About half the articles are written in English and half in German, with abstracts in both languages. The official journal of the Deutschen Ornithologen-Gesellschaft.

Journal of Avian Biology. Vol. 25– . Copenhagen: Munksgaard, 1994– . Quarterly. $162. ISSN 0908-8857. Available electronically.
Publishes articles in all areas of ornithology, with emphasis on avian ecology. Formerly titled *Ornis Scandinavica*.

Journal of Field Ornithology. Vol. 51– . Lawrence, KS: Association of Field Ornithologists, 1980– . Quarterly. $45. ISSN 0748-4690.

The journal publishes articles dealing with birds in their natural habitats, especially studies done in the neotropics. The articles are written in English, but the abstracts are in English and Spanish. The journal also publishes an annual review of current foreign ornithological literature. A publication of the Association of Field Ornithologists. Formerly titled *Bird-Banding.*

The Wilson Bulletin: A Quarterly Magazine of Ornithology. Vol. 1– . Lawrence, KS: Allen Press, 1889– . Quarterly. $40. ISSN 0043-5643. Available electronically.

For professionals and amateurs. Publishes articles, short communications, book reviews, and news in all areas of ornithology, with emphasis on the birds of the Western Hemisphere. The journal of the Wilson Ornithological Society.

Guides to the Literature

Miller, Melanie Ann. **Birds: A Guide to the Literature.** New York: Garland, 1986. 887 p. (Garland Reference Library of the Humanities). ISBN 0824087100.

An annotated guide to nearly 2,000 popular and technical books written about birds. Most of them are arranged by broad subject heading such as ecology or flight. There are also lists of statewide ornithological resources, biographies, children's literature, and more. Although the guide is outdated, it still offers the most complete listing of bird books to be found.

Biographies and Histories

Barrow, Mark V. **A Passion for Birds: American Ornithology after Audubon.** Princeton, NJ: Princeton University Press, 1998. 326 p. $90.00; $22.95 (paper). ISBN 0691044023; 0691049548 (paper).

Watching birds has been a popular pastime in the United States for a long time. This history relates the tensions between amateur bird-watchers and the emerging guild of professional ornithologists as well as outlining the continuing areas of cooperation between the two groups.

Farber, Paul Lawrence. **Discovering Birds: The Emergence of Ornithology as a Scientific Discipline: 1760–1850.** Baltimore: Johns Hopkins University Press, 1997. 191 p. $17.95 (paper). ISBN 0801855373 (paper).

Originally published in 1982, this history follows the development of ornithology as a nineteenth-century science out of the eighteenth-century tradition of natural history.

Kastner, Joseph. **A World of Watchers.** New York: Knopf, 1986. 241 p. ISBN 0394528697.

Covers the history of birding or bird-watching in North America as distinct from ornithology, although in the early years the difference was less significant. The time period covered ranges from the precolonial times (although as the author says, the Native Americans were not birders because they did not keep life lists) to Roger Tory Peterson and the modern phenomenon of birding. The book is illustrated with drawings and paintings by Louis Agassiz Fuertes, one of the best ornithological artists of all times.

Mearns, Barbara, and Richard Mearns. **The Bird Collectors.** San Diego: Academic Press, 1998. 472 p. $55.95. ISBN 0124874401.

Bird collectors, both amateur and professional, provided museums with bird specimens and were essential players in creating the modern field of ornithology. The authors discuss the activities of these individuals in the context of their times and provide brief biographies of 600 individuals from the late eighteenth century to the present who collected birds. There are also numerous photographs.

Dictionaries and Encyclopedias

Baumel, J.J., et al., eds. **Handbook of Avian Anatomy: Nomina Anatomica Avium.** 2nd ed. Cambridge, MA: Nuttall Ornithological Club, 1993. 779 p. (Publications of the Nuttall Ornithological Club, no. 23).

The purpose of this book is to establish a standard nomenclature for bird anatomy. The handbook is divided into chapters according to system (external anatomy, skeleton, cardiovascular system, etc.). Each chapter begins with a brief introduction, followed by a list of terminology, then annotations on the source and use of the terms. Appendixes provide information on Latin grammar and list the members of the International Committee for Avian Anatomical Nomenclature (ICAAN), the body that established the terminology.

Brooke, Michael, and Tim Birkhead, eds. **Cambridge Encyclopedia of Ornithology.** New York: Cambridge University Press, 1991. 362 p. ISBN 0521362059.

This encyclopedia concentrates on elucidating bird biology rather than describing bird families. It is arranged by broad topic such as anatomy, migration, and behavior and also includes a chapter on birds and humans.

Campbell, Bruce, and Elizabeth Lack, eds. **A Dictionary of Birds.** Vermillion, SD: Buteo Books, 1985. 670 p. $75. ISBN 0931130123.

Although it is called a dictionary, this is actually more of an encyclopedia with sometimes lengthy essays on a variety of topics in ornithology. Entries include terms from systematics, behavior, and biology. There are many entries discussing individual bird species listed under the common name of the family or subfamily (such as grouse or rail).

Choate, Ernest. **The Dictionary of American Bird Names.** rev. ed. Boston: Harvard Common Press, 1985. 226 p. $10.95 (paper). ISBN 0876451172 (paper).

This dictionary covers common and scientific names for North American birds and discusses their origins. It is useful for finding obscure and archaic names, and includes British names that might be encountered by Americans such as seabird names or names that are used for different birds in the two regions. The dictionary also has a biographical appendix listing American ornithologists and people who had birds named after themselves as well as an English/Latin glossary and bibliography. It is based on the American Ornithological Union's *Check-list of North American Birds,* 6th ed. (above), which is now up to the 7th edition, so it should be used with care.

Cox, Randall T. **Birder's Dictionary.** Helena, MT: Falcon Press, 1996. 186 p. $8.95 (paper). ISBN 1560444231 (paper).

This compact dictionary contains words that birders might need to define, including biological, anatomical, physiological, behavioral, and taxonomic terms. There are anatomical illustrations and appendixes listing bird orders and families of North America and the traditional and Sibley-Ahlquist-Monroe systems of classification.

Forshaw, Joseph, ed. **Encyclopedia of Birds.** 2nd ed. San Diego: Academic Press, 1998. 240 p. (Natural World Series). $39.95. ISBN 0122623401.

An oversized, colorful survey of the bird families. Introductory chapters discuss bird biology, classification, and evolution, although the bulk of the encyclopedia consists of family accounts. The accounts contain general summaries of the bird families, including interesting tidbits on the biology or behavior of the birds, plus a table summarizing the taxonomy, size, and conservation status of the family.

Gotch, A. F. **Latin Names Explained: A Guide to the Scientific Classification of Reptiles, Birds and Mammals.**

See chapter 4 for a full annotation. Explains the source of Latin terms used in avian scientific names.

Jobling, James A. **A Dictionary of Scientific Bird Names.** New York: Oxford University Press, 1991. 272 p. ISBN 0198546343.

This dictionary lists the derivation and meaning of all currently accepted scientific bird names. Some entries include the original citation; biographical terms include dates and frequently citations to major works.

Perrins, Christopher M. **The Illustrated Encyclopedia of Birds: The Definitive Reference to Birds of the World.** New York: Prentice Hall Editions, 1990. 420 p. ISBN 0130836354.

Another of the excellent encyclopedias that cover the bird species of the world. This one contains color illustrations of about 1,200 species of birds. The encyclopedia includes a brief discussion of bird biology and conservation, but the catalog section is the most lengthy. The accounts are in taxonomic order with a description of each family, followed by a brief account of selected species. The descriptions include topics such as range, habitat, size, and behavior but do not include physical descriptions.

Perrins, Christopher M., and Alex L. A. Middleton, eds. **The Encyclopaedia of Birds.** New York: Facts on File, 1985. 445 p. $45. ISBN 0816011508.

Another excellent, widely available survey of bird families with numerous color photographs and illustrations. There is more detail than in some similar encyclopedias, and many of the photographs illustrate various behaviors.

Terres, John K. **The Audubon Society Encyclopedia of North American Birds.** New York: Knopf, distributed by Random House, 1980. 1,109 p. ISBN 0394466519.

This massive compendium represents over 20 years of work by the author. Entries are listed in alphabetical order and include brief biographies of ornithologists, definitions of terms from birding, anatomy, behavior, ecology, pathology, and other fields, plus extensive "biographies" of nearly 850 species of North American birds. The species accounts are arranged by family, and they include descriptions, information on nesting, feeding, common names, oldest known individuals, range, and more. There are many excellent color photographs and black-and-white drawings.

Wrobel, M. **Elsevier's Dictionary of Bird Names: In Latin, English, French, German, and Italian.** Boston: Elsevier, 2002. 1,436 p. $245. ISBN 0444508368.

This multilingual dictionary translates 10,838 bird names, including orders, families, and species, into the major European languages. It covers birds from Europe, North America, South Africa, New Zealand, Australia, and French-speaking countries. The main portion of the dictionary is in alphabetical order by scientific name, with translations of the common name in each appropriate language. There are separate indexes for each language.

Textbooks

Gill, Frank B. **Ornithology.** 2nd ed. New York: W. H. Freeman, 1995. 763 p. $106.50. ISBN 0716724154.

The most commonly used ornithological text, this book contains extensive discussion of avian biology, from evolution to anatomy, ecology, and conservation. There is an extensive discussion of classification and phylogeny, and an appendix details the bird orders of the world. This text thus contains more information on avian biodiversity than the other texts listed below.

Pettingill, Olin Sewall, Jr. **Ornithology in Laboratory and Field.** 5th ed. Orlando, FL: Academic Press, 1985. 403 p. $59.95. ISBN 0125524552.

A classic ornithological text with only a brief discussion of taxonomy and bird families, although as part of the discussion of laboratory identification the author includes a key to the orders and families of North American birds. The emphasis is on bird anatomy, biology, and behavior. Appendixes cover ornithological methods, how to write a paper, ornithological journals, and general ornithology books.

Proctor, Noble S., and Patrick J. Lynch. **Manual of Ornithology: Avian Structure and Function.** New Haven: Yale University Press, 1993. 340 p. $60.00; $27.50 (paper). ISBN 0300057466; 0300076193 (paper).

Designed as a lab manual, this text covers the anatomy of birds in great detail. Most illustrations are of the rock dove (*Columba livia*), but many other species are illustrated as well for relevant body parts (bills, feet, and so on). The discussion of avian classification is brief but includes two tables showing competing classification systems for birds (biochemical and morphological). An appendix lists bird families according to Sibley and Monroe (above). A chapter on field techniques for studying birds completes the text.

Van Tyne, Josselyn, and Andrew John Berger. **Fundamentals of Ornithology.** 2nd ed. New York: Wiley, 1976. 808 p. ISBN 0471899658.

Although the details of higher-order avian taxonomy have changed since this text was published, the family descriptions found in the book are still useful as concise outlines of the characteristics, range, habits, food, breeding, diagnosis, and classification of each family worldwide.

Welty, Joel Carl, and Luis Baptista. **The Life of Birds.** 4th ed. New York: Saunders, 1988. 581 p. $77.31. ISBN 0030689236.

An introductory textbook that emphasizes bird biology rather than systematics, this classic text is considered by many to have the best coverage of bird biology of the ornithological texts. The discussion of avian systematics is outdated because it is pre-Sibley and Moore, but there is a nice discussion of how taxonomists go about classifying birds. Other topics covered include flight, migration, anatomy and physiology, nesting and courtship, ecology, evolution, and birds and humans.

Checklists and Classification Schemes

Austin, Oliver Luther. **Families of Birds.** Rev. ed. New York: Golden Press, 1985. 200 p. (Golden Field Guide series). ISBN 0307136698 (paper).

This widely available little guide was one of the standard popular guides to bird classification, although now that the Sibley/Monroe revision has been accepted the details of Austin's work have become out of date. However, many field guides still follow the order of bird families laid down in this volume, and the brief sketches of each order and family are still useful.

Banks, Richard C. **Obsolete English Names of North American Birds and Their Modern Equivalents.** Washington, DC: U.S. Department of the Interior, Fish and Wildlife Service, 1988. 37 p. (Resource Publication of the U.S. Fish and Wildlife Service, no. 174). URL: http://www.pwrc. usgs.gov/research/pubs/banks/obsall.htm (Accessed August 27, 2003).

The publication lists obsolete common names, as the title suggests, matching the old names to the common names listed in the *Check-list of North American Birds,* 6th ed., published in 1983. Each obsolete name is linked with the new approved common name and scientific name.

Check-List of North American Birds: Species of Birds of North America from the Arctic through Panama, Including the West Indies and Hawaiian Islands. 7th ed. Washington, DC: American Ornithologists Union Staff, 1998. 829 p. $49.95. ISBN 189127600X.

This checklist is considered to be the authoritative list of the 2,030 species of birds of North and Central America and reflects the changes in nomenclature and classification agreed on by the American Ornithologists' Union. Each species is listed with scientific and English name, original citation, habitat, distribution (summer and winter), and notes. The list of birds included in the checklist is also available on the Web at http://www.aou.org/aou/birdlist.html. Downloadable PDF and DBF versions are available from this site, which includes the latest updates not reflected in the print version.

Clements, James F. **Birds of the World: A Checklist.** 5th ed. Vista, CA: Ibis, 2000. 867 p. $39.95. ISBN 0934797161.

Follows the taxonomic sequence used in del Hoyo's *Handbook of Birds of the World* (below), this checklist is designed for birders and ornithologists. Each entry includes the standard common name in English, subspecies, and distribution along with a box to check for a life list. Appendixes list 85 recently extinct species, major references for each bird family, distribution of bird species by country, and a gazetteer. The ultimate life list for birders.

Dickinson, Edward C., ed. **The Howard and Moore Complete Checklist of the Birds of the World.** Rev. and enlarged 3rd ed. Princeton, NJ: Princeton University Press, 2003. 1,039 p. $69.50. ISBN 0691117012.

A revision of the classic, authoritative *A Complete Checklist of the Birds of the World,* by Richard Howard and Alick Moore. This edition utilizes regional experts to improve coverage and accuracy of the data. The checklist covers species and subspecies discovered since the 1980s that are not included in other world checklists. Each entry includes the scientific name, the English common name, and geographic distribution down to the subspecies level.

Lodge, Walter. **Birds: Alternative Names: A World Checklist.** New York: Sterling, 1991. 208 p. ISBN 0713722673.

This guide lists birds with several alternate common names in English that are in common use, not including local or dialect names. The names are arranged by family, then alphabetically by scientific name, and there are indexes for common names and genera.

Monroe, Burt L., and Charles G. Sibley. **A World Checklist of Birds.** New Haven: Yale University Press, 1993. 393 p. $65; $30 (paper). ISBN 0300055471; 0300070837 (paper).

This checklist covers 9,702 species of birds. Each species is covered on a single line, with scientific name, common name, and distribution. In addition, the checklist serves as a life list for dedicated birders, with a box to check off species and space for notes. The arrangement is according to the taxonomy found in Sibley and Monroe (below).

Ornithological Council. **BIRDNET: The Ornithological Information Source Presented by the Ornithological Council.** URL: http://www. nmnh.si.edu/BIRDNET/index.html (Accessed August 26, 2003).

The Ornithological Council is an umbrella group for 10 North American ornithological societies, including societies from Canada and Mexico. The site provides information on ornithology, member societies, grants and awards for ornithological research, links to birding information, and guidelines for the use of birds in research. In addition, the site provides links to Bird Accounts, http://www.nmnh.si.edu/BIRDNET/ORDERS/BIRDACCOUNTS.html, which provides an order-by-order list of bird species. The intent is to have links to species accounts, but at the time of viewing only the species lists were available.

Peters, James Lee, et al. **Check-list of Birds of the World.** Cambridge, MA: Museum of Comparative Zoology, 1931–87. 16 vol. in 17.

Volumes 1–7 of this massive work were written by Peters; the remaining volumes were edited by various individuals. The entries include the

Latin name, first description, and distribution of the birds of the world. A second edition of Volumes 1 and 11 was edited by Ernst Mayr and William Cottrell starting in 1979, but they appear to be the only volumes in the second edition. Prior to the publication of Sibley and Monroe's taxonomic revisions, Peters's checklist was the standard checklist for ornithology. Many field guides still follow Peters's taxonomic order.

Peterson, Alan P. **Zoonomen: Zoological Nomenclature Resource.** 2002. Version 4.5 (2002.08.18). http://www.zoonomen.net (Accessed August 26, 2003).

This site consists of two sections: a list of current valid scientific names for birds, based on the AOU checklist and Sibley and Monroe, and a historical analysis of avian taxonomy. The list of names includes the original citation, nomenclatural notes, and links to biographical information on the original author. The historic analysis provides graphs of various data configurations, such as number of species described per year or number of descriptions in each of the major avian taxonomy journals.

Rodner, Clemencia, Miguel Lentino, and Robin Restall. **Checklist of the Birds of Northern South America: An Annotated Checklist of the Species and Subspecies of Ecuador, Colombia, Venezuela, Aruba, Curacao, Bonaire, Trinidad and Tobago, Guyana, Suriname and French Guiana.** New Haven: Yale University Press, 2000. 136 p. $23.50. ISBN 0300087403 (paper).

Laid out in tabular form, this checklist concisely provides information on the 2,245 species of birds covered in the region. Each species is listed with scientific and English common name, number and names of subspecies, altitude range, references and comments, and presence in each country.

Wells, M. G. **World Bird Species Checklist: With Alternative English and Scientific Names.** Bushey, UK: Worldlist, 1998. 671 p. ISBN 0953242005.

The checklist is designed to provide a link between scientific and lay studies because amateurs do not always use the most up-to-date nomenclature. It includes over 18,000 alternate scientific names and 27,000 alternate English common names found in field guides and the scientific literature, representing 9,941 actual species. Species are listed in alphabetical order by scientific name, with their associated common names and alternate scientific names.

Handbooks

Attenborough, David. **The Life of Birds.** Princeton, NJ: Princeton University Press, 1998. 320 p. $29.95. ISBN 069101633X.

Written to accompany the television series of the same name, this handbook is suitable for students or the general public. Chapters cover topics such as flight, various lifestyles such as fishing or meat eating, parenthood, and responses to extreme environments. It is very heavily illustrated with splendid color photographs; in fact, the amount of space given to illustrations and text are about equal.

Bell, D.J., and B.M. Freeman, eds. **Physiology and Biochemistry of the Domestic Fowl.** New York: Academic Press, 1971–84. 5 vol. ISBN 012085001X.

This treatise covers the physiology of the chicken in detail. Volumes 1 through 3 were envisioned as a complete set; Volumes 4 and 5 update the original set.

Berthold, Peter. **Bird Migration: A General Survey.** 2nd ed. New York: Oxford University Press, 2001. (Oxford Ornithology series, no. 12). 253 p. $45 (paper). ISBN 0198507860; 0198507879 (paper).

Surveys bird migration, with most examples taken from European and African species. The author outlines the types of migration, the genetic bases for migration, methods of study, and conservation needs. Written for both researchers and students.

Bibby, Colin J., et al. **Bird Census Techniques.** 2nd ed. San Diego: Academic, 2000. 350 p. $55. ISBN 0120958317.

Provides guidance in designing and performing bird censuses. The authors discuss the standard methods for censusing birds, including line transects, point counts, catching and marking, and more.

Bird Families of the World. New York: Oxford University Press, 1995– . Price varies.

This series will cover the birds of the world and was up to 15 volumes by mid-2003. Each volume is in two parts. Part 1 provides introductory material on evolution, biogeography, natural history, conservation, and other topics. Part 2 provides detailed species accounts, including color illustrations by some of the best-known bird illustrators. Individual volumes are listed in the systematic section, below.

Chiasson, Robert B. **Laboratory Anatomy of the Pigeon.** 3rd ed. Dubuque, IA: W.C. Brown, 1984. 104 p. (Laboratory Anatomy series). $39.06. ISBN 0697049272.

A popular lab manual for pigeon dissection.

del Hoyo, Josep, et al., eds. **Handbook of the Birds of the World.** Barcelona: Lynx Edicions, 1992– . Vol. price varies.

This major new handbook is planned to consist of 10 volumes. The first volume begins with an overview of avian biology and classification, following the order in Peters's *Check-list of Birds of the World,* above. The information included in the handbook includes detailed family summaries with information on classification and natural history plus species accounts. The species accounts include classification, multiple common names, identification, natural history, distribution (including range maps), and references. There are numerous excellent color illustrations and maps for each species, plus color photographs. Currently up to Volume 7, *Jacamars to Woodpeckers.*

Dunning, John B. **CRC Handbook of Avian Body Masses.** Boca Raton, FL: CRC Press, 1993. 371 p. $169.95. ISBN 0849342589.

All known estimates of bird body mass found in the literature are listed in this handbook. The entries are arranged phylogenetically and cover 6,283 species. Each entry includes scientific name, sex and number of individuals sampled, mean, standard deviation, and range of the estimate, collecting season, and references. Section 2 lists body masses and composition for migrant birds in the eastern United States.

Farner, Donald S., and James R. King, eds. **Avian Biology.** New York: Academic, 1971–93. 9 vol. $104.00 (vol. 9). ISBN 0122494091 (vol. 9).

This treatise was designed to update A.J. Marshall's *Biology and Comparative Physiology of Birds.* It covers all aspects of bird biology except embryology. Classification schemes are discussed in Volumes 1 and 8.

Feduccia, Alan. **The Origin and Evolution of Birds.** 2nd ed. New Haven: Yale University Press, 1999. 466 p. $65; $32 (paper). ISBN 0300064608; 0300078617 (paper).

Feduccia is one of the most prominent biologists who see problems with the prevalent idea that birds evolved from dinosaurs, a point he makes in this book. However, most of the text discusses the evolution of individual bird groups, of flight and flightlessness, and other less controversial topics. There are numerous illustrations of living and extinct birds.

Fuller, Errol. **Extinct Birds.** Rev. ed. Ithaca, NY: Comstock, 2001. 398 p. $49.95. ISBN 080143954X.

The author discusses each of the more than 80 bird species that have gone extinct since 1600. The book is arranged in taxonomic order, each order discussed in a separate chapter. The chapters list rare or threatened birds in the order, then discuss the extinct species. Each account includes synonymy, size, as well as description and illustrations where available. Fuller tells what we know about each extinct species' natural history and reasons why it went extinct. The text and beautiful illustrations make it plain how much we have lost.

King, A. S., and J. McLelland. **Form and Function in Birds.** New York: Academic, 1979–89. 4 vol. $83 (vol. 3). ISBN 0124075010 (vol. 1); 0124075029 (vol. 2); 0124075037 (vol. 3); 0124075045 (vol. 4).

This treatise covers the anatomy of birds in great detail, reviewing the latest research in the field. The volumes are not divided by subject, although Volume 4 does cover respiration.

McLelland, John. **A Color Atlas of Avian Anatomy.** Philadelphia: Saunders, 1991. 127 p. $98. ISBN 0721635369.

The manual contains color photographs illustrating bird anatomy, chiefly the chicken.

Sibley, Charles G., and John E. Ahlquist. **Phylogeny and Classification of Birds: A Study in Molecular Evolution.** New Haven: Yale University Press, 1990. 976 p. $145. ISBN 0300040857.

A companion to Sibley and Monroe's *Distribution and Taxonomy of Birds of the World* (below), this text discusses the methodology used to develop a new, now generally accepted, classification of birds based on DNA hybridization. Part 1 discusses the methodology; Part 2 presents the evidence from their hybridization experiments and describes past efforts at classifying the taxon. The classification scheme itself is presented in more detail in Sibley and Monroe's work.

Sibley, Charles G., and Burt L. Monroe. **Distribution and Taxonomy of Birds of the World.** New Haven: Yale University Press, 1990. 1,111 p. $140. ISBN 0300049692.

This massive text outlines the present distribution of the bird species of the world. Each entry lists the habitat, geographical range, taxonomic notes, and one or more English common names as well as basic taxonomic information. The species are listed in a classification based on DNA-DNA hybridization (see Sibley and Alquist, above). A *Supplement* was published in 1993 with updates and corrections.

Systematic Section

Eoaves

Davies, S.J.J.F., and Mike Bamford. **Ratites and Tinamous: Tinamidae, Rheidae, Dromaiidae, Casuariidae, Apterygidae, Struthionidae.** New York: Oxford University Press, 2002. 310 p. (Bird Families of the World, vol. 9). $85. ISBN 0198549962.

See the series description (above) for more information.

Craciformes

Jones, Darryl N., René W.R.J. Dekker, and Cees S. Roselaar. **The Megapodes: Megapodiidae.** New York: Oxford University Press, 1995. 262 p. (Bird Families of the World, vol. 3). $75. ISBN 0198546513.

See the series description (above) for more information.

Galliformes

Johnsgard, Paul A. **The Grouse of the World.** Lincoln: University of Nebraska Press, 1983. 413 p. ISBN 080322558X.

Like the other volumes by the same author, this handbook covers the general biology of the grouse as well as providing detailed species accounts. The species accounts include a list of common names and subspecies as well as description and detailed information on natural history. There are range maps and black-and-white illustrations with each account, plus separate plates of color illustrations and photographs.

Johnsgard, Paul A. **The Pheasants of the World: Biology and Natural History.** 2nd ed. Washington, DC: Smithsonian Institution Press, 1999. 398 p. $55. ISBN 1560988398.

Surveys the pheasants; Part 1 describes the comparative biology, including classification, distribution, behavior, and conservation, and Part 2 provides keys and species accounts. The species accounts list synonymy, multiple common names, identification, and detailed information on ecology, biology, behavior, and reproductive biology.

Madge, Steve, and Philip J.K. McGowan. **Pheasants, Partridges, and Grouse: A Guide to the Pheasants, Partridges, Quails, Grouse,**

Guineafowl, Buttonquails, and Sandgrouse of the World. Princeton, NJ: Princeton University Press, 2002. 488 p. $45. ISBN 0691089086.

Covers 260 species of gamebirds in the orders Galliformes, Gruiformes, Charadiiformes, and Pterocliformes. Like others in this series, there are color plates in the front with brief description and range maps; species accounts include a detailed description, habitat, voice, habits, breeding, distribution, and status. The emphasis is on identification. Originally published in the UK as part of the Helm Identification Guide series.

Anseriformes

Johnsgard, Paul A. **Ducks, Geese, and Swans of the World.** Lincoln: University of Nebraska Press, 1978. 404 p. ISBN 0803209533.

Surveys the waterfowl of the world, with emphasis on the natural history of the birds rather than on identification or nomenclature. The individual species accounts list common names, subspecies and range, measurements, identification, taxonomic relationships, and detailed description of the natural history. There are range maps and black-and-white illustrations with each account plus a few color photographs.

Madge, Steve, and Hilary Burn. **Waterfowl: An Identification Guide to the Ducks, Geese, and Swans of the World.** Boston: Houghton Mifflin, 1988. 298 p. ISBN 0395467276; 0393467268 (paper).

Covers 160 species worldwide. Originally published in the UK as part of the Christopher Helm Identification Guide series. Has color plates in the front with field identification and range maps; species accounts cover identification, voice, geographical variants, habitat, distribution, and population size as well as listing common names in several languages.

Todd, Frank S. **Waterfowl: Ducks, Geese and Swans of the World.** San Diego: Sea World Press, 1979. 399 p. ISBN 0150040369.

An oversized general survey of the Anatidae, this volume illustrates almost all of the 147 species of waterfowl with beautiful color photographs, most of them of drakes in breeding plumage. The emphasis is on natural history rather than identification, and the text covers topics such as relations with humans, reproduction, feeding behavior, habitat, and more. The book, arranged by family or tribe, includes general chapters on classification, captive maintenance, conservation, and photography. There is also a "Concise Reference Guide to the Waterfowl" listing names, distribution, size, nests and eggs, and status in the wild and in captivity for each species.

Turniciformes

Johnsgard, Paul A. **Bustards, Hemipodes, and Sandgrouse: Birds of Dry Places.** New York: Oxford University Press, 1991. 276 p. $120. ISBN 0198576986.

The birds covered in this survey are relatively little studied birds of the families Turnicidae (hemipodes), Otididae (bustards), and Pteroclidae (sandgrouse). The taxonomic status of all three families is still being debated, and at present they are placed into three different orders (Turniciformes, Gruiformes, and Ciconiiformes, respectively). They do share a number of adaptations to desert life, which Johnsgard discusses in a separate chapter. The bulk of the book consists of species accounts providing varying amounts of detail about the natural history, identification, taxonomy, and status of each species.

Madge, Steve, and Philip J. K. McGowan. **Pheasants, Partridges, and Grouse: A Guide to the Pheasants, Partridges, Quails, Grouse, Guineafowl, Buttonquails, and Sandgrouse of the World.**
See main entry under Galliformes, above. Includes buttonquails.

Piciformes

Short, Lester L., and Jennifer F. M. Horne. **Toucans, Barbets and Honeygides: Ramphastidae, Capitonidae, and Indicatoridae.** New York: Oxford University Press, 2001. 526 p. (Bird Families of the World, vol. 8). $95. ISBN 0198546661.

See the series description (above) for more information.

Winkler, Hans, David Christie, and David Nurney. **Woodpeckers: A Guide to the Woodpeckers of the World.** Boston: Houghton Mifflin, 1995. 406 p. $40. ISBN 0395720435.

Contains color plates in front with information on identification; species accounts of 214 species include identification, distribution, movements, habitat, geographical variation, voice, habits, food, and breeding.

Bucerotiformes

Kemp, A. C. **The Hornbills: Bucerotiformes.** New York: Oxford University Press, 1995. 302 p. (Bird Families of the World, vol. 1). $75. ISBN 019857729X.

See the series description (above) for more information.

Trogoniformes

Johnsgard, Paul A. **Trogons and Quetzals of the World.** Washington, DC: Smithsonian Institution Press, 2000. 223 p. $49.95. ISBN 1560983884.

Like other volumes by the author, this handbook covers comparative biology of the trogons as well as providing detailed species accounts.

Coraciiformes

Erritzoe, Johannes, and Helga Boullet Erritzoe. **Pittas of the World: A Monograph on the Pitta Family.** Cambridge, UK: Lutterworth Press, 1998. 207 p. $75 (cased ed.). ISBN 0718829611; 0718828925 (ring bound); 0718828917 (cased ed.); 071882895X.

About 30 species and 67 subspecies of pittas are recognized in this volume. The introduction covers the classification, origin, general description, distribution, and natural history of the family, and individual species accounts cover the same information for each species. The species accounts also include identification, museum holdings, recent records, status, and references. There are full-page color illustrations of all 30 species, plus illustrations of the eggs of most species and a comparison plate illustrating all species on one page. An appendix lists all pitta species known to occur on each island in their range in Southeast Asia.

Fry, C. Hilary, and Kathie Fry. **Kingfishers, Bee-Eaters and Rollers: A Handbook.** Princeton, NJ: Princeton University Press, 1992. 324 p. ISBN 0691087806.

An identification guide to the 123 species worldwide. Color identification plates in front include brief description and range maps, and the species accounts in the back discuss field identification, voice, geographical variation, habitat, food, and habits. Originally published in the UK as part of the Christopher Helm Identification Guide series.

Lambert, Frank R., and Martin Woodcock. **Pittas, Broadbills and Asities.** Mountfield, UK: Pica, 1996. 271 p. $40. ISBN 1873403240.

An identification guide summarizing the state of knowledge on this little-studied group of 51 species of birds. As usual, there are color plates in front with brief descriptions and distribution information followed by detailed species accounts. The species accounts include more natural history than most similar guides, but as with other guides in this series the accounts cover identification, voice, distribution, geographical variation, habitat, status, food, habits, and breeding. There are distribution maps as well.

Psittaciformes

Forshaw, Joseph M. **Parrots of the World.** 3rd ed. London: Blandford, 1989. 672 p. ISBN 0713721340.

This massive work is one of the premier sources for information on parrots. There is an introduction discussing the fossil history, classification, anatomy, and natural history of parrots. The bulk of the book consists of species accounts, with description, distribution, subspecies, and general notes. Each account also includes a distribution map and gorgeous full-page color illustrations.

Juniper, Tony, and Mike Parr. **Parrots: A Guide to Parrots of the World.** New Haven: Yale University Press, 1998. 584 p. $55. ISBN 0300074530.

An identification guide to 350 species of parrots. Like the other guides in this series (originally published by Pica Press in the UK), this guide has color plates in front with brief descriptions and distribution followed by species accounts with range maps, identification information, voice, distribution, ecology, and geographical variations.

Apodiformes

Chantler, Phil. **Swifts: A Guide to the Swifts and Treeswifts of the World.** 2nd ed. New Haven: Yale University Press, 2000. 272 p. $40. ISBN 0300079362.

Provides information on the 96 species of swifts found around the world. As with other taxonomic identification guides, this volume has color plates in front with distribution information followed by detailed species accounts containing description, distribution, and natural history.

Trochiliformes

Johnsgard, Paul A. **The Hummingbirds of North America.** 2nd ed. Washington, DC: Smithsonian Institution Press, 1997. 278 p. $49.95. ISBN 1560987081.

Covers 47 species of hummingbirds found in the United States, Canada, and Mexico. Like other volumes by the same author, the handbook discusses comparative biology of the hummingbirds, plus detailed species accounts. There are separate keys to the identification of North American and Mexican hummingbirds, plus an appendix discussing the origin of names of hummers.

Strigiformes

Burton, John A. **Owls of the World: Their Evolution, Structure, and Ecology.** Rev. ed. Dover, NH: Tanager Books, 1984. 208 p. ISBN 0880720603.

A survey of the owls of the world, each chapter is written by a different author and covers a different group of owls. There are numerous attractive color illustrations and photographs as well as range maps for each species. Each species is described and its natural history discussed, including such topics as prey species, reproduction, voice, and habitat.

Cleere, Nigel. **Nightjars: A Guide to the Nightjars, Nighthawks, and Their Relatives.** Princeton, NJ: Yale University Press, 1998. 317 p. $40. ISBN 0300074573.

Originally published in the UK as part of the Pica Press Identification Guides series, this guide covers the 119 species of the five related families. The species accounts include distribution maps plus information on the natural history of each species.

Holyoak, D.T. **Nightjars and Their Allies: The Caprimulgiformes.** New York: Oxford University Press, 2001. 773 p. (Bird Families of the World, vol. 7). $85. ISBN 0198549873.

See the series description, above.

Hume, Rob, and Trevor Boyer. **Owls of the World.** Philadelphia: Running Press, 1991. 192 p. ISBN 1561380326.

An oversized encyclopedic guide to the owls. The book includes illustrated species accounts for 148 species, with information on identification, distribution, habitats, eggs, status, and general notes. Appendixes include distribution maps and a systematic list of owls including names, length, and distribution.

Johnsgard, Paul A. **North American Owls: Biology and Natural History.** Washington, DC: Smithsonian Institution Press, 1988. 295 p. $45. ISBN 0874745608.

As the title suggests, this book covers the comparative biology and natural history of the owls of North America. Part 1 discusses biology, including ecology, behavior, morphology, and reproductive biology. Part 2 provides detailed accounts of the natural history of 19 species of owls. There are also appendixes with keys to genera and species, to structural variations in the external ears, and to the calls of North American owls. The author also discusses the origins of the scientific and common names of owls.

König, Claus, Friedhelm Weick, and Jan-Hendrik Becking. **Owls: A Guide to the Owls of the World.** New Haven: Yale University Press, 1999. 462 p. $55. ISBN 0300079206.

Originally published by Pica Press in the UK, this identification guide provides a general overview of owl ecology and behavior, color identification plates with information on identification and distribution, and species accounts. The species accounts include range maps and cover identification, voice, movements, habitat, geographical variation, and natural history. A supplementary CD with owl vocalizations is also available.

Columbiformes

Gibbs, David, John Cox, and Eustace Barnes. **Pigeons and Doves: A Guide to the Pigeons and Doves of the World.** New Haven: Yale University Press, 2001. 615 p. $60. ISBN 0300078862.

An identification guide to the 319 species of pigeons and doves, as well as the extinct dodo and solitaires. As with the other guides originally published by Pica Press in the UK, there are color identification plates in the front with brief descriptions and distribution followed by species accounts. The species accounts cover alternative common names, identification, voice, habits, habitat, status, measurements, and geographical variation. The discussion of habits and habitat varies in length but is often fairly detailed. There are distribution maps for each species as well.

Goodwin, Derek. **Pigeons and Doves of the World.** 3rd ed. Ithaca, NY: Comstock, 1983. 363 p. ISBN 0801414342.

Covers the natural history of the pigeons and doves. After an extensive introduction covering the comparative biology of the family, species accounts provide detailed information including description, distribution, natural history, and common names. Distribution maps and black-and-white illustrations are included with each account, and color plates are scattered throughout.

Gruiformes

Johnsgard, Paul A. **Cranes of the World.** Bloomington: Indiana University Press, 1983. 257 p. ISBN 0253112559.

Surveys the state of knowledge about the cranes of the world, updating and expanding on Lawrence Walkinshaw's *Cranes of the World* published in 1973. The book contains introductory information on the comparative biology of cranes, plus detailed discussions of the natural histories of 14 crane species. Appendixes discuss the origin of scientific and common names of cranes and provides a key to the species of cranes of the world.

Ripley, Sidney Dillon. **Rails of the World: A Monograph of the Family Rallidae.** Boston: Godine, 1977. 406 p. $100. ISBN 087923198X.

This oversized (37 cm) work compiles the state of knowledge about the rails of the world up to 1975. The volume includes full-page illustrations by J. Fenwick Lansdowne in addition to the usual species accounts with multiple common names, description, measurements, distribution, status, and general notes. The author also discusses the general characteristics, distribution, and evolution of rails, and a chapter discusses the fossil rails. The volume was updated in 1985 by *Rails of the World: A Compilation of New Information, 1975–1983, Smithsonian Contributions to Zoology,* no. 417.

Taylor, Barry. **Rails: A Guide to the Rails, Crakes, Gallinules and Coots of the World.** New Haven: Yale University Press, 1998. 600 p. $50. ISBN 0300077580.

An identification guide to 145 species of the Rallidae. The book covers general information on the classification, morphology, habitat, food, voice, behavior, breeding, movements, and conservation of the rails as well as the usual color identification plates and species accounts. The species accounts discuss identification, voice, geographical variation, molt, distribution, habitat, food, habits, behavior, and breeding with more detail on natural history than in some identification guides. Originally published by Pica Press in the UK.

Ciconiiformes

Brooke, Michael. **Albatrosses and Petrels across the World.** Oxford: Oxford University Press, 2003. 448 p. (Bird Families of the World). $85. ISBN 0198501250.

See the series description (above) for more information.

Brown, Leslie, and Dean Amadon. **Eagles, Hawks and Falcons of the World.** New York: McGraw-Hill, 1968. 2 vol.

Summarizes the knowledge of the diurnal birds of prey. After general chapters discussing classification, biology, natural history, field identification, and relations with humans, there are detailed species accounts. They cover range, description, voice, general habits, food, breeding, and other information; there are full-page color illustrations of each species as well. Volume 1 contains the general chapters and species accounts from the vultures to the accipiters; Volume 2 covers the remaining species.

Ferguson-Lees, James, and David A. Christie. **Raptors of the World.** Boston: Houghton Mifflin, 2001. 992 p. $60. ISBN 0618127623.

This massive guide covers all 313 species of raptors around the world. Color identification plates in front include information on identification, habitat, and range maps; species accounts discuss distribution, movements, habitat, field characteristics, similar species, voice, food, behavior, breeding, population size, and geographical variation. There are photographs and range maps for each species account as well, and the detail given is greater than in most similar guides.

Fjeldsa, Jon. **Grebes: Podicipedida.** Oxford: Oxford University Press, 2003. 320 p. (Bird Families of the World). $85. ISBN 0198500645.

See the series description (above) for more information.

Gaston, A.J., and Ian L. Jones. **The Auks: Alcidae.** New York: Oxford University Press, 1998. 349 p. (Bird Families of the World, vol. 5). $85. ISBN 0198540329.

See the series description (above) for more information.

Grant, P.J. **Gulls: A Guide to Identification.** 2nd ed. San Diego: Academic, 1986. 352 p. $34.00; $19.95 (paper). ISBN 0856610445; 0122956400 (paper).

The emphasis in this guide, as the title suggests, is on the identification of the 31 species of gulls rather than on their natural history. There are numerous black-and-white photos and line drawings for each species as well as detailed descriptions of the various molts and plumages and distribution maps.

Hancock, James, and James A Kushlan. **The Herons Handbook.** New York: Harper & Row, 1984. 288 p. ISBN 0060153318.

Based on *The Herons of the World* (1978), this handbook discusses each of the herons of the world. Introductory material discusses classification, courtship, feeding, and identification. The species accounts cover each of the 60 heron species, including identification, distribution, migration, habitat, behavior, nest, eggs, and young, and notes. There are distribution maps and full-page color illustrations as well for each species.

Hancock, James, James A. Kushlan, and M. Philip Kahl. **Storks, Ibises and Spoonbills of the World.** San Diego: Academic Press, 1992. 385 p. $143.95. ISBN 0123227305.

An oversized handbook to the storks and relatives, this book contains full-page color illustrations for each species plus detailed information on identification, distribution, ecology, breeding, taxonomy, and conservation. An appendix provides tables of body and egg measurements as well as breeding season.

Harrison, Peter. **A Field Guide to Seabirds of the World.** Lexington, MA: Stephen Greene, 1987. 317 p. ISBN 0828906106 (paper).

This field guide features color photographs of 321 species of penguins, loons, grebes, pelicans, albatrosses, gulls, and related birds found at sea. There are identification plates in the front of the book followed by brief species accounts focusing on identification, although they include brief accounts of habits and distribution along with distribution maps for each species.

Hayman, Peter, John Marchant, and Tony Prater. **Shorebirds: An Identification Guide to the Waders of the World.** Boston: Houghton Mifflin, 1986. 412 p. $35 (paper). ISBN 0395379032; 0395602378 (paper).

Covers the Charadriiformes in the common taxonomic guide fashion with color plates and brief descriptions in one section and another with species accounts and detailed descriptions. Originally published in the UK as part of the Christopher Helm Identification Guide series.

Johnsgard, Paul A. **Cormorants, Darters, and Pelicans of the World.** Washington, DC: Smithsonian Institution Press, 1993. 445 p. ISBN 1560982160.

As with other similar books by the same author, this handbook contains extensive coverage of the comparative biology of the Pelecaniformes, followed by detailed species accounts discussing natural history and distribution. In addition, there is a central section of color photographs, keys to species, a glossary of scientific and common names, and head profile identification drawings to aid identification.

Johnsgard, Paul A. **Diving Birds of North America.** Lincoln: University of Nebraska Press, 1987. 292 p. ISBN 0803225660.

The diving birds treated in this book consist of the loons, grebes, and auks. The volume is in two main sections, one covering comparative biology and the other providing species accounts of 31 species of birds, including the extinct great auk. The species accounts are detailed and include other common names, distribution, description, measurements, identification, ecology, general biology, social behavior, reproductive biology, phylogeny, and conservation status. Appendixes list the source of scientific and common names, keys, and tables listing auk and grebe colonies.

Johnsgard, Paul A. **The Plovers, Sandpipers, and Snipes of the World.** Lincoln: University of Nebraska Press, 1981. 493 p. ISBN 0803225539.

Covers the Charadriiformes, or shorebirds, of the world. Johnsgard discusses taxonomy and reproductive biology of the shorebirds and provides a key to families and tribes as well as detailed species accounts. The species accounts list synonyms, multiple common names, range, detailed description, and natural history. There are range maps and black-and-white illustrations for each species account, plus a number of photographs. The derivation of generic and specific names is also provided.

Kushlan, James A., and James Hancock. **The Herons (Ardeidae).** Oxford: Oxford University Press, 2002. 400 p. (Bird Families of the World). $85. ISBN 0198549814.

See the series description (above) for more information.

Nelson, J. Bryan. **Pelicans, Cormorants and Allies: Pelecaniforme.** Oxford: Oxford University Press, 2003. 528 p. (Bird Families of the World). $85. ISBN 0198577273.

See the series description (above) for more information.

Olsen, Klaus Malling, and Hans Larsson. **Skuas and Jaegers: A Guide to the Skuas and Jaegers of the World.** New Haven: Yale University Press, 1995. 190 p. $40. ISBN 0300072694.

There are only seven species of skuas and jaegers, so this guide has room to cover the natural history and biology of this family in detail. As with other similar volumes, there are color plates in front to aid in identification, but with so few species to cover, the illustrations include immature and winter plumages. The species accounts include extensive information on natural history, molts, and taxonomy. First published in the UK by Pica Press.

Reilly, Pauline N. **Penguins of the World.** South Melbourne, Australia: Oxford University Press, 1994. 164 p. ISBN 0195535472.

Covers all 17 species of penguins. An introductory chapter discusses general topics in penguin distribution, taxonomy, and biology. Each lengthy species account covers description, distribution and population size, activities at sea and on land, behavior, breeding, and conservation. There are many photographs of the penguins as well as color plates for identification purposes.

Soothill, Eric, and Richard Soothill. **Wading Birds of the World.** 2nd ed. London: Blandford, 1989. 334 p. ISBN 0713721308 (paper).

A handbook to 350 species of birds that wade at some time of the year, mostly Ciconiiformes and Charadriiformes. Each account includes description, characteristics and behavior, habitat, food, voice, display, breeding, and distribution along with a distribution map. About 100 species are illustrated with a color photograph, and the remainder are illustrated with a line drawing.

Tickell, W. L. N. **Albatrosses.** New Haven: Yale University Press, 2000. 448 p. $60. ISBN 0300087411.

This handbook provides detailed information about the biology and natural history of the albatrosses. Sections cover nomenclature and classification, comparative biology, and relationship of albatrosses and humans, in addition to geographical sections discussing the albatrosses of the southern oceans, tropical areas, and the north Pacific Ocean.

Williams, Tony D. **The Penguins: Spheniscidae.** New York: Oxford University Press, 1995. 295 p. (Bird Families of the World, vol. 2). $75. ISBN 019854667X.

See the series description (above) for more information.

Passeriformes

Alström, Per, and Krister Mild. **Pipits and Wagtails.** Princeton, NJ: Princeton University Press, 2001. 260 p. $49.50. ISBN 0691088349.

A detailed guide to the 26 species of this difficult-to-differentiate family, this book provides detailed information on identifying species and subspecies. There are color plates with identification information as well as species accounts providing the usual description and natural history information. This volume is unusual in that it also includes sonagrams to assist in identifying bird calls. Originally published in the UK as part of the Helm Identification Guide series.

Baker, Kevin. **Warblers of Europe, Asia, and North Africa.** Princeton, NJ: Princeton University Press, 1997. 400 p. $57.50. ISBN 0691011699.

An identification guide to 145 species of warblers. The color plates in front include range maps and field identification; the species accounts cover identification, confusing species, geographical variation, molts, voice, habitat and behavior, and distribution. Originally published in the UK as part of the Christopher Helm Identification Guide series.

Brewer, David, and Barry Kent Mackay. **Wrens, Dippers and Thrashers.** London: Christopher Helm, 2001. 256 p. (Helm Identification Guides). $50. ISBN 0300090595.

An identification guide to 114 species; color plates include identification and distribution information followed by species accounts discussing description, geographical variation, voice, habitat, habits, distribution, breeding, food, and movements. There are range maps as well.

Byers, Clive, Jon Curson, and Urban Olsson. **Sparrows and Buntings: A Guide to the Sparrows and Buntings of North America and the World.** Boston: Houghton Mifflin, 1995. 334 p. $40. ISBN 0395738733.

Covers the 86 species of the Emberizinae. Color plates in front provide brief description and distribution information followed by species accounts. The species accounts discuss identification, sexing, molts, geographical variation, voice, habits, status, and distribution. Originally published in the UK by Pica Press.

Cheke, Robert A., and Clive F. Mann. **Sunbirds: A Guide to the Sunbirds, Spiderhunters, Sugarbirds and Flowerpeckers of the World.** London: Christopher Helm, 2001. 384 p. (Helm Identification Guides). $50. ISBN 0300089406.

An identification guide to 146 species, with an extensive introduction, color plates with distribution and brief descriptions; species accounts include identification, voice, distribution, habitat, status, movements, breeding, geographical variation, and distribution maps.

Clement, Peter. **Finches and Sparrows: An Identification Guide.** Princeton, NJ: Princeton University Press, 1993. 500 p. $29.95 (paper). ISBN 0691034249; 0691048789 (paper).

An identification guide to the 290 species of finches and sparrows worldwide. It features color identification plates in front with brief descriptions, and range maps followed by species accounts discussing identification, geographical variation, voice, status, distribution, and movements. Originally published in the UK as part of the Christopher Helm Identification Guide series.

Clement, Peter. **Thrushes.** Princeton, NJ: Princeton University Press, 2000. 463 p. $49.50. ISBN 0691088527.

Covers 162 species of thrushes. There is an extensive introduction covering the biology, behavior, and conservation of thrushes, which is followed by color plates with distribution maps and brief descriptions. The species accounts cover description, geographical variations, voice, status, movements, habitat, behavior, breeding, and molts.

Curson, Jon, David Quinn, and David Beadle. **Warblers of the Americas: An Identification Guide.** Boston: Houghton Mifflin, 1994. 252 p. $42. ISBN 0395709989.

Covers all 116 species in the Americas. Color plates in front include brief descriptions and range maps; species accounts cover description, geographical information, voice, habitat, breeding, and molts. Originally published in the UK as part of the Christopher Helm Identification Guide series as *New World Warblers.*

Feare, Chris, and Adrian Craig. **Starlings and Mynas.** Princeton, NJ: Princeton University Press, 1999. 285 p. $49.50. ISBN 069100496X.

A guide to the 114 species. Contains extensive introduction to the classification and biology of the family. Color plates include range maps and brief description; species accounts discuss identification, voice, distribution, habitat, food, breeding, behavior, and relations with humans. Originally published in the UK as part of the Christopher Helm Identification Guide series.

Frith, Clifford B., Bruce McP. Beehler, and William T. Cooper. **The Birds of Paradise: Paradisaeidae.** New York: Oxford University Press, 1998. 613 p. (Bird Families of the World, vol. 6). $110. ISBN 0198548532.

See the series description (above) for more information.

Frith, Clifford B., and Dawn Frith. **Bowerbirds: Ptilonorhychidae.** Oxford: Oxford University Press, 2003. 416 p. (Bird Families of the World). $85. ISBN 0198548443.

See the series description (above) for more information.

Goodwin, Derek. **Crows of the World.** 2nd ed. Seattle: University of Washington Press, 1986. 299 p. ISBN 0565009796.

Covers the crows, jays, and related birds of the family Corvidae. The author discusses general classification, behavior, and natural history, then provides species accounts. The species accounts include color plates, range maps, and details of the description, identification, voice, natural history, and distribution for each species.

Harrap, Simon, and David Quinn. **Chickadees, Tits, Nuthatches and Treecreepers.** Princeton, NJ: Princeton University Press, 1995. 464 p. $49.50. ISBN 0691010838.

Originally published in the UK as *Tits, Nuthatches, and Treecreepers: An Identification Guide,* part of the Christopher Helm Identification Guide Series. It has color plates with brief descriptions and distribution maps in front, detailed species accounts (including natural history) in back.

Harris, Tony. **Shrikes and Bush-Shrikes: Including Wood-Shrikes, Helmet-Shrikes, Flycatcher-Shrikes, Philentomas, Batises and Wattle-Eyes.** Princeton, NJ: Princeton University Press, 2000. 392 p. $55. ISBN 0691070369.

Covers 114 species in the closely related families Laniidae and Malaconotidae. There is a brief introductory section emphasizing shrike intraspecific communication, followed by the usual color identification plates with brief descriptions and range maps. The following species accounts cover identification and description in detail, along with geographical variation, range, movements, social organization, and breeding biology. Originally published in the UK by Christopher Helm.

Isler, Morton L., and Phyllis R. Isler. **The Tanagers: Natural History, Distribution, and Identification.** Washington, DC: Smithsonian Institution Press, 1987. 406 p. $39.95 (paper). ISBN 0874745527; 0874745535 (paper).

Covers the 242 species of tanagers. The species accounts include distribution maps and detailed information on habitat, behavior, vocalizations, and breeding. A central section of color plates includes descriptions.

Jaramillo, Alvaro, and Peter Burke. **New World Blackbirds: The Ictarids.** Princeton, NJ: Princeton University Press, 1999. 431 p. $52.50. ISBN 0691006806.

An identification guide to 103 species. Color plates in front include distribution maps and descriptions; species accounts discuss identification, voice, geographical variation, habitat, behavior, nesting, distribution, movements, molts, and general notes. Originally published in the UK as part of the Christopher Helm Identification Series.

Madge, Steve, and Hilary Burn. **Crows and Jays: A Guide to the Crows, Jays, and Magpies of the World.** Boston: Houghton Mifflin, 1994. 191 p. $40. ISBN 039567171X. Paper edition published by Princeton University Press in 1999.

An identification guide to all 120 species of the Corvini worldwide. The color plates in front include distribution information and maps; the species accounts emphasize identification but include information on geographical variation, voice, habits, breeding, habitat, and status. Originally published in the UK as part of the Christopher Helm Identification Guide series.

Orians, Gordon H. **Blackbirds of the Americas.** Seattle: University of Washington Press, 1985. 163 p. $35. ISBN 0295962534.

The blackbirds, or Icteridae, are only found in the Americas and include the orioles and oropendolas as well as blackbirds and grackles. The bulk of the book consists of a survey of the natural history and behaviors found in blackbirds organized by type of behavior rather than by species. There is a roster of icterid species and a tabular summary of blackbird habitat, diet, plumage, and social organization arranged by species.

Pratt, H. Douglas. **The Hawaiian Honeycreepers.** Oxford, UK: Oxford University Press, 2002. 336 p. (Bird Families of the World, vol. 10). $85. ISBN 019854653X.

See the series description (above) for more information.

Restall, Robin L. **Munias and Mannikins.** New Haven: Yale University Press, 1997. 264 p. $60. ISBN 0300071094.

Munias and mannikins are seed-eating birds of Asia, Australasia, and Africa. Contains an initial section of color plates and field descriptions followed by species accounts with more detailed descriptions and natural history. Published in the UK by Pica Press.

Rowley, Ian, and Eleanor M. Russell. **Fairy-wrens and Grasswrens: Maluridae.** New York: Oxford University Press, 1997. 274 p. (Bird Families of the World, vol. 4). $75. ISBN 0198546904.

See the series description (above) for more information.

Turner, Angela, and Chris Rose. **Swallows and Martins: An Identification Guide and Handbook.** Boston: Houghton Mifflin, 1989. 258 p. ISBN 0395511747.

Covering all 74 species of the Hirundinidae, this guide provides general introduction to the morphology, classification, distribution, food, behavior, and conservation status of the swallows and martins. As with other similar guides, there are color plates in front with description and distribution maps for each species; species accounts provide detailed information on identification, natural history, voice, and more.

Geographical Section

North America

Alsop, Fred. **Birds of North America.** New York: DK, 2001. 1,008 p. (Smithsonian Handbooks). $60. ISBN 0789480018.

A very hefty, beautifully laid-out handbook to 930 species of birds of North America. Although the cover states that it covers the life histories of the species, the information presented is actually rather scanty compared to the other handbooks listed below. Each species is featured on one page, with a color photograph, distribution map, diagram of flight pattern, and information on identification, song, behavior, conservation, and similar status. The handbook is also available as two separate volumes: *Birds of North America: Eastern Region* and *Birds of North America: Western Region.*

Bent, Arthur Cleveland. **Life Histories of North American Birds.** Washington, DC. U.S. Government Printing Office, 1919–50. 20 vol. (Bulletin of the Smithsonian Institution United States National Museum). Reprint, New York: Dover.

This set was considered the most comprehensive work dealing with the life histories of North American birds, although it has now been updated by *Birds of North America: Life Histories for the 21st Century,* below.

Ehrlich, Paul R., David S. Dobkin, and Darryl Wheye. **Birds in Jeopardy: The Imperiled and Extinct Birds of the United States and Canada**

including Hawaii and Puerto Rico. Stanford, CA: Stanford University Press, 1992. 259 p. $24.95 (paper). ISBN 0804719675; 0804719810 (paper).

As its title suggests, this book describes the endangered and extinct bird species for North America and Hawaii. The descriptions are arranged by the degree of jeopardy, including officially threatened, of concern but not officially listed, and extinct since 1776. There are colored illustrations of the birds' heads, plus concise information on their nesting, food, range, notes, causes of endangerment, listing, and recovery plans (for threatened species) or date of extinction. Hawaiian and Puerto Rican birds are listed separately in each chapter. The authors also discuss causes of imperilment and provide a regional list of threatened or endangered species.

Kaufman, Kenn. **Lives of North American Birds.** Boston: Houghton Mifflin, 1996. 675 p. (Peterson Natural History Companions). $35. ISBN 0395770173; 0395783224 (paper).

This handbook provides detailed information on the natural history of over 680 species of birds that breed in North America, plus less detailed information on another 230 rare visitors. Each species is illustrated with a color photograph, and the species accounts discuss habitat, feeding, nesting and reproduction, migration, and conservation status. There are also range maps. The author is a very well-known and experienced birder who has written many other books for birders.

Palmer, Ralph S. **Handbook of North American Birds.** New Haven: Yale University Press, 1962–88. 5 vol. in 6. $55. ISBN 0300040601 (vol. 5, pt. 2).

A major series detailing the natural history and identification of the birds of North America. The series was never finished and covers only the loons through the falcons.

Poole, Alan F., Peter Stettenheim, and Frank B. Gill, eds. **Birds of North America: Life Histories for the 21st Century.** Washington, DC: American Ornithologists' Union, 1992–2003. 18 vol. $175 per volume.

This series updates A. C. Bent's *Life Histories of North American Birds* (above) and contains life history accounts for over 700 species of birds issued as separate self-contained profiles. Each account contains color photograph of the species, distribution map, identification, distribution, classification, and detailed discussion of natural history and conservation, plus an extensive bibliography. The series consists of 18 volumes of 40 accounts each, and the accounts are published in no particular order. It is co-published by the American Ornithologists' Union and the Academy of Natural Sciences of Philadelphia.

Ridgway, Robert. **The Birds of North and Middle America: A Descriptive Catalogue of the Higher Groups, Genera, Species, and Subspecies of Birds Known to Occur in North America, from the Arctic Lands to the Isthmus of Panama, the West Indies and Other Islands of the Caribbean Sea, and the Galapagos Archipelago.** Washington, DC: U.S. Government Printing Office, 1911–50. 11 vol. (Bulletin of the United States National Museum, vol. 50, pt. 1–11).

Attempts to describe each species and subspecies of birds known at the time. The family descriptions include references to the taxonomic literature and keys to the genera; descriptions of genera include taxonomic references, general descriptions and ranges, and keys to the species. Species accounts include description of adult males, females, and young, plus subspecies. A classic handbook.

Sibley, David, Chris Elphick, and John B. Dunning. The **Sibley Guide to Bird Life and Behavior.** New York: Knopf, 2001. 588 p. $45. ISBN 0679451234.

A companion to the highly acclaimed *Sibley Guide to Birds* (see Identification Tools, below), this handbook tells of bird biology and behavior, and it is designed for birders who want to know more than just how to identify species. Part 1 covers bird biology, including anatomy, plumages, evolution, behavior, habitats, and conservation. Part 2, the bulk of the book, consists of family-by-family accounts of behavior. Topics include taxonomy, food, breeding, movements, conservation, and accidental species. Sibley's splendid illustrations add to the excellent text.

Africa

Brown, Leslie, Emil K. Urban, and Kenneth Newman, eds. **The Birds of Africa.** New York: Academic Press, 1982–2003. 7 vol. $205 (vol. 1); $149.00 (vol. 5); $189.95 (vol. 6). ISBN 0121373010 (vol. 1); 0121373029 (vol. 2); 0121373037 (vol. 3); 0121373045 (vol. 4); 0121373053 (vol. 5); 0121373061 (vol. 6); 012137307X (vol. 7).

The most comprehensive modern handbook of the birds of Africa, this beautifully illustrated set gives detailed information on the birds of the continent. Each species account includes original description citation, range and status, description, field characters and voice, general habits, food, breeding, map, and references. Color plates, many of them by Martin Woodcock, aid in identification. Volume 1 covers the Struthioniformes through the Falconiformes; Volume 2, the Galliformes through the Columbiformes; and Volumes 3 through 7 cover the Passeriformes.

Mackworth-Praed, W., and C. H. B. Grant. **African Handbook of Birds.** London: Longmans, Green, 1957–73. 6 vol.

This series provides a set of compact handbooks of the birds of Africa, arranged by region. The species accounts cover identification, distribution, and habits, and there are black-and-white illustrations and maps for each species. Series 1 covers the *Birds of Eastern and North Eastern Africa;* series 2, *Birds of the Southern Third of Africa;* and series 3, *Birds of West Central and Western Africa.* Each series contains two volumes.

Antarctica

Watson, George E., J. Phillip Angle, and Peter C. Harper. **Birds of the Antarctic and Sub-Antarctic.** Washington, DC: American Geophysical Union, 1975. 350 p. (Antarctic Research Series, vol. 24). ISBN 0875901247.

Although this is an identification guide to the birds found in the Antarctic and surrounding islands south of 55° latitude, it contains enough information on the natural history of the birds to count as a handbook. An introduction discusses the Antarctic environment and how to identify birds, and the main portion contains species accounts. The species accounts are quite detailed, with lengthy descriptions, plus information on the birds' habits, voice and displays, food, reproduction, migration, molt, predation and mortality, parasites, habitat, and distribution. There are color plates in a central section and black-and-white illustrations throughout.

Asia

Ali, Sálim, and S. Dillon Ripley. **Handbook of the Birds of India and Pakistan: Together with Those of Bangladesh, Nepal, Bhutan and Sri Lanka.** 2nd ed. New York: Oxford University Press, 2001. 10 vol. $295 (set). ISBN 0195655060 (set).

The second edition of this handbook was originally published from 1978 to 1999. The set covers about 2,000 species of birds found in the area. The species accounts list original author and synonyms, local common names in several languages, size, field characters, status and distribution, and natural history. Color plates are scattered throughout the volumes illustrating the species.

De Schauensee, Rodolphe Meyer. **The Birds of China.** Washington, DC: Smithsonian Institution Press, 1984. 602 p. ISBN 0874743621; 087474363X (paper).

This descriptive catalog covers 1,195 species of birds found in China. De Schauensee provides introductory material, including geography of the region and the history of ornithology in China. Colored plates illustrating the birds are found in the front of the book, followed by the species accounts. Each account includes description, range, breeding, habitat, and occasionally notes. Species that are also found in Hong Kong are noted.

Wells, David, Philip D. Round, and Uthai Treesucon. **The Birds of the Thai-Malay Peninsula: Covering Burma and Thailand South of the Eleventh Parallel, Peninsular Malaysia and Singapore.** San Diego: Academic, 1999– . vol. (AP Natural World). $125.95 (vol. 1). ISBN 0127429611 (vol. 1).

Projected to be a two-volume set. Volume 1 covers the nonpasserine birds of the region, and Volume 2 will cover the passerines and ecology of the region. The species accounts include English, Thai, and Malay common names as well as taxonomic information, range, identification, distribution, geographical variation, status, habitat, food, and so on. There are color plates.

Australasia

Coates, Brian J. **The Birds of Papua New Guinea: Including the Bismarck Archipelago and Bougainville.** Alderley, Australia: Dover, 1985–90. 2 vol. ISBN 0959025707

Unlike most handbooks, this one is illustrated with color photographs, giving it the appearance of a coffee-table book. However, it is a serious scientific work with the usual species accounts listing description, distribution, and natural history of the birds of the region. Volume 1 covers the nonpasserines; Volume 2 covers the passerines.

Marchant, S., et al., eds. **Handbook of Australian, New Zealand and Antarctic Birds (HANZAB).** New York: Oxford University Press, 1990–2001. 5 vol. in 6. $350. ISBN 0195530683 (set).

About 900 species of birds are found in this region of the world. Each species account lists scientific and common names in Dutch, English, French, German, Japanese, Malay, Maori, and Russian, and a separate appendix in Volume 5 lists Aboriginal names. The species accounts also include distribution map, field identification, habitat, distribution, movements, ecology, voice, plumages, and references. There are excellent color plates illustrating the birds as well.

Central and South America

Blake, Emmet Reid. **Manual of Neotropical Birds.** Chicago: University of Chicago Press, 1977– . vol. $130 (vol. 1). ISBN 0226056414 (vol. 1).

Only Volume 1 of this set has been published, covering the penguins through the gulls. The set was intended to cover Central and South America with the exception of Mexico and the West Indies, Galapagos, and Falkland Islands. Each family is covered in a separate chapter, with a key to genera, synopsis, and listing of species. Each species account covers description, geographical distribution, and literature citations. The volume includes color and black-and-white illustrations and range maps.

Hilty, Steven L., and William L. Brown. **A Guide to the Birds of Colombia.** Princeton, NJ: Princeton University Press, 1986. 836 p. $125.00; $52.50 (paper). ISBN 0691083711; 069108372X (paper).

This guide is either a concise handbook or a hefty field guide covering 1,695 species of the birds of Colombia. Each species account covers identification, similar species, voice, breeding, status and habitat, range, and notes. Plates in the center provide black-and-white and color illustrations for identification along with very brief description and range.

Ridgely, Robert S., and Guy Tudor. **The Birds of South America.** Austin: University of Texas Press, 1989– . vol. $85 (vol. 1), $95 (vol. 2). ISBN 0292707568 (vol. 1); 0292770634 (vol. 2).

South America is home to over 3,000 species of birds. This set is projected to cover four volumes, although only Volumes 1 and 2 have been published (Volume 2 in 1994). Existing volumes feature excellent color plates plus species accounts that include description, similar species, habitat, range, notes, and range maps. Common names are only given in English because Spanish names are not well established throughout the continent. Volumes to date include Volume 1, *The Oscine Passerines,* and

Volume 2, *Suboscine Passerines.* Projected are Volume 3, *The Nonpasserines (Landbirds),* and Volume 4, *The Nonpasserines (Waterbirds).*

Sick, Helmut. **Birds in Brazil: A Natural History.** Princeton, NJ: Princeton University Press, 1993. 703 p. $205. ISBN 0691085692.

A translation of the author's *Ornitologia Brasileira,* this handbook covers about 1,635 species of birds found in Brazil. It is in systematic order. The amount of information on each taxa varies widely, but may include description, morphology, behavior, breeding, migration, and so on. A second edition of *Ornitologia Brasileira* was published in 1997 but has not been translated into English.

Skutch, Alexander Frank. **Birds of Tropical America.** Austin: University of Texas Press, 1983. 305 p. (Corrie Herring Hooks series, no. 5). ISBN 0292746342.

An attractively illustrated guide to the natural history of 34 species of birds of Central America. The author wrote the book for a general audience and specifically chose species that were not covered in his *Life Histories of Central American Birds* (below). The accounts are extensive and include many personal observations and stories. The birds included are well known, such as the tinamous, the Groove-billed Ani, and the Resplendent Quetzal.

Skutch, Alexander Frank. **Life Histories of Central American Birds.** Berkeley, CA: Cooper Ornithological Society, 1954–69. 3 vol. (Pacific Coast Avifauna, no. 31, 34, and 35).

Covers life histories of selected species of the passerine birds of Central America. Each of the three volumes covers about 40 to 45 species and provides detailed information on the description, food, song, reproduction, and enemies of the birds. There are a few black-and-white illustrations and photographs.

Europe

Cramp, Stanley, chief ed., **Handbook of the Birds of Europe, the Middle East and North Africa: The Birds of the Western Palearctic.** New York: Oxford University Press, 1977–94. 9 vol. $165. ISBN 0198573588 (vol. 1).

One of the major handbooks, this set includes detailed species accounts for all birds found in the western Palearctic region, including the European portions of Russia. Coverage includes common names in a variety of European languages, field characters, habitat, distribution, migration, voice, plumages, measurements, weights, and geographical variations. Some of the discussions of voice include sonagrams.

Il'ichev, Valerii Dmitrievich, and Vladimir Evgen'evich Flint. **Handbuch der Vögel der Sowjetunion.** 1. Aufl. Wiesbaden: AULA-Verlag, 1985– . ISBN 3891044143 (Bd. 1); 3891044178 (Bd. 4); 3740300299 (Bd. 6/1); 3894324155 (Bd. 6/2).

A translation of the Russian *Ptitsy SSSR,* this projected 10-volume set provides detailed species accounts for the birds of the vast region of the former Soviet Union. Common names are listed in Russian, German, British English, North American English, and French. There are a number of illustrations, including black-and-white illustrations demonstrating avian behaviors.

Niethammer, Günther, et al., eds. **Handbuch der Vögel Mitteleuropas.** Frankfurt am Main, Germany: Akademische Verlagsgesellschaft, 1966–97. 14 vol.

This massive set covers the birds of central Europe in detail. Species accounts cover range, geographical variation, field identification, voice, migration, habitat, behavior, food sources, and references.

Snow, David, Christopher M. Perrins, et al. **The Birds of the Western Palearctic.** Concise ed. New York: Oxford University Press, 1998. 2 vol. $295. ISBN 019854099X (set).

This hefty two-volume set is a concise version of the nine-volume set *Handbook of the Birds of Europe, the Middle East and North Africa,* containing updated information on species covered in the earliest volumes of the original series. It covers 936 species with brief species accounts and common names in Dutch, French, German, Italian, Russian, Spanish, Swedish, British English, and North American English.

Identification Tools

CITES Identification Guide—Birds: Guide to the Identification of Bird Species Controlled under the Convention on International Trade in Endangered Species of Wild Fauna and Flora. Ottawa: Canadian Wildlife Service, 1994. 1 vol. (various pagings). ISBN 0662611837.

A multilingual guide that identifies the numerous species of birds covered by the CITES convention plus some species that might be confused with CITES species. A visual key identifies species by such features as the shape of the bill or the presence of spurs on the legs, which then leads the users to the appropriate species account. Also available on the Web at http://www.ec.gc.ca/birdsguide/Menu.asp?lang=1.

Geographical Section

North America

Baicich, Paul J., and Colin James Oliver Harrison. **A Guide to the Nests, Eggs, and Nestlings of North American Birds.** 2nd ed. San Diego: Academic Press, 1997. 347 p. (AP Natural World). $26.95 (paper). ISBN 0120728303; 0120728311 (paper).

A guide to the breeding biology of over 600 species of birds in North America, with detailed information on their breeding cycle, nest construction, breeding season, eggs, incubation, and nesting and nestling periods. The guide also illustrates nests, eggs, and nestlings.

Bull, John L., and John Farrand, Jr. **The National Audubon Society Field Guide to North American Birds, Eastern Region.** 2nd ed., fully rev. New York: Knopf, 1997. 797 p. $19.95. ISBN 0679428526.

A photographic guide to 508 species of birds east of the Rockies. The birds are arranged by color and form rather than by taxonomic order, and the plates of color photographs are separate from the species accounts. A visual key helps users zero in on the right group of birds, and there are range maps.

Elbroch, Mark, Eleanor Marks, and C. Diane Boretos. **Bird Tracks and Sign: A Guide to North American Species.** Mechanicsburg, PA: Stackpole Books, 2001. 456 p. $34.95 (paper). ISBN 0811726967 (paper).

This field guide is one of several written to allow users to identify birds by the evidence they leave, such as tracks, scats (droppings), nests, and skeletons. It is divided into sections based on the kind of sign, namely tracks, pellets (regurgitated food), droppings, signs of feeding, nests, feathers, and skulls. Within each chapter, the sign is illustrated for the most common species leaving that kind of sign and described. There are also general discussions of how the signs are made, why the birds leave that kind of sign, and so on.

Field Guide to the Birds of North America. 3rd ed. Washington, DC: National Geographic, 1999. 480 p. $21.95 (paper). ISBN 0792274512 (paper).

A very respected advanced field guide for the birds of North America north of Mexico, this guide compares with Sibley's guide (below) for popularity, but its smaller size makes it much more field friendly. It features color illustrations and distribution maps next to each description. The index can be used as a life list.

Harrison, Hal H. **A Field Guide to the Birds' Nests: United States East of the Mississippi River.** Boston: Houghton Mifflin, 1975. 257 p. (Peterson Field Guide series, no. 21). $20. ISBN 0395204348.

This field guide illustrates the nests of 285 species of birds found east of the Mississippi River.

Harrison, Hal H. **A Field Guide to Western Birds' Nests: Of 520 Species Found Breeding in the United States West of the Mississippi River.** Boston: Houghton Mifflin, 1979. 279 p. (Peterson Field Guide series, no. 25). $20. ISBN 0395276292.

A companion to Harrison's guide to eastern bird nests (above), this guide illustrates the nests of 520 species of birds.

Peterson, Roger Tory. **A Field Guide to the Birds: A Completely New Guide to All the Birds of Eastern and Central North America.** 5th ed. Boston: Houghton Mifflin, 2002. 427 p. (Peterson Field Guide series). $30 (paper); $22 (flexibound). ISBN 0395740479 (paper); 0395740460 (flexibound).

The classic field guide to eastern birds, this latest edition contains updated illustrations and range maps and includes the lower Rio Grande valley. The guide also includes a life list for birders to record their sightings.

Peterson, Roger Tory. **A Field Guide to Western Birds: A Completely New Guide to Field Marks of All Species Found in North America West of the 100th Meridian and North of Mexico.** 3rd ed., rev. and enl. Boston: Houghton Mifflin, 1990. 432 p. (Peterson Field Guide series, no. 2). $27; $18 (paper). ISBN 0395911745; 0395911737 (paper).

Like Peterson's guide to eastern birds, this field guide features color illustrations integrated with the species accounts, although all range maps are in a separate section.

Pyle, Peter, et al. **Identification Guide to North American Birds: A Compendium of Information on Identifying, Ageing, and Sexing "Near-Passerines" and Passerines in the Hand.** Bolinas, CA: Slate Creek Press, 1997– . ISBN 0961894024 (pt. 1).

Although unfinished, this advanced identification guide is an important resource for the identification not just of species, but also to the age, sex, and molts of individuals. There are no color illustrations; rather identification is based on detailed descriptions and line drawings of feathers, bills, and other anatomical details. The set is a revised edition of the author's *Identification Guide to North American Passerines.* To date, only Volume 1 has been published, covering the doves to weavers. An online errata page for Volume 1 is available at http://www.prbo.org/Errata.html.

Sibley, David. **Sibley's Birding Basics.** New York: Knopf, 2002. 154 p. $15.95. ISBN 0375709665.

A how-to guide rather than an actual identification guide, this handbook by one of the most highly regarded recent field guide authors tells how to identify birds. The author provides detailed information on what to look for such as behavior, voice, color patterns, wing structure, molts, age variation, and more. He also discusses where to find birds, taxonomy, ethics, and other issues. The numerous illustrations are by the author and very good. Although Sibley also wrote the *Sibley Guide to Birds,* the two works are independent. Another highly recommended birding guide is Kenn Kaufman's *A Field Guide to Advanced Birding: Birding Challenges and How to Approach Them* (1990), which is more advanced but covers many of the same topics.

Sibley, David. **The Sibley Guide to Birds.** New York: Knopf, 2000. 544 p. $35 (paper). ISBN 0679451226 (paper).

This highly regarded field guide is rather hefty to be taken into the field, but it is an excellent reference source for a range of users, from birders to ornithologists. Sibley provides multiple illustrations for most species, including various plumages for juveniles, males and females, and regional variations. See also the companion volume, *The Sibley Guide to Bird Life and Behavior,* above.

Udvardy, Miklos D. F. **National Audubon Society Field Guide to North American Birds, Western Region.** 2nd ed., rev. New York: Knopf, 1997. 822 p. (National Audubon Society Field Guide series). $19.95. ISBN 0679428518 (flexicover).

A photographic guide to 544 species of birds found west of the Great Plains. The format is the same as Bull and Farrand's guide to eastern birds, above.

Africa

Langrand, Olivier. **Guide to the Birds of Madagascar.** New Haven: Yale University Press, 1990. 364 p. $70. ISBN 0300043104.

A comprehensive field guide covering all 256 species, this guide features color illustrations and has extensive information on the ecology of the birds. The author also describes 17 prime bird-watching sites.

Newman, Kenneth. **Newman's Birds of Southern Africa.** 8th ed. London: New Holland, 2002. 512 p. ISBN 1868727351.

One of the most popular bird guides for this well-studied region of Africa, covering 900 species. The guide also includes a checklist.

Serle, William, and Gérard J. Morel. **A Field Guide to the Birds of West Africa.** London: Collins, 1977. 351 p. ISBN 0002192047.

This guide covers 1,000 species, although only 650 species are illustrated. The authors provide a checklist and common names in English, Spanish, French, and German.

Sinclair, Ian, P. A. R. Hockey, and W. R. Tarboten. **Illustrated Guide to the Birds of Southern Africa.** 3rd ed. Princeton: Princeton University Press, 2002. 447 p. (Princeton Field Guides). $29.95. ISBN 0691096821 (paper).

Another popular field guide for southern Africa. This guide is slightly more advanced than Newman's (above), emphasizing the identification of confusing species. It covers more than 900 species and illustrates multiple plumages (male, female, juvenile) for many of the species.

Williams, John George. **Birds of East Africa.** London: HarperCollins, 1995. 415 p. (Collins Field Guide). $22. ISBN 0002191792.

Another of the highly regarded Collins Field Guide series, this one describes 1,283 species of birds, although only 660 species are illustrated.

Antarctica

de la Peña, Martín Rodolfo, and Maurice Rumboll. **Birds of Southern South America and Antarctica.**

See full annotation under the Central and South America section, below.

Shirihai, Hadoram. **The Complete Guide to Antarctic Wildlife: Birds and Marine Mammals of the Antarctic Continent and the Southern Ocean.**
See chapter 4 for a full annotation of this guide.

Asia

Grimmett, Richard, Carol Inskipp, and Tim Inskipp. **Birds of India, Pakistan, Nepal, Bangladesh, Bhutan, Sri Lanka, and the Maldives.** Princeton, NJ: Princeton University Press, 1999. 384 p. (Princeton Field Guides). $29.95 (paper). ISBN 0691049106 (paper).

This comprehensive guide covers nearly 1,300 species of birds found on the Indian subcontinent. It is a compact field version of the authors' *A Guide to the Birds of India, Pakistan, Nepal, Bangladesh, Bhutan, Sri Lanka, and the Maldives.*

Kazmierczak, Krys. **A Field Guide to the Birds of the Indian Subcontinent.** New Haven: Yale University Press, 2000. 352 p. $35. ISBN 0300079214.

This pocket-sized guide covers about 1,300 species of birds of the region.

Kennedy, Robert S. **A Guide to the Birds of the Philippines.** New York: Oxford University Press, 2000. 369 p. (Oxford Ornithology Series). $95.00; $39.95 (paper). ISBN 0198546696; 0198546688 (paper).

The first comprehensive field guide to the birds of the Philippines, this guide identifies over 570 species, including 170 endemic species.

MacKinnon, John. **A Field Guide to the Birds of Borneo, Sumatra, Java, and Bali, the Greater Sunda Islands.** New York: Oxford University Press, 1993. 491 p. $55 (paper). ISBN 0198540353; 0198540345 (paper).

This guide covers the 820 species of birds of eastern Malaysia and western Indonesia. The introduction discusses the natural history of the region and provides bird-watching tips.

MacKinnon, John Ramsay, and Karen Phillipps in collaboration with He Fen-qi. **A Field Guide to the Birds of China.** New York: Oxford University Press, 2000. 586 p. (Oxford Ornithology series). $45 (paper). ISBN 0198549415; 0198549407 (paper).

One of the few English-language guides to this large and diverse country, this guide identifies over 1,300 species.

Massey, Joseph A., et al. **A Field Guide to the Birds of Japan.** Tokyo: Wild Bird Society of Japan, 1982. 336 p. ISBN 0870117467.

Covers 537 species of birds found in Japan.

Robson, Craig. **A Guide to the Birds of Southeast Asia: Thailand, Peninsular Malaysia, Singapore, Myanmar, Laos, Vietnam, Cambodia.** Princeton, NJ: Princeton University Press, 2000. 504 p. $59.50. ISBN 0691050120.

Covers over 1,250 species of birds found in this diverse region. The introduction discusses the ecology and conservation of the region as well as providing bird-watching tips.

Australasia

Beehler, Bruce M., Thane K. Pratt, and Dale A. Zimmerman. **Birds of New Guinea.** Princeton, NJ: Princeton University Press, 1986. 293 p. (Handbook of the Wau Ecology Institute, No. 9). $49.50 (paper). ISBN 0691083851; 0691023948 (paper).

Identifies over 700 species, 600 of them illustrated, with extensive information on the natural history of the birds. The guide also includes an ornithological gazetteer and maps of bird-watching sites.

Heather, B.D., and Hugh A. Robertson. **The Field Guide to the Birds of New Zealand.** Rev. ed. Auckland, NZ: Viking, 2000. 440 p. ISBN 0670893706.

Covers 328 species of birds found in New Zealand.

Pizzey, Graham, and Frank Knight. **The Graham Pizzey and Frank Knight Field Guide to the Birds of Australia.** Pymble, NSW: Angus & Robertson, 1999. 576 p. $24.95. ISBN 0207196915.

One of the major guides to the birds of Australia, this guide identifies 720 species of the region.

Simpson, Ken. **Field Guide to the Birds of Australia.** 6th ed. Princeton, NJ: Princeton University Press, 1999. 440 p. (Princeton Field Guides). $39.50. ISBN 0691049955.

A comprehensive guide to the 770 species of Australian birds. Includes a separate handbook section discussing each bird family.

Central and South America

Bond, James. **A Field Guide to Birds of the West Indies.** 5th ed. Boston: Houghton Mifflin, 1993. 256 p. (Peterson Field Guide Series, no. 18). ISBN 0395677017; 039567669X (paper); 0395074312.

The classic guide to the birds of the West Indies, and yes, the author is the namesake of Ian Fleming's spy.

Castro, Isabel C., and Antonia Phillips. **A Guide to the Birds of the Galápagos Islands.** Princeton, NJ: Princeton University Press, 1996. 144 p. $29.95. ISBN 0691012253.

A tourist guide to the birds of the islands, this field guide identifies all of the bird species and contains extensive information about the natural history of the Galápagos.

de la Peña, Martín Rodolfo, and Maurice Rumboll. **Birds of Southern South America and Antarctica.** London: HarperCollins, 1998. 224 p. (Collins Illustrated Checklist). $35. ISBN 0002200775.

A comprehensive guide to 1,140 species of birds found in Argentina, southern Brazil, Bolivia, Chile, Paraguay, Uruguay, and Antarctica. Common names are given in English, Portuguese, and Spanish.

Dunning, John Stewart, and Robert S. Ridgely. **South American Birds: A Photographic Aid to Identification.** Newtown Square, PA: Harrowood, 1987. 351 p. $47.50; $35.00 (paper). ISBN 0915180251; 091518026X (paper).

One of the few comprehensive guides to the 2,700 species of birds found in South America. The birds are illustrated in rather small photographs and have very brief descriptions.

Edwards, Ernest Preston. **A Field Guide to the Birds of Mexico and Adjacent Areas: Belize, Guatemala and El Salvador.** 3rd ed. Austin: University of Texas Press, 1998. 288 p. $35.00; $22.95 (paper). ISBN 0292720920; 0292720912 (paper).

Identifies the regularly occurring bird species of Mexico, Belize, Guatemala, and El Salvador, illustrating 850 species.

Howell, Steven N. G., and Sophie Webb. **A Guide to the Birds of Mexico and Northern Central America.** New York: Oxford University Press, 1995. 851 p. $39.95 (paper). ISBN 0198540132; 0198540124 (paper).

   This guide covers all 1,070 bird species of Mexico, Guatemala, Belize, El Salvador, Honduras, and western Nicaragua.

Europe

Flint, V. E., R. L. Boehme, Y. V. Kostin, and A. A. Kuznetsov. **A Field Guide to Birds of the USSR: Including Eastern Europe and Central Asia.** Princeton, NJ: Princeton University Press, 1984. 353 p. ISBN 0691082448; 0691024308 (paper).

   One of the very few guides to the birds of the former Soviet Union, this guide describes 728 species and illustrates 654 of them. It also provides information on bird-watching in this vast region.

Jonsson, Lars. **Birds of Europe: With North Africa and the Middle East.** Princeton, NJ: Princeton University Press, 1993. 559 p. $75. ISBN 0691033269; 0691026483 (paper).

   A comprehensive guide to the birds of Europe. It is based on five smaller guides prepared by the author in the late 1970s and includes distribution maps for most species along with descriptions and information on the habitat and migration of each species. Jonsson includes several pages of information on how to identify birds as well as an illustrated table of contents to help users find the right family of birds to study.

Kightley, Chris, and Steve Madge. **Pocket Guide to the Birds of Britain and North-West Europe.** New Haven: Yale University Press, 1998. 299 p. $20 (paper). ISBN 0300074557 (paper).

   Covers 386 species of birds found in Europe in a compact pocket-sized book. Multiple plumages are illustrated and similar species compared on facing pages.

Porter, R. F., S. Christiansen, and P. Schiermacker-Hansen. **Birds of the Middle East.** San Diego: Academic, 1996. 480 p. $60.95. ISBN 0856610763.

   Describes 722 species of birds found in the Arabian peninsula, Jordan, Lebanon, Israel, Syria, Iraq, Iran, Turkey, and Cyprus.

Svensson, Lars, and P. J. Grant. **Birds of Europe.** Princeton, NJ: Princeton University Press, 1999. 392 p. (Princeton Field Guides). $55.00; $29.95 (paper). ISBN 0691050538; 0691050546 (paper).

Covers 722 bird species commonly found in Europe and the Middle East as well as 23 introduced and 100 rare species. The guide includes a great deal of information on identifying birds, and there are numerous illustrations covering bird behavior as well as identification.

Pacific Islands

Pratt, H. Douglas, Phillip L. Bruner, and Delwyn G. Berrett. **A Field Guide to the Birds of Hawaii and the Tropical Pacific.** Princeton, NJ: Princeton University Press, 1987. 409 p. $52 (paper). ISBN 0691084025; 0691023999 (paper).

A comprehensive guide covering nearly 1,000 species of the Hawaiian Islands, Fiji, Samoa, Tonga, Southeast Polynesia, and Micronesia.

Associations

American Ornithologist's Union. National Museum of Natural History, Smithsonian Institution, Washington DC, 20560. Phone: 202-357-2051. Fax: 202-633-8084. E-mail: aou@nmnh.si.edu. URL: http://www.aou. org/aou (Accessed August 26, 2003).

Association of Field Ornithologists. c/o Allen Press, P.O. Box 1897, Lawrence, KS 66044-1897. URL: http://www.afonet.org/ (Accessed August 26, 2003).

Birds Australia (formerly Royal Australasian Ornithologists Union [RAOU]). 415 Riversdale Rd, Hawthorn East VIC 3123, Australia. Phone: 61 3 9882 2622. Fax: 61 3 9882 2677. E-mail: mail@birdsaustralia. com.au URL: http://www.birdsaustralia.com.au/ (Accessed August 26, 2003).

British Ornithologists' Union. The Natural History Museum, Tring HP23 6AP, United Kingdom. Phone: 44 1442 890080. Fax: 44 20 79426150. E-mail: bou@bou.org.uk. URL: http://www.bou.org.uk (Accessed August 26, 2003).

Cooper Ornithological Society. c/o Martin L. Morton, Occidental College, Biology Department, 1600 Campus Rd., Los Angeles CA 90041. URL: http://www.cooper.org/ (Accessed August 26, 2003).

Wilson Ornithological Society. University of Michigan, Museum of Zoology, Bird Division, Ann Arbor, MI 48109-1079. Phone: 734-764-0457. Fax: 734-763-4080. URL: http://www.ummz.lsa.umich.edu/birds/wos.html (Accessed August 26, 2003).

References

Gill, Frank B. 1995. *Ornithology.* 2nd ed. New York: W. H. Freeman.

Monroe, Burt L., and Charles G. Sibley. 1993. *A World Checklist of Birds.* New Haven, CT: Yale University Press.

8

Mammals

There are about 4,600 species of mammals, the smallest of the vertebrate classes. Mammals are among the most familiar animals. They have hair, three bones in their middle ears (the malleus, incus, and stapes), and produce milk. Mammals range in size from the bumblebee bat of Thailand (*Craseonycteris thonglongyai,* 2 grams) to the largest animal that ever lived, the blue whale (*Balaenoptera musculus,* over 130 tons). There are three major divisions of mammals. The smallest group is the monotremes, or Prototheria, which lay eggs rather than give birth to live young but do produce milk. The marsupials, or Metatheria, are the pouched mammals and live primarily in Australia and South America. The largest group is the placental mammals, or Eutheria, which bear live young that have been nourished in utero by a placenta.

Because we humans are also mammals, it should come as no surprise that the mammals are probably the best studied group of animals. Even so, nearly 40% of all mammals are rodents and bats that few people ever see and fewer study. In addition, large mammals are still being discovered, including a new beaked whale in 2002 and several species of deer and bovids in Southeast Asia in the 1990s.

Classification of Mammals (taken from Martin et al., 2001)

Prototheria

Monotremata (3 species)

Metatheria

Marsupials (7 orders, 270 species)

Eutheria

Insectivora (moles, shrews, hedgehogs; 375 species)

Dermoptera (Colugos or flying lemurs; 2 species)

Chiroptera (Bats; 1,000 species)

Scandentia (Tupaia or tree shrews; 19 species)

Primates (apes, monkeys, humans; 280 species)

Xenarthra (Armadillos, anteaters, and sloths; 29 species)

Pholidota (pangolins; 7 species)

Carnivora (cats, dogs, bears, seals, weasels, mongooses, and hyenas; 270 species)

Cetacea (whales, dolphins, and porpoises; 80 species)

Macroscelidea (elephant shrews; 19 species)

Lagomorpha (rabbits, hares, and pikas; 80 species)

Rodentia (rats, mice, beavers, squirrels, etc.; 2,000 species)

Tubulidentata (aardvark; 1 species)

Proboscidea (elephants; 2 species)

Hyracoidea (hyraxes; 6 species)

Sirenia (manatees and dugongs; 4 species)

Perissodactyla (odd-toed ungulates, including horses, rhinos, and tapirs; 16 species)

Artiodactyla (even-toed ungulates, including pigs, hippos, camels, deer, and cattle; 220 species)

Indexes, Abstracts, and Bibliographies

PrimateLit: A Bibliographic Database for Primatology. Madison: Wisconsin Regional Primate Research Center, 2001– . URL: http://primatelit.library.wisc.edu/. (Accessed August 26, 2003).

This database covers the scientific literature dealing with all aspects of the biology and behavior of nonhuman primates. It goes back to 1940 and indexes journals, books, book chapters, dissertations, proceedings, and other literature types. A subset of the database, *Current Primate References* (CPR), provides access to the most recent six months' worth of citations and was formerly published in print.

Smith, Charles H. **MAMMFAUN: A Bibliography Concerning the Geographical Distribution of Mammals.** 1993. URL: http://www.wku.edu/~smithch/mamm/MAMMFAUN.htm. (Accessed August 26, 2003).

Originally published as two floppy disks, this Web bibliography covers about 2,300 items such as keys, field guides, faunal monographs, and articles dealing with the geographical distribution of mammals. The bibliography, which covers only articles published up to 1993, is arranged in alphabetical order by author. In addition to the citation, the author has added geographical and taxonomic keywords.

Wahlert, John H. **Bibliography of General Works in Mammalogy.** New York: American Museum of Natural History, 1999–   . URL: http://research.amnh.org/mammalogy/biblio/. (Accessed August 26, 2003).

A handy list of resources appropriate for beginning students in mammalogy. The list is quite extensive and broken down into broad subject categories such as Keys to Mammals, Systematics and Nomenclature, and Anatomy. Most of the items are books, but a few are articles. The author works at the American Museum of Natural History.

Walker, Ernest P. **Mammals of the World.** 1st ed. Baltimore: Johns Hopkins University Press, 1964. Vol. 3.

Volume 3 of this classic encyclopedia consists of "A Classified Bibliography of Literature Regarding Mammals." It contains about 70,000 citations arranged by order, geographical area, or general subject categories. The citations refer to both popular and research articles. Another section lists about 120 periodicals that regularly publish articles dealing with mammalogy. Subsequent editions of the encyclopedia dropped the bibliography volume.

Journals

American Journal of Primatology. Vol. 1–   . New York: Wiley, 1981–   . Monthly. $2,250. ISSN 0275-2565. Available electronically.

Publishes research and review articles in all areas of the applied and basic biology of nonhuman primates. The journal also publishes the abstracts of meetings of the American Society of Primatologists in a supplementary issue and has an occasional special issue on a specific topic. The official journal of the American Society of Primatologists.

Australian Mammalogy. Vol. 1–   . Adelaide: Australian Mammal Society, 1972–   . Biannual. ISSN 0310-0049.

Publishes research articles, reviews, and brief notes on all aspects of the biology of Australasian mammals, including introduced species.

Current Mammalogy. Vol. 1–   . New York: Plenum, 1987–   . Irregular. $171. ISSN 0899-577X.

A review serial covering a broad range of subjects dealing with mammalogy, although only two volumes have been published (in 1987 and 1990).

Folia Primatologica: International Journal of Primatology. Vol. 1–   . Basel, Switzerland: S. Karger, 1963–   . Bimonthly. $557. ISSN 0015-5713. Available electronically.

Publishes Brief Reports and research articles in all areas of primatology, with emphasis on articles with a comparative or evolutionary emphasis. Articles can be in English, French, or German. The official journal of the European Federation for Primatology.

International Journal of Primatology. Vol. 1–   . New York: Kluwer, 1980–   . Bimonthly. $838. ISSN 0164-0291. Available electronically.

Publishes research articles, short articles, reviews, and book reviews in the area of basic primatology, including laboratory and fieldwork. The official journal of the International Primatological Society.

Journal of Mammalogy. Vol. 1–   . Lawrence, KS: Allen Press, 1919–   . Quarterly. $170. ISSN 0022-2372. Available electronically.

The journal publishes articles, and general notes dealing with all types of research on terrestrial and marine mammals worldwide. The official publication of the American Society of Mammalogists.

Mammalia: Journal de Morphologie, Biologie, Systematique des Mammifères. Vol. 1   . Paris: Musée National d'Histoire Naturelle, 1936–   . Quarterly. $144. ISSN 0025-1461.

Publishes original notes and research papers dealing with all aspects of mammalian systematics, biology, and ecology. Articles are written in French and English.

Mammal Review. Vol. 1–   . Oxford, UK: Blackwell Scientific Publications, 1970–   . Quarterly. $457. ISSN 0305-1838. Available electronically.

Publishes review articles on any aspects of mammalogy. A few articles are available for free at the publisher's Web site at http://www.black wellpublishing.com/journals/mam/. A publication of the Mammal Society.

Marine Mammal Science. Vol. 1–   . Lawrence, KS: Society for Marine Mammalogy, 1985–   . Quarterly. $120. ISSN 0824-0469. Available electronically.

The journal publishes research articles, review articles, notes, opinion pieces, and letters on all aspects of marine mammal biology. Volumes 1 through 13 are currently available on CD-ROM. The official journal of the Society for Marine Mammalogy.

Primates: A Journal of Primatology. Vol. 1–   . Tokyo: Springer Verlag Tokyo, 1957–   . Quarterly. $274. ISSN 0032-8332. Available electronically.

Publishes original research articles, review articles, short communications, and book reviews covering all areas of primate research.

Biographies and Histories

Birney, Elmer C., and Jerry R. Choate, eds. **Seventy-five Years of Mammalogy, 1919–1994.** Provo, UT: American Society of Mammalogists, 1994. 433 p. (Special Publication of the American Society of Mammalogists, no. 11). ISBN 0935868739.

This volume covers the history of the American Society of Mammalogists, so the emphasis is clearly on mammalogy in North America. The book is in two main sections, one covering the history of the ASM itself and the other discussing the development of the science of mammalogy. Topics covered in this section include taxonomy, biogeography, anatomy, population ecology, behavior, and conservation.

Sterling, Keir B., ed. **International History of Mammalogy.** Bel Air, MD: One World Press, 1987. vol. $25 (vol. 1, paper). ISBN 0910485003 (vol. 1); 0910485011 (vol. 1, paper).

To date, only Volume 1 has been published in this proposed series. The volume covers the history of mammalogy in Eastern Europe and Fennoscandia during the modern period.

Dictionaries and Encyclopedias

Gotch, A. F. **Latin Names Explained: A Guide to the Scientific Classification of Reptiles, Birds and Mammals.**

See chapter 4 for a full annotation. Explains the source of Latin terms used in mammalian scientific names.

Gould, Edwin, and George McKay, eds. **Encyclopedia of Mammals.** 2nd ed. San Diego: Academic Press, 1998. 240 p. (Natural World Series). $41.95. ISBN 0122936701.

A beautifully illustrated overview of mammals. The encyclopedia is in two sections, one providing an introduction to mammal classification, evolution, and biology. The second section covers mammalian diversity, discussing the distribution, classification, and natural history of each order and family.

Grzimek, Bernhard, ed. **Grzimek's Encyclopedia of Mammals.** New York: McGraw-Hill, 1990. 5 vol. ISBN 0079095089 (set).

A companion to the classic *Grzimek's Animal Life Encyclopedia,* this set provides an update to the first edition. It contains many beautiful color photographs and has a very detailed discussion of the natural history of mammalian families. There are distribution maps for many groups, plus charts comparing features such as reproduction, life cycle, size, and food preferences for related species.

Macdonald, David W., and Sasha Norris, eds. **The Encyclopedia of Mammals.** New York: Facts on File, 2001. 3 vol. (Facts on File Natural Science Library). $300. ISBN 0816042675.

A greatly expanded and updated version of a one-volume encyclopedia originally published in 1984, this encyclopedia is arranged by systematic order. For each order, there is an overview of the order, then individual chapters covering each family. Well-known species receive individual entries, and lesser-known species are covered in a general overview. There are maps and color photographs. Volume 1 covers carnivores and sea mammals; Volume 2, primates and large herbivores; and Volume 3, marsupials, insect eaters, and small herbivores.

Perrin, William F., Bernd Wursig, and J. G. M. Thewissen, eds. **Encyclopedia of Marine Mammals.** San Diego: Academic Press, 2002. 1,414 p. $139.95. ISBN 0125513402.

Contains 285 articles on all aspects of marine mammals, from anatomy to human interactions. In addition to articles on general topics, entries discuss marine mammal species, including distribution, reproduction, ecology, conservation, further reading, and cross-references to other articles. Appendixes provide biographies of marine mammal scientists and a list of marine mammal species.

Stangl, Frederick B., Peder G. Christiansen, and Elsa J. Galbraith. **Abbreviated Guide to Pronunciation and Etymology of Scientific Names for**

North American Land Mammals North of Mexico. Lubbock: Texas Tech University Press, 1993. 28 p. (Occasional Papers of the Texas Tech University Museum, no. 154).

Although the nomenclature code states that scientific names must be pronounceable, students and nonzoologists might beg to differ. This dictionary provides suggested pronunciations and etymologies for the land mammals of North America. It is arranged in checklist order, and there are no scientific or common name indexes.

Textbooks

Feldhamer, George A., et al., eds. **Mammalogy: Adaptation, Diversity, and Ecology.** Boston: WCB/McGraw-Hill, 1999. 563 p. $105.80. ISBN 069716733X.

A textbook for upper-level undergraduate and graduate courses in mammalogy, this text is in five major sections. Section 1 covers introductory material, including the history of mammalogy and techniques for studying mammals, and the remaining sections cover structure and function, diversity, ecology, and special topics such as parasitology, domestication, and conservation. Each chapter concludes with a summary, discussion questions, and suggested readings.

Martin, Robert Eugene, Ronald H. Pine, and Anthony F. DeBlase. **A Manual of Mammalogy: With Keys to Families of the World.** 3rd ed. Boston: McGraw-Hill, 2001. 333 p. $41.55 (spiral bound). ISBN 0697006433 (spiral bound).

In three sections, this manual is suitable for upper-level undergraduate or graduate courses in mammalogy. The sections include characteristics of mammals, techniques for studying mammals, and a survey of mammal families. The family surveys include keys to orders and families, and each family chapter discusses classification, distinguishing characters, the living families, and keys to families. There are black-and-white illustrations of representative species, including skulls. The manual also includes lab exercises and information on doing literature searches.

Vaughan, Terry A., James M. Ryan, and Nicholas J. Czaplewski. **Mammalogy.** 4th ed. Fort Worth, TX: Saunders, 2000. 565 p. $99.95. ISBN 003025034X.

About half of this text consists of accounts of each mammal order, discussing topics such as general characteristics, morphology, paleontology, and diversity. There are numerous illustrations and photographs both of living mammals and skulls. The authors also cover the classification, reproduction, physiology, behavior, ecology, zoogeography, and conservation of mammals. Each chapter contains a list of related Web sites, and of course there is a lengthy bibliography of more traditional sources.

Checklists and Classification Schemes

American Society of Mammalogists. **State Lists: State-Specific Lists of Indigenous Mammals.** URL: http://www.mammalsociety.org/statelists/index.html (Accessed August 26, 2003).

This site links to state mammal lists, with plans to add Canadian and Mexican lists as well. At the time of viewing, about half the state lists were complete. The lists include common and scientific names, higher taxa, status and distribution, and whether a photograph is available from the society's mammal image library, and the species account number from *Mammalian Species,* below.

Anderson, Sydney, and J. Knox Jones, Jr., eds. **Orders and Families of Recent Mammals of the World.** New York: Wiley, 1984. 686 p. ISBN 047108493X.

This handbook discusses the orders and families of living mammals. Each taxon is covered in detail, with information including diagnosis, distribution, a list of families or genera, habits, and general notes. There are distribution maps and illustrations of skulls for most taxa as well.

Corbet, G.B. **The Mammals of the Palaearctic Region: A Taxonomic Review.** Ithaca, NY: Cornell University Press, 1978. 314 p. (Publication of the British Museum [Natural History], no. 788). ISBN 0801411718.

This checklist was co-published by the British Museum (Natural History) and covers the mammals of Europe and Asia north of the Himalayas along with Africa north of the Sahara. Species are listed in taxonomic order, with subspecies, range, and remarks. A *Supplement* was published in 1984 as no. 944 of the museum's publication series.

Corbet, G.B., and J.E. Hill. **A World List of Mammalian Species.** 3rd ed. New York: Oxford University Press, 1991. 243 p. ISBN 0198540175.

This list provides a comprehensive list of mammalian species. Each entry includes scientific name, English common name, and geographical range, with selected line drawings.

Honacki, James H., Kenneth E. Kinman, and James W. Koeppl, eds. **Mammal Species of the World: A Taxonomic and Geographic Reference.** Lawrence, KS: Allen Press and the Association of Systematics Collections, 1982. 694 p. ISBN 0942924002.

One of the standard checklists of the mammalian species of the world. Each brief entry includes original author and citation, comments, type locality, distribution, conservation status, and ISIS number (the International Species Inventory System).

International Species Inventory System (ISIS). URL: http://www.isis.org (Accessed August 26, 2003).

A system to record information on all animals held in captivity, ISIS holds data on over 1.65 million individuals from 10,000 species, including pedigrees and population demographics. The data was formerly published as *ISIS Mammalian Taxonomic Directory* in loose-leaf format. The ISIS numbers are frequently included in other mammalian handbooks.

Mammalian Species. No. 1– . American Society of Mammalogists, 1969– . Irregular. $50. ISBN 0076-3519.

This serial publication consists of individual species accounts for the mammals of the world. About 25 to 30 are published per year, over 700 by early 2003, and each number covers one species. The information provided for each species includes species name, diagnosis, general characters, distribution, ecology, etymology, function, reproduction, behavior, genetics, and literature cited. Most are illustrated with distribution maps, skulls, and line drawings. An index and PDF files of the first 631 accounts have been made available by Virginia Hayssen at URL: http://www.science.smith.edu/departments/Biology/VHAYSSEN/msi/

McKenna, Malcolm C., and Susan K. Bell. **Classification of Mammals above the Species Level.** New York: Columbia University Press, 1997. 631 p. $198; $52 (paper). ISBN 023111012X; 0231110138 (paper).

A revision of George Gaylord Simpson's classic mammalian classification system published in the *Bulletin of the American Museum of Natural History* in 1945, this system lists all names that have been used for recent and extinct mammalian groups above the species level, whether currently accepted or not. In addition to the classification system itself, the authors provide a lengthy and detailed discussion of the history and theory of classification. There are several appendixes, listing mammalian characters, extinct close relatives to the mammals, and taxonomic suffixes denoting rank.

Nowak, Ronald M. **Walker's Mammals of the World.** 6th ed. Baltimore: Johns Hopkins University Press, 1999. $99.95. 2 vol. ISBN 0801857899.

A revision of Ernest P. Walker's classic, this handbook covers mammals to the generic level. Orders, families, and genera are described, including natural history and distribution, and the species are listed within each genus. There are photographs illustrating each genus. The amount of information available for each genus varies widely; some are covered in half a page; others such as *Canis* have much more extensive accounts. The 5th edition of the handbook is also available online by subscription only.

Szalay, Frederick S., Michael J. Novacek, and Malcolm C. McKenna, eds. **Mammal Phylogeny.** New York: Springer-Verlag, 1993. 2 vol. $96 (vol. 1); $108 (vol. 2); $185 (set). ISBN 0387978542 (vol. 1); 0387978534 (vol. 2); 0387976760 (set).

The information presented in these volumes is based on a symposium sponsored by NATO in 1984. Volume 1 covers the phylogeny of extinct groups, monotremes, and marsupials, and Volume 2 covers placentals.

Wilson, Don E., and F. Russell Cole. **Common Names of Mammals of the World.** Washington, DC: Smithsonian Institution Press, 2000. 204 p. $19.95. ISBN 1560983833.

Contains a list of the standard common names for 4,629 species of mammals, introducing many new names. The list is arranged in phylogenetic order and includes order and family names as well as those of genera and species.

Wilson, Don E., and DeeAnn M. Reeder, eds. **Mammal Species of the World: A Taxonomic and Geographic Reference.** 2nd ed. Washington, DC: Smithsonian Institution Press, 1993. 1,206 p. $80. ISBN 1560982179.

A checklist to the mammals of the world, this is the standard classification guide for mammals. It provides original citation, type locality, distribution, status, synonyms, and comments for each species. An appendix lists the species accounts found in numbers 1–402 of the serial publication *Mammalian Species,* above. Also available on the Web at URL: http://www.nmnh.si.edu/msw/.

Handbooks

Animal Care and Use Committee. **Guidelines for the Capture, Handling, and Care of Mammals as Approved by the American Society of Mammalogists.** s.l.: American Society of Mammalogists, 199?. 47 p.

This pamphlet provides guidelines for research with mammals, including field studies, capture, and specimen collection. The pamphlet also discusses topics such as the researchers' responsibility for dependent offspring, euthanasia, transporting captive animals, and more. It is available for no charge at the American Society of Mammalogists' Web site, at http://www.mammalsociety.org/committees/commanimalcareuse/98acu guidelines.PDF.

Attenborough, David. **The Life of Mammals.** Princeton, NJ: Princeton University Press, 2002. 320 p. $29.95. ISBN 0691113246.

Published in conjunction with a television series by the same name, this colorful volume provides information on the natural history and evolution of mammals. It is arranged roughly by lifestyle into chapters such as plant predators, return to the water, and life in the trees. Although written for the general public, it offers a nice overview of mammalian behavior and ecology. The photographs are particularly attractive. The author also wrote *The Life of Birds* (see chapter 7), which is quite similar in its aim and format.

Bookhout, Theodore A., ed. **Research and Management Techniques for Wildlife and Habitats.** 5th ed. Bethesda, MD: Wildlife Society, 1994. 740 p. $40. ISBN 0933564104.

This edition of a highly regarded manual is in four parts, covering experimental design, field and laboratory techniques, population analysis and management, and habitat analysis and management. Many of the techniques are aimed at land mammals, but other groups are included as well. A revised edition of *Wildlife Management Techniques Manual.*

Chiasson, Robert B. **Laboratory Anatomy of the White Rat.** 5th ed. Dubuque, IA: W.C. Brown, 1988. 129 p. (Laboratory Anatomy series). $39.06. ISBN 0697051323.

A laboratory manual for rat dissection.

Gilbert, Stephen G. **Pictorial Anatomy of the Cat.** Rev. ed. Seattle: University of Washington Press, 1975. 120 p. $20. ISBN 029595454X.

One of the standard anatomical atlases for the cat; also available in an abridged version (*Outline of Cat Anatomy*).

Hafner, Mark S., et al. **Mammal Collections in the Western Hemisphere: A Survey and Directory of Existing Collections.** Lawrence, KS: Printed by Allen Press for the American Society of Mammalogists, 1997. 93 p. ISBN 0893380555.

Presents the results of a survey of mammal collections taken in 1995. The authors present summary information on the collections, including size, taxa represented, presence of catalogs or various policies, and similar data. The directory itself provides contact information and a brief summary of the size and special strengths of the collection. There are several appendixes covering such topics as a bibliography of type specimen catalogs, publication series associated with mammal collections such as *Fieldiana: Zoology,* and basic standards. Also available on the Web at http://www.mammalsociety.org/committees/commsyscollection/collsurvey.pdf.

Hayssen, Virginia, Ari van Tienhoven, and Ans van Tienhoven. **Asdell's Patterns of Mammalian Reproduction: A Compendium of Species-Specific Data.** Ithaca, NY: Comstock, 1993. 1,023 p. $95. ISBN 0801417538.

This handbook provides species-specific data on the reproductive biology of mammals, with the exception of well-known domesticated and laboratory species such as cows and rats. It is arranged in the standard taxonomic sequence. The data include items such as neonatal mass, neonatal size, weaning mass, litter size, sexual maturity, cycle length, gestation, lactation, interlitter interval, and seasonality. A revised edition of S. A. Asdell, *Patterns of Mammalian Reproduction,* 2nd ed. (1964).

Lawlor, Timothy E. **Handbook to the Orders and Families of Living Mammals.** 2nd ed. Eureka, CA: Mad River Press, 1979. 327 p. $22.95. ISBN 091642216X.

Provides keys and diagnostic descriptions of the orders of mammals from around the world. An introductory section discusses mammalian bones, especially skulls, and their importance for identification. Each order is described along with diagnostic features such as number of digits, dental formula, and size.

Michaud, Steve L. **Virtual Pig Dissection.** URL; http://mail.tkchs.sad27. k12.mc.us/fkchs/vpig/. (Accessed August 26, 2003).

This Web site provides labeled drawings of pig anatomy, including external anatomy, respiratory system, circulatory system, digestive system, and male and female reproductive systems. Anatomical names are linked to brief definitions. The quality of the illustrations is reasonably good, but not as clear as most print lab manuals.

Nagorsen, D. W., and R. L. Peterson. **Mammal Collector's Manual: A Guide for Collecting, Documenting, and Preparing Mammal Speci-**

mens for Scientific Research. Toronto: Royal Ontario Museum, 1980. 79 p. $16.57. ISBN 0888542550.

This small handbook provides methods of collecting mammals in the field, including documentation, preservation, and how to ship specimens.

Silva, Marina, and John A. Downing. **CRC Handbook of Mammalian Body Masses.** Boca Raton, FL: CRC Press, 1995. 368 p. $149.95. ISBN 0849327903.

This handbook contains data on nearly 2,600 species of mammals. The data were gathered from thousands of published sources, and the tables include columns for taxa, sex, mass, minimum and maximum size, country and location, and reference number.

Wilson, Don E., et al, eds. **Measuring and Monitoring Biological Diversity. Standard Methods for Mammals.** Washington, DC: Smithsonian Institution Press, 1996. 409 p. (Biological Diversity Handbook series). $55.00; $29.95 (paper). ISBN 1560986360; 1560986379 (paper).

This handbook provides methods for studying mammalian populations. The authors describe techniques for a variety of research projects, including diversity, population size, capture, marking, and more. Appendixes cover ethics, the preparation of voucher specimens, vendors of supplies useful for mammalogists, and a table of random numbers as well as several additional techniques.

Systematic Section

Monotremata and Marsupalia

Archer, Michael, ed. **Possums and Opossums: Studies in Evolution.** Chipping Norton, NSW, Australia: Published by Surrey Beatty & Sons in association with the Royal Zoological Society of New South Wales, 1987. 2 vol. ISBN 0949324051.

Despite the title, this set covers the entire range of marsupials around the world. It contains papers originally presented at a symposium of the Royal Zoological Society of New South Wales. Chapters present a new classification system for marsupials as well as detailed information on both living and extinct Australian marsupials. The non-Australian marsupials are more briefly summarized.

Bethge, Philip. **Platypus and Echidna.** Department of Anatomy and Physiology, University of Tasmania. URL: http://www.healthsci.utas.edu.au/medicine/research/mono/monotremehp.html (Accessed August 26, 2003).

Although this site had not been updated for several years at the time of viewing, it contained detailed information on the biology of the monotremes. For each group, the site is divided into three areas covering the basics, physiology, and ongoing research projects. There is also an extensive bibliography and list of links for each group.

Griffiths, Mervyn. **The Biology of the Monotremes.** New York: Academic Press, 1978. 367 p. ISBN 0123038502.

This treatise surveys the biology of the platypus and echidnas. The author covers classification and distribution, physiology, reproduction, lactation, and neurobiology as well as discussing four views of the evolutionary relationship of monotremes to the other mammals.

Hunsaker, Don, ed. **The Biology of Marsupials.** New York: Academic Press, 1977. 537 p. ISBN 0123622506.

Discusses the biology of marsupials, with emphasis on the North American species. Topics covered include classification, cytogenetics, ecology, central nervous system, behavior, immune system, and diseases. There is also a bibliography of New World marsupials and notes on the nomenclature used.

Marshall, Larry G. **The Families and Genera of Marsupialia.** Chicago: Field Museum of Natural History, 1981. 65 p. (Fieldiana Geology, new ser., no. 8; Publication of the Field Museum of Natural History, no. 1320).

This catalog reviews marsupial systematics and provides a list of the recognized families and genera of living and extinct marsupials. The list includes synonyms, references, and ranges.

Oldfield, Thomas. **Catalogue of the Marsupialia and Monotremata in the Collection of the British Museum (Natural History).** London: Printed by Order of the Trustees, 1888. 401 p.

The catalog lists and describes 151 species of marsupials plus three monotremes, along with keys to family, genus, and species. The species accounts consist of very detailed physical descriptions along with distribution, location of type specimens, and type location. There are 28 plates at the end of the volume illustrating selected specimens and/or skulls, some of them hand colored.

Saunders, Norman, and Lyn Hinds, eds. **Marsupial Biology: Recent Research, New Perspectives.** Sydney, NSW, Australia: UNSW Press, 1997. 413 p. $127.25. ISBN 0868403113.

Summarizes the latest research on the biology of marsupials, including reproduction and development, general ecology, pathology and homeostasis, and developmental neurobiology.

Stonehouse, Bernard, and Desmond Gilmore, eds. **The Biology of Marsupials.** Baltimore: University Park Press, 1977. 486 p. (Biology and Environment). ISBN 0839108524.
Unlike Hunsaker's volume by the same name, above, this treatise emphasizes the biology of Australasian species. One chapter provides an annotated list of the living marsupial species worldwide.

Marine Mammals

Berta, Annalisa, and James L. Sumich. **Marine Mammals: Evolutionary Biology.** San Diego: Academic Press, 1999. 494 p. $62.95. ISBN 0120932253.
This volume covers the evolution and systematics of the pinnipeds, cetaceans, sirenians, and other marine mammals as well as discussing their biology, ecology, and behavior. An appendix covers the classification of marine mammals, including distribution and descriptions at the family level.

Hoelzel, A. Rus, ed. **Marine Mammal Biology: An Evolutionary Approach.** Malden, MA: Blackwell Science, 2002. 432 p. $73.95. ISBN 0632052325.
This textbook covers a range of topics in marine mammal biology, including sensory systems, vocal anatomy, feeding ecology, energetics, life history strategies, problem-solving abilities, and conservation. An initial chapter discusses diversity and distribution of marine mammals, providing a nice overview of their classification.

Nowak, Ronald M. **Walker's Marine Mammals of the World.** Baltimore: Johns Hopkins University Press, 2003. 336 p. $22.95 (paper). ISBN 0801873436 (paper).
Like the other volumes in this series, the text for this book was taken from *Walker's Mammals of the World,* 6th ed. (above), with a new introduction.

Reynolds, John E., III, and Sentiel A. Rommel, eds. **Biology of Marine Mammals.** Washington, DC: Smithsonian Institution Press, 1999. 578 p. $75. ISBN 1560983752.

This text provides an integrated introduction to the biology of marine mammals, including pinnipeds, cetaceans, and sirenians. An introductory chapter surveys the classification and diversity of marine mammals; subsequent chapters discuss functional morphology, physiological solutions to living in water, sensory systems, energetics, reproduction, communication, behavior, ecology, and the effects of environmental contaminants on marine mammals.

Rice, Dale W. **Marine Mammals of the World: Systematics and Distribution.** Lawrence, KS: Society for Marine Mammalogy, 1998. 231 p. (Special Publication of the Society for Marine Mammalogy, no. 4). ISBN 1891276034.

Updates Dale W. Rice's *A List of the Marine Mammals of the World,* 3rd ed. The volume provides a list of names of recent species of marine mammals, each entry including scientific and English common names, a review of published studies on geographical variation, and geographical distribution. Appendixes provides a list of bats and nonpinniped carnivores that are considered marine mammals as well as a classification of living and fossil marine mammals.

Ridgway, Sam H., and Richard J. Harrison, eds. **Handbook of Marine Mammals.** New York: Academic Press, 1981–98. 6 vol. Price varies.

This treatise covers the biology and life history of marine mammals, as well as their distribution and identification. Each volume covers a group of related mammals.

Insectivora

Churchfield, Sara. **The Natural History of Shrews.** Ithaca, NY: Comstock, 1990. 178 p. (Natural History of Mammals series). $47.50. ISBN 0801425956.

In addition to covering the natural history of shrews, this volume discusses the diversity and evolution of the 266 species of shrews found around the world.

Gorman, Martyn L., and R. David Stone. **The Natural History of Moles.** Ithaca, NY: Cornell University Press, 1990. 138 p. (Natural History of Mammals series). $41.95. ISBN 0801424666.

In addition to the extensive discussion of natural history of moles, this book includes a discussion of the classification of moles. The authors also talk about getting rid of moles, mole ectoparasites, and keeping moles in captivity.

Chiroptera

Altringham, John D. **Bats: Biology and Behaviour.** New York: Oxford University Press, 1996. 262 p. ISBN 0198540752.

Designed for the use of students, this treatise covers bat biology and general research trends. It is arranged by topic, rather than taxonomically, and discusses topics such as evolution and classification, flight, echolocation, hibernation, reproduction, behavioral ecology, community ecology, and conservation. The section on classification outlines bat diversity to the family or subfamily level.

Fenton, M. Brock. **Bats.** Rev. ed. New York: Checkmark Books, 2001. 224 p. $45. ISBN 0816043582.

This survey of the bats of the world is suitable for the general public. It discusses topics such as echolocation and bats and humans as well as how to identify and photograph bats. The survey of bat species includes information on natural history and range, and there are many color photographs.

Miller, Gerrit S. **The Families and Genera of Bats.** Washington, DC: U.S. Government Printing Office, 1907. 282 p. (Bulletin of the United States National Museum, no. 57).

Although dated, this catalog of the bats is still one of the most complete works on the Chiroptera. The author provides a historical summary of the various classification systems used for the bats as well as information on bat anatomy. The individual family and genus descriptions include keys to genera, synonymy, and detailed descriptions including type species, distribution and variation, characters, dental formulas, and illustrations of skulls.

Nowak, Ronald M. **Walker's Bats of the World.** Baltimore: Johns Hopkins University Press, 1994. 287 p. $20.95 (paper). ISBN 0801849861 (paper).

The text of this handbook was adapted from *Walker's Mammals of the World,* 5th ed., above, with an expanded introduction.

Wilson, Don E. **Bats in Question: The Smithsonian Answer Book.** Washington, DC: Smithsonian Institution Press, 1997. 168 p. $55.00; $24.95 (paper). ISBN 1560987383; 1560987391 (paper).

The first section of this guide covers general bat facts presented in a question-and-answer format, covering bat sounds, colonies, why bats hang upside down, and other questions that the general public might ask. There is also a taxonomic section surveying bat families and subfamilies and a final section covering bats and humans. An appendix lists the conservation status of each species of bats around the world, including common names.

Wimsatt, William A., ed. **Biology of Bats.** New York: Academic Press, 1970–77. 3 vol. ISBN 0127580034 (vol. 3).

This treatise covers all aspects of chiropteran biology, from evolution to relations with humans. Classification is covered very briefly in Volume 1 as part of the discussion of bat evolution.

Scandentia

Lyon, Marcus Ward. **Treeshrews: An Account of the Mammalian Family Tupaiidae.** Washington, DC: U.S. Government Printing Office, 1913. 188 p. (Proceedings of the U.S. National Museum, vol. 45).

Still the only lengthy review of the tree shrews, this classic catalog discusses background information on the study of the tree shrews, their distribution and classification, and species accounts. There are keys to species. The species accounts cover the usual detailed listing of type locality, type specimen, distribution, diagnosis, description, and remarks. There are several black-and-white plates of drawings, photographs of study skins, and skulls.

Primates

Fleagle, John G. **Primate Adaptation and Evolution.** 2nd ed. San Diego: Academic Press, 1999. 596 p. $59.95. ISBN 0122603419.

This textbook provides an introduction to primate natural history, biology, and evolution. Initial chapters discuss general topics followed by chapters on each of the major groups of living primates. These chapters are followed by discussion of evolution and the fossil primates.

Hershkovitz, Philip. **Living New World Monkeys (Platyrrhini): With an Introduction to Primates.** Chicago: University of Chicago Press, 1977. vol. $140 (vol. 1). ISBN 0226327884 (vol. 1).

Only one volume of this set has been published to date. It was designed to assist taxonomists with identifying all known species of callitrichid and callimiconid primates. As part of that mission, the author provides an introduction to primatology, including general classification and evolution of primates. He also discusses evolutionary and comparative morphology of the New World monkeys and then provides very detailed accounts of the systematics, evolution, and biology of the monkeys. The accounts include direct quotes from a number of authorities covering everything from pregnancy to habitat and food sources. There are numerous photographs and illustrations of living monkeys, skulls, and anatomical features.

Hill, W.C. Osman. **Primates: Comparative Anatomy and Taxonomy.** New York: Interscience, 1953–74. 8 vol. (Edinburgh University Publications: Science and Mathematics, no. 3).

This massive set covers the anatomy and classification of the primates in great detail. Each higher-order taxa is described, including structure, development, behavior, taxonomy, and distribution. Species accounts focus on the anatomy of each individual species, from external anatomy to viscerals.

Jacobsen, Larry, coord. **Primate Info Net.** URL: http://www.primate. wisc.edu/pin/ (Accessed August 26, 2003).

This site is maintained by the Wisconsin Primate Research Center (WPRC) Library at the University of Wisconsin, Madison, and contains a variety of links and information for people interested in primatology. Among the resources found on the site is a set of Primate Fact Sheets covering the natural history and taxonomy of the living primates.

Kavanagh, Michael. **A Complete Guide to Monkeys, Apes and Other Primates.** New York: Viking Press, 1984. 224 p. ISBN 0670435430.

This handbook describes the genera of primates, including representative or interesting species. Each account includes excellent color photographs and a distribution map, and discusses the natural history and behavior of members. Many of the primate species were (and are) little studied, so the length and amount of detail varies widely. The appendix covers the classification of primates, with a note of those that are threatened or endangered.

Napier, J.R., and P.H. Napier. **The Natural History of the Primates.** Cambridge, MA: MIT Press, 1985. 200 p. ISBN 026214039X.

Provides a detailed discussion of the natural history of primates, including general characteristics and classification, origins, structure and function, and social behavior as well as discussing human evolution. There are also generic-level accounts that contain information on the distribution and natural history of each group of primates. These accounts include black-and-white photographs and drawings of the primates along with some color photographs.

Nowak, Ronald M. **Walker's Primates of the World.** Baltimore: Johns Hopkins University Press, 1999. 224 p. $20.95. ISBN 0801862515 (paper).
   The text and photographs in this handbook were adapted from *Walker's Mammals of the World,* 6th ed., above, with a greatly expanded introduction.

Preston-Mafham, Rod, and Ken Preston-Mafham. **Primates of the World.** New York: Facts on File, 1992. 192 p. $35.00; $19.95 (paper). ISBN 0816027455; 0713727918 (paper).
   Provides an overview of primates, covering 60 species. The authors discuss individual species, then cover primate natural history and conservation in general. Suitable for students and the general public.

Rowe, Noel. **The Pictorial Guide to the Living Primates.** East Hampton, NY: Pogonias Press, 1996. 263 p. $79.95; $59.95 (paper). ISBN 0964882507; 0964882515 (paper).
   This handbook illustrates and describes the living primates of the world. Each species is covered in one to two pages, with several color photographs, range maps, and text including taxonomy, description, habitat, diet, life history, locomotion, social structure, behavior, vocalizations, and sleeping sites.

Wolfheim, Jaclyn H. **Primates of the World: Distribution, Abundance, and Conservation.** Seattle: University of Washington Press, 1983. 831 p. $57.50. ISBN 0295958995.
   As the title suggests, this volume provides detailed information on the status of the world's primates. Each species account covers taxonomic notes, geographical range, abundance and density, habitat, factors affecting populations, and conservation action. There are range maps but no illustrations. The amount of information available varies, of course, but the volume is a useful source of information on the distribution and pressures affecting primate numbers.

Xenarthra

Montgomery, G. Gene, ed. **The Evolution and Ecology of Armadillos, Sloths, and Vermilinguas.** Washington, DC: Smithsonian Institution Press, 1985. 451 p. $51. ISBN 0874746493 (paper).

The results of a symposium on the evolution and ecology of Xenarthra, this volume contains papers on the biology, ecology, and evolution of the members of this odd order. Initial chapters discuss the history of the classification of the order and the identification and distribution of the known species. The species accounts in this chapter cover the usual nomenclature, range, measurements, and comparisons. There are range maps plus illustrations of skeletal features plus a key to species. The articles are written in English, but the abstracts are in English, Portuguese, and Spanish.

Carnivora

Alderton, David. **Foxes, Wolves, and Wild Dogs of the World.** New York: Facts on File, 1994. 192 p. $29.95. ISBN 0816029547.

This nicely illustrated book surveys the canines of the world. After discussing general topics such as wild dogs and humans, anatomy, reproduction, and evolution, the author surveys the canids of the world by region. The species accounts cover distribution and natural history, and there are range maps. A checklist lists common names and subspecies as well as scientific names.

Alderton, David. **Wild Cats of the World.** New York: Facts on File, 1993. 192 p. $32.95. ISBN 0816027366.

Surveys the felines of the world, with emphasis on their natural history, reproduction, and evolution. About half of the book consists of discussion of feline biology, with the other half containing species accounts for each wild cat. Each species account includes a range map and information on the habitat, behavior, conservation status, and more. Most cats are illustrated with a color photograph as well.

Bonner, W. Nigel. **Seals and Sea Lions of the World.** New York: Facts on File, 1994. 224 p. $32.95. ISBN 0816029555.

This general survey of the pinnipeds of the world is suitable for students or the general public. The emphasis is on the biology and behavior of the seals and sea lions, but there are detailed species accounts of each of the 33 species. The volume is arranged by pinniped family, and there are distribution maps for most of the species. Several chapters discuss the relationships between seals and humans.

Craighead, Lance. **Bears of the World.** Stillwater, MN: Voyageur Press, 2000. 132 p. $29.95. ISBN 0896585034.

A survey of the bears of the world, this book discusses eight species of bears in detail. There are distribution maps, color photographs, and detailed information on natural history.

Ewer, R. F. **The Carnivores.** Ithaca, NY: Cornell University Press, 1998. 500 p. $27.95 (paper). ISBN 0801484936 (paper).

First published in 1973, this classic handbook to the biology, natural history, and classification of the carnivores is still used. The author discusses skeletal anatomy, anatomy of the soft parts, food, social organization, reproduction, fossil species, and classification.

Fox, Michael W., ed. **The Wild Canids: Their Systematics, Behavioral Ecology, and Evolution.** New York: Van Nostrand Reinhold, 1974. 508 p. (Behavioral Science series). ISBN 0442224303.

As suggested by the subtitle, this classic handbook covers a range of topics in the classification, behavioral ecology, social behavior, genetics, and evolution of the wild dogs of the world.

Gittleman, John L., ed. **Carnivore Behavior, Ecology, and Evolution.** Ithaca, NY: Comstock, 1989–96. 2 vol. $43.50 (vol. 1, paper); $99.95 (vol. 2); $43.50 (vol. 2, paper). ISBN 080142190X (vol. 1); 0801495253 (vol. 1, paper); 0801430275 (vol. 2); 080148216X (vol. 2, paper).

Covers the behavior, ecology, and evolution of carnivores, as the title suggests. An appendix in Volume 2 lists the classification of mammals, based on Honacki's *Mammal Species of the World,* above.

King, Judith E. **Seals of the World.** 2nd ed. Ithaca, NY: Cornell University Press, 1983. 240 p. ISBN 0801415683 (paper).

A summary of knowledge about the 34 species of seals, sea lions, and walrus. The book covers the classification and diversity of pinniped species, plus pinniped biology. The species accounts discuss the distribution, description, breeding, predators, feeding, exploitation by humans, behavior, and population size of each species, and they are illustrated by color photographs. An appendix gives the origins of the scientific names.

Reeves, Randall R., Brent S. Stewart, and Stephen Leatherwood. **The Sierra Club Handbook of Seals and Sirenians.** San Francisco: Sierra Club Books, 1992. 359 p. ISBN0871566567.

A companion to Leatherwood's *The Sierra Club Handbook of Whales and Dolphins* (see below), this handbook covers the seals, sea lions, walrus, manatees, and dugongs of the world. The species accounts are detailed, including nomenclature, description, distribution, natural history, conservation status, and references. There are black-and-white illustrations and some photographs as well. Appendixes list pinniped species with their dental formulas and show the breeding ranges of the major oceanic regions.

Sunquist, Melvin E., and Fiona Sunquist. **Wild Cats of the World.** Chicago: University of Chicago Press, 2002. 452 p. $45. ISBN 0226779998.

Covering all 36 species of wild cats found around the world, this handbook provides a general introduction to cat biology, behavior, taxonomy, and conservation as well as information on how to study the wild cats. The very detailed species accounts include information such as description, distribution, ecology and behavior, status in the wild and in captivity, and an extensive list of references. Most of the accounts include tables of data such as weights, prey items, and so on.

Ward, Paul, and Suzanne Kynaston. **Wild Bears of the World.** New York: Facts on File, 1995. 191 p. $32.95. ISBN 0816032459.

One of the excellent handbooks in this series, this book surveys the bears of the world with emphasis on their natural history. One chapter discusses ursine classification and biology; the bulk of the book consists of discussion of the various bear species.

Cetacea (see also Marine Mammals, above)

Bonner, W. Nigel. **Whales of the World.** New York: Facts on File, 1989. 191 p. ISBN 0816017344.

This handbook surveys the whales and is arranged taxonomically. There is extensive information on their natural history, and an appendix lists whale classification.

Ellis, Richard. **The Book of Whales.** New York: Knopf, 1980. 202 p. $35 (paper). ISBN 0394509668; 0394733711 (paper).

This oversized handbook contains very detailed information on the whales. Each account includes at least one black-and-white illustration, range map, and an extensive summary of our knowledge of the whale. A separate section of color illustrations shows 13 species of whales in a natural setting, all done by the author. The companion volume, *Dolphins and Porpoises,* below, covers the remaining cetaceans.

Ellis, Richard. **Dolphins and Porpoises.** New York: Knopf, 1982. 270 p. $35 (paper). ISBN 0394518004; 0679722866 (paper).

Similar in format to the author's *Book of Whales,* above, this handbook covers the 43 species of dolphins and porpoises. The species accounts are as detailed and comprehensive, and this volume also includes nine color plates illustrating species in the wild. The references are extensive.

Leatherwood, Stephen, and Randall R. Reeves. **The Sierra Club Handbook of Whales and Dolphins.** San Francisco: Sierra Club Books, 1983. 302 p. ISBN 087156341X; 0871563401 (paper).

This small guide to the world's cetaceans provides detailed information on each species. The accounts include the scientific and common names plus their derivation, distinctive features, description, natural history, distribution and conservation status, and similar species. There are color illustrations and black-and-white photographs.

Mead, James G., and Joy P. Gold. **Whales and Dolphins in Question: The Smithsonian Answer Book.** Washington, DC: Smithsonian Institution Press, 2002. 200 p. $55.00; $24.95. ISBN 1560989556; 1560989807 (paper).

One of a series of similar answer books, this volume provides information for the general public about the cetaceans. It is written in a question-and-answer format, covering topics such as how whales are different from and similar to other mammals, migration, tracking, food sources, conservation, and more. Whale evolution and diversity is covered in a separate chapter that surveys the types of whales and discusses their natural history and conservation status. An appendix outlines cetacean classification.

Lagomorpha

Chapman, Joseph A., and John E.C. Flux, eds. **Rabbits, Hares, and Pikas: Status Survey and Conservation Action Plan.** Gland, Switzerland: International Union for Conservation of Nature and Natural Resources, 1990. 168 p. $27. ISBN 2831700191.

Reviews the state of knowledge about the lagomorphs and provides an action plan for their conservation. It is arranged in three sections: an introduction and classification, species accounts, and a conservation action plan.

Rodentia

Alderton, David. **Rodents of the World.** New York: Facts on File, 1996. 192 p. $32.95. ISBN 0816032297.

One of several similar handbooks aimed at the general public, this volume discusses the rodents found around the world. Because rodents have had such an impact on human societies through disease and food destruction, the section on rodents and humans is extensive, but the volume also discusses rodent biology, evolution, and diversity. There is a checklist of rodent families as well as separate chapters on each of the three rodent suborders, the Sciuromorpha (squirrels), Myomorpha (mice and rats), and Caviomorpha (cavies).

Ellerman, John Reeves. **The Families and Genera of Living Rodents.** London: Printed by Order of the Trustees of the British Museum, 1940–49. 3 vol.

This catalog covers all 343 rodent genera known at the time and is the only comprehensive survey of the Rodentia. Each entry lists author, type species, range, number of species or subspecies, characters, and remarks, along with a list of the species or subspecies for each genera. There are illustrations of skulls and teeth for about 90 species. The author also discusses the Rodentia order and various classification systems previously used for the order. The catalog is in two parts: volume 1, Rodents Other Than Muridae and volume 2, Family Muridae. An untitled volume 3, pt. 1 includes additions and corrections to the previous volumes.

Proboscidea

Shoshani, Jeheskel, ed. **Elephants.** Rev. ed. New York: Checkmark Books, 2000. 240 p. $39.95. ISBN 0816042942.

This oversized volume provides an introduction to the two species of elephants, including their evolution, biology, behavior, conservation, and interactions with humans. It is suitable for students and the general public and has only a brief bibliography. The Frequently Asked Questions appendix provides a handy source of quick facts such as how long elephants live, how thick is their skin, and so on.

Sirenia (see also Marine Mammals, above)

Reeves, Randall R., Brent S. Stewart, and Stephen Leatherwood. **The Sierra Club Handbook of Seals and Sirenians.**

See full annotation in the Carnivores section, above.

Ripple, Jeff. **Manatees and Dugongs of the World.** Stillwater, MN: Voyageur Press, 1999. 144 p. $29.95. ISBN 0896583937.

A survey of the four living manatee and dugong species, including natural history and conservation.

Ungulates (Perissodactyla and Artiodactyla)

Geist, Valerius. **Deer of the World: Their Evolution, Behaviour, and Ecology.** Mechanicsburg, PA: Stackpole Books, 1998. 421 p. $60. ISBN 0811704963.

A survey of the natural history of the deer, this handbook discusses deer evolution as well as covering natural history by group rather than by species. The appendix contains numerous tables covering size, reproductive biology, and other data.

Groves, Colin P. **Horses, Asses, and Zebras in the Wild.** Hollywood, FL: R. Curtis Books, 1974. 192 p. ISBN 0883580085.

Reviews the wild horses and relatives, exclusive of the domesticated horse. Each wild species is described, with habitat, physical characteristics, and distribution.

Huffman, Brent. **The Ultimate Ungulate Page: Your Guide to the World's Hoofed Mammals.** 1996. URL: http://www.ultimateungulate. com/ (Accessed August 26, 2003).

This site provides information on the ungulates or hoofed mammals, including the Tubulidentata, Hyracoidea, Proboscidea, Sirenia, Perissodactyla, and Artiodactyla orders. There are species accounts for about half the ungulate species, following the basic format of *Mammalian Species* (above), and they include classification, description, ecology, behavior, distribution, conservation status, and general remarks. There are distribution maps and photographs as well, many of them taken by the author.

Vrba, Elisabeth S., and George B. Schaller, eds. **Antelopes, Deer, and Relatives: Fossil Record, Behavioral Ecology, Systematics, and Conservation.** New Haven: Yale University Press, 2000. 341 p. $70. ISBN 0300081421.

The emphasis in this volume is on the past, present, and future of the ruminants, the Cervidae (deer) and Bovidae (cattle and relatives). The introduction includes a checklist of artiodactyls, including the nonruminants such as pigs, hippos, and camels, and several chapters cover the phylogeny of various taxa.

Geographical Section

North America

Banfield, A. W. F. **The Mammals of Canada.** Toronto: Published for the National Museum of Natural Sciences, National Museums of Canada by University of Toronto Press, 1974. 438 p. $47.50. ISBN 0802021379.

Still the only comprehensive handbook to the mammals of Canada, this volume provides popular accounts of 196 species. Scientific names are given for each species, along with English and French common names, description, habits, habitat, reproduction, economic status, range map, distribution, and references. There are appendixes showing skulls, dental formulas, number of digits and mammae, and a glossary. It will be updated by the *Handbook of Canadian Mammals.*

Cockrum, E. Lendell. **Mammals of the Southwest.** Tucson: University of Arizona Press, 1982. 176 p. ISBN 0816507600; 0816507597 (paper).

An attractive little handbook to the mammals of the southwestern United States and northwestern Mexico. Although 171 species are found in the region, only one species from each of the 80 or so "major types" (for example, pocket mice) is illustrated and described, with other similar species mentioned briefly. The information provided for the "major types" includes identifying features, measurements, habitat, habits, and distribution maps. The black-and-white illustrations are quite attractive.

Forsyth, Adrian. **Mammals of North America: Temperate and Arctic Regions.** Buffalo, NY: Firefly Books, 1999. 350 p. $40. ISBN 155209409X.

This oversized, colorful handbook provides detailed information on the natural history of the mammals of most of North America, excluding tropical regions. The species accounts include color photographs, etymology of names, description, longevity, gestational length, diet, habitat, predators, dental formulas, and distribution. There are also short essays on various topics of interest.

Hall, E. Raymond. **Mammals of North America.** New York: Wiley, 1981. 2 vol. ISBN 0471054437 (vol. 1); 0471054445 (vol. 2); 0471055956 (set).

The set summarizes the results of taxonomic studies on living mammals of North America, covering 3,607 species and subspecies. The species accounts include technical description, skulls, and distribution maps for most species and line drawings for some. There are keys to genera and species.

Ingles, Lloyd G. **Mammals of the Pacific States: California, Oregon, and Washington.** Stanford, CA: Stanford University Press, 1965. 506 p. $22.95 (paper). ISBN 0804718431 (paper).

This classic handbook was designed to be used by students and laypeople, either as a reference or textbook. It provides general information on mammals and their ecology, evolution, and study as well as the species accounts. Keys to skulls and to living specimens are also included. The species accounts are often brief for animals such as the innumerable rodents, but the author also includes more detailed information on families or closely related genera. The handbook is illustrated with black-and-white photographs and illustrations, and there are distribution maps and illustrations of many skeletal features as well. Appendixes explain how to collect and prepare specimens, how to identify scats (droppings), lists, dental formulas, and outlines the classification of the mammals of the region.

Jones, J. Knox, Jr., David M. Armstrong, and Jerry R. Choate. **Guide to Mammals of the Plains States.** Lincoln: University of Nebraska Press, 1985. 371 p. ISBN 0803225628; 0803275579 (paper).

Covers the mammals of North Dakota, South Dakota, Nebraska, Kansas, and Oklahoma. The concise species accounts cover distribution, description, habits and habitat, reproduction, and suggested references. In addition, there are distribution maps, black-and-white photographs, keys to species, and a checklist of all 138 native and 8 introduced species covered in the handbook.

Kurta, Allen. **Mammals of the Great Lakes Region.** Rev. ed. Ann Arbor: University of Michigan Press, 1995. 376 p. $18.95 (paper). ISBN 0472094971; 0472064975 (paper).

This handbook is a revised edition of William Henry Burt's classic by the same title. It includes information on the natural history, distribution, and description of the mammals of the Great Lakes region of North America. Each species account includes a black-and-white photograph and suggested references, and appendixes cover studying and identifying mammals of the region including keys to skulls and whole specimens and dental formulas.

Maser, Chris. **Mammals of the Pacific Northwest: From the Coast to the High Cascades.** Corvallis: Oregon State University Press, 1998. 406 p. $26.95. ISBN 0870714384.

A handbook to the mammals of the Pacific Northwest, particularly Oregon. Each species is described, its natural history discussed, and the author's own encounters presented. There are black-and-white photographs of the mammals, nests, scats, tracks, and so on.

Van Zyll de Jong, C.G. **Handbook of Canadian Mammals.** Ottawa: National Museum of Natural Sciences, National Museums of Canada, 1983– . vol. $19.95 (vol. 1); $19.95 (vol. 2). ISBN 0660103281 (vol. 1); 0660107562 (vol. 2).

This handbook is designed to update and expand on A.W.F.'s *The Mammals of Canada.* To date, only the first two volumes have been published (the last in 1985), covering marsupials and insectivores in Volume 1 and bats in Volume 2. The volumes are in taxonomic order, containing descriptions of each taxa. Species accounts include common names in English and French, descriptions, distribution, systematics, and biology. There are black-and-white drawings, distribution maps, and keys as well.

Whitaker, John O., and William J. Hamilton, Jr. **Mammals of the Eastern United States.** 3rd ed. Ithaca, NY: Comstock, 1998. 583 p. $57.50. ISBN 0801434750.

A guide for students and interested laypeople, this handbook covers the land mammals found east of the Mississippi River. The species accounts are semitechnical and include description, tooth formula, distribution, habitat, natural history, and subspecies. There are distribution maps and black-and-white photographs for each species, plus a section of color photographs illustrating many species. There are also keys to orders, families, genera, and species plus an appendix listing endangered and threatened species.

Wilson, Don E., and Sue Ruff, eds. **The Smithsonian Book of North American Mammals.** Washington, DC: Smithsonian Institution Press, 1999. 750 p. $75. ISBN 1560988452.

Published in association with the American Society of Mammalogists, this oversized handbook to the mammals of North America north of Mexico provides detailed species accounts for all native species. The accounts were written by authorities who often have done extensive research on the species, and they include information on the mammals' natural history and range as well as size, identification, synonyms, other common names, subspecies, status, and references. There are color photographs and range maps. Appendixes list common and scientific names of plants mentioned in the text and a glossary.

Zeveloff, Samuel I. **Mammals of the Intermountain West.** Salt Lake City: University of Utah Press, 1988. 365 p. ISBN 0874803276; 0874802962 (paper).

This handbook covers the 151 species of mammals found in the region between the Sierra Nevada and Rocky Mountains. The species accounts are listed in systematic order. Each includes size, ecology, reproduction, general notes, distribution map, and references. Most of the larger species are also illustrated, some in color. The author also provides a checklist.

Africa

Harrison, David L., and Paul J. Bates. **The Mammals of Arabia.** 2nd ed. Sevenoaks, Kent, UK: Harrison Zoological Museum, 1991. 354 p. ISBN 0951731300.

This second edition of a classic catalog was written for professional mammalogists and provides more detailed information on the classification and description of mammal species than Kingdon's handbook, below.

Kingdon, Jonathan. **Arabian Mammals: A Natural History.** San Diego: Academic Press, 1991. 279 p. $104. ISBN 0124083501.

This attractively illustrated handbook covers the mammals of the Arabian peninsula. Each species account includes drawings by the author, a distribution map, and information on the natural history of the mammal. About 50 species are featured in full-page color illustrations, with captions in Arabic and English. The author also provides a checklist of Arabian mammals and a list of national parks and nature reserves in the region.

Kingdon, Jonathan. **East African Mammals: An Atlas of Evolution in Africa.** New York: Academic Press, 1971–82. 3 vol. in 7. $146 (vol. 1); $146 (vol. 3C). ISBN 0124083013 (vol. 1); 0124083021 (vol. 2A); 0124083420 (vol. 2B); 012408303X (vol. 3A); 0124083439 (vol. 3B); 0124083447 (vol. 3C); 0124083455 (vol. 3D). Reprinted by University of Chicago Press, 1984–89.

Provides an atlas and inventory of the mammals of East Africa (Kenya, Tanzania, and Uganda). Each species is treated in great detail, with local common names, distribution maps, and an extensive discussion of the biology and natural history of the animals. The most striking feature of the series is the illustrations, all done by the author. They include charming drawings of the mammals in natural poses, as well as skeletons and musculature.

Meester, J. A. J., and Henry W. Setzer, eds. **The Mammals of Africa: An Identification Manual.** Washington, DC: Smithsonian Institution Press, 1971. 1 vol. (loose-leaf). ISBN 0874741165.

Despite its age, this is still one of the few comprehensive guides to the identification and taxonomy of the mammals of Africa. The parts of the manual were published out of order as a loose-leaf volume, but follow a standard format. Identification is based on dichotomous keys rather than illustrations, and there are brief species accounts listing original author, distribution, notes on identification or taxonomy, and ecology.

Skinner, John D., and Reay H. N. Smithers. **The Mammals of the Southern African Subregion.** 2nd ed. Pretoria, Republic of South Africa: University of Pretoria, 1990. 771 p. ISBN 0869798022.

Covers the mammals of Africa south of the Zambezi River, including Namibia, Botswana, Zimbabwe, part of Mozambique, and the Republic of South Africa. The species accounts include scientific and common names in English and Afrikaans, taxonomic notes, description, distribution, habitat, and natural history. There are keys to species as well as distribution maps and black-and-white illustrations, plus separate color plates illustrating most of the species. The authors also include information on species such as the quagga and blue antelope that have become extinct in historical times. The bibliography is very extensive.

Asia

Allen, Glover M. The **Mammals of China and Mongolia.** New York: The American Museum of Natural History, 1938–40. 2 vol. (Central Asiatic Expeditions of the American Museum of Natural History; Natural History of Central Asia, vol. 11).

This classic handbook is still one of the few comprehensive publications covering the mammals of China. It is in two sections, the first providing an introduction to the history of the study of mammals in China as well as a description of the region. The remainder of the two volumes consists of a systematic account of the mammals. There are a few illustrations and black-and-white photographs, but most species are not illustrated, although there are keys.

Corbet, G. B., and J. E. Hill. **The Mammals of the Indomalayan Region: A Systematic Review.** New York: Oxford University Press, 1992. 488 p. ISBN 0198546939.

Covers the area of southeast Asia from India to China and south to Borneo. The species accounts include black-and-white illustrations and distribution maps plus information on synonymy, range, ecology, variation, and remarks. There are several appendixes, listing recent species, new names proposed in the volume, biographical notes on collectors and describers, glossary, and additions to maps.

Heaney, Lawrence R., et al. **A Synopsis of the Mammalian Fauna of the Philippine Islands.** Chicago: Field Museum of Natural History, 1998. 61 p. (Fieldiana Zoology new series, no. 88).

This handbook covers 201 species of mammals of the Philippines. Species accounts include citation to the original description, English common name, distribution, habitat, and conservation status. An updated version is also available at http://www.fmnh.org/philippine_mammals/ Precursor.htm.

Australasia

Australian Mammal Society. **Australian Mammal Species Files.** Australian Mammal Society, 2001. URL: http://www.australianmammals. org.au/ (Accessed August 26, 2003).

This site will contain species accounts for all Australian mammals when complete, although at the time of viewing only a few were available.

Flannery, Tim F. **Mammals of New Guinea.** Rev. and updated ed. Ithaca, NY: Comstock/Cornell, 1995. 568 p. $87.50. ISBN 0801431492.

Covers 212 species of mammals, many of them endemic to New Guinea. Much of the information presented in the species accounts comes from the author's own fieldwork. The accounts include English and Bahasa Indonesian common names, local names, scientific names, distribution maps, conservation status, habitat, identification, taxonomy, museum specimens, natural history, and illustrations. Most of the illustrations are color photographs of live animals, but some are of study skins from museums. A gazetteer, glossary, references, and skull photographs are also included.

Flannery, Tim F. **Mammals of the South-West Pacific and Moluccan Islands.** Ithaca, NY: Comstock/Cornell, 1995. 464 p. $87.50. ISBN 0801431506.

A handbook to 230 species of mammals of the region extending from just east of Sulawesi, north to Micronesia, and south to New Zealand, including Micronesia, Samoa, Fiji, and the Moluccas. This volume excludes New Guinea, which is covered by the author's *Mammals of New Guinea.* Species accounts cover the description, distribution, holotype, local names, status, synonyms, and etymology for each species. There are some color photographs, often of study skins, and some information on natural history as well, although many of the species are not well studied.

King, Carolyn M., ed. **The Handbook of New Zealand Mammals.** New York: Oxford University Press, 1990. 600 p. ISBN 0195581776.

Covers the 46 species of land mammals in New Zealand, including native and introduced mammals. The authors provide an introduction and key to skulls as well as detailed species accounts. The species accounts include scientific and multiple common names, description, field sign, measurements, variation, history of colonization, distribution, habitat, and natural history. There are black-and-white photographs and range maps for each species as well.

Strahan, Ronald, ed. **Mammals of Australia.** Rev. ed. Washington, DC: Smithsonian Institution Press, 1995. 756 p. $75. ISBN 1560986735.

This handbook covers the marsupial and placental mammals of Australia. There are detailed, authoritative species accounts for each mammal featuring color photographs, range maps, natural history, and descriptions. It is suitable for researchers or amateurs.

Central and South America

Eisenberg, John Frederick. **Mammals of the Neotropics.** Chicago: University of Chicago Press, 1989–99. 3 vol. $40. ISBN 0226195422.

The set is arranged by region; within each volume the species accounts are arranged in taxonomic order and include distribution maps, black-and-white illustrations, and detailed information on distribution, range, natural history, and notes. The geographical coverage is as follows: Volume 1, The Northern Neotropics: Panama, Colombia, Venezuela, Guyana, Suriname, French Guiana; Volume 2, Chile, Argentina, Uruguay, Paraguay; and Volume 3, The Central Neotropics: Ecuador, Peru, Bolivia, Brazil. Volumes 2 and 3 are by Kent H. Redford and John F. Eisenberg.

Europe

Bjärvall, Anders, and Staffan Ullström. **The Mammals of Britain and Europe.** London: Croom Helm, 1986. 240 p. ISBN 0709932685.

A beautifully illustrated handbook for the general public, this handbook covers the natural history of the native and introduced species of European mammals. There are distribution maps covering Britain and Europe west to the western edge of the Caspian Sea and south to the northern Mediterranean Sea.

Corbet, G. B., and Stephen Harris, eds. **The Handbook of British Mammals.** 3rd ed. Boston: Published for the Mammal Society by Blackwell Scientific Publications, 1991. 588 p. ISBN 0632016914.

This handbook was designed to identify species and stimulate interest in their study. The species accounts are detailed, covering description, distribution, variation, habitat, natural history, and relations with humans. There are illustrations of the animals and their skulls and a checklist of species.

Heptner, V. G., A. A. Nasimovich, and A. G. Bannikov. **Mammals of the Soviet Union.** Washington, DC: Smithsonian Institution Libraries and National Science Foundation, 1988. 2 vol. in 4.

This set is a translation of *Mlekopitaiushchie Sovetskogo Soiuza,* originally published in Moscow in 1961. It is a successor to S. I. Ognev's *Mammals of the U.S.S.R. and Adjacent Countries,* below. To date, not all volumes of the original Russian publication have appeared, but the following translations are available from various publishers: Volume 1, Artiodactyla and perissodactyla; Volume 2, pt. 1a., Sirenia and Carnivora (sea cows; wolves and bears); Volume 2, pt. 1b, Carnivora (weasels, additional species); Volume 2, pt. 2, Carnivora (hyaenas and cats); Volume 2, pt 3, Pinnipeds and toothed whales.

Niethammer, Jochen, and Franz Krapp, eds. **Handbuch der Säugetiere Europas.** Wiesbaden, Germany: Akademische Verlagsgesellschaft, 1978–93. 6 vol. in 9. Price varies.

This series covers the mammals of Europe. Volume 1 contains an introduction covering mammalian systematics, anatomy, paleontology, and ecology as well as species accounts. The species accounts include description, taxonomy, distribution, geographical variation, paleontology, and ecology. The volumes are arranged as follows: Volumes 1 and 2, rodents and perissodactyls; Volume 2, artiodactyls; Volume 3, insectivores, lagomorphs and primates; Volume 4, bats; Volume 5, carnivores; and Volume 6, pt. 1–2, marine mammals. A supplementary volume covers the threatened mammals of Europe.

Ognev, S.I. **Mammals of the U.S.S.R. and Adjacent Countries.** Jerusalem: Published for the National Science Foundation, Washington, D.C., by the Israel Program for Scientific Translations, 1962–67. 9 vol.

A translation of the Russian original *Zveri SSSR i prilezhashchikh stran,* written between 1928 and 1950. Volumes 1 and 2 of the English translation were published as *Mammals of Eastern Europe and Northern Asia (Zveri vostochnoi Evropy i severnoi Azii).* This groundbreaking series covered the mammals of this vast region in more detail than other previous works. Ognev died before he was able to complete the project, but the following volumes are available in translation: Volume 1, *Insectivora and Chiroptera;* Volumes 2 and 3, *Carnivora;* Volumes 4 through 7, *Rodents;* Volume 9, *Cetacea.* Volume 8, intended to cover the mice, hamsters, and gerbils, was never published.

Identification Tools

Brunner, Hans, and Brian J. Coman. **The Identification of Mammalian Hair.** Melbourne: Inkata Press, 1974. 176 p. ISBN 0909605017.

Although this volume focuses on the identification of hair from Australian mammals, it has a wider use because of the extensive discussion of how to identify unknown hairs. The authors discuss the structure of hairs, methods for studying hair structure, and how to develop a system for hair identification. The handbook also contains photographs of the hairs of 75 species of native and introduced mammals of the state of Victoria, arranged by cross-sectional appearance. This includes such widely distributed mammals as domestic pigs, humans, cats, dogs, sheep, and house mice. Teerink, below, provides a similar work for European mammals. Although there are articles from the 1930s and later identifying the hair of American mammals, there is no similar book-length guide for American mammals.

Jefferson, Thomas A., Stephen Leatherwood, and Marc A. Webber. **Marine Mammals of the World.** Rome: UNEP/FAO, 1993. 320 p. (FAO Species Identification Guide). $60. ISBN 9251032920.

This identification guide covers 119 species of marine mammals as well as freshwater seals and sirenians. The introduction discusses marine mam-

mals and includes an illustrated glossary and keys to species of living specimens as well as keys to skulls. The species accounts include identification,
illustrations of the whole animal, its skull, and appearance at the surface
(for cetaceans), plus confusing species, size, distribution, biology and
behavior, exploitation status, and conservation status. There are multiple
common names in English, French, and Spanish and range maps as well.

Reeves, Randall R., et al. **Guide to Marine Mammals of the World.** New
York: Knopf, 2002. 527 p. (National Audubon Society Field Guides).
$26.95. ISBN 0375411410.

This colorful guide discusses the marine mammals, including cetaceans,
pinnipeds, sirenians, sea otter, and polar bear. The authors provide introductory material on ranges, behavior, reproduction, food, conservation status, and how to watch marine mammals as well as detailed species
accounts. The species accounts include color illustrations and photographs,
range maps, descriptions, range and habitat, similar species, behavior, and
status. Appendixes include a glossary, regional assemblages, and diagrams
of marine mammal morphology. Comparative plates help users identify
similar species.

Teerink, B.J. **Hair of West-European Mammals: Atlas and Identification Key.** New York: Cambridge University Press, 1991. 224 p. $70.
ISBN 0521402646.

Identifies the hair of 73 species of European mammals. The book is in
three parts, consisting of introductory material on how to identify hairs,
keys to species, and the atlas, which contains photographs of hair and
cross sections. There is a species list with common names in English, German, French, Dutch, and Danish. See also Brunner and Coman, above, for
a similar discussion for Australian mammals.

Geographical Section

North America

Booth, Ernest S. **How to Know the Mammals: Pictured-Keys for Determining to Species, All of the Mammals of the United States and Southern Canada.** 4th ed. Dubuque, IA: W.C. Brown, 1982. 198 p. (Pictured
Key Nature series). $20.50. ISBN 0697047814.

This key identifies 400 mammal species found in North America and
includes background information on identifying mammals. There are
black-and-white illustrations and range maps as well.

Burt, William Henry, and Richard Philip Grossenheider. **A Field Guide to the Mammals: Field Marks of All North American Species Found North of Mexico.** 3rd ed. Boston: Houghton Mifflin, 1976. 289 p. (The Peterson Field Guide series, no. 5). ISBN 0395240824; 0395240840 (paper).

The classic field guide to North American mammals, this guide features larger range maps and more information on the natural history of the mammals than Kays and Wilson's guide, below. Covers 380 species and includes illustrations of skulls and tracks as well as a table of dental formulas.

Jones, J. Knox, and Richard W. Manning. **Illustrated Key to Skulls of North American Land Mammals.** Lubbock: Texas Tech University Press, 1992. 75 p. $11.95 (paper). ISBN 0896722899 (paper).

A student's guide, this spiral-bound key to mammalian skulls of North America north of Mexico excludes the marine mammals. Most genera are illustrated with black-and-white photographs and there are many line drawings as well. An illustrated glossary helps define the technical terms.

Kays, Roland W., and Don E. Wilson. **Mammals of North America.** Princeton, NJ: Princeton University Press, 2002. 240 p. (Princeton Field Guides). $49.50; $19.95 (paper). ISBN 069108890X; 0691070121 (paper).

This major new field guide is a worthy competitor to Burt and Grossenheider's classic Peterson field guide, with very attractive illustrations and a "Quick Mammal ID Chart" to help users find the right family. Includes plates of marine mammal dive sequences, as well as illustrations of scats and tracks. It covers 442 native and introduced species, and the descriptions contain only brief descriptions and habitat information. The range maps are generally quite small, but the guide contains the latest information on ranges and scientific names.

Murie, Olaus Johan. **A Field Guide to Animal Tracks.** 2nd ed. Boston: Houghton Mifflin, 1975. 375 p. (Peterson Field Guide series, no. 9). $18. ISBN 0395910943 (paper).

Because most mammals are very elusive, often the only way to know they are around is by the tracks they leave behind. This classic field guide not only illustrates tracks and track patterns but also discusses other types of signs, such as burrows, scats, and sounds. Murie also covers tracks of some birds, reptiles and amphibians, and insects.

Searfoss, Glen. **Skulls and Bones: A Guide to the Skeletal Structures and Behavior of North American Mammals.** Mechanicsburg, PA: Stackpole Books, 1995. 277 p. $19.95 (paper). ISBN 0811725715 (paper).

Mammals can be very elusive creatures, and often the only evidence of their presence are traces such as tracks, scats, or bones. This guide helps students and researchers identify the major bones of common mammal species and shows how to infer lifestyle of the animal based on its skeleton. The author also tells how to create a bone collection and provides exercises.

Africa

Kingdon, Jonathan. **The Kingdon Field Guide to African Mammals.** San Diego: Academic Press, 1997. 464 p. (AP Natural World). $39.95. ISBN 0124083552 (paper).

Covering the mammals of the entire African continent, this field guide by a very well-known mammalogist also features some of the most attractive and witty illustrations found in any field guide. In addition to the usual descriptions, distribution maps, and brief natural history information, the author provides a phylogenetic chart for each order.

Antarctica

Shirihai, Hadoram. **The Complete Guide to Antarctic Wildlife: Birds and Marine Mammals of the Antarctic Continent and the Southern Ocean.**

See chapter 4 for a full annotation.

Australasia

Menkhorst, Peter. A Field Guide to the Mammals of Australia. New York: Oxford University Press, 2001. 269 p. $35. ISBN 019550870X (flexi).

A guide to 379 species of Australian mammals, this volume includes keys and color illustrations of each species. The descriptions include natural history, similar species, range, and more.

Central and South America

Emmons, Louise H. **Neotropical Rain Forest Mammals: A Field Guide.** Chicago: University of Chicago Press, 1990. $54.00; $25.95 (paper). ISBN 0226207161; 0226207188 (paper).

Covers 315 species of lowland rainforest mammals from Central and South America. The species accounts cover identification, similar species, sounds, natural history, geographical range with distribution map, conservation status, and local names. There are color plates in the center of the book illustrating most species. Appendixes provide keys to families and genera, illustrations of tracks of larger mammals, a glossary, and information on classification and biogeography of rainforest mammals.

Reid, Fiona. **A Field Guide to the Mammals of Central America and Southeast Mexico.** New York: Oxford University Press, 1997. 456 p. $35 (paper). ISBN 0195064003; 0195064011(paper).

This guide covers the 400 species of the region and includes multiple common names in English, Spanish, and other local languages. In addition to the usual descriptions and natural history, the guide includes information on the major parks of the area and has lists of animals found in each.

Europe

Macdonald, David W., and Priscilla Barrett. **Mammals of Britain and Europe.** Princeton, NJ: Princeton University Press, 2001. 312 p. (Princeton Field Guides). $24.95 (paper). ISBN 0691091609 (paper).

Originally published by HarperCollins, this guide identifies 230 species of land and marine mammals of Europe. The descriptions include tracks and signs, natural history, and distribution maps.

Associations

American Cetacean Society. P.O. Box 1391, San Pedro, CA 90731. Phone: 310-548-6279. E-mail: acs@pobox.com. URL: http://www.acsonline.org (Accessed August 26, 2003).

American Society of Mammalogists. c/o Duane Smith, 290 MLBM, Brigham Young University, Provo, UT 84602. Phone: 801-378-2492. URL: http://www.mammalsociety.org/ (Accessed August 26, 2003).

Australian Mammal Society. c/o Dr Rod Kavanagh, State Forests of New South Wales, P.O. Box 100, Beecroft, NSW 2119, Australia. E-mail: rodk@sf.nsw.gov.au. URL: http://www.australianmammals.org.au/ (Accessed August 26, 2003).

Mammal Society. 15 Cloisters House, 8 Battersea Park Rd, London SW8 4BG, UK. Phone: 44 207 4984358. Fax: 44 207 6228722. E-mail:

enquiries@mammal.org.uk.   URL: http://www.abdn.ac.uk/mammal/ (Accessed August 26, 2003).

Society of Marine Mammalogy. URL: http://www.marinemammalogy. org/ (Accessed August 26, 2003).

Reference

Martin, Robert Eugene, Ronald H. Pine, and Anthony F. DeBlase. 2001. *A Manual of Mammalogy: with Keys to Families of the World.* 3rd ed. Boston: McGraw-Hill.

INDEX

Africa: amphibians and reptiles, 227–28, 242–43, 249–50; birds, 290–91, 299; fishes, 204–5, 214–15; mammals, 336–37, 344

Agnatha, handbooks, 197

All Species Foundation, 6

American Arachnological Society, 170

American Cetacean Society, 345

American Elasmobranch Society, 217

American Entomological Society, 169

American Fisheries Society, 217

American Malacological Society, 89

American Mosquito Control Association, 172

American Ornithologist's Union, 304

American Society of Ichthyologists and Herpetologists, 217, 252

American Society of Mammalogists, 345

American Society of Parasitologists, 88

American Zoo and Aquariums Association, 51

Amphibians: bibliography, 220–21; checklists, 227–28; classification, 220; generally, 219–20; handbooks, 232–35; Web site, 220–21

Amphibians and reptiles: Africa, 242–43, 249–50; Asia, 243–44; Australasia, 244, 250–51; biographies and histories, 223; Central and South America, 244–46, 251–52; checklists and classification, 225–31; dictionaries and encyclopedias, 223–24; Europe, 246; handbooks, 231–46; identification tools, 246–52; journals, 221–22; literature, 222; North America, 240–42, 247–49; Pacific Islands, 252–53; references, 253; textbooks, 224–25; Web sites, 221, 222, 225, 246–48

Animal Behavior Society, 51

Animals, defined, 1

Annelida: classification, 65; handbooks, 75–76

Anseriformes, 273

Antarctica: birds, 291, 299–300; fishes, 205–6; mammals, 344

Apodiformes, handbook, 276

Apterygota: checklists and classification, 121; handbook, 138; identification, 160–61

Arachnida: associations, 170; checklists and classification, 118–19; handbooks, 130–33; identification, 159; journals, 104

Aristotle, 2

Arthropods: associations, 169–72; biographies and histories, 109–12; checklists and classification, 117–29; classification of, 92–93; dictionaries and encyclopedias, 112–14; generally, 91–92; handbooks, 129–54; identification tools, 154–69; indexes, abstracts, and bibliographies, 93–97; journals, 97–107; literature, 25–27; references, 172; textbooks, 114–17; Web sites, 107, 108

Asia: amphibians and reptiles, 243–44; birds, 291–92, 300–301; mammals, 337–38

Association of Field Ornithologists, 304

Associations: amphibians and reptiles, 252–53; arthropods, 169–72; birds, 304–5; fishes, 217; general, 51–52; invertebrates, 88–89; mammals, 345–46; vertebrates, 182

Australasia: amphibians and reptiles, 244, 250–51; birds, 292–93, 301–2; fishes, 206–8, 215–16; general references, 49; mammals, 338–39, 344

Australian Mammal Society, 345

Binomial nomenclature, 4

Biographies and histories: amphibians and reptiles, 223; arthropods, 109–12;

About the Author

DIANE SCHMIDT is Biology Librarian and Associate Professor of Library Administration, University of Illinois at Urbana–Champaign.